AR MAR 2012
VE CC b14

Loves of

HARRIET
BEECHER STOWE

by Philip McFarland

Loves of

HARRIET
BEECHER STOWE

Philip McFarland

GROVE PRESS

New York

Engraved portrait of Harriet Beecher Stowe, from a photograph taken in 1868, courtesy of the Schlesinger Library, Radcliffe Institute, Harvard University.

Published simultaneously in Canada
Printed in the United States of America

FIRST EDITION

ISBN-10: 0-8021-1845-3
ISBN-13: 978-0-8021-1845-5

Grove Press
an imprint of Grove/Atlantic, Inc.
841 Broadway
New York, NY 10003

Distributed by Publishers Group West

www.groveatlantic.com

07 08 09 10 11 12   10 9 8 7 6 5 4 3 2 1

for

Don Cantor
and
Charlie Burlingham

dear loyal friends for more than fifty years

CONTENTS

Contents

CALVIN

*"If you were not already my dearly loved husband,
I should certainly fall in love with you."*

Harriet Beecher Stowe to Calvin Stowe, 1842

CALVIN ELLIS STOWE, C. 1840
Harriet Beecher Stowe Center, Hartford, Connecticut.

WESTWARD BOUND

Start with a coach lumbering westward over country roads and its occupants singing. The year is 1832, in mid-October. "After a week in Philadelphia," one of those travelers would recall some seventy years later, "we chartered a big, old-fashioned stage, with four great horses, for Wheeling, Virginia, and spent a week or more on the way, crossing the Alleghenies, before ever a railroad was thought of, and enjoyed every minute of the way. At least we children did, with brother George on the box shouting out the stories he got from the various drivers, and leading us all in singing hymns and songs." Fully alive and fresh from Yale at age twenty-three, George was keeping busy in the breeze topside, chatting with the stage driver, urging papers of religious uplift on chance passersby, and leading his family below in song, up to nine voices in their chorus all together. Another of the number, twenty-one-year-old Harriet Elizabeth Beecher, described the same scene with the journey still in progress: the "obliging driver, good roads, good spirits, good dinner, fine scenery, and now and then some 'psalms and hymns and spiritual songs,' for with George on board you may be sure of music of some kind." She, too, spoke of her older brother's distributing his tracts along the highway, "*peppering* the land with moral influence"; and after they had stopped for the evening at a village inn, Harriet took care to account for the party present one by one. She was writing back home and wanted her sister's family in Hartford to picture the scene.

See them, then, gathered in the front parlor of a Pennsylvania tavern. Father is opposite, seated at the table reading. Kate is writing a letter to that married sister who has chosen to stay behind in her settled life in Connecticut. Young Thomas, eight years old, sits beside his father making an entry in a journal of his own; and, wrote Harriet, ten-year-old Isabella—who will recall this odyssey after three-quarters of a century—"has her little record" too. George meanwhile stands ready to begin his contribution to the letter that Kate is composing, while, unmentioned, Aunt Esther, along with Harriet's stepmother and the youngest, James at four, may have been off in their bedchamber resting, all of them after a day's travel stopped at the village of Dowington, some thirty miles beyond Philadelphia.

They were bound for a new life together in the Queen City of the West, still many days ahead at the end of a long road. Father was fifty-seven. Thus advanced in age, the indomitable Lyman Beecher had picked up these of his family who wanted to come and was setting out to begin life anew in Cincinnati. Earlier, he and Kate—his eldest daughter, Catharine—had scouted out the lay of the land, venturing west this past spring of 1832, and had liked what they saw. "I know of no place in the world," Catharine had written, well pleased, from the scene, "where there is so fair a prospect of finding every thing that makes social and domestic life pleasant." Already a couple of relatives from back east were established with their families in the thriving riverport of 30,000 people. "Indeed," Catharine had reassured her correspondent at home, Cincinnati "is a New England city in all its habits, and its inhabitants are more than half from New England." As for Father, "I never saw," she went on, "such a field of usefulness and influence as is offered to him here."

All his adult life Catharine's father had made himself useful, first as the minister in a remote Long Island village during ten years at the start of the century; next for sixteen years as the minister of Litchfield, a prosperous town in western Connecticut; then over these past six years as minister of the Hanover Street Church in Boston's North End. But now, toward the end of his sixth decade, the nationally known Reverend Lyman Beecher had been offered a new, wonderful opportunity to serve both God and his country. For some time he had been thinking about the West in any case— "If we gain the West, all is safe," he assured Catharine in 1830; "if we lose it, all is lost"—when word reached him of a new seminary being established in Cincinnati, Ohio. A benefactor out there had donated sixty acres of land two miles beyond the city on which to erect the Lane Theological Seminary, and $70,000 had been pledged for buildings and staff, provided that the celebrated Dr. Beecher could be persuaded to come from Boston to teach in and serve as president of the institution; "as he is the most prominent, popular, and powerful preacher in the nation, he would immediately give character, elevation, and success to our seminary, draw together young men from every part of our country, secure the confidence and co-operation of the ministers and churches both east and west of the Alleghany Mountains, and awaken a general interest in the old states in behalf of the West."

Dr. Beecher learned of the trustees' hopes to his enormous joy. "I had felt and thought, and labored a great deal about raising up ministers"—what work could be more useful than that?—"and," he remarked of the invitation later, "the idea that I might be called to teach the best mode of preaching to the young ministry of the broad West flashed through my mind like lightning. I went home, and ran in, and found Esther alone in the sitting-room." Esther was his maiden half sister, who lived with the family. "I was in such a state of emotion and excitement I could not speak, and she was frightened. At last I told her. It was the greatest thought that ever entered my soul; it filled it, and displaced every thing else."

During these early years of the nineteenth century, the rapidly changing West was creating abundant work for the likes of a devout evangelical such as Lyman Beecher. Catholics, newly arriving, appeared to threaten all that vast region; the Mississippi Valley must be saved for the old faith, for Beecher's brand of Protestantism. Cincinnati, for instance, founded along the Ohio River in 1788, had already become home to a congregation of some 100 Roman Catholics in scarcely three decades, by 1819; and in the single, more recent year of 1829, the swelling band of German and Irish proselytizers had managed to lure 150 Protestants of the river town over to popery, to that gaudy theological despotism whose laity were not even allowed to read the Bible, whose doctrines of celibacy and distaste for the flesh seemed at war with the family, whose allegiance ultimately was paid to a potentate in far-off Rome. A vast number of Americans viewed all this as a matter of the gravest concern. Dr. Beecher's "great motive in going to Cincinnati," his daughter Harriet would later flatly aver, "was to oppose the influence of the Roman Catholic church in every way." For Beecher was a Protestant evangelical, and thus his job, his duty, his life's work was the saving of souls; on those terms he would wage battle against the Catholics out west, proselytizing for his own faith with a vigor that surpassed their own.

He was elected president of Lane Theological Seminary on October 22, 1830. Ecclesiastical matters detained him in Boston (Hanover Church had burned down, and a new church was being built on Bowdoin Street); but with his eldest daughter Catharine, then in her early thirties, he went west at last, for the first time, in April 1832, to look over the terrain. What the two found delighted them both. "I never saw a place so capable of being rendered a paradise by the improvements of taste as the environs of this city," Catharine wrote after visiting Walnut Hills, site of the struggling school—"so elevated and cool," she jested, "that people have to leave there to be sick." The seminary was located on a hill that was picturesque enough, even if only a couple of bare buildings had so far been erected alongside the forest, and although city and river were hidden from view. Soon the Beechers had chosen the spot among woodlands "where our house shall stand in case we decide to come."

They did decide in favor of making the tremendous move, so that in early October 1832, various members of the family were congregating in New York City: the patriarch with his second wife, his three young children by her, and his half sister down from Boston; the grown Catharine by his first wife over from Hartford; and his son George from New Haven and Yale, determined to finish his ministerial studies out west at Lane. "Well, my dear," another emigrating daughter, Harriet, wrote from New York on October 6, 1832, "the great sheet is out and the letter is begun." Through their varied lifetimes, these Beechers would each abundantly demonstrate a facility with language, but Harriet wrote perhaps most easily of all, and she would be the one to make entries over the great sheet of this present letter, recording events of the journey from here to Cincinnati, transmitting the whole back to Hartford once the party had arrived.

The travelers assembling in New York were apportioned among homes of Christian well-wishers. "I don't know, I'm sure, as we shall ever get to Pittsburgh," Harriet confided to her sister back home.

"Father is staying here begging money for the Biblical Literature professorship; the incumbent is to be C. Stowe. Last night we had a call from Arthur Tappan and Mr. Eastman." The rich merchant Tappan was a benefactor of Lane; part of the delay in New York was to allow Dr. Beecher, when not preaching at churches and theaters, to solicit money from such wealthy people directly. He persuaded the landowner Stephen Van Rensselaer, for instance, to subscribe $1,000 for the new seminary on the spot. "Father has been this morning in high spirits," Harriet reported. "He is all in his own element—dipping into books—consulting authorities for his oration—going around here, there, and every where—begging, borrowing, and spoiling the Egyptians—delighted with past success and confident for the future." The argument to be advanced in support of the Lane enterprise went like this: "Cincinnati, now at the heart of four millions, and in twenty years to be at the heart of twelve millions, is the most important point in our nation for a great central theological institution of the first character." That was how the emissary Franklin Vail, trustee of Lane, had put the matter when traveling east to recruit Dr. Beecher; and "the good of the Church, the awakening of the East in behalf of the West," Vail had insisted besides, "loudly demanded that one of their best generals should occupy the very seat of Western warfare while the enemy was coming in like a flood." The general to stanch that flood of papists and infidels was precisely this same exuberant Congregational pastor, summoned down from Boston to solicit New York money before resuming his journey west with a part of his numerous progeny.

"Well, we did get away from New York at last," Harriet in Philadelphia was able to add to her letter two weeks later, "but it was through much tribulation." They had traveled the second leg of the journey by water. New York truckmen delivered the family baggage to the wrong wharf, however, "and, after waiting and waiting on board the boat, we were obliged to start without it, George remaining to look it up." By the time of their arrival in Philadelphia, with the weather turned dull and drizzly, the travelers had grown disconsolate, "poor Aunt Esther in dismay—not a clean cap to put on—mother in like state—all of us destitute. We went half to Dr. Skinner's and half to Mrs. Elmes's—mother, Aunt Esther, father, and James to the former; Kate, Bella, and myself to Mr. Elmes's. They are rich, hospitable folks, and act the part of Gaius in apostolic times."

Gaius played host *"to me and to the whole church,"* the apostle Paul writes in Romans 16:23. As for the misguided trunks, they caught up with the Beechers next morning. "Father stood and saw them all brought into Dr. Skinner's entry, and then he swung his hat and gave a 'hurrah,' as any man would whose wife had not had a clean cap or ruffle for a week." Philadelphia newspapers meanwhile were noting the presence in their city of so remarkable a group: "'this distinguished brother, with his large family, having torn themselves from the endearing scenes of their home,' etc., etc., 'were going, like Jacob,' etc.—a very scriptural and appropriate flourish," Harriet adjudged the allusion, to a reverent Old Testament émigré who had led his own large family into Egypt. "A number of the pious people of this city," she added, "are coming here this evening to hold a prayer-meeting with reference to the journey and its object," intent upon sending the Beechers on their way well blessed.

Thus in their great carriage the party rumbled overland next day toward Dowington, toward Harrisburg and Pittsburgh and, after many more days than anticipated, up into the Alleghenies and down to Wheeling on the Ohio River. Brother George explained the late delay in their progress. "We had poor horses in crossing the mountains. Our average rate for the last four days to Wheeling was forty-four miles. The journey which takes the mail-stage forty-eight hours, took us eight days." Moreover, having reached the Ohio River at last, at Wheeling (still in Virginia in those antebellum years), the Beechers were advised to linger. They had meant to push on at once by riverboat, but Asian cholera had broken out at their destination. For months the disease had been anticipated with dread, newspapers full of its horrors in Europe, then in England, then relentlessly over the Atlantic to New York and inland. Now the mysterious cholera, with its spectacular symptoms that led so often and promptly to death, had reached Cincinnati and was running a dreadful course there, in this first of its several outbreaks as a scourge of nineteenth-century America.

So the Beechers delayed for a week at Wheeling, where Dr. Beecher improved his hours preaching with great success eleven times, before setting out with his family in the chartered stage overland once more as far as Granville, Ohio. There George himself preached five times, his father four. "The interest was increasingly deep and solemn each day," the younger man was pleased to notice, "and when we left there were forty-five cases of conversion in the town, besides those from the surrounding towns. The people were astonished at the doctrine, said they never saw the truth so plain in their lives."

In that fruitful manner these Beechers concluded their ebullient journey westward, from Granville over corduroy roads to Columbus and on from there finally to Cincinnati, which they reached safely on Wednesday, November 14, 1832, delighted to discover that their furniture had arrived the day before.

Lyman Beecher would bring to these new responsibilities the zeal with which he had undertaken earlier pastoral tasks in East Hampton, at Litchfield, and in Boston. "All at the West is on a great scale, and the minds and the views of the people correspond with these relative proportions," he exulted with characteristic spirit. "The West is a young empire of mind and power and wealth and free institutions, rushing up to a giant manhood, with a rapidity and a power never before witnessed below the sun." Likewise his family, looking back on the same early times at Walnut Hills, would recall an intense enthusiasm, remembering their then new household—a rambling brick home at the edge of the primeval forest—as "replete with moral oxygen—full charged with intellectual electricity." The Beechers insisted years later that theirs had been a glorious life out there while it lasted, although what Harriet set down soon after the arrival sounds often more beclouded. For at the time, she wrote back east of feeling depressed in these new surroundings, of feeling homesick, of lamenting a persisting tendency to withdraw into herself. "I am trying," Harriet Beecher explained wistfully from Cincinnati early on, "to cultivate a general spirit of kindliness towards everybody, instead of shrinking into a corner to notice how other people behave. I am holding out my hand to the right and to the left, and forming casual or incidental acquaintances with all who will be acquainted with me."

Shrinking into a corner, watching how others behave: by nature this seventh of the Beecher offspring was reserved, observing. Only with difficulty did the brilliant young woman make friends, and thus her true friends were few. Georgiana May back in Hartford was one such. To Georgiana, Harriet wrote candidly, in the spring of 1833, of ill health and low spirits since coming to Cincinnati.

Her new surroundings appeared somehow less substantial than the old. "About half of my time I am scarcely alive, and a great part of the rest the slave and sport of morbid feeling and unreasonable prejudice." But why, surrounded by family and with so much to sustain her, was she not more content with her lot? Harriet's few close friends were back east, and to the closest of them she wrote on another occasion, in an undated letter of the period, of having returned from a little party of twelve or so after talking all evening. "When I came to my cold, lonely room," she wrote to the absent Georgiana May, "there was your letter lying on the dressing-table. It touched me with a sort of painful pleasure, for it seems to me uncertain, improbable, that I shall ever return and find you as I have found your letter." In the new silence, what had made Harriet Beecher's room appear so lonely, so cold was her sense of leaving New England for good. Born and reared in Litchfield, at home as well in Boston and Hartford, deeply attached to her native region and yearning for her few and dearest friends there—: "Oh, my dear Georgy," the emigrant burst out with unrestrained candor, "it is scarcely well to love friends thus. The greater part that I see cannot move me deeply. They are present, and I enjoy them; they pass, and I forget them. But those that I love differently; those that I *love*, and oh, how much that word means! I feel sadly about them. They may change; they must die; they are separated from me, and I ask myself why should I wish to love with all the pains and penalties of such conditions?" Even to this dear friend Harriet hesitated about expressing such a feeling, pausing because "so much has been said of it by the sentimental, who talk what they could not have felt. But," she pressed on, "it is so deeply, sincerely so in me, that sometimes it will overflow."

2

CINCINNATI

*H*arriet Beecher was a woman of strong and varied emotions; yet the contrast persists between her later radiant recollections—of Cincinnati, say—and the drabber feelings that she recorded at the time. She would remember a childhood, for instance, spent in "a great household inspired by a spirit of cheerfulness and hilarity." And has anyone ever written more appealingly than she, more vividly and with keener humor, about the domestic warmth of early New England? Yet during that childhood—born in Litchfield, Connecticut, in June 1811, she was young into the third decade of the nineteenth century—living through those years, Harriet as a girl gave poignant witness to her unhappiness. She was emphatically a middle child, as if adrift in the midst of five older siblings and what would become five younger siblings as well. A slight, plain girl, she appeared to live much of the time in an inner world of her own, in her corner observing. She was bright, as were the Beechers generally; so that during the fall of 1824, her oldest sister having set up a school twenty-five miles from Litchfield, at Hartford, Harriet— just entering her teens—came there first as a student, then, still very young, as a teacher. At this Hartford Female Seminary she met Georgiana May, herself one in a family of many children and a leading scholar at the new institution, "older and graver . . . but between her and me," the future author recalled, "there grew up the warmest friendship, which proved lifelong in its constancy."

Catharine Beecher's school at Hartford was a thriving success, and Harriet worked conscientiously to help make it so. Yet the work seemed hardly fulfilling. Some of the young teacher's discontent was inherent in adolescence; some arose from stresses of the Reverend Lyman Beecher's Calvinism, imposed on the family by a strong-willed father. At fourteen, as a sample of her anguish, "My whole life is one continued struggle," Hatty lamented. "I do nothing right. I yield to temptation almost as soon as it assails me. My deepest feelings are very evanescent." And again, early in 1827, visiting her father at his new church in Boston, Harriet (she is fifteen now) writes back to Catharine in Hartford: "I don't know as I am fit for anything, and I have thought that I could wish to die young, and let the remembrance of me and my faults perish in the grave, rather than live, as I fear I do, a trouble to every one. You don't know how perfectly wretched I often feel: so useless, so weak, so destitute of all energy. Mamma"—this was her stepmother, Lyman Beecher's second wife—"often tells me that I am a strange, inconsistent being. Sometimes I could not sleep, and have groaned and cried till midnight, while in the daytime I tried to appear cheerful and succeeded so well that papa reproved me for laughing so much. I was so absent sometimes that I made strange mistakes, and then they all laughed at me, and I laughed, too, though I felt as though I should go distracted. I wrote rules; made out a regular system for dividing my time; but my feelings vary so much that it is almost impossible for me to be regular."

In her early twenties she accompanied her family to Cincinnati, where sister Catharine, eleven years her senior and now a widely known educator, had determined to set up another academy, the Western Female Institute. In this new land Harriet for her part resolved, as she said, to come out of her inner world "and live in the external one." The particular external world into which she was emerging would have appeared attractive in many respects, along the sparkling Ohio River in the sixth largest city in America, situated on its plain and highlands that had been forest and canebrake a mere forty years before. During her earlier exploratory visit to Cincinnati, Catharine had reported having "become somewhat acquainted with those ladies we shall have most to do with, and find them intelligent, New England sort of folks." New Englanders were in abundance out here, and had helped make of the riverport a solid city of brick buildings and macadamized roadways, so that other visitors were for the most part impressed. Harriet Martineau, prolific English author, was to spend time in the town two or three years after the Beechers arrived and be delighted with it, feeling constantly exhilarated. "For more reasons than one," Martineau wrote enthusiastically, "I should prefer Cincinnati as a residence to any other large city of the United States. Of these reasons not the last would be that the 'Queen of the West' is enthroned in a region of wonderful and inexhaustible beauty."

To be sure, another foreign resident felt differently, responding perhaps rather more the way we might if, from our twenty-first century, we were set down in the Cincinnati of the early 1830s. Anthony Trollope's mother had come to America (the future novelist a miserably unhappy twelve-year-old at school back in England) to repair the family fortunes, persuaded that a bazaar out west would be a moneymaking proposition, just the thing for an elder son, Henry, to manage. Ascending the Mississippi, she, that hopeful son, and two daughters arrived at Cincinnati's Public Landing in February 1828. Frances Trollope spent two of the four years that followed in the town, unsuccessful at fulfilling any mercantile ambitions but finding another way to prosper when, upon returning to England, she published an account of her travels, *Domestic Manners of the Americans,* to wide notice and much indignation, in 1832, short months before the Beechers aboard their great chartered coach were rumbling westward through Pennsylvania toward a new life.

Mrs. Trollope had liked little of what awaited those travelers at their destination: the spitting everywhere, so that this Englishwoman had found it impossible to keep her skirts clean of other people's spit; the public eating with dinner knives thrust straight into gorging mouths, and such rapid eating! without one word spoken through each graceless, hasty meal; the impertinent, egalitarian pretensions of servants—never "servants," however, always "help"—the total lack of refinement and culture (only at the Reverend Timothy Flint's home had Mrs. Trollope located culture in Cincinnati); the monotonous hills surrounding, from the crests of which every view was obscured by trees and thick brush; back in town a uniform lack of drains, with decaying garbage piled high in the center of streets, its horrific stench entwined with the stink from overflowing alleyway privies; and everywhere, the hogs wandering free, their obtrusive snouts "fresh dripping from the kennel." Everybody noted Cincinnati's hogs. Garbage-consuming hogs were a feature of most cities at the time, but nowhere were they so plentiful as in this Porkopolis, alive with its polyglot immigrant chatter along the waterfront, its peddlers, its homesteaders in transit westward, its shaggy flatboatmen and southern planters bringing their black slaves over from Kentucky, its Indians and trappers and French down from northern wilds. The New England influence that Catharine Beecher had observed appeared well diluted by now, as waves of immigrants from Europe and elsewhere kept coming. An Englishman, William Proctor, came over and set up a candle factory; the Irishman James Gamble had his little candle factory also. Those two, having married sisters, were about to join forces momentously, in 1837. The Austrian Rudolph Wurlitzer meanwhile came with his fiddle to Cincinnati and established a musical instrument shop. Andrew Jergens from Germany built a soap factory; and Charles and Maximilian Fleischmann, Hungarians, erected their distillery here and introduced Americans to fresh compressed yeast, which traffic on the river spread widely.

But above all, there to make people wealthy were the hogs, as Harriet Beecher at her own arrival had promptly noted. To her stay-at-home older sister Mary, established in residence in Hartford, Harriet was writing, within weeks of the family's settling in on Fourth Street, of seeing their four-year-old brother Jamie "parading by the house with his arm over the neck of a great hog, apparently on the most amicable terms possible; and the other day he actually got upon the back of one, and rode some distance. So much for allowing these animals to promenade the streets, a particular in which Mrs. Cincinnati has imitated the domestic arrangements of some of her elder sisters, and a very disgusting one it is."

Disgusting, true; but highly profitable. Salt pork was the staple of a sailor's diet, and the British government had earlier contracted to get much of its mess pork from Cincinnati. From that boon had arisen industries associated with a pork-packing city: slaughterhouses, smokehouses for curing bacon and hams, tanyards, lard-renderers, glue factories, bone-fertilizer factories, soap and candle makers. In years ahead the riverport would become "literally speaking, a *city of pigs*," according to yet another English visitor, a Mrs. Houstoun: "a monster piggery," as she called it. "Alive and dead, whole and divided into portions, their outsides and their insides, their grunts and their squeals, meet you at every moment." Or as

Mrs. Trollope put it (that "learned lady," whom Americans, smarting from having read her tart opinions of them, recalled as "short, thick and vulgar-looking" and "much given to being slovenly and slipshod. She might be seen ever and anon in a green calash and long plaid cloak dragging at her heels, and walking with those colossian strides unattainable by any but English women")—the opinionated Mrs. Trollope had recorded a stroll she had taken in the countryside around Cincinnati with the expectation of pressing her feet to "the flowery sod," yet even in so bucolic a setting having been forced to step over hillside brooks running red with pigs' blood, her way actually "entangled in pigs'-tails and jawbones," so that "the prettiest walk in the neighbourhood was interdicted for ever."

Nevertheless, out of all that Cincinnati pork, pigs' flesh, lard, and hide, from those unsightly bones, feet, bristles, and corpses of gray swine piled in warehouses, fortunes were being made and mansions and riverfront villas were rising, with wealth fostering a substantial culture despite Mrs. Trollope's failure to find it. In fact, the town's intellectual life, of New England origins, was already remarkably ample, having preceded the boom in hogs; and to this cultural Cincinnati the privileged children of Reverend Lyman Beecher, president of Lane Theological Seminary, would gain prompt access.

A prominent manifestation of local culture was the Semi-Colon Club, founded this year of 1832 by, among others, two transplanted relatives of the Beechers, Samuel Foote and his brother John. Members of the club included Judge James Hall, editor of the *Western Monthly*; Professor Hentz, the naturalist; his wife, the novelist Caroline Lee Hentz; Professor O. M. Mitchel, the astronomer; General Edward King—all those names of such consequence then, so deep in oblivion now—Mrs. Peters, afterward founder of the Philadelphia School of Design; C. P. Cranch, the poet; Charles W. Elliott, historian of New England; Dr. Daniel Drake, physician and author; his brother Benjamin, author of biographies of Black Hawk and Tecumseh; Edward D. Mansfield, author and editor; Professor James W. Ward, poet and naturalist; James H. Perkins, poet, essayist, and editor; William Greene, political writer; U. T. Howe, newspaper wit; as well as the two poets Charles D. Drake and C. B. Brush. One member of the Semi-Colon Club did transcend local fame to become a name that we recognize: Salmon P.

Chase, young Cincinnati lawyer who would evolve into Lincoln's secretary of the treasury and chief justice of the United States Supreme Court. Catharine Beecher, educator, was yet another member of the club, as was her younger sister Harriet. And Calvin Stowe, the new professor of biblical literature at Lane, for whose salary Dr. Beecher had been raising funds in New York City on his way west, joined the Semi-Colons too, bringing along his young wife, who would become Harriet's friend.

The club met on alternate weeks either at Samuel Foote's house at Third and Vine streets or at Dr. Drake's, where members enjoyed discussions, musical interludes, and the reading of papers aloud. Harriet Beecher took an active part. To Georgiana back in Hartford she reported of writing a piece to be read next Monday evening at the club, at Uncle Sam's, he being the brother of Harriet's own mother, Dr. Beecher's late first wife. What the younger Miss Beecher's effort would provide for the society's amusement was an imitation of the orotund prose of Dr. Samuel Johnson, the eighteenth-century lexicographer, with the result that the parodist had been "stilting about in his style so long that it is a relief to me to come down to the jog of common English." Nor was this Harriet's debut contribution to the literary pleasures of Cincinnati's poets, wits, and intellectuals. She had submitted, first, a parodic letter in the manner of Bishop Butler, "written in his outrageous style of parentheses and fogification. My second a satirical essay on the modern uses of languages." Moreover, she had prepared a response to gentlemen of the club who had been jesting on the tired subjects of matrimony, bachelordom, and spinsterhood. That playful reproof took the form of "a series of legislative enactments purporting to be from the ladies of the society, forbidding all such allusions in future." It was in fun, of course, and only for circulation among the Semi-Colons gathered in Samuel Foote's parlor. "I try not to be personal," the spinster Miss Beecher wrote, "and to be courteous, even in satire."

But on a Monday evening in November 1833, a member entertained the group by reading aloud Harriet's latest offering, entitled "A New England Sketch." That humorous description of a farmer back home in Connecticut so pleased everyone in attendance that Judge Hall, fellow member as well as editor of the *Western Monthly*, urged its author to submit the sketch in a contest sponsored by his magazine. Her entry easily took the prize, a substantial fifty dollars and publication—Harriet E. Beecher's first such bearing her name—in the April 1834 issue of the journal.

Earlier she had been teaching at her sister's Western Female Institute. "Since writing the above," Harriet had complained to her friend Georgiana the previous spring, in those months soon after arriving in the West, "my whole time has been taken up in the labor of our new school, or wasted in the fatigue and lassitude following such labor. To-day is Sunday, and I am staying at home because I think it is time to take some efficient means to dissipate the illness and bad feelings of divers kinds that have for some time been growing upon me." Since then, Miss Beecher had found a way to allay bad feelings by writing, even earning money doing so. With her older sister's encouragement she had taken weeks away from teaching to write a geography textbook for children, published to considerable success under the educator Catharine's name. And Harriet was making new friends as well, notably the wife of Lane's recently appointed professor of biblical literature, the accomplished Mrs. Eliza Tyler Stowe, Harriet's age, a gifted singer, a popular member of the Semi-Colons, and the daughter of the president of Dartmouth College.

So young Mrs. Stowe was yet another properly pedigreed New Englander come west. Like the Stowes, the equally proper Beechers had been living early on in town, in sight of hogs and close to where the Semi-Colons assembled, while their new residence was made ready on campus two miles off. When it was finished, the family moved into the spacious brick building set among acacias, rosebushes, and honeysuckle atop elevated Walnut Hills at the edge of the forest, the most comfortable home that any of them had ever known. Dr. Beecher for his part was addressing his duties all this while by educating Presbyterian ministers and doing battle with Catholics in America.

But Beecher's attacks on the religious foe had grown less strident than formerly. What tempered his words was a public calamity back in Boston, where a Protestant mob on a Monday in August 1834, in the aftermath of widespread anti-Catholic preaching and under the gaze of impassive authority, set about terrorizing ten religious sisters and their fifty-five boarding-school girls ages six to fourteen, by burning to the ground the Ursuline Convent on

Mount Benedict, across the river in what was then Charlestown. Responding to that and similar antipapist outrages, Lyman Beecher, in his *Plea for the West,* dealt more temperately than in the past with the Catholic church, against which he now insisted that he had no ecclesiastical quarrel. Indeed, in his lecture, delivered repeatedly on a fund-raising trip in the East, Beecher regretted any infringement of the civil and religious rights of Catholics, whose present practitioners should be spared blame for what had occurred in the church's name in the Middle Ages. Against living Catholics, "a declamatory, virulent, contemptuous, sarcastic, taunting, denunciatory style is as unchristian," Lane's president insisted, "as it is in bad taste and indiscreet." As for Catholic beliefs, Dr. Beecher would make no more complaints, but he did reserve the right to criticize matters of church policy: of the church's strivings to gain political power, of Catholic parents refusing to send their children to public schools. To those and other such practices, President Beecher continued to regard it his duty to call attention.

Yet the enemy that threatened Lane Seminary and the West was hardly Catholicism. Times were changing, and Cincinnati, looking directly across the river to slaveholding Kentucky, was no longer undilutedly a New England town. By now the riverport was more of a southern city, its trade of lumber, wheat, and pickled pork flowing southward down the Ohio and Mississippi as far as New Orleans. Southern Illinois, southern Indiana, and indeed southern Ohio itself were peopled by merchants and farmers willing to accommodate the South and its peculiar institution, as much from a shared revulsion toward black Americans as from an interest in commercial prosperity.

The proximate southern way of life, and some few New Englanders' strong, rising objections to it early in Dr. Beecher's tenure, would come to threaten—far more than any Catholic threat—the very survival of Lane Theological Seminary. In the opening months of 1834, a group of idealistic seminarians at Lane, many of them older than their counterparts today, met in Walnut Hills to urge their slaveholding neighbors south of the Ohio River to live by the spirit of the gospel. Those divinity scholars were in earnest, assembling on eighteen successive nights for two and a half hours each to debate an issue that most of their countrymen would rather see left alone. The issue was what to do about slavery. Should freed slaves be set up in colonies overseas, and should steps be taken to abolish the institution of slavery altogether—and if so, gradually or all at once, and by persuasion or direct action? Seventeen seminarians who had witnessed slavery's inhumanities firsthand—half of them sons of slaveholders, one a former slaveholder himself—spoke at the Lane Debates. The leader of the agitation was Theodore Weld of Connecticut, then in his early thirties; and when the discussions and the heartfelt testimony were finally ended, the group of students and future ministers voted to reject any idea of settling former slaves and free blacks in overseas colonies, voted in fact to establish an antislavery society at once and to push for the immediate abolition of slavery, while pledging themselves to found schools for blacks and lecture far and wide on slavery's evils.

Trustees of Lane were profoundly displeased, with twenty-one supporters of colonizing blacks abroad seated among their board of twenty-five. As professional men, fifteen of those trustees enjoyed dealings with the South. Moreover, students of future classes at Lane would necessarily be recruited in large measure from the border South or from farmers and merchants in the North who conducted trade with southern states. Accordingly, on August 16, 1834, with President Beecher away in the East raising money for the seminary, Lane's trustees suppressed the nascent antislavery society and decreed that any other student groups unrelated to the curriculum would be prohibited from convening. On his return Dr. Beecher tried to explain and moderate the effects of the trustees' actions, but thirty-nine defiant students, including Weld himself, left the seminary in disgust anyway.

The blow of such wholesale departures proved a crippling one to Lane, and all but fatal. The antislavery students took themselves off to Oberlin in northern Ohio, enrolling at that new college under the tutelage of Beecher's evangelical rival Charles Grandison Finney. Behind them in Cincinnati they left a diminished institution, about which friends of slavery now detected the taint of abolition and anarchy, while slavery's opponents could see at Lane only the death of free speech and an absence of Christian charity. From classes of forty students at its inception, enrollment at the seminary shrank over the following decade to as few as five.

Harriet Beecher's letters of the time, in the mid-1830s, scarcely mention these contentious matters. She was away herself in the summer of 1834, having set off for a first visit back to New England since coming west two years earlier. She was twenty-three years old, traveling with her friend Mary Dutton by stage, steamboat, canal boat, and railroad up through Ohio and along Lake Erie to glorious Niagara ("I felt as if I could have *gone over* with the waters; it would be so beautiful a death; there would be no fear in it"), and from Buffalo on across New York to western Massachusetts, to attend the graduation from Amherst College of yet another brother, Henry, younger and closest to her in age.

While in the East, she was to receive grim news from her family in Cincinnati. Amid the hogs and filth, cholera had come back to the Queen City that summer. The causes of its reappearance were no better understood on this visitation than when the disease had first raged here two years earlier. In that earlier summer the governor of New York, observing the plague spreading devastation westward through cities of his own state, could offer fellow citizens no more satisfactory explanation for their sudden grief than that "an infinitely wise and just God has seen fit to employ pestilence as one means of scourging the human race for their sins, and it seems to be an appropriate one for the sins of uncleanliness and intemperance," inasmuch as God's punishment hit hardest among the squalidly, drunkenly poor. Yet in its new manifestation, the blight from far-off Asia was invading the outskirts of Cincinnati as well, so that by July 1834 it had moved up to formerly salubrious Walnut Hills, where thirty students of Lane Theological Seminary fell ill, eight gravely so.

Another sufferer was "our dear Mrs. Stowe," Professor Stowe's wife, Harriet's new friend. Twenty-five years old, Eliza Tyler Stowe had been stricken with dysentery "the very day you left," Harriet was to read in a letter from the Beecher household. "The disease yielded to medicine well & on the following sabbath she was apparently entirely relieved & the Dr said she would be well in a day or two." But Dr. Drake was wrong about that; next morning Eliza Stowe was grappling with a severe relapse. Her condition grew desperate. "She set all her affairs in order, gave messages to Mr Stowe for her friends & than said she wished to talk no more about these things." The twenty-third psalm was read aloud for her, repeatedly, and the patient took comfort from it. But on the following day she was discovered "struggling with death," brows knit, deadly pale, exhibiting "distressing movements of convulsive throes I thought O Lord God can we go through with this!"

Relating their ordeal, Harriet's stepmother would spare her reader nothing. "Mr. Stowe said O my love, remember, remember The Lord is my shepherd I shall not want, he leads me in green pastures . . ." And near the last the dying woman was heard to exclaim, "O, how delightful! Her whole countenance brightened & glowed She waved her hands with joy, saying (I cannot tell how many times) O, how delightful." Then, utterly exhausted, Eliza sank into a lethargic sleep, as for two hours the watchers at bedside prayed and read hymns and scriptures aloud over the victim, during which "the only apparent change was she ceased to breathe."

Calvin Stowe had been left a childless widower, and on her return from the East Harriet Beecher sought to console her friend's husband for his loss. A minister's sensitive daughter proved effective at consoling; in time, Professor Stowe became dependent on Harriet's comfort. "I thank God," he was writing to her during the months that followed, "that he has given me a female friend to whom I can open my heart. There are some feelings which a man cannot exercise, and my heart cannot rest in masculine friendship alone. I must be within reach of woman's love, or my own feelings will suffocate me." Within a year of Eliza Stowe's death, the widower was declaring his love for her living friend. "My affection for you is no sudden caprice," Calvin wrote to Harriet in May 1835, "and no sudden caprice will change it. It is of slow and natural growth, & true to its object as the needle to the polar star." These new feelings he would express even more graphically, feelings of what he called "*inseperableness,* as though my blood somehow circulated through your veins, and if you were to be torn from me I should *bleed to death.*"

The widower and his late wife's friend, Calvin Stowe and Harriet Beecher, were married on January 6, 1836. On her wedding morning the bride found time to write to Georgiana May back in Hartford. "Well, my dear G.," Harriet began, "about half an hour more and your old friend, companion, schoolmate, sister, etc., will cease to be Hatty Beecher and change to nobody knows who. My dear, you are engaged, and pledged in a year or two to encounter a similar fate, and do you wish to know how you shall feel? Well, my dear, I have been dreading and dreading the time, lying awake all last week wondering how I should live through this overwhelming crisis, and lo! it has come," she frankly confessed, "and I feel *nothing at all.*"

3

PROFESSOR STOWE

*T*he groom ("Well, here comes Mr. S.," his bride, Harriet Elizabeth Beecher, had written on the wedding morning to her
friend in Hartford, "so farewell, and for the last time I subscribe,
Your own, H. E. B.")—the Calvin Stowe approaching to change
Miss Beecher's name for good was an extraordinary human being.
No surviving evidence suggests that the twenty-four-year-old woman,
for all her intelligence and wit, had ever had any other man express
a romantic interest in her. The man who finally did—undashing
though his round self might appear—had distinctively romantic
traits about him, in addition to being in a number of other ways
exceptional.

Six years after their wedding, while Harriet was visiting her
younger half sister Isabella in Connecticut, she would write to her
husband, "I was telling Belle yesterday that I did not know till I
came away how much I was dependent upon you for information.
There are a thousand favorite subjects on which I could talk with
you better than with any one else. If you were not already my dearly
loved husband I should certainly fall in love with you." And for his
part, Calvin, those several years into their marriage, in the summer
of 1842, would write to the absent Harriet: "And now, my dear wife,
I want you to come home as quick as you can. The fact is I cannot
live without you, and if we were not so prodigious poor I would
come for you at once. There is no woman like you in this wide world.
Who else has so much talent with so little self-conceit; so much
reputation with so little affectation; so much literature with so little
nonsense; so much enterprise with so little extravagance; so much

tongue with so little scold; so much sweetness with so little soft-
ness; so much of so many things and so little of so many other
things?"

He had been born in Natick, Massachusetts, in April 1802—this
erudite professor at Lane Seminary—the son of the village baker. "I
very early learned to read," Professor Stowe recorded in adulthood,
"and soon became immoderately attached to books. In the Bible I
read the first chapters of Job and parts of Ezekiel, Daniel, and Revelation, with most intense delight, and with such frequency that I could
repeat large portions from memory long before the age at which boys
in the country are usually able to read plain sentences."

But even more distinctive than such precocity in a village boy
was the nature of the private world that Calvin Stowe inhabited. "I
have often thought," he wrote in a paper read to Cincinnati's Semi-
Colon Club in 1834, a year and more before his second marriage,
"I would communicate to some scientific physician a particular
account of a most singular delusion under which I lived from my
earliest infancy till the fifteenth or sixteenth year of my age, and
the effects of which remain very distinctly now that I am past
thirty"—effects that would last through his long life. From very early
in that life he had shared his world with apparitions, of such cred-
ibility that the child presumed everyone else lived surrounded by
similar phenomena. As late as when he was nine or ten years old,
he tells us, Stowe "never doubted the real existence of these phantoms, nor had I ever suspected that other people had not seen them
as distinctly as myself. I now, however"—for the first time, not
earlier than when he was nine!—"began to discover with no little
anxiety that my friends had little or no knowledge of the aerial
beings among whom I have spent my whole life; that my allusions
to them were not understood, and all complaints respecting them
were laughed at. I had never been disposed to say much about them,
and this discovery confirmed me in my silence. It did not, however, affect my own belief, or lead me to suspect that my imagina-
tions were not realities."

Such enlightenment had to wait a while longer, until the boy
reached his mid-teens. In the meantime, the apparitions that were
uniquely visiting this sickly, highly sensitive child of the early nineteenth century would prove on occasion reassuring and at other
moments horrifying in the extreme. Professor Stowe was able to

date the various appearances of the visions from crucial events in his childhood: the family's move from one house to another when he was four, his father's death when Calvin was six, another move thereafter into his grandmother's home. The earliest of his bedrooms in the three successive residences was upstairs in front. There, a door in one wall opened on an unfinished closet, low and narrow, and in that closet his phantoms would congregate. Not yet four, lying alone in the darkness, he watched them without uneasiness, persuaded that they were as real as his parents were, as the bench downstairs in the kitchen was. The child did recognize a difference between phantoms and what he could touch and feel, "but to me this difference was no more a matter of surprise than that which I observed between my mother and the black woman who so often came to work for her; or between my infant brother and the little spotted dog Brutus of which I was so fond." Life, after all, that early was filled with wonders.

"One night"—a single specimen among several recollected—"as I was lying alone in my chamber with my little dog Brutus snoring beside my bed, there came out of the closet a very large Indian woman and a very small Indian man, with a huge bass-viol between them." The woman wore a loose black gown, Stowe could recall with precision thirty years later, and a gray fur cap like a lady's muff. The Indian man was dressed in a shabby overcoat and a black, close-fitting hat. "They took no notice of me, but were rather ill-natured towards each other, and seemed to be disputing for the possession of the bass-viol." The man grabbed the instrument and played a few audible, harsh notes that "seemed to vibrate through my whole body, with a strange, stinging sensation." Only very rarely did the child's visions emit such sounds—or any noise at all. The Indian woman now took the viol back "and appeared to play very intently and much to her own satisfaction, but without producing any sound that was perceptible by me." Soon the apparitions left Calvin's bedroom, and he watched them—for his phantasmagoria was visible through walls— go down to the back kitchen, where they lingered to play their silent music and talk with the child's mother. Afterward, the phantoms went out the back door, leaped upon a heap of straw and beans in the yard, and "with a strange, rumbling sound" disappeared.

The same intrusion was repeated thereafter night after night with hardly a variation. What struck Calvin as oddest about the recurring visits was that, though every night beans and straw were heaped in the yard beyond the back door, the pile was nowhere to be seen in the daytime. He asked his mother about it, "but as I was not as yet very skillful in the use of language, I could get no satisfaction out of her answers, and could see that my questions seemed to distress her. At first she took little notice of what I said, regarding it no doubt as the meaningless prattle of a thoughtless child. My persistence, however, seemed to alarm her, and I suppose that she feared for my sanity. I soon desisted from asking anything further, and shut myself more and more within myself."

The family moved to the second dwelling, a one-story house where the child's new bedroom was off the kitchen. The room was unfinished, its wall boards in some places not reaching the ceiling. One opening between ceiling and wall was directly in Calvin's line of sight as he lay in bed; and each evening, after the candle had been removed, a human face, which bore a striking resemblance to an older boy in the village whom the four-year-old feared and hated, appeared in the opening above a board. But in this private darkness the face looked pleasant, friendly. His visitor "would peer at me over the top of that board," Stowe recalled, "and gradually press forward his head, neck, shoulders, and finally his whole body as far as the waist, through the opening, and then, smiling upon me with great good-nature, would withdraw in the same manner in which he had entered. He was a great favorite of mine; for though we neither of us spoke, we perfectly understood, and were entirely devoted to, each other."

These visits the child looked forward to and always welcomed. But one night, alone in his room, Calvin was frightened by vast black tunnel-shaped clouds whirling about him in great agitation. "This alarmed me exceedingly, and I had a terrible feeling that something awful was going to happen." Soon the human face of his phantom friend appeared between wall and ceiling, "cautiously peeping at me through the aperture, with an expression of pain and terror on his countenance. He seemed to warn me to be on my guard, but was afraid to put his head into the room lest he should be touched by one of the clouds, which were every moment growing thicker and more numerous."

The phantom withdrew, leaving Calvin alone with the clouds. Then, "on turning my eyes towards the left-hand wall of the room,

I thought I saw at an immense distance below me the regions of the damned, as I had heard them pictured in sermons." The dreaded clouds were rising out of those depths, while nearer at hand, at only a little space from his bed, Calvin discovered several stout, well-dressed devils with hairless, ash-colored faces wrestling with what he recognized as a Natick ne'er-do-well named Brown, a village fixture "unprincipled and dissipated," of whom for a long time the boy had stood in great fear. From his bed, trembling from head to foot, he watched as the terrified Brown and the devils struggled, until one of the clouds grazed the reprobate's hand, which immediately grew black and shriveled. Brown was in a panic, his face contorted horribly. A devil appeared with a pair of rollers of the sort used in iron mills, whereupon his satanic companions seized the man and put his feet to the rollers and cranked his body relentlessly in. "Not a word was spoken, not a sound heard, but the fearful struggles and terrified, agonizing looks of Brown were more than I could endure. I sprang from my bed," writes Stowe in his thirties, remembering, "and ran through the kitchen and into the room where my parents slept, and entreated that they would permit me to spend the remainder of the night with them." Those Calvinists heard their son out unmoved. "'Poh! poh! you foolish boy,' replied my father, sternly. 'You've only been dreaming; go right back to bed, or I shall have to whip you.'" And Calvin was obliged to do so, trudging across the kitchen "with all the courage I could muster," entering his room to find neither cloud, nor devils, nor anything else out of the ordinary. But thenceforth he meant to keep his troubles to himself.

After his father's death, the family lived with Calvin's grandmother, and there in that third bedroom, "a neatly furnished upper chamber," the child, now six or seven, could see through his wall at night a pleasant meadow with a grove of trees at its farther end, out of which would emerge a little female figure, "about eight inches high and exquisitely proportioned," with long black hair and wearing a black silk robe. The figure would approach to the plane of the wall, smile at Calvin, "raise her hands to her head and draw them down on each side of her face," then abruptly turn and withdraw in haste. Her visits would be repeated as many as three times in an evening. And on another occasion, on a bright moonlit night, Calvin awoke to find beside him in bed a full-length human skeleton, ashy blue in color. The child screamed in horror, and others in the household hurried to his aid. "I refused to tell the cause of my alarm, but begged permission to occupy another bed, which was granted."

Finally he would realize that such phantoms as he lived with daily and nightly were quite absent from other people's lives; and at a still later date, in his mid-teens, he would come to understand that the apparitions had no reality. Yet they would never leave him, however skilled Stowe as an adult might become in ignoring their presence. A singular instance, years after his marriage to Harriet Beecher, discloses their casual ubiquity. Harriet had set out from the family's rural home to catch a train but had missed it. She returned to wait through the several hours for the next scheduled train and, with work to do, entered the house quietly to retire to her writing desk in the couple's bedroom. A half hour went by, and Professor Stowe came in, gazing about with a preoccupied air. He said nothing to his wife but continued with his own concerns. Thinking his behavior strange, Harriet diverted herself for a while observing him. Finally the situation became so odd that she started to laugh. Her husband turned from the bookshelves and stared at her. "Why, is that you?" he exclaimed in utter surprise. "I thought it was one of my visions!"

His father's untimely death had left young Calvin Stowe to grow up in Natick in straitened circumstances, so that the child had had to work from an early age. Feeble in health, he was apprenticed to a papermaker, this village oddity immoderately attached to books, given to long walks alone in the evenings. "The most lonely fields, the woods, and the banks of the river, and other places most completely secluded, were my favorite resorts, for there I could enjoy the sight of innumerable aerial beings of all sorts, without interruption." Stowe's visions animated all of nature around him, gave each trembling leaf a soul. The moody young romantic assigned names to the solitary places that he haunted. "Moonlight was particularly agreeable to me, but most of all I enjoyed a thick, foggy night." Often in those years he suffered an indefinable melancholy, living always vividly, intensely, experiencing at times "a morbid love for my friends that would almost burn up my soul, and yet, at the least provocation from them, I would fly into an uncontrollable passion and foam like a little fury. I was called a dreadful-tempered boy; but the Lord knows that I never occasioned pain to any animal, whether human or brutal, without suffering untold agonies in consequence of it." Even years later, as a more rational adult, he recalled with sorrow those "alternate fits of corroding melancholy, irritation, and bitter remorse" that had darkened a romantic adolescence.

Fortunately, wide reading and a superior intellect earned the apprentice papermaker a scholarship to college, which the church in the village provided. Thus Stowe as a young man set out from Natick to the frontier settlement of Brunswick, in the just created state of Maine. From Bowdoin College, founded two decades earlier, Calvin Ellis Stowe graduated as valedictorian in the class of 1824. (A classmate, the future president Franklin Pierce, had proved considerably less able academically; and in the class behind—in a single small, remote young college—were one adept scholar and another less so: Henry Wadsworth Longfellow and Nathaniel Hawthorne.) After graduating, Stowe lingered a year in Brunswick as librarian at Bowdoin, then resumed his studies, at Andover Theological Seminary, before taking a position in Hanover, New Hampshire, as professor of Greek at Dartmouth.

"In 1830," he would later explain, "I got hold of 'Faust,'"—in the original German—"and for two gloomy, dreary November days, while riding through the woods of New Hampshire in an old-fashioned stagecoach, to enter upon a professorship in Dartmouth College, I was perfectly dissolved by it." Forever after, Stowe would be a devoted scholar of Goethe, as invariably this tireless reader would carry with him in his pockets copies of the New Testament in Greek and of Dante's *Divine Comedy* in Italian. For Calvin Stowe was a superlative linguist, fluent in addition in Spanish, Latin, Hebrew, and Arabic. All seven of those languages he read as easily as he read English. And he was, moreover, or would soon become, the foremost biblical scholar in the America of his day.

Like many of us, he was sometimes unclear about what were his strengths and weaknesses. "From the hour of my birth I have been constitutionally feeble, as were my parents before me, and my nervous system easily excitable. With care, however, I have kept myself in tolerable health"—this hypochondriac who, after repeated alarms about his approaching demise, would die finally in his eighty-fifth year. Professor Stowe frankly admitted having no talent or taste for writing poetry or fiction, with barely enough imagination to enjoy other people's efforts in those departments of literature. His own writing style, he declared, was "remarkable for its dry, matter-of-fact plainness"; and yet, writing on the most abstruse theological subjects, he still managed to express himself with homely vigor. He was a wonderful lecturer, of great liveliness, able to mimic a wide range of dialects, a gifted storyteller with a huge fund of stories and a most marvelous memory; but in his own words, "the only talent of a higher kind which I am conscious of possessing is a turn for accurate observation of men and things, and a certain broad humor and drollery."

That is far too modest. We have already witnessed Stowe's skill in observation combining with his retentive memory to recall childhood visions of astonishing preciseness. While at Dartmouth, and courting his future wife Eliza Tyler, he was in addition doing editorial work for a Boston journal, *The Recorder,* and in Boston would attend Hanover Street Church in the North End. That church's pastor, Reverend Lyman Beecher, readily recognizing Stowe's many gifts, persuaded this professor of Greek to join him out west and teach biblical literature at the newly founded Lane Theological Seminary. In August 1832, Stowe received his appointment to the Lane faculty. There in Cincinnati, he was to lose his beloved wife of two years to cholera, then grieve and be comforted in his grief by the late Mrs. Stowe's young female friend Harriet Beecher, ending by making that friend his second wife in early January 1836.

"Three weeks have passed since writing the above," the new Mrs. Stowe would continue her as yet unsent letter to Georgiana May, begun on the couple's wedding day, "and my husband and self are now quietly seated by our own fireside, as domestic as any pair of tame fowl you ever saw; he writing to his mother, and I to you." By then, the newlyweds had had their honeymoon, such as it was, up to Columbus. "Ohio roads at this season are no joke," Harriet assured her friend back east, recalling the midwinter journey brought about by Mr. Stowe's being summoned to deliver a lecture in the state capital—"and I had too much adhesiveness not to go too." On the basis of that lecture, on Prussian education, to the Western College of Teachers, the Ohio legislature commissioned the professor to investigate and report on aspects of European public schooling that might help children in this young western state. In part to fulfill that charge, in part to purchase books in Europe for

Lane Theological Seminary, Professor Stowe would be leaving America soon. Thus promptly the new husband and wife were to be separated, as they would be often in years ahead. On this present occasion, Calvin Stowe sailed from New York on June 8, aboard the *Montreal* bound for London. His bride, who would have liked very much to go east with him, to see him off and visit family and friends in Hartford, stayed in Cincinnati instead, taking up residence with the numerous Beechers of Walnut Hills. By then it would have been imprudent to embark on any further travels over the roads of the time, for Harriet Beecher Stowe was already pregnant. With Mr. Stowe still absent overseas, she gave birth in late September 1836, one week short of nine months after the wedding, to twin girls, the first of the couple's seven children.

4

EARLY MARRIED LIFE

*H*alf a year later the new mother was able to report that "tho I scarcely slept a wink last night & tho I have had one of two babies in my arms all day—tho money is scarce & times hard yet I never was happier on the whole than I am now." She had taken to motherhood. That surprised those who knew this second Mrs. Stowe best, including her own family. The Beechers regarded the former spinster, married late by the lights of the time, as the cleverest among numerous, very bright siblings; as an intellectual, in fact, even a genius. An admiring sister-in-law put it plainly, without irony, regarding Harriet's having given birth to twins: "you are a genius, and therefore can't be expected to walk in a beaten track." Or as Catharine a little later, in this same spring of 1837, wrote of her younger sister's parenting, "Harriet manages better than folk would expect who are wont to think a genius & a blue stocking cannot be good for anything else." Later still, her half sister Isabella, after ample time to observe Harriet's skills at child rearing and housekeeping, would remark that whatever imperfections they might display were "clearly traceable to the very qualities which render her so superior to most."

For there were imperfections in Mrs. Stowe's homemaking, and Professor Stowe, returning from his book-buying expedition in Europe, would find occasion to point them out. Having been ten months away, the scholar of biblical literature disembarked in New York in January 1837, and only then learned of his wife's having given birth to twins five months earlier. "Bravo, you noble creature," he wrote proudly to Cincinnati on landing. The twins must be named for his first wife and his second, Eliza and Hattie. Incidentally, Calvin Stowe's trip overseas had proved a great success. He came back with enrichment for the library at Lane Theological Seminary to the extent of eight big crates containing 5,000 volumes, including writings by Greek and Latin church fathers from Justin Martyr in the second century to Bernard in the twelfth, as well as all the proceedings of the various Catholic church councils from the fourth century to the seventeenth, along with works of such consequential religious figures as Huss, Wyclif, Luther, Calvin, and Melanchthon. And what pleasure it must have given this learned book lover to be rooting through collections in Germany, France, and England in order to choose suitable titles at Lane's expense: 200 volumes of Greek and Roman classics, various works of ancient and modern history, encyclopedias, fifty volumes of *Memoirs of the French Academy,* 160 volumes of Royal Society proceedings, seventy volumes of British poetry, fifty-six volumes of German and French poetry, illustrated books of costumes and of architecture, plus works of all the standard European theologians and historians. Well satisfied, Lane Seminary gave a picnic in the summer to display its new bibliographic treasures on the lawn. And by then the flourishing professor, who was also Lane's librarian, had submitted to the Ohio legislature his other charge, a *Report on Elementary Instruction in Europe* that was printed and widely distributed in several states beyond Ohio to influence the shaping of public school education throughout the Old West.

Back home at last this spring of 1837, his mission overseas successfully completed, Professor Stowe helped around the house when he could. During the daytime he would lecture at the seminary with his usual effectiveness, then would look after "one baby or another nights," according to his wife, "in consequence of which he is often tired & sleepy at both periods."

Twins, of course, put strains on the marriage. The Stowes did find much to talk about, this new mother and father, as they always would. "I believe," Calvin ventured, "there are very few husbands and wives in the world, who have so many real good talks together on such matters as we have"—both of them book lovers, both intellectual, both similarly and devoutly religious, both with a keen sense of humor and a ceaseless relish for the peculiarities of human speech and behavior. But temperamentally the two differed.

In the course of their talks and their fluent letters to each other during times apart, Calvin made those differences abundantly, even systematically clear. "1) I am naturally anxious," he wrote, "to the extent of needlessly taking much thought beforehand. You are hopeful, to the extent of being heedless of the future, thinking only of the present." That difference might not be all bad, but "2)," this husband continued itemizing, striving all the while to be fair, "I am naturally very methodical as to time and place for everything, and anything out of time or out of place is excessively annoying to me. You have," he told Harriet bluntly, "no idea of either time or place." Which seems true: all her life Harriet Beecher Stowe was famously detached, daydreamingly remote, in her own word *absent*. "I," Calvin went on, "want prayers and meals at the particular time, and every piece of furniture in its own place. You can have morning prayer anytime between sunrise and noon without the least inconvenience to yourself, and as to place, it seems to be your special delight to keep everything in the house on the move, and your special torment to allow anything to retain the same position a week together. Permanency is my delight,—yours, everlasting change."

Other contrasts individuated them: "3) I am naturally particular, you are naturally slack," so that Calvin had already suffered inexpressible torment, as he put it, from his wife's innocent habit of mishandling his newspapers, "instead of folding them properly and putting them in their place, either dropping them all sprawling on the floor, or wabbleing them all up into one wabble, and squulching them on the table like an old hen with her guts and gizzard squeezed out." And for a fourth point, Mrs. Stowe was in her husband's view extravagant, hiring help when times were hard.

For times had become very hard. Practical steamboats plied the Ohio well before 1830, the same year that a canal was opened to bypass the rapids at Louisville and not long before the Beechers in their lumbering stagecoach, late in 1832, were arriving from the East. From 1830 on, then, with traffic chugging upstream on the river as well as all the way down, Cincinnati's fortunes exploded. It had become the premier riverport in America, America's first boomtown, growing from maybe 6,000 people in 1815 to more than twelve times that many three decades later, and to as many as 115,000 by 1850, nearly half (51,000 of those mid-century Cincinnatians) foreign-born. Already by the mid-1830s, with Dr. Beecher installed as Lane's

president at nearby Walnut Hills and with his daughter about to
marry a member of Lane's faculty, the city was a national wonder,
its dry goods and jewelry stores, its grand shops of furs, millinery,
silverware, and other merchandise for sale on such an ample scale
as to leave visitors agape. Cincinnati in that respect appeared the
equal of Paris and London, as one traveler insisted; its elegant
emporiums were as well supplied "with the best English and French
goods," according to another, "as in the largest cities in the East."
Wealth from hogs and pork and trade upriver and down was achieving all that.

Yet during this same 1837, in the spring of Calvin Stowe's return from abroad to take on responsibilities as the father of twins
and resume his lecturing at Lane, banking houses downriver in New
Orleans were suddenly failing, to the catastrophic sum of $1.5 mil-
lion, and their failure was sending economic shock waves all over
the Union. Panic ensued, the first deep depression in American history, caused by recent changes in federal monetary policies, by years
of too much borrowing on the part of people speculating wildly in
western lands, and by apprehensive creditors abruptly calling in
loans. As always in such instances, the causes of the Panic of 1837
appear complex and abstract in the telling; the effects, however,
were concrete and simple. Back in Hartford, for instance, the only
stay-at-home Beecher, Mary, after nine years of comfortable marriage to her lawyer husband, Thomas Perkins, was all at once to see
her beautiful piano and the other furnishings of a beloved parlor sold
to satisfy creditors, as Aunt Esther, visiting from Cincinnati, reported.
The plight of the beset attorney Perkins was even "more trying now
than at his former failure," Esther Beecher wrote, because "then he
had but two children and a regular salary of a thousand dollars a year
for their support and his office rent free—now he has four children
no salary and hires an office at a hundred dollars a year," with heavy-
booted draymen in his residence confiscating his assets. Closer to
home, at the corner of Third and Vine streets in Cincinnati, the affluent Samuel Foote, brother of Harriet Beecher Stowe's late mother,
was feeling the pinch as well; he would have to sell his commodious
mansion and move to smaller quarters, closing for good the parlor
where the Semi-Colon Club used to meet: "our *last* Semi-colon," as
Mrs. Foote would write sorrowfully on March 6, and indeed the club
never did come together again.

Closer still: Lane's principal benefactor was the New York merchant Arthur Tappan, who like so many others had felt the force of the current panic. For one consequence, the bank was declining to honor Lyman Beecher's draft on Mr. Tappan for his salary as president of Lane Seminary. Already Lane had been reeling, ever since that substantial group of seminarians, intent on extending ideals of brotherhood to include blacks in an essentially southern city, had walked out of classes for good three years ago, in 1834, leaving behind a stain of abolitionism to besmirch the school's reputation. Enrollment was down in any case, and money tight, so that there seemed no prospect any time soon of Professor Stowe's getting the home that his family had been promised. He and his wife and the twins would have to make do with their present "miserable accommodation," much less ample than housing that other professors at Lane enjoyed. By the summer of 1837 this mild-mannered scholar of biblical literature was ready to "throw Lane Seminary to the dogs if they do not justice to me in this respect, and you may tell them so." That to his wife, daughter of Lane's president. A cramped cottage to live in; "the covenant-breaking conduct of the board"; how Stowe was treated compared with other professors: all that "has been the cause of three fourths of my unhappiness since I returned from Europe."

School trustees were meanwhile doing what they could under trying circumstances. They managed to find Professor Stowe an extra $250 to atone in part for his living conditions, and from other school funds they somehow put together President Beecher's salary for the current year. Yet from now on, year after year would be the same. Effects of the Panic of 1837 extended far into the 1840s, and the history of Lane through that grim period would be one of hand-to-mouth uncertainty, of scouring about for money and for students to augment whatever money could be found. Calvin's salary of $1,200 a year would soon be cut to $1,100—later it was cut more drastically still—and his father-in-law's salary be cobbled together from uncertain sources, in one instance partly from a contribution by the George Beechers. George, the former divinity student who earlier had led hymn-singing atop the family's chartered stagecoach headed west, had since gone on to become a minister himself and marry well. He and his wealthy wife Sarah Buckingham would send along $200 to help make up President Beecher's modest remuneration.

But though money problems persisted, and Lane Seminary's reputation went on suffering from the ill fame that student defections over abolition had stirred up years earlier and that wouldn't die down, Mrs. Stowe, still in her cramped cottage, wife of a disgruntled husband and mother of twins, was trying with characteristic optimism to put the best face on things. "We are rather better," she noted succinctly at the end of 1838, "in that we now know *exactly* the state of our accts—We are in debt—& embarrassed but have good hope by management to pay off—But few students—traveling expences great—cant afford to come from the east & not many to be found in this ungodly west—Must retrench."

Retrenching, however, was what Harriet found hard to do. That, as we have seen, was the fourth point on which she and her husband differed. Professor Stowe, who needed little else from life beyond a book in his hand, found Mrs. Stowe extravagant. He meant to read his way through these rough times and wait for the Tappan mercantile enterprises back east to recoup their losses. But his wife could scarcely do likewise. Chores in the cottage demanded constant attention. Tending the babies, managing the larder, cooking, baking, sewing, washing, ironing, the unending dusting and cleaning —all the business that Aunt Esther summed up with images of brooms and flatirons, bread trays and knitting needles—had been keeping Harriet's hands perpetually occupied.

Then, precisely two years and a week into her marriage, in January 1838, she was to give birth to a son, Henry Ellis Stowe. There were now three children under eighteen months old. "My Dear, Dear Georgiana," the new mother found time at last, six months later, to write to her Hartford friend: "Only think how long it is since I have written to you, and how changed I am since then—the mother of three children! Well, if I have not kept the reckoning of old times, let this last circumstance prove my apology, for I have been hand, heart, and head full since I saw you." She would provide specifics. "Now, to-day, for example"—Harriet set out to describe for Georgiana one day in detail. She had waked at 4:30 this morning, and already it was almost light outside. The nurse must be got up to start breakfast. "So out of bed I jump and seize the tongs and pound, pound, pound over poor Mina's sleepy head, charitably allowing her about half an hour to get waked up in." By now baby Henry is awake as well: "quâ, quâ, quâ, so I give him his breakfast, dozing meanwhile and soliloquizing as follows: 'Now I must not forget to tell Mr. Stowe about the starch and dried apples'—doze—'ah, um, dear me! why doesn't Mina get up? I don't hear her,'—doze—'a, um,—I wonder if Mina has soap enough! I think there were two bars left on Saturday'—doze again—"

Suddenly it is broad daylight. Harriet must make sure about breakfast. Moving to do so she wakes the baby, who starts crying loudly, "fisting the bedclothes." Half-dressed, the harried mother fetches pillows to prop up her infant before hurrying to check downstairs. Then back in the nursery she remembers this is washing day, with "a great deal of work to be done." She gets busy at once, applying herself "vigorously to sweeping, dusting, and the setting to rights so necessary where there are three little mischiefs always pulling down as fast as one can put up."

This from a woman who, as her husband bears witness, lacked natural gifts for setting homemaking matters to rights. The other two children by now are "chattering, hallooing, or singing at the tops of their voices," while the adults lay out breakfast. That is served in good time and eaten, and the meal cleared away. Professor Stowe is then "dispatched to market with various memoranda of provisions, etc., and the baby being washed and dressed, I begin to think what next must be done."

Harriet will cut out some children's dresses. She is just figuring their measurements when Master Henry, five months old, "makes a doleful lip" and starts crying. While his mother attends to that, one of the twins rummages through the sewing box, and the other chews coals and plays in ashes at the hearth. Deterred, the twins fall to quarreling. "Number two screams: that frightens the baby and he joins in." One gets scolded, the other consoled, and before long the reprimanded toddler is washing her apron in the slop jar. Finally Mina comes up from sweeping to help restore order, allowing their mother to return to cutting out frocks.

"But let this suffice, for of such details as these are all my days made up. Indeed, my dear, I am but a mere drudge with few ideas beyond babies and housekeeping."

That wasn't quite true. For a long while, ever since before her marriage, Harriet had made time in her day to write and was earning money doing so. In such straits as these, writing seemed all the more necessary, for health of mind and to supplement a growing family's shrinking income. Back in Semi-Colon days she had first published locally in Judge Hall's *Western Monthly*, then later had begun selling her work to periodicals farther afield, to the *Evangelist* in New York and to *Godey's Lady's Book* in Philadelphia; sometimes those magazines would pay her as much as a penny a word. By now Harriet E. Beecher Stowe might make in a single year up to $300 to augment the family's meager finances.

But she took that money and spent it on what her husband must learn was not an extravagance—hiring additional help to do the house chores, in order that Mrs. H. E. B. Stowe might set aside even more time for writing.

This was a period in Ohio, as elsewhere in the middle to late 1830s, of prolonged public outcry against abolitionists, when respectable citizens—clerks, merchants, farmers in town—felt moved to rally indignantly and give their support to mobs that, in one instance, howled threat-filled protests outside the office of an antislavery newspaper editor setting up his print shop in Cincinnati. That particular mob ended by destroying the abolitionist's newsprint and trays of type, throwing his printing press into the Ohio, and eventually driving this James G. Birney—a former slave owner who had experienced a change of heart—to depart the riverport and find a new career, leaving his newspaper, the *Philanthropist*, in the hands of the more moderate Dr. Gamaliel Bailey to edit and publish. (Birney would go on to become the Liberty Party candidate for president in 1840.) But about such civic turmoil close at hand Harriet E. Beecher Stowe had little to say. She was writing instead of what she knew well, and loved, and remembered, and of what with sharp intuition she guessed that her audience wanted to read.

Those latter efforts intended to please the reader—edifying essays on frankness, the good consequences of children obeying their parents, the perils of theatergoing, the virtues of temperance, the moral risks in dancing—now please hardly at all. But the remainder of Stowe's early writings, which includes vivid evocations of canalboat travel and of remembered New England characters ("Aunt Mary," "Old Father Morris"), still have life in them, and humor, and here and there a freshness that lingers after these many years. Moreover, during their own day her sketches were appearing widely enough that this self-effacing scribbler, in an era when female authorship was still a suspect enterprise, felt moved to write back east as if in apology: "if you see my name coming out every where, you may be sure of one thing, that I *do* it for *the pay*."

Yet she fretted. The twins and little Henry needed their mother's care. "Our children," she wrote Calvin, "are just coming to the age when everything depends on my efforts"—at nurture, of course, not at literature. "They are delicate in health, and nervous and excitable, and need a mother's whole attention. Can I lawfully divide my attention by literary efforts?" But her husband proved supportive after all. He had learned to be grateful for the money: *Godey's Lady's Book*, for example, was paying his wife $15 a page, and that, the professor calculated, was "making money very fast."

It was more than that, though. Calvin Stowe loved his wife, and depended on her, and believed in her, and was very proud of her. "You must be a *literary woman*," he would come to insist. "It is so written in the book of fate. Make all your calculations accordingly, get a good stock of health, brush up your mind, drop the E out of your name, which only encumbers it and stops the flow and euphony, and write yourself only and always, *Harriet Beecher Stowe*, which is a name euphonous, flowing, and full of meaning; and my word for it, your husband will lift up his head in the gate, and your children will rise up and call you blessed."

The scholarly Mr. Stowe adored his clever wife, so that in the end she could do and have whatever she wanted. Was it a room of her own? "There is one thing I must suggest," she informed the doting Calvin. "If I am to write, I must have a room to myself, which shall be *my* room." Harriet had thought it all out, in her mind devising a space at home where she could put in a stove and set down a cheap carpet already purchased and move spare furniture, and the only other thing she asked was "that you will let me change the glass door from the nursery into that room and keep my plants there, and then I shall be quite happy." Her carpet constituted more expense during hard times, but of course she would be allowed to move the door. His wife would have her way. Only the new room was to be for writing. When the day's writing was done, husband and wife must as always sleep together in their shared bedroom.

For the ordained minister and professor of sacred literature had, pronouncedly, his carnal side. "Though I have, as you well know, a most enthusiastic admiration of fresh, youthful female beauty," he would remind his wife candidly at a future time, "yet," he would go on—and this after nearly a decade of marriage—"it never comes anywhere near the kind of feeling I have for you. With you, every desire I have, mental and physical, is completely satisfied and filled up, and leaves me nothing more to ask for. My enjoyment with you is not weakened by time nor blunted by age, and every reunion after separation is just as much of a honey-moon as was the first month after the wedding." He asserted it categorically: "No man can love and respect his wife more than I do mine."

The more reason, perhaps, to regret that they were often apart. Professor Stowe might be sent east to look for godly students and pursue the hateful task of fund-raising—and on one such expedition become aware of a spate of scandalous behavior in the Protestant ministry: a pastor in Exeter, New Hampshire, seducing a kitchen girl and committing adultery with a member of his congregation; two Episcopalian ministers in Philadelphia, one concupiscent and the other, a bishop, exposed as a drunk, who "while half boozled has caught young ladies who were so unfortunate to meet him alone, and pawed them over in the most disgusting manner, and actually attempted to do them physical violence. This has been going on for years until it could be borne no longer, and now it all comes out against him," Stowe reported in horror, "to the dishonor of religion, his own unspeakable shame and anguish, and the distress unutterable of his wife and children." The case provided matter for reflection. "Bless the Lord, O my soul," Calvin wrote to his own wife fervently, "that with all my strong relish for brandy and wine, and all my indescribable admiration and most overflowing delight in handsome young ladies, no offences of this kind have yet been written down against me in God's book."

Harriet responded with both sympathy and dismay. By this time she had a father, seven brothers, and a husband in the ministry or soon to be and so must wonder, "could it be, that the great Enemy has prevailed against any of you"? Endowed as was one particular daughter, sister, and wife with "a most horrible vivid imagination," she had been led by her husband's letter to imagine—"nay saw as in a vision all the distress and despair that would follow a fall on your part." Oh, but "What terrible temptations lie in the way of your sex," she wrote to her absent Calvin; "till now I never realised it— for tho I did love you with an almost *insane* love before I married you I never knew yet or felt the pulsation which showed me that I could be tempted in that way—."

Being male (such was the thinking), her husband did feel the pulsation. Through the coming years their frequent separations— with Stowe going off on business for Lane; or his wife, taking the sturdier twin, traveling east to see editors and visit family and friends in Hartford—would end each time in blissful reunions. Come back, the distressed Calvin would implore meanwhile, and he might tempt Harriet with the prospect of their reading aloud in intimacy from the Bible, specifically from the Song of Songs, which is Solomon's: *Behold, thou art fair, my love. Thy lips are like a thread of scarlet, and thy speech is comely. Thy two breasts are like two young roes that are twins, which feed among the lilies. Thy lips, O my spouse, drop as the honeycomb; honey and milk are under thy tongue. . . .*

Whereupon, following nuptial-like comings-together, Harriet would again find herself pregnant, as in September 1839, and in time would be giving birth, as in May 1840, now to a fourth child, her second son, Frederick. And on this occasion, even more so than earlier, the physically slight mother regained her health only slowly. For two months she was bedfast, and for long months afterward she was very feeble, so that with 1840 winding down at last, the convalescent was driven to explain to her friend Georgiana back east: "For a year I have held the pen only to write an occasional business letter such as could not be neglected." Which means that through all that while, whatever literary fancies may have entered Harriet's mind had vanished unrecorded.

5

AGONIES

George Beecher, the former Yale student who in 1832 had accompanied those of his family migrating westward through
Pennsylvania—he singing atop their chartered stagecoach—up into
the Alleghenies and on finally to Cincinnati, had there finished his
divinity studies at Lane Seminary before being ordained and setting out to preach. George's first church was at Batavia, New York,
where he married into a prosperous family. Later the Reverend Mr.
Beecher moved with his wife Sarah Buckingham to a church in
Rochester, and later still to Chillicothe, in southern Ohio. The young
minister—he was born in 1809, two years before Harriet—was at
Chillicothe, engaged in his pastoral duties, working to finish repairs
on his new home, and taking pride in his carefully cultivated garden, when his oldest sister Catharine came calling in the summer of
1843. She arrived on June 30 in time for evening prayers.

This eldest of the Beecher children found everyone at her
brother's household "in unusual health & prosperity—George had
come in from his Friday lecture and seemed in very cheerful spirits." The next morning, July 1, the parson rose before daylight, went
to market, and brought home provisions for his family. But birds
outside were molesting his beloved garden, flocking in trees and
eating the fruit. He took his shotgun and went to scare them away.

At breakfast time he hadn't returned. A servant, sent to call him,
found the Reverend Mr. Beecher "lying on the ground with his
double barreled gun in his hand—apparently the charge had passed
through his cheek & up through the top of his head which was
shattered." Shattered as well, and very soon after, was any peace

for the surviving Beechers. "Poor Sarah—the first that she saw of him that morning was his lifeless bleeding form on the sofa"; the suddenly widowed woman knelt beside her dead husband "with his hand in hers in heartless despair till she was at last forcibly carried into another room—The intelligence was immediately spread." Lyman Beecher, the dead man's father, heard the dreadful news back east where he was fund-raising, when somebody blurted it out on a city street, leaving Lane's elderly president (now nearing his seventies) breathless, speechless, before he burst into tears: "they were not the tears of the father which flowed first, but the tears of disappointed hope for so much and so needed usefulness in the cause of Christ cut off." A father's tears flowed afterward. As for Harriet, George's next younger sibling, "Why is it when we know that our Redeemer liveth," she wrote in her anguish at the time, ". . . that I can only weep and mourn & feel so sick at heart—I thought I knew the entire emptiness of this world & why is it so distressing to see one more proof of what I knew before!" Later she would elaborate: "The sudden death of George shook my whole soul like an earthquake; and as in an earthquake, we know not where the ground may open next, so I felt an indistinct terror," adding that such "unexpected, stunning agonies show us heart secrets before undreamed of."

Those years in the 1840s appear harrowing for the Stowes, although perhaps living through their successive days was less relentlessly bleak than the grim written remains of the times indicate. Harriet herself was of a generally hopeful nature, full of fortitude and possessed of a religious temperament that gave her a deeply felt confidence in the ultimate direction of mortal affairs. Moreover, moments of stated happiness survive in the record, as for example during festivities in June 1844 to celebrate the tenth anniversary of Lane Seminary, where friends and family assembling "have talked," according to Lyman, "one or two or all together every waking hour—We are all in good health & spirit & are quite garrulous & filled with laughter." Yet even then, even there, Harriet was burdened with four additional adults and ten children (including the widow Sarah Buckingham and little Georgy) to provide for around her table, leaving Calvin to grumble about his wife's taking on so much: "Will no experience and no suffering teach you, that there are certain boundaries which you have no right to pass over?"

The family was very poor, prodigious poor, in Professor Stowe's phrase. Lane Seminary continued to struggle semester after semester into its uncertain future, with Lyman out rustling up whatever students he could come across, and Calvin, discouraged, morose, heading east to raise funds in a frame of mind that made fundraising certain to fail. He had a nervous breakdown, in fact, writing to his wife in Cincinnati of doing nothing but lolling in bed or reading the newspaper or straggling over fields; he had lost his voice, was "very nervous, my throat is sore, my lungs are weak, my stomach is exceedingly sensitive and rebellious," and he was mending very slowly. Back in Ohio, the Stowe children got whooping cough, and typhoid raced through Lane Seminary, bringing sixteen feverish students down. One died. For a month, Harriet—who was taking in boarders for what little that chore might add to the family income—nursed another student through his fever. A mysterious ailment afflicted her, for a considerable while depriving this writer and homemaker of the use of her hands. Was it her blue pills, liberally prescribed: calomel, toxic with mercury? She had given birth, some weeks after George's suicide, to a girl, named Georgiana in honor both of her dead brother and of her lifelong friend in Hartford; and after this fifth child's arrival the mother's indisposition proved especially severe: "my babe was eight weeks old this Tuesday & yet I am far from being fully restored." A wet nurse was brought into the household, "for alas after all my efforts & sufferings I am deprived of the ability to nourish her myself." But the child remained sickly, the nurse was unstable, and the mother continued anxious and harassed. Housework overwhelmed her. "If I should sew every day for a month to come I should not be able to accomplish a half of what is to be done, and should be only more unfit for my other duties."

Calvin had set off, in the summer of 1845, to attend a ministers' convention in Detroit when Harriet wrote to him, despondent, on June 16. "My Dear Husband,—It is a dark, sloppy, rainy, muddy, disagreeable day, and I have been working hard (for me) all day in the kitchen, washing dishes, looking into closets, and seeing a great deal of that dark side of domestic life which a housekeeper may who will investigate too curiously into minutiae in warm, damp weather." Her candor here confirms, at any rate, the consistently honest nature of the Stowes' relationship. "I am sick of the smell of sour milk," Harriet writes, "and sour meat, and sour everything, and then the clothes *will* not dry, and no wet thing does, and everything smells mouldy; and altogether I feel as if I never wanted to eat again." As for her health, "it gives me very little solicitude," she reported indifferently, "although I am bad enough and daily growing worse. I feel no life, no energy, no appetite, or rather a growing distaste for food; in fact, I am becoming quite ethereal." Moreover, she was still suffering from what she terms a distress in the brain, "as I have done more or less since my sickness last winter, a distress which some days takes from me all power of planning or executing anything; and you know that, except this poor head, my unfortunate household has no mainspring, for nobody feels any kind of responsibility to do a thing in time, place, or manner, except as I oversee it."

She had, however, relished Calvin's recent letter, "which was neither sour nor mouldy," Harriet assured her husband, but "formed a very agreeable contrast to all these things; the more so for being unexpected. I am much obliged to you for it." Yet it was hard to stay long off the demands that preoccupied her. "Georgiana is so excessively weak, nervous, cross, and fretful, night and day," and the older children—the four of them—"are, like other little sons and daughters of Adam, full of all kinds of absurdity and folly."

It was most discouraging. "When the brain gives out, as mine often does, and one cannot think or remember anything, then what is to be done? All common fatigue, sickness, and exhaustion is nothing to this distress." Was it more of the unsuspected aftereffects of her supposedly therapeutic blue pills, those overprescribed toxins of the time? Still, she would soldier on; for what sustained Harriet, daughter of a minister, sister of ministers, devout believer herself, was faith in her God. "Yet do I rejoice in my God," she assured Calvin, her minister husband, "and know in whom I believe, and only pray that the fire"—the flames of her current afflictions—"may consume the dross; as to the gold, that is imperishable. No real evil can happen to me, so I fear nothing for the future, and only suffer in the present tense."

God would provide. "As to a journey"—travel being her great cure-all—"I need not ask a physician to see that it is needful to me as far as health is concerned, that is to say, all human appearances are that way, but I feel no particular choice about it. If God wills I go. He can easily find means. Money, I suppose, is as plenty with Him now as it always has been, and if He sees it is really best He will doubtless help me."

Such was one woman's faith, and events appeared to justify her adhering to it. Calvin came home and worked at developing his skills as nurse and father—"You would laugh to see him in his spectacles gravely marching the little troop in their nightgowns up to bed, tagging after them, as he says, like an old hen after a flock of ducks"; and money abruptly arrived as though from nowhere, from New York in fact, in the form of $50 from Mrs. G. W. Bull—moved by the sickness in the Stowe family—and from Raleigh, North Carolina, where a Mrs. Devereaux sent another $50, with others adding their smaller sums. "For all I have had trouble," Harriet wrote the following March, "I can think of nothing but the greatness and richness of God's mercy to me in giving me such friends, and in always caring for us in every strait. There has been no day this winter when I have not had abundant reason to see this. Some friend has always stepped in to cheer and help, so that I have wanted for nothing."

Harriet's health continued miserable, but through other people's generosity—a measure of the esteem in which the couple were held—the feeble wife had been able to travel with her Calvin back to Hartford, Boston, and Natick last summer, in 1845; and now, in this spring of 1846, with the children distributed among various friends and relatives, Harriet would once more take her ailing self off, accompanied by her sister Kate this time, by steamer up the Ohio and overland 900 miles for a stay of eleven months in Brattleboro, Vermont.

Much effort had gone into making such a momentous decision: family conferences, letters back and forth, professional consultations, weighings of pros and economic cons. But in Brattleboro was Dr. Wesselhoeft's grand water sanitarium, among the very best of many such in a reform-minded age. And Harriet Beecher Stowe, for all her devout focus on a millennial future, remained alert throughout her lifetime to the fads and enthusiasms of the shifting present, of which watercures in the 1840s furnished a striking example.

They were something new under the American sun, the earliest of them having been established in New York City as recently as 1843; Wesselhoeft's at Brattleboro had opened a year before

Harriet's arrival as a patient. These watercures—the methodology was imported from Europe—seem wonderfully emblematic of their era, in an America progressing through the mid-nineteenth century confidently forward toward perfection. The state of medicine then practiced accounts in part for the astonishing success of watercures, which sprang up fast in the 1840s all across the North and Northwest, and which would flourish in one form or other as far as the Pacific until the end of the century. At Wesselhoeft's establishment alone, patrons included Martin Van Buren's son and niece, John C. Calhoun's son, the nearly blind Francis Parkman, Henry Longfellow, Julia Ward and Samuel Gridley Howe, Richard Henry Dana, Senator Fessenden of Maine, Philip Hone, James Russell Lowell, and James Parton and his wife Fanny Fern, as well as various retired military officers and ministers, counts, and barons from overseas. All had tried conventional medicine to no avail. Henceforth those sufferers meant to forgo dramatic therapeutics, eschewing cuppings and bleedings, leeches, boluses, blisterings, and the all-purpose doses of laudanum and mercury-laden calomel, in favor of a different kind of treatment, noninterventional.

The benighted practice of medicine then current, along with fried foods in overabundance and a widespread, long-standing, overgenerous indulgence in alcohol, brought patients with their mercury poisoning, their diseased livers and kidneys, flocking to the watercures. This was an age that was bound on betterment in any case, busy reforming its schools, prisons, insane asylums, diets, and ways of living together, as in such utopian communitarian societies as New Harmony, Brook Farm, and Oneida. Watercures provided additional, non-utopian opportunities for people to live together, therapeutically, some 390 patients having gathered at Dr. Wesselhoeft's establishment by the time of Harriet's arrival. For of a piece with its other impulses toward reform was America's sudden enthusiasm for hydropathy, for this newfangled means of accompanying spiritual strivings with aspirations to physical perfection.

In Brattleboro, at Dr. Wesselhoeft's sanitarium on Elliot Street, one encountered two handsome buildings: Paradise Row to the east for women, and the west building fitted out for men. These were set amid lawns, fountains, and woodland paths. Inside, beyond a veranda, were a well-ventilated dining hall and a music salon, as well as offices, laundry, bathing facilities, a bowling alley, a billiard room, and a carpenter's shop. Inside as well a new life awaited, and by our lights much about that life appears sensibly designed to restore health. Most obviously, women who attended—Harriet (to repeat) would remain there nearly a year—were granted a reprieve from the endless exhaustion of childbearing. Unburdened of homemaking responsibilities as well, ladies could form their own society, establishing new friendships among genteel patrons in carefree circumstances. Their diets were changed at once. John Knight, a Mississippi merchant, came to Dr. Wesselhoeft's shortly after Harriet Beecher Stowe departed and wrote back to his wife in Natchez itemizing the plain food: brown or rye bread, butter, hominy or mush, milk, chocolate or cocoa, and water for breakfast; roasted or boiled meat, vegetables, rice pudding, and water for dinner; bread, butter, and milk for supper—and more water. All the patients were encouraged, in fact, to flush out the system by drinking at least ten glasses of water a day. They were also urged to exercise morning and afternoon along the many woodland walks, which varied from half a mile to four miles in length. They were urged to avoid overstimulation—no tea or coffee, certainly no alcohol—and they were all urged to get plenty of rest, going to bed early each evening.

But the core of the treatment was water, not only inside the patient, through many glasses drunk daily; but outside, with purifying water applied repeatedly in wraps, sweats, sitzes, douches, plunges, showers, and sprays from early morning until bedtime. Wet sheets were the primary oft-repeated therapy. The patient, having been set in cold water—all the water was cold, never warm—or submerged in cold water, or doused in cold water that fell from fifteen feet overhead, was then wrapped in cold wet sheets and left for the body heat to sweat out various types of asthma, fevers, enlarged heart or liver, gout, hernia, measles, pleurisy, rheumatism, ringworm, scarletina, smallpox, syphilis, tumors, and other ailments that racked our nineteenth-century forebears. After each such dousing and sweating, the patient was unwrapped and would don loose-fitting clothes (not cotton or flannel, which were thought to enfeeble the skin) and would socialize quietly in the well-ventilated surroundings, knitting, bowling, playing non-gambling games, eating simply, and retiring early to bed.

Such was the routine, and Harriet prospered under it. In those sociable, salutary days she was bound to find happy hours, with her sister Catharine on hand and another sister—Mary, up from Hartford—enrolled as a patient as well. "Not for years, have I enjoyed life as I have here—real keen enjoyment—everything agrees with me." She exercised faithfully, even on bad days walking no less than three miles and on good days up to seven—"& not suffered for it." Although homesick and longing to see her children, she twice postponed her date for returning to Cincinnati. She meant to arrive home entirely cured of her various ailments, in firmer health "than I have had these ten years—comfort your heart with this," she urged her impatient husband: "weeks fly fast—March will soon be here & we will come together again."

Calvin did languish under his wife's absence but would suffer more from her presence, he vowed, unless she were in better health than she had been over the last year of their living side by side: during that time "you well know what has been the state of things both in regard to yourself & me." It had been "almost 18 months since I have had a wife to sleep with me," he complained less obliquely. "It is enough to kill any man, especially such a man as I am." Indeed, out there in Cincinnati when it got too bad, when "I get desperate," he wrote candidly to his wife, "& cannot stand it any longer, I get dear, good kind hearted Br Stagg to come and sleep with me, and he puts his arms round me & hugs me to my hearts' content"— that brotherly neighbor innocently comforting Professor Calvin Ellis Stowe through the worst of his sexual disquiet.

After nearly a year of daily exercise, of purging the toxic effects of far too many blue pills taken earlier, of submitting to sitz baths and what she called terrible douches as well as innumerable wrappings in sheets, of eating simply and playing charades or joining her reading circle over herbal drinks in the evenings, Harriet did come home at last, well rested and in good health, in April 1847. Nine months later almost to the day, in January 1848, she gave birth to her sixth child, a boy, Charley. But this birth was not like previous ones; the mother recovered promptly, and the infant was healthy and unfretful: "after ten years of trial God at length has given me a baby that I can *nurse myself,*" she exulted. "My little Charlie is larger & more thriving than any child I ever had—I nurse him exclusively & use both breasts (one you know I never used before with any of my other children) & have abundance for him."

The child turned out to be a delight, Harriet's "pride and joy," sweet-tempered, beautiful, and thriving. She would feel his little fingers clutching in the nighttime and take comfort, loneliness passing out of her with the warmth of the baby's touch. Calvin had gone away again. His own health ever precarious, the professor set out six months after Charley's birth for a stay of his own at Brattleboro. Before leaving Vermont, Harriet had discussed the matter with Dr. Wesselhoeft, so that her husband would be able to benefit from the watercure at special rates—as it happened, through fifteen months, from June 1848 to a year from the September that followed. And early on in that extended stay Calvin wrote back to a doting Harriet, in mid-July soon after his arrival: "You are so proud of your baby, one would think you never saw a baby before. Well," he concluded indulgently, "you had trouble enough with the infancy of the others— I am right glad you can take comfort with this one."

During his long time away from home, the absent husband would eventually have recourse to comfort of a different if not unfamiliar sort. He missed his children; he missed his wife. The couple wrote regularly back and forth, Calvin's letters full of health concerns but alluding to the pride he took in Harriet's competence, as she managed the unceasing demands of a bustling household alone. He yearned to be back with her at Walnut Hills. A full year had passed; another July had rolled around. At the end of that month, on July 31, 1849, Calvin wrote chattily from Brattleboro about a fellow patient at the sanitarium, a Mr. Farber from Newton, Massachusetts, engaged to be married and at the watercure for treatment of a disease of the eyes that had postponed his wedding. Farber had taken it "into his little black-curly pate to fall desperately in love with me," this absent husband wrote in good humor, "and he kisses and kisses upon my rough old face, as if I were a most beautiful young lady instead of a musty old man. The Lord sent him here to be my comfort." But what could the yearning Calvin know as he wrote to his wife far away? "He will have me sleep with him once in a while," he told Harriet all unknowing from Vermont's green simplicities in that fatal, horrible month, "and he says, *that is almost as good as being married*—the dear little innocent ignorant soul."

What could any of them know? In the United States of our own times, there has been not one indigenous, active case of cholera for nearly 100 years. Today, the disease is of scarcely more than historic interest to American medical practitioners. But not until 1883, thirty-four years after the dreadful month of July 1849 in Cincinnati, did the director of a German scientific commission to Egypt succeed in isolating the bacterium that causes the illness, a comma-shaped, motile organism that kills about half of the humans whose intestines it manages to enter. *Vibrio cholerae* enters most often by means of polluted food or water.

If diagnosed in time, cholera might have been treated, even in 1849 and even though doctors disagreed on the treatment; but in an age when dysentery and diarrhea were common—Calvin's "exceedingly sensitive and rebellious" stomach being hardly unusual—the swift-moving disease could establish itself in the victim before it was recognized. Symptoms rapidly grew acute: excruciating cramps, violent spasmodic vomiting, dehydration, skin turning a frightening blue, face pinched, hands and feet puckered and cold. Death often followed in hours.

The causes of such a calamity were no better understood in America in 1849 than they had been when cholera first appeared here in 1832, raging through Cincinnati as the Beechers were reaching Wheeling, bound from the East in their great chartered stagecoach. For prevention, people in 1849, as earlier, took brandy, garlic, castor oil, camphor pills, huge doses of the nefarious calomel, uncomprehending. Did the disease arise from too much electricity in the atmosphere? Were animalcules or the spores of fungi to blame? Coal fires were lit in the streets of Cincinnati to rid the air of infusorians, so that heavy smoke lay over the city during that summer of 1849. Through the darkened streets hearses began to rumble on their way to the cemetery; soon new graveyards were being hastily laid out, and wagons were recruited—drays, carts, anything that rolled and could carry off the multiplying corpses. Undertakers and grave diggers kept busy day and night.

In the end, 7,500 people in the one city perished. Those in the country air had thought themselves safer, yet cholera came to the countryside too, past the slaughterhouses and tanyards and fertilizer factories at the edge of Cincinnati on up Montgomery Road the two miles to Walnut Hills. July 10: "Yesterday," wrote Harriet to her absent husband, "little Charley was taken ill, not seriously, and at any other season I should not be alarmed." She had wrapped her child—a year and a half old by then—in hydropathic sheets, and he seemed to get better, beginning to fuss. "Never was crossness in a baby more admired." For a week thereafter Charley's condition continued to improve. Calvin from his great distance could follow only at a lapse of time, helplessly, and encourage: "In a day of calamity you are worth having," he wrote to his wife; "yours is a heart that never fails."

Death meanwhile stalked all around. The Stowes' dog Daisy died. Old Frankie, who did the family laundry, died; and the Stowe twins, Eliza and Hattie, now twelve, helped make the poor woman's shroud. The day after, July 16, Charley came down with what this time was unmistakably cholera. For days and nights through a week his small body suffered, his mother hovering in anguish. She wrote to Calvin on July 23: "At last, my dear, the hand of the Lord hath touched us. We have been watching all day by the dying bed of little Charley, who is gradually sinking." The family did not expect him to survive the night. "All will be over," she wrote, "before you could possibly get here, and the epidemic is now said by the physicians to prove fatal to every new case."

Calvin must stay where he was, even as his youngest son, formerly so healthy, lived on in torment another three days. Through that ordeal Harriet looked down on her child's "imploring face when I could not help nor soothe nor do one thing, not one, to mitigate his cruel suffering, do nothing but pray in my anguish that he might die soon."

The small victim did die at last. And out of that private agony—a mother in Cincinnati crushed at her dead Charley's bedside—would arise directly Harriet Beecher Stowe's forthcoming astounding globewide public triumph.

6

CALL TO BOWDOIN

Calvin Stowe returned from Brattleboro in September, a month and a half after Charley's death, to Walnut Hills and the grave site near the family home and the flowers that Harriet had planted there.

It is perhaps too easy to judge this scholar severely. In appearance he was hardly prepossessing—increasingly roly-poly with the passing decades—and his appetite for food, brandy, pretty girls, arcane books, and a wife's connubial favors has contributed its touch of ludicrousness to the surviving portrait. As for favors, he who deplored enforced abstinences might better, we feel, have abstained more often. At crucial times Calvin was away from home, leaving the running of a large, drastically underfunded household to a wife distracted, frail, and frequently ill. When he did come home, a number of his domestic decisions proved misguided, so that increasingly he let the more practical Harriet determine what was best for their family. His "endless studying & reading," as she put it, resulted in only minimal public benefit. "I get out of patience that he wont write with all this reading. He is a cormorant and keeps all to himself," Harriet later complained, adding, "If I had it"—in this case, her husband's vast biblical knowledge—"wouldn't I make it flare and flame." Indolent, self-absorbed, impractical, often ineffective in dealing with life's challenges, crumbling in crises, Professor Stowe was moreover perpetually ailing, with ailments that a life stretching into his overweight eighties would finally belie. For all that, he groused continually about the delicacy of his constitution, as during days lying directly ahead, when, in February 1850 (having recently spent fifteen months looking after himself in Brattleboro), he lamented from Cincinnati, "My health has not been good this winter and I do not suppose that I should live long were I to stay here"—this in his late forties, with another thirty-six years of life before him.

Yet the abundant ailments of which Calvin Stowe regularly complained felt no doubt real and alarming to the sufferer; we in health must learn to suppress our impatience with those less lucky. And Cincinnati, particularly in the hot, humid summer months, was in truth hazardous; Calvin gave point to his views of the place by insisting that just last summer 9,000 people had perished from cholera within a three-mile radius of the Stowe home. Meanwhile, with all his flaws, the man exhibited solid virtues. He might observe pretty girls with pleasure, but he left them alone, remaining faithful and devoted to his plain-featured wife. Nor is there any evidence that now or later the professor experienced the least jealousy—experienced anything but pride in his wife's productivity and subsequent, unparalleled success as a writer. Harriet in turn felt gratefully affectionate toward Calvin, for his love, his knowledge, his support, and his sense of fun. People in general liked Professor Stowe immensely, a learned gentleman who told droll stories filled with mimicry and color; his letters crackle with anecdotes relayed in the accurately re-created dialects of acquaintances and strangers overheard. Harriet listened to Calvin's stories and used them in her writing; that was only one of the ways he gave her aid. And he was a legitimate and most erudite scholar in a field that she valued above all others, this Professor Calvin Ellis Stowe, known and admired equally for his expertise about the Bible and for the lively clarity with which he imparted his knowledge in classrooms and lecture halls.

His alma mater down east in Maine had come to value the achievements of so able an alumnus; so that just this past fall, in 1849, Bowdoin College had offered its valedictorian of the class of 1824 a newly established faculty chair, as Collins Professor of Natural and Revealed Religion. Calvin accepted the offer with alacrity. He would have to stay on at Lane through the present academic year until a replacement could be appointed, but he meant to leave for New England as soon as possible. By now his having come west at all must have seemed a mistake with regard to his career. Looking back on his arrival in Cincinnati, the aging Stowe would have recalled a young teacher in his early thirties full of scholarly gifts and high hopes—the vast West to be won; the glorious book-purchasing expedition to Europe, from which he had returned with 5,000 volumes for Lane's now splendid library; the much admired report on the Prussian school system that the young academic had written for a grateful Ohio legislature. But what had been achieved since then? After seventeen years of obscurity at Lane, underpaid amid broken promises, Stowe, nearing fifty, found himself living hand to mouth, at an institution still wobbly, in a city where one risked one's life and the life of one's large family by remaining. He jumped at the chance to get out and back east when he could.

Harriet would go first, in springtime before the germ-laden summer, visiting family and friends along the way and getting things ready in Maine, with her husband to follow at the end of the school year. Six months' pregnant, traveling with three of her children and Aunt Esther, Harriet Beecher Stowe set out from Cincinnati in April 1850. Behind her she was leaving Charley's grave and the flowers that a grieving mother had planted; yet like her husband, she must have been more than ready to go, and very glad to return to New England. As the twenty-one-year-old unmarried daughter of Lane Seminary's newly appointed president, Miss Beecher had come west eighteen years before, in 1832. Thereafter through a long residence (she was now about to turn thirty-nine) she had married, endured illnesses and miscarriages, given birth to six children, buried her youngest child, and—although writing little these last five years—had made a kind of professional name for herself by writing and selling sketches and stories to magazines. Some of what she wrote had even been gathered together and published, in 1843, through her sister Catharine's enterprise, as a book, *The Mayflower,* a collection that earned for its author a modest national fame. By no means did it approach her husband's more substantial, clerical eminence, yet she had won recognition enough to cause readers of fiction back east to take notice.

Incidentally, despite the author's years in Ohio, during which her sketches were written, those fifteen in *The Mayflower* deal not at all with the West. Not one among the sketches concerns the great issues of the day that the Queen City appeared to be illustrating through its brief, brash history: nothing about settlers and traders, backwoodsmen, the waves of immigrants, southerners with their black slaves strolling the riverport's pungent streets, pioneers head-ing farther west still. Rather, what *The Mayflower* contained, in addition to conventionally sentimental essays, were more memo-rable evocations of an earlier New England, the seminal region of America that Harriet Beecher Stowe had re-created from far off with an exile's undimmed vision—the region to which, at last, she was returning to stay.

Her traveling party of two women, two girls, and a boy—Harriet and Aunt Esther; thirteen-year-old Hattie (the more robust of the twins); Freddie, age ten; and her daughter Georgie, age seven—set off from Cincinnati's Public Landing to journey by riverboat up the Ohio as far as Pittsburgh, arriving in the afternoon between four and five on Wednesday, April 24, 1850. From there they trans-ferred to a canal boat on the Pennsylvania Canal for "a quiet and agreeable passage" ever farther east in what were the terminal days of such leisurely travel. At five the next morning all were out on deck sightseeing, the children exclaiming with "unbounded delight" about mountain scenery more dramatic than those young eyes had ever beheld. At a canal lock Harriet disembarked and, feeling good health returning, strolled along the towpath to rejoin the boat at the next lock down.

"We reached Hollidaysburg about eleven o'clock, and at two o'clock in the night were called up to get into the cars at Jacktown." The cars were railroad cars, and it must have been here, as a world-famous author would later recall, that the weary, bedraggled, un-kempt travelers were ushered from inside a depot to wait outside in the night, because an official of the railroad had persuaded him-self that he was dealing yet again with beggarly immigrants milling about. The story stretches credulity; but if true, it furnishes a stark enough image—two unescorted women, one visibly pregnant, with three children adrift in a strange place at an early hour—to set alongside scenes soon to form, of adoring multitudes in noisy hom-age wildly cheering the celebrity that one of those women was about to become. The bleak Pennsylvania scene and the early hour rein-force, as well, our sense of the hardships of travel back then. Know-ing nothing different, of course, travelers put up with it; those people of the mid-nineteenth century (including the previous year's forty-niners, innocently spreading cholera westward) loved being on the move. Certainly Harriet did; nor was this her first time making the journey east. Despite illnesses, near indigence, and a large family to look after, she had managed to travel from Ohio to Connecticut on five earlier occasions. This was the sixth, as she and her aunt and the children during the last full week of April 1850 rode the railroad from Jacktown to Philadelphia, which they reached finally at three on Friday afternoon, April 26. From there they went by boat and railroad on to New York, to arrive very tired between ten and eleven at night, having covered 300 miles since two o'clock that morning. A cousin met them at the station and accompanied them over to Brooklyn.

In Brooklyn lived Harriet's next-younger sibling, her brother Henry, with his wife Eunice, who had been set up comfortably these past couple of years at Plymouth Church in Brooklyn Heights. Henry was doing very well. His congregation, as Harriet reported back to her husband, "are more than ever in love with him and have raised his salary to $3,300"—three times what Bowdoin was offering Calvin—"and given him a beautiful horse and carriage worth $600." Not bad for a minister of God still in his mid-thirties; and Calvin Stowe at forty-eight could have hardly received the news indifferently. The professor had himself been negotiating about salaries through the spring. Stowe had been offered $1,500 by Lane "and a good house besides" to stay where he was—this from an institution that all these years had been crying poor and paying less than promised, now suddenly able to put its hands on money that substantially improved on the offer from Bowdoin. And, Professor Stowe wrote his mother in Natick, "to-day I have had another offer from New York city of $2,300." Nothing came of that last, but the post at Bowdoin was what he wanted anyway, and had written and told the college so; "if they will give me $500 free and clear in addition to the salary, I will accept the proposition, and I suppose that there is no doubt that they will do it."

Harriet, meanwhile, delaying in Brooklyn with her brother Henry through a week in early May, was thinking of finances too. In the East at last to stay, she felt her muse awakening; for that matter, the family would need whatever money she could earn with her pen. The Stowes had taken a house in Maine, in Brunswick on Federal Street, that cost more than Calvin's salary had allowed for; Harriet meant to make up the difference writing for magazines, for which purpose she was calling on publishers during her stopover in New

York. "My health is already improved by the journey," she assured Calvin from Brooklyn, going on to tell of her arrangements with editors here that might earn them additional income. "As to furniture, I think that we may safely afford an outlay of $150, and that will purchase all that may be necessary to set us up, and then we can get more as we have means and opportunity." When he next wrote, her husband should let her know if any money had come in for the pieces she had written and submitted already. "My plan," she went on, "is to spend this week in Brooklyn, the next in Hartford, the next in Boston, and go on to Brunswick in May or June."

In Hartford were two married sisters: the younger, Isabella—a half sister in her late twenties, married to Mr. Hooker—and the older, a full sister, Mary Perkins, with whom the travelers stayed. Harriet visited with her school friend Georgiana May (now Mrs. Sykes) as well, before pressing on to Boston in mid-month, at the start of a new week. There she and the children were welcomed by an older brother, the Reverend Edward Beecher, and his family. And from Edward's home in Boston on May 18, Harriet wrote to Calvin of having spent all her time since arriving "busily engaged in the business of buying and packing furniture." She meant, she said, to set off for Maine Tuesday night on the Bath steamer. "My traveling expenses, when I get to Brunswick, including everything, will have been seventy-six dollars." And here she took a moment to appeal to her husband's understanding, breaking off to urge that he "reflect calmly how great a work has been imposed upon me at a time when my situation particularly calls for rest, repose, and quiet"—only six or eight weeks from giving birth to her seventh child. "To come alone such a distance with the whole charge of children, accounts, and baggage; to push my way through hurrying crowds, looking out for trunks, and bargaining with hackmen, has been a very severe trial on my strength, to say nothing of the usual fatigues of traveling."

The note of self-pity, however justified, occurs only now and then in the correspondence of Harriet Beecher Stowe. Despite her many exertions—of "seeing to bedsteads, tables, chairs, mattresses," as she would soon be writing to Georgiana May Sykes from here, of "thinking about shipping my goods and making out accounts," and with a trunk still to pack "as I go on board the Bath steamer this evening"—despite all those cares, more typical than any whining is the tone she conveys while writing yet again to Calvin before setting out on this final leg of the journey: "You are not able just now to bear anything, my dear husband"—for again he was ill—"therefore trust all to me; I never doubt or despair." Take whatever money her earlier pieces might have earned "and use it as you see necessary"; should editor Wright reject them, be sure to bring the pieces along when you come East. "I am strong in spirit," she wrote, "and God who has been with me in so many straits will not forsake me now."

A storm was raging as the travelers reached Brunswick at last, on Wednesday, May 22, a northeaster that met them stepping off the steamer and would blow in torrents for the rest of the week. A faculty wife was on hand to meet them as well, to take the weary party home with her to rest while the various Boston purchases were in transit and the Titcomb house that the Stowes had rented was made ready. "Mrs. Upham has done everything for me," a grateful Harriet wrote Calvin after a week in Brunswick, on May 29, "giving up time and strength and taking charge of my affairs in a way without which we could not have got along at all in a strange place and in my present helpless condition." And she added gratefully: "This family is delightful, there is such a perfect sweetness and quietude in all its movements. Not a harsh word or hasty expression is ever heard."

The Stowes did get set up in their home on Federal Street, a house that Calvin had remembered from his undergraduate days at Bowdoin, when Henry Longfellow and Longfellow's brother Stephen lived there as students. Much remained to be done to make it habitable: painting and furnishing rooms, getting the kitchen in working order, putting down carpets, upholstering furniture. In the midst of those manifold chores Calvin wrote from Cincinnati, telling his wife, as she noted, that "he is sick a bed—& all but dead—dont ever expect to see his family again wants to know how I shall manage in case I am left a widow—knows we shall get in debt & never get out—wonders at my courage—thinks I am very sanguine—warns me to be prudent as there wont be much to live on in case of his death &c &c. I read the letter," a resolute Harriet in her new health in New England concludes, "& poke it into the stove, & proceed—"

In her grand ramshackle dwelling, on July 8, 1850, another Charley Stowe was born, the last of Harriet's children. The earlier

Charley, Samuel Charles, lay in his grave in Cincinnati; this new infant, Charles Edward, was here in his mother's arms. He was "so like" the other; but, Harriet would confess to a near neighbor out west who had also lost a child, "I do not feel him the same nor do I feel for him that same love which I felt for Charley—It is a different kind—I shall never love another as I did him—he was my '*summer child.*'" She could not look into a little drawer that held her dead Charley's clothes "without feeling it thro my very heart."

The school year at Lane having ended, Calvin with the two other Stowe children arrived in Brunswick shortly before the birth of this latest baby. Sister Catharine came down to Brunswick as well, to help with the housework and with home schooling. Chores never ceased, but whenever she could, Harriet made time to write, and with a fluency not felt since her early years out west, when she had written for the now-defunct Semi-Colon Club. Now as invariably in need of money, she sent her work off to magazines, but was suddenly writing a great many lively letters besides to relatives and friends, spending hour after hour at her writing desk. Not that there weren't interruptions. "Since I began this note I have been called off at least a dozen times—once for the fish-man, to buy a codfish—once to see a man who had brought me some barrels of apples—once to see a book man—then to Mrs. Upham to see about a drawing I promised to make for her—then to nurse the baby—then into the kitchen to make a chowder for dinner & now I am at it again for nothing but deadly determination enables me ever to write—it is rowing against wind and tide."

In December Calvin set off once more for Cincinnati, having somehow been persuaded to teach the winter term at Lane Seminary; the trustees out there had yet to find a replacement for him. Bowdoin College granted a leave of absence to let its Collins professor do so; but despite that consideration, Stowe was planning to forsake Bowdoin's low-paying appointment as soon as he could, in order to seize yet another academic opportunity that had come his way. Andover Theological Seminary, the premier institution of its kind in America, had offered Professor Stowe its chair of sacred literature, with living accommodations and with a salary twice that of Bowdoin's, or of Lane's either. Move to Andover and he would be set for good. He must teach the winter term in Cincinnati (safe, at least, from the riverport's summertime health risks) and a full year at Bowdoin to fulfill his contract in Maine. But after scrimping through so many underpaid hours in the classroom, the professor was bent now on ending his career adequately remunerated in Massachusetts, on Andover's prestigious campus. Accordingly, Stowe was gone from Bowdoin part of the time up to the summer of 1852, when he joined the faculty of Andover Seminary at last, for the rest of his working life.

Harriet, meanwhile, with her sister Catharine's help continued managing matters in Brunswick. As an economy measure she had let the cook go, so was doing the cooking herself and writing for the magazines—"more than anybody or I myself would have thought"— besides cleaning, shopping, haggling with tradesmen, painting, refinishing furniture, and teaching an hour a day in the Beechers' home school. In addition to all that, "I have read two hours every evening to the children"—the novels of Sir Walter Scott: *The Talisman, The Abbot, Ivanhoe, Kenilworth*—"yet I am constantly pursued & haunted by the idea that I dont do anything."

A relative by marriage would have her do more. "Hattie," the wife of her brother Edward importuned her from Boston, "if I could use a pen as you can, I would write something that would make this whole nation feel what an accursed thing slavery is."

The letter moved its recipient to make a vow: she would approach that horrific subject as soon as she could.

7

POLITICS

She wouldn't be able to write what she wanted while baby Charley was sleeping with her. In December, with 1850 winding down, Harriet sent word to Calvin: "As long as the baby sleeps with me nights I can't do much at any thing—but I shall *do it at last.* I shall write that thing if I live." Doubts that had formed during her time of poor health lingered, leaving this author, wife, and mother uncertain of the future; even now a breast infection required her to engage yet another wet nurse. But the bracing Maine air was proving salutary. Winter storms whipped down on Brunswick and caused . the old Titcomb house to groan, reminding a nighttime occupant within of her childhood home in Litchfield, which used to rattle and groan just like this, and creak under storms like nothing she had heard in eighteen years out west. She was back in New England and, despite the hard work and the troublous times, was enjoying it—the happiest, healthiest years of her life, she would judge the Maine years in retrospect. In daylight Harriet got outside sometimes with the older children and threw snowballs and sledded, rosy-cheeked as though a child herself, down Federal Street.

Moreover, as noted, she had been writing abundantly for the eastern magazines, for two specifically: the *New-York Evangelist,* in the pages of which her work from Cincinnati had long been welcomed; and for the *National Era* in Washington, D.C. The editor in Washington was Gamaliel Bailey, who had earlier, in Cincinnati in the mid-1830s, taken over *The Philanthropist* from the abolitionist James G. Birney, after a mob had thrown Birney's printing press into the Ohio River. Since then Dr. Bailey had himself left Cincinnati and come east and as early as this last August was publishing a sketch by Harriet Beecher Stowe in his *National Era*, the first of four such printed over the fall that included a typically innocuous account of a professor's only somewhat successful tending of a vegetable garden: "A Scholar's Adventures in the Country." Summing up months at her desk in late 1850, Harriet could boast of having through such fugitive pieces earned a substantial supplement to her husband's income; the Stowes would have $1,800 this year, which for a wonder came close to meeting their expenses. Even so, "I don't want to feel obliged to work as hard every year as I have this," she wrote to Calvin at year's end. Even though she might earn $400 annually with her pen, "I don't want to feel that I must, and when weary with teaching the children, and tending the baby, and buying provisions, and mending dresses, and darning stockings, sit down and write a piece for some paper."

As for that, the state of the Stowes' finances was on the point of changing, astoundingly. It is doubtless true about any such sudden change: causes of an extraordinary event will seem, after the fact, so numerous and disparate as to invest their coming together with the aura of a miracle. Not far into the future, in February 1853, Harriet Beecher Stowe was to describe herself thus: "I am a little bit of a woman,—somewhat more than forty, about as thin and dry as a pinch of snuff; never very much to look at in my best days, and looking like a used-up article now." She went on to explain that, inasmuch as she had married at twenty-five and borne seven children, her "principal fields of labor" had been in the nursery and the kitchen. From such a diminutive, domesticated source, at just this time, how did the far-ranging, passionate, and nation-shattering marvel of *Uncle Tom's Cabin* arise?

And in just this place. The place, in fact, was profoundly important, not only because Stowe was back in New England, after wholesome months at a watercure in Vermont and at present in the invigorating climate of coastal Maine. It is, incidentally, a notable fact that henceforth through her four remaining decades of life, this author would suffer few of the abundant complaints that had relentlessly plagued her during the years out west. Managing the stress of writing her first novel and living the totally different life that followed would go more easily in good health, and for the most part she was destined to enjoy health at least relatively good.

Yet beyond the good health that it fostered, this place—
Brunswick, Maine—lay near Boston, where Harriet's abolitionist
brother Edward Beecher lived; and Boston, more than any other
city in the Union, had exploded with fury over what Edward's wife
described as the "terrible things" happening in America in 1850. For
Boston was a port city in a free state, to which slaves who managed to escape from the South had long made their way in order to
disappear among menial black laborers in freedom, as cooks, ste-
vedores, coachmen, helping the city to function. Moreover, Boston was in Massachusetts, and Massachusetts was, for the times,
unusually liberal, with a tradition of liberalism that stretched back
long before the American Revolution. In Massachusetts, for instance, five years earlier, by 1845, black children had already been
admitted without discrimination to the public schools of Lowell,
Nantucket, New Bedford, Salem, and Worcester; within a decade
the state legislature was to enact, in 1855, a law that forbade distinctions on the basis of race or religious beliefs in admitting children to public schools statewide.

Which is not to say that the condition of free people of color in
Boston in the mid-nineteenth century was easeful. Hardly anywhere
in the Union could blacks find ease then. Throughout the North,
whites had passed laws at every level—federal, state, and municipal
—that insisted on African-Americans' inferiority. In some "free"
states blacks were forbidden to settle at all; and virtually every state
in the North isolated them through custom and ordinances that
not only denied blacks additional opportunities but shrank what
few they had. They could not vote. They were not allowed to enter
hotels and restaurants except as servants. They were forbidden to
board stagecoaches, omnibuses, steamboats, or railroad cars—or,
in the instances where they could board such vehicles, they were
allowed only in segregated sections. Blacks had to live in their separate parts of town and pray in their own churches or in designated
Negro pews of white churches. They had to sit in remote parts of
theaters. Their crimes sent them to inferior black prisons; their
illnesses got them treated in inferior black hospitals; their deaths
relegated them to inferior black cemeteries.

We (blind in our own ways) stare back in amazement at the
extreme, ubiquitous racism of antebellum America. The failure of
imagination on the part of nearly every white person in the 1850s,

including the very best and best-intentioned of northerners—
Theodore Parker, Wendell Phillips, Samuel Gridley Howe, Salmon
P. Chase, Abraham Lincoln, all of whom deplored slavery—lay in
a general inability to visualize the black and white races living together as social equals. Granted, the often degraded condition of
free people of color in the North—let alone slaves in the South—
made so vast an imaginative leap a challenge; not even the abolitionists, with one or two bright exceptions, were able to accomplish
it. Thus when we read even so brilliant and sensitive a thinker as
Parker addressing the enormity of slavery, we find him consistently
failing to empathize with blacks—scarcely a word about black slaves'
suffering. Theodore Parker's outrage, like that of so many others,
arose from what slavery was doing to whites: how slavery corrupted
the slaveholder and how its advance into federal territory would
undercut free white labor. Thence followed a general desire to
exclude low-wage free blacks from northern states, and thence the
efforts, in the late 1840s, to keep no-wage slavery out of western
territories newly acquired as the fruits of victory in the Mexican
War just ended.

During the civic turmoil that followed that war, Harriet Beecher
Stowe found herself in the right place, in Brunswick, not far from
seething Boston. And she was in Maine at the right time, too, having come east from Cincinnati in April and May of 1850. Through
that same spring, Congress in Washington was struggling to fashion a compromise between North and South on precisely the issue
of slavery in the new western territories. What had brought matters to a head was the gold rush of the preceding year, which had
abruptly, massively swollen the population of California. Populous
California was ready to enter the Union, and as a free state, but
the South objected. Heretofore the numbers of slave states and free
had been roughly in balance; admitting a new free state would throw
that balance off.

Thus into the spring of 1850 debates raged on the Senate floor:
an aged Henry Clay striving for compromise; Daniel Webster declaring his Ichabod faith in the sanctity of the Union; feeble old
John C. Calhoun, near death, glowering as a colleague read aloud
the great man's final, unyielding defense of southern values. Out
of those viewpoints and amid high feeling, the senators managed
to craft legislation that sought to placate both South and North.

Their measures ended by satisfying neither; yet opposition to the proposal as a whole was disarmed by means of introducing its parts one bill at a time, and thus the so-called Compromise of 1850 was passed by early fall and received President Fillmore's signature. California would be admitted free of slavery. The other territories—those incipient states—could be opened to slavery (even while the Great American Desert was deemed inhospitable to crops that slave labor harvested). And the South, having won in principle one major concession, was granted another: a new fugitive slave law with teeth in it, to replace a seldom invoked and circumventable act on the books since 1793.

The new law enjoining the recapture of runaway slaves was what had enraged Boston, and by no means Boston alone. People throughout the North had watched the bill take shape and knew what it signified. While Harriet that May, on her way to Maine, lingered in her abolitionist brother Edward's household in Boston, shopping for furniture and shipping her purchases off to Brunswick, she would have been exposed to an abundance of Beecher family ire; and even if her letters during the trip are silent about it—speaking only of the mundane chores that moving with young children from west to east required of her—she would have listened. Here as on other occasions she held her peace: listening, observing. But in later years her sister-in-law, Edward's wife, remembered the spring of Hatty's visit and the summer and fall of 1850 that followed it, and spoke of those indignant times to the Reverend Charles Stowe—little Charley of Brunswick all grown up to become (almost as a matter of course) a minister—and his mother's biographer as well. To the biographer Charles Edward Stowe, Mrs. Edward Beecher supplied her recollections, she who had been filled with the abolitionist spirit ever since the 1830s. "Those terrible things which were going on in Boston," she told Mrs. Stowe's youngest son nearly four decades after 1850, "were well calculated to rouse up this spirit. What can I do? I thought. Not much myself, but I know one who can. So I wrote several letters to your mother"—to Harriet in Brunswick that fall—"telling her of various heartrending events caused by the enforcement of the Fugitive Slave Law."

Such events were unfolding close at hand. That was because the Slavepower, not content to possess the South, remained on the move. Five years earlier the Republic of Texas had joined the Union, with slavery extended into that enormous acreage. Now, by the terms of the newly enacted Compromise of 1850, slavery's appalling blight was poised to spread legally across the free soil of the Utah and New Mexico territories. But, asked the South, why should it not? Slaves were property, chattel, like cows and other livestock. A slave owner was entitled to take his property wherever he went in the Union. And what was wrong with slavery anyhow? Slaves in the South were better provided for than were their wretched black counterparts up North, better off, indeed—enjoying happier lives—than white wage slaves that northern factories ground down as immigrant labor. Moreover, like the poor, the institution of slavery had been with us forever, and in societies far and wide. Old Testament patriarchs owned slaves; Moses provided regulations for managing slavery; Saint Paul in the New Testament counseled the slave Onesimius to return to his master; Jesus said not one word against slavery. Could it be evil, then? And could an institution be evil that furnished the means of clothing America, an institution—Cotton is King!—on which the economy of America depended? So much depended on slavery. Again (as the South continually reiterated), the Bible sanctioned it; history sanctioned it; the economy sanctioned it, triumphantly; and the Constitution sanctioned it: the Founding Fathers had woven slavery into the law of the land.

But now that law had been enlarged in a way that permitted the Slavepower to send its agents northward pursuing runaway slaves into the very heart of freedom, into the streets of Boston. Worse yet: those same scoundrelly slave catchers, by the terms of the new Fugitive Slave Law, could enjoin any northern citizen to help them seize and return blacks to bondage. Not only did the new law prohibit Bostonians from aiding the fugitive slave; Bostonians must actively help the slave *catcher* or be heavily fined and imprisoned. Moreover, the slave catcher's word and documentation were enough: that black man or woman over there is a runaway, and the accused was forbidden to testify in his own defense or even to know who his accuser was, and commissioners adjudicating such cases would be paid better—by law, $10 instead of $5—when they found for the plaintiff, the slave owner.

Already in Boston, agents and their deputies had been slouching about, asking questions. Blacks had fled; those remaining lived in fear, and some whites were wondering whether as Christians they could, if ordered, play a part in sending people of color back into bondage. But that was the law: "all good citizens are hereby commanded to aid and assist in the prompt and efficient execution of this law whenever their services may be required"; and anyone obstructing slave catchers or hiding or otherwise helping alleged "persons owing service or labor" to escape from an agent of the Slavepower would pay court costs and be "subject to a fine not exceeding one thousand dollars, and imprisonment not exceeding six months," penalties severe enough to give the most humane of northerners pause.

Boston that fall was accordingly filled with resentment, raucousness, and suspicion. Blacks and whites were joining forces to form a Committee of Vigilance, and blacks formed their own League of Freedom. On both sides of the issue newspapers railed, some urging resistance at whatever cost, others counseling citizens to preserve the Union, abide by the law, and maintain the lucrative peace. In October abolitionists met at Faneuil Hall in noisy assembly, as anti-abolitionists would gather some weeks later at the same site in support of the Union. And on October 19, three gentlemen from down South checked into the United States Hotel on Beach Street. The three were bent on seizing William and Ellen Craft and taking that respectable black couple back with them to Georgia. But officials in Boston proved reluctant; friends of the Crafts rallied around; and Messrs Hughes, Knight, and Beal were forced finally to leave town empty-handed.

The new year, 1851, had scarcely begun, however, before another attempt at rendition was set in motion, this one more artfully managed. A constable Caphart arrived in town quietly, on behalf of the slave owner John DeBree of Norfolk, Virginia. Moving with expedition, the constable showed federal authorities DeBree's documents of ownership, then promptly, at ten on the morning of February 15, accosted one Shadrach Minkins as he was serving coffee in the Cornhill Coffeehouse. The constable and his deputies forced the terrified Minkins into the street. The day was so wet that, one observer noted dourly, watercure staffers would have only to "hold their patients out of a window, & they would get sufficiently moist." Through the dismal square the officials led Shadrach— in his shirtsleeves, in full view of the morning crowds—across to the courthouse. Inside, in a mobbed courtroom on the second floor, the runaway heard his fate decided. Mr. DeBree's documents were in order; Minkins must return to slavery in Virginia. The hearing ended. The courtroom was cleared.

More than 200 Bostonians had meanwhile gathered outside; some were making their way into the courthouse and up the stairs. Suddenly the courtroom door sprang open, and twenty blacks rushed at deputies who were lingering inside with Shadrach. The intruders seized the accused and managed to hurry him downstairs and out into nearby Cambridge Street—"two huge negroes bearing the prisoner between them with his clothes half torn off"—on down to Garden Street and into the maze on the far side of Beacon Hill that was the black section of town. Thus Shadrach got away—and would live out the rest of his life in Montreal—to the vast satisfaction of some in the North and to the dismay and disgust of many others, throughout the breadth of the South, of course, but in Boston too: law-abiding Bostonians who had hoped for an end to all this agitation over slavery and for the prosperous resumption of business as usual.

During the tense fall of 1850 that preceded Shadrach's rescue, Edward Beecher's wife had been writing her letters to Brunswick. "I remember distinctly," she later told Harriet's biographer son, "saying in one of them, 'Now, Hattie, if I could use a pen as you can, I would write something that would make this whole nation feel what an accursed thing slavery is.'" A sibling, unnamed but old enough at the time to recollect the moment later, would tell Charles Stowe of the very day that the letter reached Brunswick. In the parlor on Federal Street their mother read aloud to the family what Aunt Isabella had written. Coming upon the passage—"I would write something"—she "rose up from her chair," that eyewitness testified, "crushing the letter in her hand, and with an expression on her face that stamped itself on the mind of her child, said: 'I will write something. I will if I live.'"

Not only was this the right time, then, and not only was it the right place for the assigning of such a high charge. Harriet Beecher Stowe would prove to be the right person to take on the task, this "little bit of a woman . . . about as thin and dry as a pinch of snuff" the one person in all of America who could do it. And not simply because at the moment she happened to be in the midst of reading aloud to her children for two hours each evening Sir Walter Scott's fiction—and would in November be reading *David Copperfield* aloud—thus instructing herself through example about how novels (which she had never written before) are put together. That was important, but equally important was the long apprenticeship this author had already served, rendering character and dialect in sketches published in periodicals over sixteen years. More important still was her having spent those years in Cincinnati, out west, looking south across the river into slave country.

True, she had visited the South only once, and then only its fringes and a long time ago, when she was still Harriet Beecher, not long after her arrival in Ohio. In 1833, she and a fellow teacher at her sister Catharine's Western Female Institute had stayed in Kentucky with the slaveholding family of one of their students. Her traveling companion later recalled that "Harriet did not seem to notice anything in particular that happened, but sat much of the time as though abstracted in thought. When the negroes did funny things and cut up capers, she did not seem to pay the slightest attention to them"—an attitude, in this absent, observant author, that hardly surprises us. "Afterwards, however," Mary Dutton continues, "in reading 'Uncle Tom,' I recognized scene after scene of that visit portrayed with the most minute fidelity, and knew at once where the material for that portion of the story"—the section on the Shelby family, at the start—"had been gathered."

That said, Cincinnatians of those times hardly needed to cross the river to know about blacks and slavery. Slaves came to them as fugitives. In one instance Harriet's husband and her brother Henry helped a runaway slave flee farther north. In another, a black woman working in the household confided to Mrs. Stowe that she, too, was a fugitive, and her master was in town looking for her. Of course Harriet sheltered the poor creature. And other stories about slave life she would hear from black domestics whom she came to know and care for. This New Englander was versed, too, in abolitionist testimony from the Lane Debates and from their leader Theodore Weld, as well as in newspaper coverage of the abundant racial tensions in Cincinnati during her years there. Riots had broken out against the abolitionist Birney ("that night," of July 30, 1836, she had written at the time, "the mob tore down his press, scattered the types, dragged the whole to the river, threw it in, and then came back to demolish the office"). And later, in 1841, an ugly riot had filled several summer days in the Queen City and threatened Lane Seminary, which was suspected of harboring blacks whom drunken Irish were pursuing. (If they show up, President Beecher decreed, seminarians may defend themselves; but "aim low," he told his boys bracingly, "and hit 'em in the legs! hit 'em in the legs!")

That was the Beecher spirit; and perhaps—in preparing Harriet for the task ahead—more important than was her familiarity with Scott and Dickens, or her long experience as a writer of sketches, or her residence among blacks in Cincinnati, or her present residence near Boston just at this time, was the fact that she was a Beecher. As such, she had been born bright; she had grown up driven; she was assured; she had wit and a highly developed moral sense; and she was well supported. Beechers stood by one another. Her younger brother Charles, who had lived in New Orleans (and abhorred what he saw there), furnished Harriet with eyewitness accounts of slavery up close; one such account inspired the vivid, archetypal portrait of the slaveowner Simon Legree. Another younger brother, Henry, her favorite, urged her on in her efforts, as did her older brother, Edward. Her sister Catharine, meanwhile, was furnishing immediate aid by living in Brunswick and helping manage the household.

Harriet's husband supported her, too. Back in Cincinnati to teach the winter term at Lane, he could check local details useful in her narrative. Besides, he believed in her as a writer, believed her clever and disciplined enough to do anything. Moreover, Professor Stowe helped his wife indirectly, in a manner unintended, for theirs was a typically fecund Victorian marriage—again, begun at the right time, as a young princess was about to ascend the British throne. Harriet thus found herself out west in a Victorian household where, attending to the needs of a large family, she came to understand much about bondage firsthand, this brilliant woman enslaved day by day to domestic duties, through long years of menial drudgeries in nursery and kitchen.

Yet as important as all that was—the place, the time, the person, the family—one further condition proved most crucial of all, so much so that her novel could not have been written without it. Harriet Beecher Stowe wrote *Uncle Tom's Cabin* out of the abiding agony that she felt over the loss of her summer child, her beautiful first Charley, whose image in a white shift even now survives, hauntingly, with his fair hair, his delicate features, his eyes forever closed. An existing postmortem daguerreotype shows Charley at peace hours after the filthy, protracted horrors of cholera had finally killed him. A pillow surrounds the well-shaped head; the fingers hold a dark, irregular object. Is it a flower? Aspects of a brief, sweet life and of its ending had made this mother's loss consummately excruciating; at the last Charley screamed in such protracted torment that Harriet could only pray for death to take him. She could no longer speak of it. Yet of all that suffering the surviving image registers not a trace.

And as terrible as Harriet's loss had been, her child was now in a better world. But what of slave mothers separated from *their* children, black children whom white greed tore away and sent down the river to feel slavery's full, lashing horrors on the racks of the rice swamp, the sugar plantation, the cotton field? A woman of color who had worked for the Stowes in Cincinnati and whom Harriet had come to cherish had told of having each of her several children by a white master taken from her. "I beseech you," the author Harriet Beecher Stowe, at the end of a novel even now forming in her mind, would directly address white mothers North and South, "pity the mother who has all your affections, and not one legal right to protect, guide, or educate, the child of her bosom! By the sick hour of your child; by those dying eyes, which you can never forget; by those last cries, that wrung your heart when you could neither help nor save; by the desolation of that empty cradle, that silent nursery,—I beseech you, pity those mothers who are constantly made childless by the American slave-trade! And say, mothers of America, is this a thing to be defended, sympathized with, passed over in silence?"

8

UNCLE TOM'S CABIN

*A*t the start of a new year—and with so many women publishing now—Harriet felt grateful to receive a message from
Gamaliel Bailey of the *National Era*. To her husband she reported
on January 12, 1851: "I was just in some discouragement with regard to my writing; thinking that the editor of the 'Era' was over-
stocked with contributors, and would not want my services another
year, and lo! he sends me one hundred dollars, and ever so many
good words with it." At once the author's scarcely repressible optimism surged again. "Our income this year will be seventeen hundred
dollars in all," she gloated for Calvin's benefit out in Cincinnati,
"and I hope to bring our expenses within thirteen hundred." Thus,
financially, the Stowes might finally be getting a little ahead.

And now, with an editor's encouragement and moved by the
turmoil of the year just ended, Harriet would try to write that something about slavery. She envisaged sketches on the order of those
she had composed from the beginning, a few pages each of homely
description and characterization, in this instance tied together by
one common thread, that of humanizing black people while depict-
ing the range of slave life. Last year's fiery debates in Congress, the
passage of the Fugitive Slave Act, the appearance of the Slavepower's
agents in Boston: all were moving her to face the evils of bondage
head-on. Yet what could one woman hope to do, addressing an
apathetic American reading public about an institution deeply
entrenched, politically dominant, and commercially indispensable?
"In fact, it was a sort of general impression upon her mind," the
author herself writes in the third person, looking back, "as upon

that of many humane people in those days, that the subject was so dark and painful a one, so involved in difficulty and obscurity, so utterly beyond human hope or help, that it was of no use to read, or think, or distress one's self about it."

A month passed during the winter in Brunswick, with demands persisting in the Stowe household on Federal Street: of child rearing, housekeeping, school tending. But the plight of people of color remained on Harriet's mind. On the first of February she wrote to her brother Henry in Brooklyn: "Would to God I could do something even the humblest in this cause—I have actually and really found tears dropping on my pillow when I have thought of the wrongs and sorrows of those oppressed ones." This was the month when slave catchers in Boston, entering the Cornhill Coffeehouse, apprehended the fugitive Shadrach Minkins, whereupon his fellow blacks charged the courtroom, rescued the prisoner, and—amid public commotion on both sides—hied him off to safety in Montreal. On a Sunday morning in that same February, Harriet Beecher Stowe attended communion in Brunswick, Maine. In the First Parish Church she sat drifting in a dreamlike state where sometimes her mind would wander. All at once an image appeared to her, like a diorama in ghastly motion, of three men looming over a fourth on the ground. The man on the ground was a black slave, whom two other blacks were mercilessly, mortally flogging while a white man goaded them on. That was the brutal, inexplicably vivid picture that seemed to have come out of nowhere; and so strongly was Harriet affected by it that only with difficulty could she restrain herself from sobbing aloud. After the service she hurried home and sat down at once and wrote out what she had seen: a vision "blown into her mind as by the rushing of a mighty wind." Later Calvin came upon her scribbled pages in a drawer. Write toward that, he urged his wife; there is the climax of the book you've been speaking of.

In a fateful letter of March 9, 1851, to Gamaliel Bailey, editor of the *National Era*, Harriet Beecher Stowe explained: "I am at present occupied upon a story which will be a much longer one than any I have ever written, embracing a series of sketches which give the lights and shadows of the 'patriarchal institution,' written either from observation, incidents which have occurred in the sphere of my personal knowledge, or in the knowledge of my friends." She intended, she told the editor, to "show the *best side* of the thing, and something *faintly approaching the worst."* And she stressed that this would be different from what she had done before. "Up to this year I have always felt," Harriet wrote, "that I had no particular call to meddle with this subject, and I dreaded to expose even my own mind to the full force of its exciting power. But I feel now that the time is come when even a woman or a child who can speak a word for freedom and humanity is bound to speak." She went on to specify how she proposed to handle so tremendous a subject. "My vocation," she said, "is simply that of a painter, and my object will be to hold up in the most lifelike and graphic manner possible Slavery, its reverses, changes, and the negro character, which I have had ample opportunities for studying." And why had she settled on presenting her readers with images merely? "There is no arguing with *pictures,"* she insisted, "and everybody is impressed by them, whether they mean to be or not." That was her plan, then— sketches, verbal images of slavery—and she was writing about it to the editor in timely fashion "because I know that you have much matter to arrange, and thought it might not be amiss to give you a hint. The thing may extend three or four numbers. It will be ready in two to three weeks."

The winter just ending had been fierce in Brunswick, and the house where the Stowes were staying was drafty throughout. "The cold has been so intense," Harriet had reported around the new year, "that the children have kept begging to get up from table at mealtimes to warm feet and fingers." Heat from their airtight stove never reached the floor: "heat your head and keep your feet freezing. If I sit by the open fire in the parlor my back freezes, if I sit in my bedroom and try to write my head aches and my feet are cold." Under those inauspicious conditions, "I am projecting a sketch for the 'Era,'" she told Calvin, "on the capabilities of liberated blacks to take care of themselves. Can't you find out for me how much Willie Watson has paid for the redemption of his friends, and get any items in figures of that kind that you can pick up in Cincinnati?" But trying to write in winter was hard; trying to write at any time in the home on Federal Street was a forbidding enterprise. "When I have a headache and feel sick, as I do to-day, there is actually not a place in the house where I can lie down and take a nap without being disturbed. Overhead is the school-room, next door is the dining-room, and the girls practice there two hours a day. If I lock my door and lie down some one is sure to be rattling the latch before fifteen minutes have passed."

Springtime improved matters only somewhat. Household chores were unending, and a writer's lack of privacy persisted. Harriet meanwhile had begun sketching a slave purchase in words: a Kentucky gentleman in dire financial straits feels driven to sell a beloved family retainer to a trader in slaves. The two men—the slave owner Shelby and the slave trader Haley, studies in contrast—sit dealing together over their brandy. And a real-life constable Caphart, having come up from Norfolk to Boston this recent February to seize the runaway Shadrach Minkins, was providing his uncouth part of a Brunswick housewife's inspiration as she created her memorable scene, furnishing her—so she would write to Richard Henry Dana—with "an insight into the character of a negro catcher." By such means, from whatever sources, she sought to draw her verbal pictures: from current news, from remembered conversations with black domestics, from a single visit years ago to Kentucky, from what she could learn from Calvin in Cincinnati or from her brother Charles Beecher recalling his months as a clerk in New Orleans, from what she might read about slavery, from what she was all this while feeling profoundly.

"The thing may extend three or four numbers," she had warned the editor, Gamaliel Bailey, in March. "It will be ready in two to three weeks." But the thing kept growing in size and taking longer to write than expected, so that not until May 8, 1851, did a headline appear in Bailey's weekly announcing "A New Story by Mrs. Stowe." The notice informed readers that "Week after next we propose to commence in the *Era,* the publication of a new story by Mrs. H. B. Stowe, the title of which will be, 'UNCLE TOM'S CABIN, OR THE MAN THAT WAS A THING.' It will probably be of the length of the Tale by Mrs. Southworth, Entitled Retribution." In case some readers of the *Era* were innocent of the fact, "Mrs. Stowe is one of the most gifted and popular of American writers," the notice affirmed. "We announce her story in advance, that none of our subscribers, through neglect to renew their subscriptions, may lose the beginning of it, and that those who desire to read the production as it may appear in successive numbers of the *Era,* may send us their names in season."

The author meanwhile was growing obsessed with her subject. Day and night she thought about the swelling narrative and its many scenes indoors and out: a Kentucky tavern, a slave auction block, the icebound Ohio, travel in early spring on corduroy roads out west. And she brooded on the characters, black and white, male and female, young and old, crude and genteel, rich and poor, who thronged her ever more numerous sketches. Her imagined world became a reality lived with so intensely that she needed only a little while each day to get her vivid apparitions down on paper. Mostly she wrote in the morning, at a desk in the dining room at Brunswick, warding off interruptions as best she could. After Calvin returned from Ohio to assume his duties on the Bowdoin faculty, Catharine got her sister away from home distractions: "At eight o'clock we are through with breakfast and prayers and then we send off Mr. Stowe and Harriet both to his room in the college. There is no other way to keep her out of family cares and quietly at work and since this plan is adopted, she goes ahead finely." Sometimes the author traveled to Boston; Mrs. Edward Beecher remembered that a few installments of *Uncle Tom's Cabin* were written there, upstairs in the Reverend Edward Beecher's study, and that Harriet would read those numbers aloud in the evenings to her brother's family.

She was writing from the heart. The effort took a great deal out of her, often moving her to tears as she imagined the humble lives of her slave creations: their deprivations, the inhumanities visited upon them, their resilience. All her life seemed to have been preparing for this: her childhood stance as a bystander in the midst of a large family under a domineering father, her introverted Calvinist upbringing, two decades of her gifts subjected to domestic bondage out west with a husband often absent and not always helpful, her means and hopes ever restricted by a lack of money, her nature oppressed by a frontier society commercial and assertively male. Blacks in that society, whom life in Litchfield and Cincinnati had allowed her to know, appeared—whatever their gender—to partake more of womankind's virtues as then insisted on: humility, patience, compassion, docility, faith. Accordingly she sympathized with them in their subjugation, felt she knew and understood the quality of African-Americans, was moved to show them for the first time in our literature not as comical properties but as people. Her original subtitle for *Uncle Tom's Cabin*—"The Man That Was A Thing"— she would change finally, in acknowledgment of the novelty of her subject matter, to "Life Among the Lowly."

Stowe's method of writing the novel—in moments when she could manage it, in segments for weekly publication—posed problems. The *National Era* was published in Washington, D.C., some 550 miles from Brunswick. It took a couple of days at least— sometimes three or four days—to get copy from author to editor. Nor was there time for corrections in the relentlessness of the schedule; she scarcely ever saw proofs. Harriet would mail her weekly segment from Portland, or occasionally from Boston or even New York, though in the long course of writing her serial she never visited the editorial offices in Washington—would mail off one number and get busy at once on the next. And despite domestic impediments and the growing demands of the story, she got the job done, faithfully fulfilling her obligations to editor Bailey and her readers week after week while the narrative swelled, from matter for three or four issues as originally envisaged to the more than forty numbers in total that appeared in successive weekly editions of the *Era* from June 5, 1851, to April 1, 1852. Upon receiving her proposal, Bailey had offered $300 for those original four sketches of slave life, a handsome financial reward under the circumstances; but with ten times four total submissions in hand the editor reconsidered. Mrs. Stowe should name her price: what more did he owe her? Harriet thought and came up with a figure: an additional, very modest $100, which Dr. Bailey willingly paid.

Her sister had been scouting around for a book publishing house that might take an interest in Harriet's emerging novel. In the early fall of 1851, with *Uncle Tom's Cabin* still in progress, Catharine Beecher approached a firm that had published her own work, but Phillips, Sampson & Company declined this new opportunity. Hundreds of slave narratives and abolitionist tracts were already in print. The public had grown weary of them; and, in any case, so stale a subject had better be avoided rather than risk offending southern readers: "no discussion of it could be held in the free states without impinging upon the sensibilities of the slave states, to whom alone the management of the matter belonged." But that fall the wife of a publisher of religious literature—an abolitionist whose publishing house had already relinquished any readers down South— sat at home with her husband relishing the latest installment of *Uncle Tom's Cabin* in the *National Era*. Like so many others, Mrs. Jewett was profoundly stirred that week—all but shattered—when, in the narrative, Tom's friend Little Eva died. John P. Jewett must get in touch with so wonderful a writer and secure the rights to publish her story. Jewett had already brought out some sermons by Harriet's brother Henry Ward and would soon announce, this very December of 1851, the first of six projected volumes of the collected works of Harriet's father, Lyman Beecher. The morning after his wife's suggestion, he accordingly wrote to Mrs. Stowe and by return mail "received her reply, informing me that she and her husband would be in Boston in three weeks and would be pleased to make arrangements with me for publishing the story."

For all that, Jewett had his reservations, having to do with length and subject matter. The subject of *Uncle Tom's Cabin* was unpopular; readers might countenance one volume about black people in slavery, but a tale—a "ladies' tale" at that, about which this publisher of solid sermons had doubts—would run perhaps fatal commercial risks if extended into a second volume. Mrs. Stowe should wrap up her story at once. However, if she was willing to assume the risks herself—pay the expenses of printing— her publisher stood ready to split with her fifty-fifty whatever profits or losses might eventuate. But the Stowes had no money for such an investment, so Jewett would be obliged to take on all the risk himself, with the author accordingly receiving the cus- tomary ten percent of whatever sales might develop. And all the while the novel kept growing.

Wealthy as a Brunswick housewife was about to become, Harriet Beecher Stowe would have been a great deal wealthier if she could have scraped together the means to pay for the printing of *Uncle Tom's Cabin*. Jewett himself, doubtful in the fall, had come to sus- pect, even as the novel was burgeoning through its second volume, that very good money was to be made from it after all. By the spring of 1852 he had determined on an initial printing of—at the time an enormous expression of confidence—no fewer than 5,000 copies. Moreover, he would be printing from stereotype, a method more expensive than the movable type usual with novels, but one that would end up saving the publisher money if, as he obviously be- lieved, the reading public should call for further copies to be is- sued beyond the original 5,000. In addition, he had commissioned six engravings to be inserted in the text and was planning to offer *Uncle Tom's Cabin* in various bindings.

And he did more than that. However much he would eventually earn for his efforts—and for them John P. Jewett was paid extraordinarily well—he worked hard to promote the book, and in unprecedented ways. He sought out the abolitionist poet John Greenleaf Whittier to write a poem about Little Eva, then found a composer to set Whittier's poem to music. Before publication, he saw to it that the novel was mentioned in dozens of newspapers. He even traveled to Washington to talk *Uncle Tom's Cabin* up with members of Congress. These were years when a mass middle-class, mostly female reading market was for the first time emerging in America, at prosperous mid-century after the depression that had followed the horrific Panic of 1837. In Boston, the innovative genius of the editor James T. Fields—publisher of Hawthorne, Longfellow, Emerson, Holmes, and Whittier himself —was even now showing the way to gratify and enlarge such a widespread readership; but not even the great Fields could have matched the ingenuity of his fellow publisher Jewett in the promotion of at least this one commodity, this unusual story—still unfolding serially through the winter and into the spring of 1852— that depicted life among the lowly as imagined by a housewife in Maine.

The final number of *Uncle Tom's Cabin* appeared in the April 1, 1852, issue of the *National Era*. On March 20 of that same year, John P. Jewett of Boston had sent out to the bookstores his two-volume edition, price $1.50, of the new novel by Mrs. Harriet Beecher Stowe on the great moral question of the age. To Horace Mann that same day, the author herself, referring perhaps to emended copy for the *Era*, wrote: "To day I have taken my pen from the last chapter of 'Uncle Tom's Cabin' & I think you will understand me when I say that I feel as if I had written some of it almost with my hearts blood—." She would come to believe, of the long, trancelike period during which the novel emerged, that God had composed it, that she was merely His vessel, listening and, as it were, writing to dictation (a not uncommon feeling among authors in the throes of inspiration, setting down what they never knew they knew). And after those final proof sheets left her hands—or at least she would remember it thus and write of the moment in a later preface to the novel—"it seemed to her that there was no hope, that nobody would hear, nobody would read, nobody would pity; that this frightful system, which had already pursued its victims into the free states, might at last even threaten them in Canada."

Maybe that spring she did feel so: no hope, with nobody to hear or read of or pity the victims for whom she had tried to speak. She was, after all, only one woman: a daughter, sister, wife, and mother who had written a first novel seeking to persuade the Union that it must disentangle itself from an institution of colossal economic importance with which its fate had been lucratively intertwined since before the founding. What chance was there that an appeal in such a form, from such a source, could make a difference? But many years later, when the publisher J. C. Derby remarked to Mrs. Stowe of Jewett's once telling him that at its first appearance its author had had little confidence in her novel's prospects, she responded sharply: "What Jewett says about Uncle Tom is false. I was not altogether such a fool as he represents, although I confess I was surprised at the *extent* of the success."

9

RECEPTION

*T*he success of *Uncle Tom's Cabin* was immediate and phenomenal, unprecedented in the history of our literature. Published two years earlier, *The Scarlet Letter,* Nathaniel Hawthorne's most profitable work by far up to that time, would garner for its author a total of $1,500 over the fourteen years of life remaining to him. For *Moby-Dick* (1851), Herman Melville earned a total of $556.37 during the forty years elapsing until his death. By contrast, within its first *three months* as a book, *Uncle Tom's Cabin* earned Harriet Beecher Stowe $10,300, and the money kept pouring in. Three thousand copies were sold on the initial day of publication, the entire run of 5,000 within ten days, 300,000 within nine months. No other writer in America had come anywhere close to such a commercial triumph before. Four Adams power presses ran full speed day and night to gratify the clamor for Uncle Tom, and up to 200 bookbinders were kept busy binding the volumes. Already in the *National Era* of January 27, 1853, with the history of the bound novel not yet a year old, its publisher, Jewett, was able to announce that *Uncle Tom's Cabin* had sold a million copies so far in America and England, and the demand for it was showing no sign of abating.

Masses of readers adored the story, the famous as well as the less so, here and around the world. Dickens in England saluted Stowe's achievement as "a noble work; full of high power, lofty humanity, the gentlest, sweetest, and yet boldest, writing." In France George Sand reviewed the novel promptly and enthusiastically, praising its author for possessing something more than talent —for possessing genius, "the genius of goodness, not that of the man of letters, but of the saint." Tolstoy in Russia would cite *Uncle Tom's Cabin* as an example of "the highest order of art." In Germany Heine compared the book favorably to the Bible. Nearer at hand, in the very midst of the furor surrounding this sudden literary phenomenon, Rufus Choate, an influential Boston attorney whose sympathies lay with a commercially prosperous status quo, bemoaned the fact that a single work of fiction was likely to create a troublemaking "two millions of abolitionists." Longfellow—by contrast, no friend of the South's peculiar institution—recorded in his journal of having begun "'Uncle Tom'—a pathetic and droll book on slavery," which after two weeks of reading aloud in the evening was to move him and his wife deeply: "we read ourselves into despair in that tragic book, 'Uncle Tom's Cabin.' It is too melancholy, and makes one's blood boil too hotly." Like everyone else, the poet gaped in amazement at the rocket ascent of Stowe's reputation; within a year his journal records this exclamation: "How she is shaking the world with her 'Uncle Tom's Cabin!' At one step she has reached the top of the staircase up which the rest of us climb on our knees year after year. Never was there such a literary *coup-de-main* as this." Emerson would speak of the novel's vast appeal "to the universal heart." The Quaker Whittier, arch abolitionist, went so far as to venture thanks for the horrid Fugitive Slave Law, "for it gave occasion for 'Uncle Tom's Cabin.'" Even the fastidious Henry James would recall Stowe's clarion blast in his youth as "a triumphant work," wondrous as a fish that flies and blessed with "the extraordinary fortune of finding itself, for an immense number of people, much less a book than a state of vision, of feeling and of consciousness, in which they didn't sit and read and appraise and pass the time, but walked and talked and laughed and cried."

The esteem in which the novel was held from the start, in the North certainly, and very soon worldwide, persisted beyond the Civil War. After the war, the excellent, underrated John W. De Forest, himself a novelist, asserted that nowhere else but in *Uncle Tom's Cabin* would one find American life portrayed "so broadly, truly and sympathetically"; and in 1882, fourteen years after that utterance, De Forest was still insisting that Mrs. Stowe belonged "at the head of all living novelists, especially in the characteristics of power and sincerity, both of feeling and style." The recently founded

Nation had concurred in the earlier year 1868, with De Forest's opinion, pronouncing the elusive Great American Novel to have achieved embodiment at last in Stowe's fictional creation. And as further corroboration, no less a critic than William Dean Howells, writing at the end of the nineteenth century, concluded that *Uncle Tom's Cabin* was "almost the greatest work of imagination that we have produced in prose," albeit its principal virtue lay "in the address to the conscience, and not its address to the taste; to the ethical sense, not the aesthetical sense"—to morality, that is, rather than to art.

Its addressing the conscience helps account for the novel's decline in critical standing once the Civil War had abolished the evil of slavery that *Uncle Tom's Cabin* indicted. Moreover, after the war, with Reconstruction forsaken and a new harmony sought among whites nationwide, the North chose to lay aside memories of antebellum discord; yet even so, even if forgetfulness marked the official stance from the 1880s onward, the sheer vigor of its narrative would make Stowe's novel as late as 1899 the most frequently checked out of all the volumes in the New York Public Library.

Thus among readers in the North. Those in the South felt differently about *Uncle Tom's Cabin*—and about saintly Mrs. Stowe as well. In January 1853, within a year of publication, the author would report what a cousin living in Georgia had told her: "that the prejudice against my name is so strong that she dares not have it appear on the outside of her letters, and that very amiable and excellent people have asked her if such as I could be received into reputable society at the North." The previous October, in the pages of the distinguished *Southern Literary Messenger*, Mrs. Stowe had been taken sternly to task for "a shameless disregard of truth and of those amenities which so peculiarly belong to her sphere of life"; she had thus "forfeited the claim to be considered a lady, and with that claim all exemption from the utmost stringency of critical punishment." Criticism was accordingly meted out at length, of a novel filled (the reviewer, George F. Holmes, declared) with implausibilities and untruths, whose black characters were uniformly favored over the whites; indeed, every white face that the authoress limns contains "something sinister and repulsive," whereas the Negro "under her brush invariably becomes handsome in person or character, or in both, and not one figures in *Uncle Tom's Cabin,* no matter how benighted or besotted his condition, who does not ultimately get to heaven"—much of which judgment is manifestly untrue. Similarly, in the *Southern Quarterly Review* of January 1853, Louisa S. C. McCord, a well-known writer in her time, professed to have recoiled before "the lothsome rakings of a foul fancy" that was Mrs. Stowe's, appalled by "the foul imagination which could invent such scenes" as were depicted in *Uncle Tom's Cabin* "and the malignant bitterness (we had almost said ferocity) which, under the veil of Christian charity, could find the conscience to publish them." Others of repute in the South would describe the novel as "a guidebook to the marketplace of abomination," and its author as unprincipled to the extent that "never before was anything so detestable or so monstrous among women as this." Hers was "a filthy, lying book," and she herself "as ugly as Original sin—an abomination in the eyes of civilized people." More specifically, the diminutive Mrs. Stowe was to be recognized as a "tall, coarse, vulgar-looking woman—stoop-shouldered with a long yellow neck, and a long peaked nose—through which she speaks." From elsewhere came comments on the author's voice, which was "probably harsh," and on Stowe's "big, scrawling hand, with the letters all backwards, avoiding neatness with painstaking precision," and—worst of all—on "the man Harriet," who had "unsexed herself" by leaving her proper, domestic, private world to meddle in the public masculine world of politics. In the "odious notoriety" resulting from such a betrayal, she possessed "too much mind not to comprehend the wicked injustice and dangerous consequences of the distorted picture she has drawn of slave life and Southern morals." Mrs. Stowe's "unseemly and mischievous labors" in writing such a book have degraded talents that "might have been usefully and gracefully devoted to delicate and womanly compositions"—all of these labors undertaken, patently, "for the sake of gain." She had, in short, "written one of the most abominable libels which the age has produced, full of all manner of calumnies and uncharitableness; and provocative of mischief beyond her power to check, if she would. Such a desecration of woman's nature is a sorry and a rare sight, even in this age of feminine aspirations to rivalry with man in all his harshest of traits, and all his most unamiable pursuits."

In that vein the South had responded at the time of publication, and its hostility thrived through the 1850s and the war that followed to continue strong into the twentieth century. Novels were written, a veritable genre—*Aunt Phillis's Cabin, Life at the South, The Planter's Northern Bride,* many others—in quite inferior refutation of what had occasioned them, southern authors choosing to depict life for the slave bathed in hues far mellower than Stowe's. As for that, the author of *Uncle Tom's Cabin* had fulfilled her promise to show the best as well as no more than a hint of the worst of plantation living, populating her pages with attractive white southerners (the most despicable character in the novel comes from Vermont) and limiting her condemnation to the inhuman institution that had deformed the South, while conveying throughout her fondness for southerners as people and her compassion for slavery's victims, whether black or white.

Hence she was quite unprepared for the intensity of southerners' reaction to her novel. Most assuredly Harriet Beecher Stowe would have been ill prepared for the eloquent intensity of one African-American in the North, reacting in the mid-twentieth century to this fiction out of a different time, nearly 100 years old by then. As a child the novelist James Baldwin (1924–1987) had loved *Uncle Tom's Cabin,* but during the course of a brilliant, tortured adulthood he learned to despise—in post–World War II America before *Brown* v. *Board of Education*—what for him by then had grown into a "very bad novel." Writing in 1949 in the *Partisan Review,* Baldwin deplored the narrative's "catalogue of violence," its sentimentality, its sanctimonious whitening of blackness, and above all the servility and sexlessness of its hero. The evangelical spirit "that breathes in this book, hot, self-righteous, fearful, is not different," concluded this subtle northern African-American reader, "from that spirit of medieval times which sought to exorcize evil by burning witches; and is not different from that terror which activates a lynch mob." In sum, the aim of such protest fiction as was exemplified by *Uncle Tom's Cabin* appeared to the mature Baldwin to resemble "the zeal of those alabaster missionaries to Africa to cover the nakedness of the natives, to hurry them into the pallid arms of Jesus and thence into slavery."

Others among Baldwin's twentieth-century contemporaries were reading a far different novel. Edmund Wilson, reconsidering

Uncle Tom's Cabin in his own maturity, in the 1950s, discovered "a much more impressive work than one has ever been allowed to suspect." This most astute, discerning white critic praised the book's "eruptive force," its taut intent objectivity, its "desperate candor that shook South and North alike." Kenneth Lynn, another perspicacious critic of American literature, would find to praise "the shrewdness, the energy, the truly Balzacian variousness of Mrs. Stowe's characterizations," as well as her ability to arouse emotion "not for emotion's sake alone—as the sentimental novelists notoriously did—but in order to facilitate the moral regeneration of an entire nation." Most strikingly, the American novelist Jane Smiley, writing in 1996, went to the lengths of implying that Stowe's novel is more salutary as antislavery fiction than Mark Twain's later masterpiece: "I would rather my children read *Uncle Tom's Cabin*, even though it is far more vivid in its depiction of cruelty than *Huck Finn*, and this is because Stowe's novel is clearly and unmistakably a tragedy. No whitewash"—as in *Adventures of Huckleberry Finn*—"no secrets, but evil, suffering, imagination, endurance, and redemption —just like life." Stowe's novel is filled, says Smiley, with "the power of brilliant analysis married to great wisdom of feeling." And incidentally, according to yet another admiring reader, the British novelist Anthony Burgess, writing in 1966, *Uncle Tom's Cabin* "has done more than any work of literature to make Negro servitude in the South seem not only the type of all slavery but the only one we ought to feel guilty about. We can forget what happened to the Jews, or what is still going on under Islam, or that a greater white novelist"—Cervantes—"was a galley-slave. Thanks to Harriet Beecher Stowe, colour has become for all time the colour of the oppressed."

About the "Uncle Tom," meanwhile, whose alleged obsequiousness has so infuriated reformers of the civil rights era and afterward, "we all," according to Jane Smiley, "know what an 'Uncle Tom' is, except we don't. The popular Uncle Tom sucks up to the master and exhibits bovine patience. The real Uncle Tom," whom Stowe's novel in fact depicts, "is both a realist and a man of deep principle." Youthful, brawny, he allows himself to be sold—rather than fleeing to freedom, as he easily could have done—in order to save the financially strapped plantation on which live his own wife, family, and friends, as well as his kindly master and mistress. Later, Tom submits to the fatal beating that brings the novel to its horrendous climax—that flogging of Stowe's vision at communion in Brunswick—because to do differently would have betrayed others and damned his own soul. Nor is Tom's suffering there so different in intensity from the passion of Jesus, whom above all others Harriet Beecher Stowe (and Tom) adored. Anyway, what course besides the one he followed would have bestowed on him more self-respect? Or, as Burgess wonders, "What palliative ought a progressive slavery novel to make available to Legree's victims"—to Tom above all—"(abolitionist pamphlets? gems from Tom Paine?)? Visions of secular reform have always been pie in the sky; a man entering the gas chamber needs heaven."

One easily identifiable source accounts for the contrast between the shuffling, meek old "Uncle Tom" who lives in the popular imagination and the vigorous young Uncle Tom of Stowe's novel. *Uncle Tom's Cabin* appeared in the spring of 1852. Some months later, in November, the first production of a play called *Uncle Tom's Cabin* was warmly received in Troy, New York; it soon moved to New York City and thence across the nation and overseas at the start of a remarkable stage history. Stowe herself had nothing to do with the play and profited not a penny from its stupendous success. For during every week that passed from its opening in 1852 through close to ninety years, far into the 1930s, somewhere in America some professional company was performing *Uncle Tom's Cabin*. For each person who read the book, fifty people, maybe as many as a hundred, saw the play; and the play, unhindered by any need for fidelity to what had inspired it, became quite early something very different.

"Take the children," urged the playbills, "and give them an ideal and lasting lesson in American history. It is delightful, wonderful, instructive and moral." Morality provided one great attraction. In the mid-nineteenth century, people who would have avoided a theater's disreputable precincts—the catcalls, the prostitutes, the apple cores tossed from the gallery—felt for the first time willing to pay to see a production as right-minded as this, with, moreover, something to please the entire family: the melodrama of evil Simon Legree snapping his snake whip and of Eliza crossing the ice floes of the Ohio with bloodhounds in hot pursuit (no bloodhounds pursue her in the novel); the pathos of Tom's agonizing death; the spectacle of little Eva soaring heavenward on a milk-white dove;

the comedy of chawing, teetotalling Phineas Fletcher (who scarcely appears in the novel), of Miss Ophelia with her scorn of the shiftless, of black Topsy dancing her breakdowns. Soon the characters had diverged into stereotypes, as the play in postbellum years moved farther away from any mention of slavery or condemnation of the South in favor of what became ultimately pure entertainment, a modified minstrel show directed increasingly toward children, with comical field hands and elderly Uncle Tom, age imparting dignity and making the black man safely asexual as he and Little Eva, that lovely white child, played out their affecting scenes together. In time would come the first movie ever made from a novel, in 1903, with other screen versions to follow. Shirley Temple would play a ringleted Little Eva; Judy Garland, in blackface, a Topsy.

All of which—long-running play ("America's Greatest Hit!"), numberless traveling companies, ballets, various silent and sound versions on the screen—tell us only a little about *Uncle Tom's Cabin*, by Harriet Beecher Stowe.

10

DARK PLACES

S towe's novel begins with that sketch of two men over brandy engaged in a business transaction. Goodhearted, imprudent Arthur Shelby, the Kentucky planter, has run up debts. A major creditor is the coarse Dan Haley, who sits now, Shylock-like, claiming his pound of flesh. Haley deals in slaves as others deal in coal or potatoes; he will take as payment Shelby's exemplary Tom, strong, pious, faithful, trustworthy. But a bit more than even that valuable commodity will be needed to pay off the Kentuckian's indebtedness and thus save his plantation. Throw in the slave child Harry there. Harry's mother, the light-skinned Eliza Harris, gets wind of the proposed sale of her boy and determines to flee with him in the nighttime northward. An intelligent, well-treated house servant, Eliza is able—with her benevolent mistress's collusion—to gather up little Harry and escape on foot through the perils of slaveholding Kentucky to the Ohio River. On the river's far bank lies freedom. Meanwhile, Eliza's husband, the proud George Harris, a slave on a neighboring plantation, has vowed to flee from his own master, who is as cruelly spiteful as that other planter, Shelby, is ineffectually kind.

Eliza's and George's separate adventures, before their fortuitous reunion in Ohio and subsequent flight together to carry themselves and their child beyond the reach of even the Fugitive Slave Law, form one of the two paths of Stowe's spacious plot. That path lies northward toward freedom. The other plot direction, which follows Tom after he is sold to Haley, turns southward, descending the Mississippi River ever more deeply into slave country. Stowe moves her narrative back and forth, maintaining interest and suspense by tracing the Harrises' experiences alternately with Tom's. Haley has put his new acquisition aboard a steamboat bound for the slave marts of New Orleans; but on the boat along the way the kindly Tom is befriended by a young white child of five or six, returning with her father from a visit to New England. In the course of the voyage the child, Eva, slips over the side of the deck into the river, and Tom rescues her; whereupon her grateful father, Augustine St. Clare, is moved to purchase the black man to be a servant in his household. Thus Tom finds himself well situated in comfortable circumstances in New Orleans, as coachman to a kindly master.

The brilliant, articulate St. Clare has brought back with him from Vermont a spinster cousin, Miss Ophelia, to help look after his daughter Eva in the absence of a mother's care; for the mother, the vividly realized Marie St. Clare, languishes in self-absorbed invalidism, leaving her husband, Ophelia, and the servants to manage as best they can. Out of pity, St. Clare buys and introduces into his New Orleans home a little black child, Topsy, whom previous owners have flagrantly mistreated. Ophelia is urged to exercise her New England philanthropy on this new charge. Thus the comically misbehaving Topsy; prim Miss Ophelia; beautiful, warmhearted little Eva; indolent, skeptical St. Clare; the querulous valetudinarian Marie St. Clare; and various sharply drawn black servants, including Tom, proceed through their interactions to instance varieties of southern urban life as a complement to the representation of southern rural life that the Shelbys of Kentucky have earlier enacted.

But disaster awaits the St. Clares. The much loved little Eva falls ill with consumption and dies, although not before persuading her father to free their dear friend Tom from bondage, however benign. The grieving St. Clare is in the process of doing so when, while breaking up a public fight in the city, he is mortally wounded. His family is thrown into turmoil, and the egregious widow sells off the servants to liquidate her assets and leave New Orleans. Thus Tom, instead of returning—as he had hoped—a free man to his wife and children in Kentucky, finds himself on the auction block after all. And now his luck runs out utterly: he is purchased by the execrable Simon Legree.

Like Ophelia, the sadistic Legree was born in Vermont, but there any resemblance between the two ceases. This slave owner, down from the North, who embodies the very worst of the South's paternal institution, takes Tom and another acquisition, the lovely fifteen-year-old quadroon Emmeline, off up the Red River to dark places deep in the Louisiana backwoods. There, on Legree's isolated, forlorn plantation, with only a master's whim for law, the gentle, powerful Tom is set to work in the cotton fields. As in Melville's later *Billy Budd,* the very goodness of the black man soon provokes Legree's hatred, which leads in the end to Tom's being flogged to death, ostensibly for refusing to betray what he knows about young Emmeline's flight from her monstrous oppressor. Tom, thus, at the end of his long journey lies martyred while evil abides; although Eliza and George Harris, having completed travels in the opposite direction, succeed in reaching their distant goal, stepping onto Canadian soil with the certainty of a future in freedom for them and their descendants.

Such a brief summary of the five years that the novel encompasses offers but a faint suggestion of Stowe's rich achievement as revealed through her well-structured scenes. At the start, her title signals that *Uncle Tom's Cabin*—for all its geographical range, sociological breadth, and political acumen—will be a domestic novel, focused sharply on the home. The story's overarching concern, repeated again and again, is with the breaking up of that home: the severance—or the threatened severance—of, in particular, mothers from their children. "I well remember," the author recalled for her biographer son Charles in his adulthood, "the winter you were a baby and I was writing 'Uncle Tom's Cabin.' . . . I remember many a night weeping over you as you lay sleeping beside me, and I thought of the slave mothers whose babes were torn from them"—as in Cincinnati an earlier Charley (the image of this child asleep beside her) had been torn from Harriet Beecher Stowe. In *Uncle Tom's Cabin,* Eliza flees from home clutching little Harry to save him. Good Mrs. Bird, the Quaker who succors Eliza in her flight through Ohio to freedom, has recently lost to death her own child, whose clothes she gives to Harry. Traders seize the child of a slave aboard the steamboat headed south with Tom (himself wrenched from his family), causing the bereft mother to leap overboard into the night, a suicide. Old Prue, who delivers bread to the

St. Clares' kitchen, has been turned into a scowling drunk, having earlier been kept by a white master "to breed chil'en for market" who were sold "as fast as they got big enough"; a last child, whom Prue particularly loved, was allowed to die through her owner's appalling selfishness. The St. Clares lose their Eva. Legree's supplanted mistress, the quadroon Cassy, has had her two children taken from her. Separation and loss are everywhere in the novel, contributing to its urgency, its poignancy, and its unfaltering power.

And to the novelty of *Uncle Tom's Cabin*. Slave narratives had appeared before 1852, earnest, stock accounts of cruelties in bondage and escapes to freedom. But Stowe's story offered something new by fleshing out the lives of black people, by consciously and for the first time humanizing their ordeal. Her original subtitle, "The Man That Was A Thing," stressed the chattel aspects of a so-called patriarchal but actually inhuman institution: slaves as property, denied their freedom, denied education, denied all legal and family rights. The altered subtitle—"Life Among the Lowly"—emphasized the humanity of black people, the fact that they were *people,* which many of her white readers were being led to feel emotionally only now, in absorbing this stirring narrative. Indeed, Stowe's forceful grip on her readers' sympathies helps account, perhaps above all other explanations, for the novel's prompt and unprecedented popularity.

Humor provides another explanation, no doubt, for the novel's vast appeal, the appeal of this "droll" *Uncle Tom's Cabin,* as Longfellow described its early pages. The form that Stowe's humor assumed was a novelty too. She had begun by painting pictures— "sketches"—and the story that grew out of those sketches exhibits both the failings and the strengths of such a narrative approach. Despite the artful structuring, transitions are sometimes abrupt, the movement from scene to scene on occasion more mechanical than organic. But the scenes themselves are wonderfully vivid, either inside slave quarters, or within a carriage tossed about in flight over ragged roads, or on a Mississippi steamboat, or in the St. Clares' raucous kitchen, or at a slave auction house, or up the dark river to Legree's ramshackle beweeded plantation. Moreover, the characters that populate those and many other such scenes are fully drawn—Balzacian in truth—each one, white or black, individualized. Each speaks in his or her own distinctive way, whether—

among the whites—in that of the insinuating Haley, or the compassionate Mrs. Shelby, or the cultured St. Clare, or the pampered whiny Marie St. Clare, or the pragmatic Vermonter Ophelia, or the Ohio Quaker abolitionists theeing and thouing, or the thuggish Marks and Loker, or the brutal Legree. And among the black characters—but what a roster it is! unprecedented in American letters up to that time—among all those sharply individuated black people we hear the articulate, bright Harrises and the pretentious Adolph and the mild Uncle Tom and the embittered Prue and the well-reared Cassy and the comfortably authoritarian Chloe and Dinah and the irrepressible stable hand Sam and the zestfully disingenuous Topsy. Each has his own voice, and out of those voices arises much of the humor of *Uncle Tom's Cabin.*

Some of that humor has traveled poorly over the decades. Stowe's original readers would have chuckled where we will not, for of course the author, like virtually all her white contemporaries, was—when judged by our lights—a racist. The chance of her being otherwise was infinitesimal. Virtually every white person of Stowe's era subscribed to racial doctrines that have since been discredited: that Anglo-Saxons, for example, are inventive, courageous, and enterprising; that Africans, by contrast, are by their very nature childlike, servile, and comical. Hence the ease with which black speech and behavior could be made to appear humorous to white readers of the mid-nineteenth century and for many long years afterward.

In the course of her life Stowe knew, worked with, and felt genuine affection for many black people. She admired them; nowhere else in all of American literature before *Uncle Tom's Cabin* can blacks be found portrayed so humanly, variously, and sympathetically. But the author was a child of her times, subscribing to the era's misconceptions. The hugely esteemed William Ellery Channing, for instance, spoke of blacks as *by nature* "affectionate, easily touched . . . among the mildest, gentlest of men"—an estimate with which Stowe readily concurred, to the extent that her language expressing such complacent attitudes will make us of a different era wince: blacks as exotics "of the most gorgeous and superb countries of the world"—she is speaking of Africa—and hence despite their untrained taste possessed of a racial passion "for all that is splendid, rich, and fanciful," their temperament displaying a "childlike simplicity of affection, and facility of forgiveness," their habits inclining "to repose on a superior mind and rest on a higher power." That last inclination gives blacks a religious sense finer than the Anglo-Saxon's, as Stowe and a great many of her northern countrymen believed—no small recommendation for people of color in the opinion of a daughter, sister, and wife of ministers. Tom, we read elsewhere in the novel, is possessed of "the soft, impressible nature of his kindly race, ever yearning toward the simple and child-like," and hence naturally drawn to the white child Eva. And, like his piety, Tom's humility, his docility—traits understood to be characteristic of all blacks—were in the dichotomous world of mid-nineteenth-century America regarded as attributes more feminine than masculine, affiliated more with the higher, moral home than with the lower, amoral marketplace.

All of that made blacks appealing to Stowe, if often for reasons that we now dismiss as misguided. The author meanwhile took pains to bring humor into her story in order to brighten what would otherwise have been an account of an abhorrent social system too dark for her readers to tolerate. Of that system, the southerner St. Clare remarks with biting irony: "Why, because my brother Quashy is ignorant and weak,—and I am intelligent and strong,—because I know how, and can do it,—therefore, I may steal all he has, keep it, and give him only such and so much as suits my fancy." This same religious skeptic pursues his analysis of southern society with disinterested clarity: "Here is a whole class,—debased, uneducated, indolent, provoking,—put, without any sort of terms or conditions, entirely into the hands of such people as the majority in our world are; people who have neither consideration nor self-control, who haven't even an enlightened regard to their own interest,—for that's the case with the largest half of mankind. Of course, in a community so organized, what can a man of honorable and humane feelings do, but shut his eyes all he can, and harden his heart? I can't buy every poor wretch I see. I can't turn knight-errant, and undertake to redress every individual case of wrong."

Only when leavened with humor will the depiction of such a horrendous social order be tolerable. Stowe strives, for all that, to describe the South as fair-mindedly as possible, writing a legitimately national novel, offering the balance that abolitionist tracts, slave narratives, and certainly southern apologias for slavery lacked. Not only are her fully realized black people of all sorts: male, female, young, old, as virtuous as Tom, as warmly tender as Tom's wife Chloe, as vain as Rosa in the St. Clare household, as pitiful as poor Prue, as good-hearted as Sam, as angry as George Harris, as horrific as the brutal Quimby and Sambo on Legree's plantation. But among Stowe's southern whites are some who are thoughtful, generous-spirited, and genuinely distressed by a social system they never made and don't know how to mend.

From that mass of imagined humanity have arisen characters so vivid as to achieve the status of myth and archetype: Topsy, Eva, Legree, Tom himself. As for Tom, described as "a perfect behemoth," "large, broad-chested, powerfully made," his behavior under the ruthless Legree's taunts and goadings near the end of the novel exhibits less of servility than of the highest courage. Even when threatened with being roasted alive Tom refuses to do his master's bidding. "Mas'r Legree, . . . I can't do it. I did only what I thought was right. I shall do just so again, if ever the time comes. I never will do a cruel thing, come what may." Tom's sufferings for declining to shed other people's blood, as Legree has ordered him to by flogging a fellow slave ("What! ye blasted black beast! tell *me* ye don't think it *right* to do what I tell ye! What have any of you cussed cattle to do with thinking what's right?")—Tom's sufferings, like his ultimate forgiveness of his tormenters, exemplify not so much submissiveness as the nonviolent response to injustice that Martin Luther King, Jr. would later fashion into an effective tool for civil revolution. Indeed, Tom's behavior at the last, as the text insists again and again, echoes nothing so clearly as the passion "of one crowned with thorns, buffeted and bleeding."

The novel has its faults. Those of racism and sentimentality are attributable to the times in which it was written; a tendency to sermonize can be traced to the evangelical who wrote it. Moreover, by the end the blacks still alive whom we care most about, except Cassy, have made their way to Africa, thus sparing readers any need to confront whatever social tensions would surely result from a mass emancipation of slaves bent on living free among white people. Stowe no more than her readers was able to imagine that outcome. And in making Legree a bachelor, she spared those readers the pain of contemplating yet another dark side of slavery: the effect on their white wives and families of husbands bedding slave mistresses. Such evasions in the story were, however, hardly faults to its early audience, either here in America or in lands far overseas, where *Uncle Tom's Cabin* was soon translated into numerous foreign tongues, its author—that "little, feeble, timid-looking woman," as Mrs. Longfellow described her—known promptly and admired worldwide.

So popular, in fact, did her book become internationally that Charles Edward Stowe, her son and biographer, was able in time to collect editions in twenty-six languages (a number now grown to fifty-eight) of *Uncle Tom's Cabin*—the author of which meanwhile, having finished her amazing novel, would spend some of its early earnings renovating a stone house in Andover, Massachusetts, to which her family moved from Brunswick in the fall of 1852, Calvin Stowe having been installed by then as professor of sacred literature at Andover Theological Seminary.

LYMAN

"I fear we have too much in this world to love
& that we love it too well
How precious have been the gifts of the Lord unto us
what a father!
and he still lives."

Harriet Beecher Stowe of Lyman Beecher, 1843

LYMAN BEECHER, C. 1838
portrait by Edward Dalton Marchant,
Harriet Beecher Stowe Center, Hartford, Connecticut.

II

TO ENGLAND

Calvin Stowe and his wife, the now internationally famous Harriet Beecher Stowe, sailed for Liverpool via Halifax aboard the steamship *Canada* in late March 1853, precisely a year after *Uncle Tom's Cabin* first appeared as a book. The Stowes' traveling party included Sarah Buckingham Beecher—the affluent widow of Harriet's late older brother George (dead by his own hand a decade earlier in Chillicothe, Ohio)—along with Sarah's son, the eleven-year-old Georgy, and her adult brother William. Those last three traveled at their own expense, but Calvin and Harriet were sailing as guests of English admirers in the antislavery movement, with Charles Beecher, Harriet's younger brother, along as factotum. Charles was charged with keeping a record of the trip in the form of a journal, which he started at sea east of Halifax on April 1.

That morning half the party has settled in on deck abaft the smokestack. The other three are elsewhere about the ship: "his grace the duke of Buckingham"—Sarah's brother William—leaning over the railing seasick far astern; young Georgy seasick as well; Calvin, veteran of Atlantic crossings and in the best of health for once, below in his cabin comfortably reading his German. Here topside the wind is raw, the temperature in the thirties. Most of the other passengers have, like Professor Stowe, forsaken the deck; the few men remaining are in muffs and greatcoats. "Hatty and Sarah are the only ladies out," Charles reports, "and they occupy settees with pillows and are enveloped in nameless and numberless articles of apparel": petticoats, dresses, shawls, cloaks, wrapping gowns. For all that, the bundled travelers are in high spirits and—despite cold winds, a snowstorm, no fires below, and tall waves relentlessly pummeling the ship—will remain so throughout the twelve days of the voyage.

"All round the whole horizon now we see not land, naught but a boundless level desert," Charles exults that Friday, "but, oh, how beautiful! I could spend years and never tire gazing on this still, yet moving, this somber, yet gay, this green, gray, blue-black, foamy sparkling sea." The diarist of this present adventure is a minister like George, the Beecher brother deceased, and as his five other living brothers are or will become. Four years younger than his sister Harriet, Charles is one of the several sons in the Beecher family who entered the ministry reluctantly. He attended Lawrence Academy in Groton, went to Bowdoin, studied at Lane in Cincinnati, and through it all felt more love for music than for divinity. To his minister father's dismay Charles had taken his religious doubts to New Orleans and taught music down there and worked as a clerk in a cotton factory. The experience gave the young man a view up close of slavery, which he learned promptly to loathe; but his vivid recollections of slave marts and slave dealers furnished his older sister later with characters and scenery for her recently published *Uncle Tom's Cabin*. Returning north from New Orleans in the early 1840s, Charles was ordained at last and proceeded to pursue his calling in churches in Indiana and New Jersey. He married and had five children but never made much money. Charles's beliefs were somewhat heterodox; indeed he would later be convicted of heresy, and his opposition to the Fugitive Slave Act in 1850 was vociferous enough to alarm his congregation in Newark. Preach disobedience to the law of the land? Now, at thirty-nine, he was sailing away from worshippers' grumblings to serve as support for his sister Hatty on what promised to be a most clamorous tour abroad, where help would be needed managing luggage, dealing with invitations, keeping accounts, responding to correspondents, and generally easing a famous author's progress overseas.

At present, though, on board the *Canada* as it plows east at ten knots toward England, days are carefree and unencumbered. Chess helps pass the hours, and reading, snoozing, walking the deck, playing shuffleboard. And the travelers sing, as the Beechers sang together two decades earlier in a great stagecoach headed west toward Cincinnati. "Hatty and Stowe *sing* in the midst of the roaring winds and waves, and the officers and men pretend not to notice it, only I know that they stop talking and keep very quiet till we get through." Stowe, his wife, and the others sing "John Anderson, My Jo," "Hark, the Goddess Diana," "Amazing Grace," and "The Sea, the Sea, the Open Sea," all of them amused by lyrics in that last: "With the blue above and the blue below, And silence whereso'er I go"—for they've met with no such thing, Charles protests in good humor, considering "such a thrashing, clattering, roaring, howling, banging, creaking, squealing, boozling, storming, and unutterably noisy time as we have had from the first moment we started."

Yet they are having a grand voyage. Professor Stowe insists he has been "as happy as a goose all the way, never had such a fine time." They are off the Irish coast now, and here Hatty is "in high spirits on the sunny deck, spying with the rest. Saw Skibbereen, where the famine was." The weather has improved dramatically. "We have a warm southwest wind. The sun is warm and bright. All are in raptures at this brilliant finale." The men on deck play a game of "monkey": "A noose is suspended from the yardarm, and the individual enacting the monkey puts it about his middle and runs about after the rest, and they hit him with knotted handkerchiefs, and he them. If he hits you, you have to be monkey." Charles reports of laughing at their play "till I could hardly stand. All the ladies were spectators. I was monkey twice."

Now, finally, they are sliding past tolling bell buoys, past a lighthouse, ships, other steamers, at nine on a Sunday morning, April 10, 1853, up the muddy Mersey to Liverpool. The pilot aboard compliments them on their good fortune in arriving in sunshine, after a week of gales that drenched the port. "Stowe is in full life and glory. Hatty, by his side, looks literally seven ways of a Sunday. All is bustle, animation, exaltation." And at this very moment: "There go the Stars and Stripes to the fore. Before us lies the great city."

Charles's journal lets us hear the voices of the travelers gaping by the railing. Stowe: "No old cathedrals, castles, etc. All New Yorkish." Hatty: "I wonder if they'll fire from the fort!" Stowe: "How green the grass looks." The ship drops anchor. A tender comes alongside. Baggage has been piled on deck; in the saloon passengers rise as their names are called. "Mr. Stowe." "Here." "Anything contraband here, Mr. Stowe? Any cigars, tobacco, etc., etc.?" "Nothing, sir." Unlocks it, fumbles through the case, shuts it up.

A porter seizes the luggage: "To the Adelphi." The piece is marked with red chalk. After a wait, the tender takes passengers ashore. On the solid dock cabs sit amid the crowds, who are pushing and rushing about. "Where's Mrs. Stowe?" "Which is she?" To Sarah: "Are you Mrs. Harriet Beecher Stowe?" And soon away the American party rides in two carriages, "chased by a crowd, men, women, and boys." Mr. and Mrs. Stowe will be honored guests of a wealthy local merchant; Charles and the Buckingham contingent ride in a different carriage, bound for their hotel. The conveyances stop side by side at a canal bridge to await a ship's passing. "Hatty looks out at us and laughs and we telegraph back and forth. Crowd have it all their own way. A line forms and marches past her window." Some few spectators feign well-bred reserve; others allow themselves a frank, long stare; many bow. A child climbs on the cab wheel and peers through the window directly into the face of England's acclaimed visitor from overseas.

"Now the bridge is clear and away we thunder."

Mrs. Stowe has been invited—"a voyage to Great Britain and back free of expense"—by the Committee of the New Ladies' Anti-Slavery Society in Glasgow and the Glasgow New Association for the Abolition of Slavery. She must come, also, to receive in her own person a most remarkable document, "An Affectionate Address," beautifully illuminated and engrossed on vellum, from the women of Great Britain and Ireland to the women of the United States. The document, composed by Lord Shaftesbury, urges those latter, as sisters, wives, and mothers, to raise their voices against Negro slavery, which has denied an entire race the rights and joys of marriage as well as the benefits of education in the truths of the gospel. The address is signed by British women from all walks of life, from the highest to the humblest, more than 500,000 signatures bound in twenty-six massive blue-leather folio volumes. "We acknowledge," the half million signatories conclude, "that our forefathers introduced, nay, compelled the adoption of slavery in those mighty colonies. We humbly confess it before Almighty God, and it is because we so deeply feel and so unfeignedly avow our own complicity that we now venture to implore your aid to wipe away our common crime and our common dishonour." On behalf of her fellow countrywomen Mrs. Stowe must come accept that affecting address, along with the thanks of a grateful nation, which has been more enthusiastic about *Uncle Tom's Cabin* than even the Americans; a million copies of her book from eighteen different publishers (only one of whom will share any profits with the author) have been sold here in England in the first eight months after publication.

But before setting out on what was to prove the most stupendous triumphal tour ever accorded an American in Great Britain up to that time, Harriet Beecher Stowe had delayed at home in Andover in order to complete a task begun near the end of last year. Opponents had accused her novel not only of containing willful lies but also of exhibiting rank ignorance about conditions under slavery in the South. A Beecher would not submit tamely to any such accusations—in this instance, that one of the family had published untruths and implausibilities. On the contrary, Mrs. Stowe was not at all ignorant of her subject; and far from exaggerating harsh conditions under slavery, she had rather mitigated the system's horrors. To rebut her critics, she meant to provide unanswerable facts in support of every charge that her book had leveled.

The result, *A Key to Uncle Tom's Cabin: Presenting the Original Facts and Documents upon Which the Story Is Founded, Together with Corroborative Statements Verifying the Truth of the Work,* was put together under great pressure and despite many distractions, in three months of intense labor that ended in the early spring of 1853, before the *Canada* set sail for England. Even so, the collection is more than half again as long as the novel it defends. "I write it," the author reported that February, "in the anguish of my soul, with tears and prayer, with sleepless nights and weary days. I bear my testimony with a heavy heart, as one who in court is forced by an awful oath to disclose the sins of those dearest."

One source of Stowe's defense was the harrowing *Slavery As It Is* by Theodore Weld (who had led the exodus of abolitionist students from Lane Seminary in the mid-1830s). Published in 1839, Weld's book of over 200 closely printed double-column pages provides testimony of eyewitnesses—each witness's character vouched for—to the inhumanities of the South's peculiar institution, as well as extracts from newspaper advertisements and other contemporary sources, clearly identified and dated, verifying the grim living conditions, inadequate food, horrendous punishments, and almost routine mutilations of slaves, by branding or by extracting a sound front tooth for easy identification should the gaptooth choose to flee. In addition to such authentic evidence already in print, at her request the author of *Uncle Tom's Cabin* had been inundated with materials of all sorts—letters, memoirs, sermons, newspaper articles, court records, abolitionist tracts, slave narratives—from a multitude of sources and acquaintances, exposing slavery's manifest iniquities. By consulting Weld's pioneer work, selecting from this new wealth of heart-sickening material, and taking into consideration her and her family's own recollections, Stowe was able to assemble a volume in four parts that, even at this far remove, still chills the blood.

Part One of *A Key to Uncle Tom's Cabin* considers the challenged veracity of scenes and characters in her novel. Were the characters, as the *New York Courier and Enquirer* charged, exceptional cases (if ever existing at all) whom the author has misleadingly presented as representative? Rather, Stowe insists, each of her characters—taking the principals one by one—is by design a type, standing in for a large group of people; each is a composite of individuals whom the author knew personally or was reliably informed about. The second part of *A Key* deals with southern law, which defenders of slavery insisted protected slaves from mistreatment by their masters. Here Stowe reviews a number of atrocious court cases that expose the utter helplessness of black slaves entangled in the South's legal system. Slaves enjoyed no rights, none at all. "THE POWER OF THE MASTER MUST BE ABSOLUTE, TO RENDER THE SUBMISSION OF THE SLAVE PERFECT," as one judge ruled, appallingly; otherwise, the entire social order would founder. Part Three of Stowe's *Key* addresses public opinion, which slavery's defenders represented as an unfailing safeguard against cruelty to blacks, even if the law were not. Here the author furnishes and witheringly comments on abundant evidence that demonstrates the terrors of extralegal white mobs at lynchings and while expelling from their midst fellow whites judged too friendly to Negroes. In addition, she provides evidence for the scandal of free blacks kidnapped into slavery and the abiding widespread discontent among slaves longing for freedom no matter how gentle the terms of their servitude. Southern opinion indulged each separate inhumanity. The fourth, concluding part of *A Key* deplores not only the failure of Protestant churches to agitate for ending so shockingly immoral

a social blight—"NO INFLUENCES OUT OF THE CHURCH COULD SUS-
TAIN SLAVERY AN HOUR, IF IT WERE NOT SUSTAINED IN IT"—but also
their failing to agitate for the legalization of slaves' marriages, and
their failing to get laws repealed that forbade the education of slaves,
and their failing to stop the internal slave trade, and the churches'
failing even to prevent the growth and spread of slavery.

"We have got used to things that might stir the dead in their
graves," Stowe tells her readers; and with vigor and eloquence,
skillfully wielding such rhetorical weapons as irony, analogy, cita-
tion, anecdote, dialogue, and emphatic repetition, the author seeks
to prod those readers out of their numb complacency. *A Key*, in
fact, is a strikingly effective performance, devastating in its expo-
sures and condemnations. Moreover, it would prove to be another
extraordinary commercial success, on both sides of the Atlantic.
Within a month after its publication in the spring of 1853, even as
Mrs. Stowe was on the high seas bound for England, the volume
had already sold 90,000 copies, a figure only the less astonishing
because the novel it spoke for had previously been such a phenomenon, "the most marvelous literary phenomenon that the world has
witnessed"—or so *Blackwood's Edinburgh Magazine* would assert
this very year.

The British had taken to Stowe's story on slavery in whatever
form, overwhelmingly. As early as December 1852, eleven different
dramatizations of *Uncle Tom's Cabin* were competing on the London stage. Sheet music memorialized scenes from the novel. Shops
called themselves after its characters. Infants in abundance were
named Eva. English mothers bought their children Topsy dolls.
Wallpaper displayed Tom, Miss Ophelia, and the others in characteristic attitudes. Available for purchase were Uncle Tom's coffee; Uncle Tom's china; Uncle Tom's jigsaw puzzles, board games,
card games, sugar toys.

Explanations for such enthusiasm in the British Isles for an
American novel from an author previously unknown are numerous: Great Britain's history earlier in the century of having liberated its own West Indian slaves and abolished slavery throughout
the empire; its consequent philanthropic interest in matters concerning slavery generally; the recent invention of the steam press,
which made cheap books possible; the expansion of railroads to
speed such books nationwide; a new, prosperous female middle

class eager to encounter sentiment, humor, and uplift on the printed page; the satisfaction that English readers felt in learning through Stowe's gripping chapters of the moral delinquencies of their American cousins—that boastful Union's ugly underside—along with the titillation derived from reading of slavery's depravities, physical and sexual, in such an entertaining, religiously sanctioned context. Those were some of the reasons for the extraordinary reception that greeted Harriet Beecher Stowe and her party upon their arrival in Liverpool in April 1853.

She had not expected it: "much to my astonishment, I found quite a crowd on the wharf," the author wrote to her children back home, describing what had confronted the travelers as they alighted from the tender off the *Canada*, "and we walked up to our carriage through a long lane of people, bowing, and looking very glad to see us." Thereafter, in the weeks ahead, crowds would appear wherever this slight, often pictured American with the distinctive curls showed herself. From Liverpool her party took the train to Glasgow, then to Edinburgh, then to Aberdeen and Dundee—as they rode along singing "Bonnie Doon," "Scots Wha Hae," and "Auld Lang Syne," exulting all the while in the miracle of finding themselves among place-names as familiar, from the much loved fiction of Sir Walter Scott, as were places at home. Returning to Edinburgh they entrained at last, bound south toward Stratford, Birmingham, and London. News of their progress had meanwhile preceded them into village after village along the way. "People came and stood in their doors, beckoning, bowing, smiling, and waving their handkerchiefs, and the carriage was several times stopped by persons who came to offer flowers." These were tributes, Mrs. Stowe noted, "not mainly from the literary, nor the rich, nor the great, but the plain common people." Everyone, it seemed, in this literate nation had read her novel. Many commented to that effect; servants in her hosts' homes would ask if the author might step to the rear and let them see her, while outside, the "butcher came out of his stall, and the baker from his shop, the miller, dusty with his flour, the blooming, comely, young mother, with her baby in her arms, all smiling and bowing."

And during the many stops from Liverpool on, Mrs. Stowe was beset with dinners, soirees, receptions, excursions, breakfasts, teas. Glasgow gave a tea for her that accommodated, to her amazement,

2000 people. On April 25, a dinner at Glasgow's city hall seated 3,500 and lasted for seven hours. Addresses were delivered from Leeds, Dalkeith, and Berwick-upon-Tweed. Deputations were received from Paisley, Greenock, and Belfast. Gifts were bestowed on her: books, verses, music, a bracelet, a gold-lined bog-oak casket, flowers, an inkstand, statuary, penny offerings from her legions of humble readers—each one contributing a single cent in gratitude—the sum presented on a silver salver in the form of 1,000 sovereigns, $5,000. Attempting to leave Edinburgh, the Stowe carriage was besieged in the yard "for an hour before we started with a crowd of men, women, and children, standing, climbing, clinging, dripping, and soaking and steaming in the rain and cold."

It was of course exhausting. "I wish I could get her out of this vortex," Charles Beecher fretted solicitously. "And yet, it is not for ourselves. It is for the cause. A great and glorious cause"—of antislavery —so that the movement might prosper. "And the work we have to do is a real one." Through it all Hatty amazed her brother by her manner: her artlessness, her good cheer, and "her own roguish funny way of taking things." Drily, she regretted that her fans, for all their looking, didn't have "something pretty to look at," as she was entertained by a recurring sense, from people meeting her for the first time, that the celebrity appeared to them rather less homely than her many public depictions had indicated. Charles for his part loved gazing at his sister: ever modest, self-possessed, and somehow amused through all the uproar. "It is a privilege to be near her," he concluded early on, and as late as London was still marveling: "She is the same everywhere. Nothing seems to disturb her serenity."

Charles himself felt overwhelmed, working each morning before breakfast and till two some afternoons, reading, digesting, and answering letters: "Letters of all sorts, sizes, descriptions. Presents of books, verses, music. Requests to dedicate to her. Invitations to dine. Invitations to this place and that. And pamphlets, newspapers, and handbills." People pleaded for his sister's autograph. Mountainous piles of letters and gifts all had to be acknowledged. By the time they reached London the factotum was sighing, "I never was so tired in my life."

Nor did the clamor over Mrs. Stowe abate when the travelers reached the capital, in early May. As at Edinburgh, as at Dundee and Aberdeen and Birmingham, but even more so here in London, crowds would break into cheers at the mere sight of the American author. She attended a huge dinner in her honor at Exeter Hall, the mass of guests wildly calling out as she arrived in the gallery, rising en masse to wave hats and handkerchiefs and umbrellas and anything else at hand "for the space of two or three minutes. I never saw the like," Charles recorded in amazement. At the Mansion House, the residence of the lord mayor of London, Mrs. Stowe dined opposite Dickens, whose work she knew very well but "whom I now beheld for the first time, and was surprised to see looking so young"; the two enjoyed a "very pleasant, friendly conversation." She was entertained on one grand occasion at Stafford House, the duchess of Sutherland's magnificent residence opposite Buckingham Palace, where the author was presented with that illuminated "Affectionate Address" from the women of one nation to those of another, along with the twenty-six leather-bound volumes of more than half a million signatures.

The duchess and Mrs. Stowe became fast friends. Others of England's aristocracy were proud to claim the friendship of this physically insignificant woman who three years earlier, mistaken for a penniless immigrant, had been expelled from a train depot at two o'clock in the morning in Jacktown, Pennsylvania. Lord Carlisle, Lord John Russell, Lord Palmerston, the duke of Argyll, Lord and Lady Shaftesbury, and the archbishop of Canterbury all were most cordial. Lord Chief Baron Pollock told the author of being dismayed, in her *Key to Uncle Tom's Cabin*, by Judge Ruffin's astounding opinion—"THE POWER OF THE MASTER MUST BE ABSOLUTE, TO RENDER THE SUBMISSION OF THE SLAVE PERFECT"—which had made "a deep impression on his mind." The duchess of Argyll embraced Mrs. Stowe in tearful gratitude for her having written the fourth part of *A Key*, about the failure of Protestant churches in the United States to fight against slavery's enormities.

But of the many people she met in Scotland and England, one impressed the American above all others. In late May, Calvin Stowe had been obliged to return home to resume his academic duties at Andover Theological Seminary. Soon after his departure, his wife was writing to her professor of sacred literature, on May 31, to tell him about the encounter. Three days before, she had gone to lunch at Oxford Terrace, where, "among a number of distinguished guests, was Lady Byron, with whom I had a few moments of deeply interesting conversation." Lady Byron! Here, in 1853! The meeting had moved Harriet profoundly. "No words addressed to me in any conversation hitherto," she confided to her husband, "have made their way to my inner soul with such force as a few remarks dropped by her on the present religious aspect of England,—remarks of such quality as one seldom hears."

12

CULTURE

*B*ut Lady Byron, in this very room! She could not get over it. "I often think," Harriet Beecher Stowe would write to that fabled Englishwoman four years later, "how strange it is that I should *know* you—you who were a sort of legend of my early days—," yet "that I should love you," she went on, "is only a natural result." Stowe's love amounted to more than hero worship, for the two women had deep feelings in common. Both were cultured, philanthropic, and devoutly religious; indeed, their religious biographies were not dissimilar. Born into Calvinist households, both in their maturity forsook the sterner aspects of Calvinism for a more merciful gospel of love. Actually, over her lifetime some of Lady Byron's religious beliefs had grown more liberal than those of Mrs. Stowe: that the priesthood should give way to a lay ministry, that creeds of whatever sort are enchaining, that it is a sin "to *make* a child say, '*I believe.*'"

But Byron's widow! To be able to touch the hand that had touched *his* hand! Forty-two years earlier, Harriet Beecher Stowe had been born in the Connecticut village of Litchfield, on June 14, 1811. A mere month after her birth, precisely on July 14, on the other side of the Atlantic, a nobleman at age twenty-three was stepping ashore at Portsmouth, returning to England at the end of a couple of years of travel through foreign lands: Portugal, Spain, Greece, Albania. In his luggage he carried an explosive manuscript, his narrative poem describing some of those travels that, when published the following February, in 1812, would turn out to be the very sort of literary phenomenon, on both sides of the Atlantic, that Mrs.

Stowe's prose narrative about slavery in the American South proved to be four decades later. Suddenly, overnight, the young man, George Gordon, Lord Byron, was, like Stowe at a later time, sensationally famous. "The subject of conversation, of curiosity, of enthusiasm almost, one might say, of the moment," an observer on the scene during that spring of 1812 noted, "is not Spain or Portugal, Warriors or Patriots, but Lord Byron!" The irresistible young aristocrat's *Childe Harold's Pilgrimage* "is on every table, and himself courted, visited, flattered, and praised wherever he appears." Handsome, cultivated, astoundingly gifted, Byron "is really the only topic almost of every conversation—the men jealous of him, the women of each other."

Childe Harold's Pilgrimage, which had caused the sensation, relates the adventures of a contemporary young English aristocrat who, spurning the virtuous life, chooses rather to drink and revel day and night in disreputable company:

> Whilome in Albion's isle there dwelt a youth,
> Who ne in virtue's ways did take delight;
> But spent his days in riot most uncouth,
> And vex'd with mirth the drowsy ear of Night.
> Ah, me! in sooth he was a shameless wight,
> Sore given to revel and ungodly glee;
> Few earthly things found favour in his sight
> Save concubines and carnal companie,
> And flaunting wassailers of high and low degree.

Much like Byron himself, "Childe"—or young nobleman—Harold grows satiated with self-indulgence and, to relieve his boredom, sets forth on a journey to exotic places, first to Portugal and Spain, at the time the scene of battles between British and Spanish forces allied against Napoleon's occupying French army, and from there to Greece and Constantinople and into the unknown wilds of Albania. Such far-ranging travels would be vividly described (the archaic diction soon set aside as the poem unfolds) in two cantos comprising some 200 stanzas that form a travelogue with commentary. In the course of nearly 1,900 lines, stay-at-home Londoners might visit the pageantry of a blood-drenched bullfight; ponder a battlefield strewn with corpses and anonymous heroism;

enjoy a sunset over an Albanian village square peopled with color-ful Turks, Greeks, Moors, and Nubians, while "the deep war-drum's sound announc'd the close of day"; and partake of numerous other picturesque settings that bestir the solitary Harold's observations and responses. Those reveal one young aristocrat's distinctive personality —fated to enrapture the world's imagination—of a brooding, sensi-tive, rootless sensation seeker bearing some unnamed "secret woe" that has corroded his youth and joy but cannot prevent his feeling a shifting array of emotions, marvelously expressed, which include scorn, cynicism, compassion, anger, idealism, tenderness, and suf-fering. "I remember well," Harriet Beecher Stowe in maturity would write of the initial impact that Byron's verses had on her, as on tens of thousands of others, "the time when this poetry, so resounding in its music, so mournful, so apparently generous, filled my heart with a vague anguish of sorrow for the sufferer, and of indignation at the cold insensibility that had maddened him."

In the years that followed immediately upon his literary triumph, young Byron, still in his mid-twenties, would go on to compose a series of eastern tales in verse—*The Giaour, The Bride of Abydos, The Corsair, Lara*—set for the most part in unfamiliar regions of the Ottoman Turks, amid minarets, rugged landscapes, piracy at sea, strange beliefs and customs, and shockingly barbarous behav-ior. The tales limned other incarnations of this new Byronic hero: a social outlaw, handsome, laconic, melancholy, solitary, brave. And each tale was wildly popular. *The Corsair,* for example, sold an unprecedented 10,000 copies on the day it was published, in Feb-ruary 1814, and went through eight editions before the year ended. Later, overseas, near a parsonage in far-off Litchfield, Connecti-cut, Harriet Beecher as an intellectually precocious ten-year-old in her Aunt Esther's parlor devoured *The Corsair,* "astonished and electrified," although one verse, in Canto 2, at line 514, did trouble the young reader: "From one I never loved enough to hate." What did that mean? "Oh, child, it's one of Byron's strong expressions," her aunt responded evasively.

Whatever his meaning, this poet was extraordinary. Byron's abundant productions—narratives, dramas, lyrics—all wrung the heart. And the man was so fully alive, had lived more intensely, seen more, felt and done more in twenty-five years than the rest of us might hope to experience in thrice that span of days. Handsome beyond measure, he was a poet of fascinating paradoxes: a glamorous, proud lord who was both a snob and a friend of prizefighters; a noble clubfoot imbued with an abhorrence of cant, hypocrisy, and the corruptions of power; an aristocratic foe of tyrants and champion of freedom; an athlete who struck some as an effeminate dandy; moodily shy yet utterly, winningly charming when he chose to be; a prolific laborer at his craft, yet one much of whose life was wasted—it was rumored—in debauchery and depravity. For Lord Byron's behavior was already famously scandalous: Lady Caroline Lamb, the wife of Victoria's future prime minister Melbourne, had grown besotted, making a public fool of herself for the poet's love, while Lady Oxford was only one of many others similarly smitten in the London of those palmy days.

Then, abruptly, he was to be married. Byron's bride was the adored only child of Sir Ralph and Lady Milbanke, twenty-two-year-old Annabella, proper, chaste, well-read, spiritual. The wedding took place on January 2, 1815, and through the social season that followed in the spring, Lord and Lady Byron were seen often together in public, at dinners and the theater, he "hanging over the back of her chair, scarcely talking to anybody else, eagerly introducing his friends to her." That summer, Napoleon—England's enemy; Byron's hero as a foe of the old, corrupt order—was crushed a final time at Waterloo. In December, the Byrons had a daughter. Then in January the young mother set out with her infant from their London home, at 13 Piccadilly Terrace, bound for her own mother's family seat at Kirkby Mallory, a hundred miles north in Leicestershire.

She never returned. "The separation of Lord and Lady Byron," one observer noted not long after, "astonished the world, which believed him a reformed man as to his habits and a becalmed man as to his remorses." The couple's separation grew bitter, grew public, although the public had few certainties from which to fashion its surmises. Byron's married half sister, Augusta Leigh, sought to make peace as a warm friend of both husband and wife. Byron's other friends became involved. Lawyers intervened. But Annabella's counselors were adamant that she must not reenter the poet's household.

In March 1816, two months after the separation, Byron's publisher printed fifty copies of a poem for private circulation—soon reprinted in a newspaper and thus read widely:

Fare thee well! and if for ever—
Still for ever, fare *thee well*—
Even though unforgiving, never
'Gainst thee shall my heart rebel.—
Would that breast were bared before thee
Where thy head so oft hath lain,
While that placid sleep came o'er thee
Which thou ne'er can'st know again. . . .

A month later, in April 1816, Byron left England, never to return. Never again would he see his wife, never again his child, never set foot again on English soil. From Dover he crossed to Ostend, visited Waterloo, journeyed on to Geneva, there to linger with the poet Shelley, Shelley's teenage mistress (and future wife) Mary Godwin, and Mary's stepsister Claire Clairmont—another of Byron's pursuing lovers, pregnant with his child.

From Geneva the poet passed into Italy, where he made his way to Venice, to delay there through three years of dissipation and literary fruitfulness. British tourists gaped at his lordship and gossiped. Word reached London, from returning travelers and through the poet's own marvelous, candid, unsuppressible letters to friends, of his shocking flouting of convention, his sexual excesses, his putting on of weight, his bitterness toward England and toward his estranged wife's intransigence. He did write to Lady Byron, mostly unanswered letters about their daughter; and meanwhile the grand, fresh, bold, and inspired poetry continued to pour forth: *Beppo, Mazeppa,* two more cantos of *Childe Harold's Pilgrimage.* "Heaven knows why," he mused at the time to his half sister Augusta back in England, "but I seem destined to set people by the ears."

Then, after copulations that by his own count came to number in the hundreds, Lord Byron was reported to have settled down. He was in constant attendance on the lovely young Countess Teresa Guiccioli, whose elderly husband appeared to be indulging this close friendship as long as discretion was observed. The intimacy with Guiccioli endured. And the poet had lost weight, and was writing what his countryman Shelley recognized at once as the greatest poem of their time, although others reading it in segments in England were scandalized by the subject matter, the cynicism, the wildly shifting tone of this massive, satirical, irreverent, epical *Don Juan.*

Next, abruptly, having supported Italy's aspirations to independence from foreign and native tyrannies that occupied the peninsula, Byron suddenly appeared in Greece, armed, bringing volunteers and substantial amounts of his fortune to further Greek strivings for freedom after centuries of Turkish rule. And in Greece, just as suddenly, unexpectedly, the poet turned man of action lay ill with fever at swampy Missolonghi. His baffled doctors could do little but bleed him, excessively and against their patient's will, the beautiful body—he was thirty-six—grown enfeebled, sallow, much diminished, dead.

The poet's demise, on April 19, 1824, echoed across all of Western culture. "I am deeply affected by Byron's death. He was the one person with whom I felt a real affinity," Heinrich Heine wrote. To Victor Hugo, Byron's passing was a personal loss, no less than a "domestic calamity." Pushkin, Lamartine, Mazzini, Delacroix, Rossini, Carlyle ("Poor Byron! Alas poor Byron! The news of his death came down upon my heart like a mass of lead"), the young Brontës, Disraeli, Bulwer-Lytton ("We could not believe that the great race was run. So much of us died with him, that the notion of his death had something of the unnatural, of the impossible")— all in their different ways, in their different countries, groaned under the news. While overseas, in America, in the parsonage at Litchfield, Lyman Beecher with tears in his eyes announced solemnly to his second wife: "My dear, Byron is dead—*gone*." And that lady's stepdaughter, just turning thirteen, therewith shared in the universal dismay; Hatty Beecher took her basket and went out with the doleful news to a nearby hill to pick strawberries, but instead she "lay down among the daisies, looking up into the blue sky, and wondered how it might be with his soul." Lord Byron was dead. The sensualist and idealist, scoffing satirist and poet of the tenderest sentiment, immoralist and fighter for freedom, Byron was no more.

But by no means would he be forgotten. On the contrary, in America through the 1820s and 1830s, the poet's influence seemed ubiquitous. Young men dressed like him; young women tearfully sang his lyrics: "Fare thee well! And if for ever . . ." Longfellow, under Byron's influence himself, fretted nonetheless, in 1832 in the pages of the *North American Review*, about the village Byrons throughout the land who were imitating "his sullen misanthropy and irreligious gloom." Some were stirred by the Englishman's daring skepticism, others by his scandalous outraging of convention; but all in America could concur in their admiration for the late poet's commitment to freedom, the courage and idealism with which he had (it was understood) given his life for liberty, to disenthrall Greece from its longtime Turkish masters.

His abiding popularity was enhanced when Americans—those lovers of liberty—recalled the high regard that Byron had expressed for General Washington and for Simón Bolívar, heroes of a new world. The poet, himself on the titanic scale of those statesmen and of his other hero, Napoleon, had—like them—helped sweep away the cobwebs of the past, opening windows and letting sunlight and fresh air into the stale mansions of culture, as those three leaders of Europe and of both North and South America had cleansed from their houses of state debris accumulated during eras of privilege and tyranny. For here in this new century, romanticism—of which Byron, for all his scoffing at fellow romantic poets, was a major exponent—had replaced the aridities of classicism that had dominated the tastes of a previous age. In the 1700s, under classicism, reason had been extolled, and symmetry, order, restraint: the values of ancient Greece and Rome, of community, of the typical, the generality (all men are created equal in this more perfect union). Now, under romanticism, in place of reason came a fascination with feeling, impulse, passion, the *irr*ational. The particular took precedence over the general; the individual over the community; the atypical, exotic, heroic, sublime over the familiar contours of the everyday. Instead of the symmetry and balance of classical architecture, romantics valued such atmospheric asymmetries as the Gothic cathedral, with medievalism emerging from the "Dark Ages" into favor (Childe Harold on his pilgrimage evoking in diction and subject matter just such exotic, medieval preferences). It was a world perceived afresh, and no longer so often in the rational light of noontime as rather at misty morning, or at twilight, or amid the solitude of distant, moonlit ruins. Young Calvin Stowe, for instance, chose solitude during these early years of the nineteenth century: "the most lonely fields, the woods, and the banks of the river, and other places most completely secluded, were my favorite resorts," as we recall his saying. "Moonlight was particularly agreeable to me," Stowe remembered of a romantic childhood, "but most of all I enjoyed a thick, foggy night." So too did thousands of others in the early years of the newly awakened century.

Such distinctions as these oversimplify complex cultural matters; but if we wonder, as well we might, how off in puritanical America, the inhibited daughter of a Calvinist minister, wife of a minister, sister of ministers, mother of a minister-to-be, could have written—in pauses from incessant quotidian duties of kitchen and nursery—a novel so passionate and so intimate with evil as *Uncle Tom's Cabin*, the answer is: Byron. To be sure, other circumstances contributed to Harriet Beecher Stowe's accomplishment, as noted earlier: Sir Walter Scott's romantic fiction taught the housewife techniques for telling a long prose story; an extended residence in Cincinnati put her in touch with her subject matter; little Charley's excruciating death from cholera—a child torn from a mother's arms—provided her with the anguish to feel slavery's horrors fully. But it was Byron's poetic melodramas that legitimated her depictions of such atrocities of bondage as old Prue's grotesque death, in squalor and alone, where "the *flies had got to her*"; or as the bereft slave mother Lucy's desperate midnight plunge to her death in the Mississippi; or as Cassy's shuddering accounts of her own sexual enslavement and the mercy murder of her infant. And it was Byron's heroes and his distinctive person who authorized such characters in *Uncle Tom's Cabin* as the dashing, handsome, swarthy George Harris, in flight in his cape and gloves, his bearing evoking a Spanish grandee more than the slave that he was; or the prepossessing Augustine St. Clare, with his high intelligence and debonair skepticism; or even the egregious Simon Legree, embodiment of Byronic villainy.

Stowe the artist had worshipped at Byron's shrine long after his popularity began to wane in America, in the 1840s, eclipsed by a more congenial romantic, Wordsworth, whose verses celebrated the virtues of childhood, of the domestic affections, of quiet communion with nature. So Mrs. Stowe, arriving in London at Oxford Terrace in May 1853, found herself enthralled in the very room with the poet's widow, now past sixty: Lady Byron in person (tiny as the American visitor), in a lavender dress, her plain widow's cap over silvery hair, serene late in a life of much suffering. Never remarried, her lord three decades dead, this noblewoman seemed proof against travail, devoting her days to bestowing an abundance of benefactions on the worthy poor.

Her American admirer, newly possessed of means to bestow her own benefactions (including a total of $20,000 in cash that the British had collected for Mrs. Stowe to take home and dispose of as she thought fit in alleviating the high costs of slavery), was enchanted by even this brief encounter with Lady Byron. Soon after their meeting, Harriet left England to complete her European adventure with a summer of travel on the continent. There the child of romanticism felt duly awed in the presence of Gothic cathedrals, "Alpine," as she called them, "vast, wild, and sublime," the Alps themselves dazzling her with their own sublimity. Visiting Geneva, Stowe took pains to hunt down any vestiges of Byron, boating on Lake Leman, where he had boated; visiting the castle of Chillon, scene of a memorable poem by Byron; and having brother Charley carve her name, at their guide's request, on the dungeon pillar below where Byron had carved his.

Afterward, the travelers pressed on to Cologne, Leipzig, Antwerp, and Paris. In Paris, the Buckingham contingent traveling with them—Sarah, William, and Georgy—went their own way for yet more touring. But Harriet and her brother, having briefly returned to England, cut short their travels at the behest of their impatient families back home in Andover and Newark. By that time, in addition to the $20,000 (which would soon be "melting away like snow before the summer's sun," Calvin warned his wife, unless she proved a more conscientious accountant than heretofore), Mrs. Stowe had acquired the fruits of much shopping, including souvenirs for her large and extended family—"bronzes, vases, statuettes, bonbons, playthings"—as well as those antislavery mementos bestowed by well-wishers at numerous stops in the course of her travels. Some of the acquisitions were sent home; the rest were collected aboard ship at Liverpool—the site of Harriet Beecher Stowe's triumphal reception five months before—where now a group of her many new friends had gathered on Wednesday morning, September 7, 1853, waving their best wishes and blessings from shore and from tender as the steamship S.S. *Arctic*, with the world-famous author of *Uncle Tom's Cabin* among its passengers, weighed anchor to descend the Mersey bound for the open sea.

13

LOOKING BACK

*H*er father came to visit that fall, after Harriet's return from her rewarding tour of Britain and the continent. By then, Lyman Beecher had moved back east and was living in Boston, having retired from the presidency of Lane Theological Seminary three years earlier, about the time the Stowes left Cincinnati for Brunswick, Maine. Now his daughter Harriet and son-in-law Calvin were in residence near Boston, in Andover, Massachusetts, at another seminary, in a two-story gabled cottage that the earliest earnings from *Uncle Tom's Cabin* had allowed them to renovate. In this "Stone Cabin"—sixteen windows in the front and a spacious parlor the width of the house, with deep window seats, many pillows and plants, and much light—the Reverend Dr. Beecher, seventy-eight, was made welcome through the autumn of 1853 for a leisurely stay.

In retirement the old man had been putting together his *Works*, writings that had accumulated over a fecund lifetime. John P. Jewett of Boston, the publisher of *Uncle Tom's Cabin*, had earlier arranged with Mrs. Stowe's distinguished father to issue as many as six volumes of those writings, which would comprise, as their author projected them, a description of his theological system, an ample selection of his sermons, a goodly number of lectures, and other miscellaneous matter of general interest, the whole to conclude "with a history of my life and times." In introducing the first of his volumes, Dr. Beecher had explained that the documents not yet published "are thoroughly digested and well considered, as the result of frequent revisions, and in their order, plan, and definitions and expositions, are such as . . . may easily and rapidly be fitted for the press, and given to the public."

His gift proved not so easy to bestow on the public after all. The filing of a lifetime of paperwork, diligently preserved, turned out to have been haphazard; and all the while Dr. Beecher's mind as he neared eighty had been growing increasingly fuzzy. Somehow he had managed through 1852 to get a second and a third volume produced, but nothing yet had appeared in print about the minister's times and colorful life. So Lyman Beecher had come to Andover in the fall of 1853 in order, with the help of his grown children, to remedy that failing. In the Stowes' parlor, Catharine, Edward, Hatty, Henry, and Charles would variously read aloud from sheaves of papers, Charles transcribing their father's response to this letter or that sermon, with an occasional question or comment to prod the memory of an old man still physically vigorous but mentally "subject to deep lapses of abstraction," as they discovered, "in which he would forget all about the reading, and wander off into a reverie."

Earlier it had been different. Seated here with his children, Dr. Beecher was led, as an example, to remember one time forty years before at Litchfield, around 1812 (with London all astir over Lord Byron's newly published *Childe Harold's Pilgrimage*), when the Connecticut minister had been bursting with exuberance at the start of yet another religious awakening: "lectured sometimes nine times a week," he reminisced, "besides going in the morning to converse with the awakened. I knew nothing about being tired. My heart was warm, and I preached with great ease. If any ministers happened along, I did not want them to help me. Did not ask them, not a single one. They would strike forty miles behind. My mind and the mind of the congregation were in such a state they could not come up to us."

So much joy had filled this man's days, so much ardor, with his world forever safe in the keeping of a benevolent God. For of God's benevolence Lyman never doubted; that was the bedrock on which he built his life. Of course he knew suffering: Beecher saw it all around him, grieved over sin and the loss of loved ones, was himself prone to spells of depression. Of one such period, "How mysterious are the ways of God!" he had exclaimed from Litchfield in the spring of 1813, "and yet we can not doubt their perfect wisdom and perfect goodness." True, clouds and darkness swirl about

God's path, "and His footsteps are in the great deep. What He does we know not now, but we shall know hereafter. If this world were the whole of His empire, He would doubtless govern it very differently; but it is only a *speck* in His immeasurable dominions, though what He does here does chiefly illustrate His glory, and fill His boundless realms with light, and joy, and praise."

How had a fallible human being come to know such tremendous truths for a certainty? Beecher's evidence, both scriptural and empirical, appeared conclusive. He knew what he knew because the Bible, the inspired word of God, revealed it to be so; and he knew it because the world all around him confirmed the fact of God's goodness. To be sure, his was a more beautiful world than ours—no strip malls, plastic, blare of advertising, no mass-produced tastelessness—an agrarian world far less comfortable than ours but demonstrably more beautiful; and the denizens of that world, for all its undeniable squalor, responded more directly than we do to nature's diurnal and seasonal rhythms, made aware in doing so of God's omnipresence. In their suffering, too, they felt God near; for as a good parent, filled with love, must punish his refractory child, even so a beneficent Father punishes His wayward children. Suffering implemented a divine plan cosmic beyond human comprehension; yet as for humanity's waywardness, its utter depravity without God's grace, that was everywhere in evidence. To find it, look no farther than upon the selfish willfulness of a two-year-old at any family hearth.

For his part, assured of God's benevolence, Lyman Beecher must spread the good news, must help that willful child and all the rest of the family, all the people in the village, in the parish, in cities and countryside far and wide, to recognize their own sinfulness and make themselves one with the Father. What else mattered when placed alongside the issue of their conversion to God and their souls' salvation through all eternity? Live for that, preach for that, pray for that: for the saving of souls. As one who knew him well would sum up, Dr. Beecher's "controlling desire was to promote the cause of human happiness and salvation, and thus advance the Divine glory. In no man did I ever see this characteristic more prominent."

So dynamic a force dominated the upbringing of Harriet Beecher Stowe; and "was there ever a parent," her sister Catharine would wonder in adulthood, "who, in the first period of family training, more perfectly exhibited the happy combination of strong and steady government with the tenderest love and sympathy, or whose children were better prepared to transfer the love and obedience of an earthly father to a Heavenly One?"

Legends would hover around this larger-than-life family man like moths about lamplight: of the sandpile that Lyman shoveled from wall to wall in his cellar to ease stress and keep himself fit; of the fiddle he would play for the children, delighting them by sometimes climbing in his stocking feet atop a table to dance a double shuffle; of the honor bestowed on the current youngest among those children, allowed at breakfast time to waken Papa with a pinch of the nose and many kisses, after which Dr. Beecher would feign fear of a lion under the bed until his child had looked and succeeded in reassuring him, so that only then was the reverend doctor willing to be led by the finger laughingly to the breakfast table amid cheers of the family gathered around.

He had been born in New Haven, Connecticut, in 1775. The son and grandson of blacksmiths, Lyman Beecher was raised on an uncle's farm at North Guilford nearby. The young man, bright and articulate, escaped from farm labors by getting himself into Yale College, where he graduated in 1798 and proceeded directly to what passed for Yale's divinity school—"there was no such seminary as Andover then." Is matter eternal? Can there be infinite succession? Can the existence of an eternal first cause be proved from the light of nature? Profundities such as those he and his fellow candidates at the divinity school wrote of and debated through nine months, by which means they became qualified to fill pastoral needs—in Lyman's case at a parish across the Sound from New Haven, at East Hampton village on the outer edge of Long Island.

He would remain as minister at East Hampton for a decade, from 1799 to 1810, until a burgeoning family and a parsimonious if devoted congregation combined to drive him back to the mainland. Beecher outgrew the $400 annual salary that East Hampton provided. Soon after establishing himself on Long Island he had married Roxana Foote, a pious Episcopalian whom he had met on a holiday from Yale. By all accounts Roxana was extraordinary. "I never witnessed a movement of the least degree of selfishness," her husband recalled of her many years afterward, seated with his children in the parlor at Andover; "and if there ever was any such thing.

in the world as disinterestedness, she had it." Others who knew Mrs. Beecher remarked on her unvarying kindness, her artistic gifts, her quite unusual scientific interests, her devotion as a wife and mother, and spoke of their never having seen or heard her angry— in short, of her near sanctity. The couple would have nine children, eight of whom grew to maturity. Harriet was one of those eight, born the year after the Reverend Mr. Beecher had accepted a call to the more lucrative parish of Litchfield, Connecticut.

By then, in 1811, the minister was known extensively, far better known than might have been expected of a parson not long removed from a remote village at the outer edge of Long Island. In the wake of Aaron Burr's murder of Alexander Hamilton, Beecher had published, in 1806, a sermon against dueling that had attracted wide notice; with equal fervor he had been chastising Sabbath breakers, extolling temperance, and repeatedly—through evangelical rhetoric vivid and memorable—awakening his and neighboring congregations to their peril. The man was afire with his convictions, for, as he had written to Roxana at the very start of his ministry: "Every thing is at stake. Immortal souls are sleeping on the brink of Hell. Time is on the wing. A few days will fix their eternal state. Shall I hide the truth?"

To Litchfield, then, he brought his truth, to that beautiful, prospering village in the hills of western Connecticut, where in June of the year after his arrival, his daughter Harriet, the seventh of his children, the sixth surviving, would be born, in 1811. And in Litchfield five years later, Harriet's mother (the memory of whose goodness would pervade the rest of her husband's long life, as it would the lives of all her progeny) took ill. In a lucid interval during her final, feverish hours Roxana expressed a heartfelt desire that "her children might be trained up for God," trusting as well that God would provide for Mr. Beecher another companion to "more than fill her place." Thus, selflessly, Roxana Beecher died of consumption in a "heavenly" state of mind—so a grief-stricken husband reported—her sorrow turned to joy, on September 25, 1816, in her forty-second year.

"It is a most moving scene," a neighbor wrote at the time, "to see eight little children weeping around the bed of a dying mother, but, still, it was very cheering to see how God could take away the sting of death, and give such a victory over the grave."

That, incidentally, was the year when Lord and Lady Byron separated and the poet went into exile overseas. In America, precisely twelve months after his first wife's death, Lyman Beecher did arrive home with another life's companion, from Boston, where he had gone to deliver a rousing sermon against the Unitarians. Miss Harriet Porter, of a distinguished family from Portland, Maine, was, like the first Mrs. Beecher, pious. So socially prominent a young lady in her mid-twenties might have paused before accepting the marriage proposal of an ill-paid village parson in his forties and the father of eight children; but as she explained to Catharine Beecher, the eldest stepdaughter awaiting her arrival at Litchfield: "In my view, a minister of the Gospel fills a most honorable station. He is to be considered a messenger from the court of Heaven. His happiness is to be regarded, his comfort to be promoted in every possible way. To be an instrument of good to such is also honorable; it is a preferment, I think, far above the distinctions which usually give pre-eminence in this life."

So Miss Porter, now Mrs. Beecher—"so fair, so delicate, so elegant," as the adult Harriet Beecher Stowe would recall her first sight of her—arrived at Litchfield. There at a wholesome altitude she found handsome buildings along wide, tree-lined streets ("It surpasses in pleasantness any thing I have seen except Boston Mall"); a society singularly eminent (Judge and Mrs. Reeve, Colonel Tallmadge, Mrs. Gould); and a parsonage "of great cheerfulness and comfort," full of singing children, "as lovely children as I ever saw, amiable, affectionate, and very bright." In the months that followed, those young Beechers would furnish absent family members with their own glimpses of each other—and of a now workaday "Mamma," settled in after a year or so, who "don't laugh any more than she used to." Seven-year-old Harriet "makes just as many wry faces, is just as odd, and loves to be laughed at as much as ever." Or this, two years farther along, from Edward, reporting in 1821: "Harriet reads every thing she can lay hands on, and sews and knits diligently." Much later, Hatty herself would record impressions of those years of her childhood, in "a great household inspired by a spirit of cheerfulness and hilarity, and of my father, though pressed and driven with business, always lending an attentive ear to any thing in the way of life and social fellowship." For, as Catharine in a postscript had reminded her brother away at college: "Never mind this, Ned"—of their reverend parent's contributing a gently written reproof about too much levity in the letter just ended—"for papa loves to laugh as well as any of us, and is quite as much *tickled* at nonsense as we are."

There was some sadness, of course, amid the many happy group scenes of hunting rabbits and picking berries, of going fishing together, of reading aloud in the evenings and splitting logs for the winter. Harriet Porter, the second Mrs. Beecher, proceeded to have four children of her own, the first of whom died as an infant. Money remained a problem—scraping together enough to educate all those boys. The Beecher children were slow to come to Christ. And the battle to be waged against false faiths never ended: against Roman Catholics, Unitarians, Methodists, and even Old School Calvinists, who frowned upon the more liberal Lyman Beecher's New School ways as heretical.

Lord Byron, born into an Old School Calvinist household, as Beecher had been, ended by renouncing so stern a faith entirely; "I am nothing at all," the poet declared, "but I would sooner be a Paulician, Manichean, Spinozist, Gentile, Pyrrhonian, Zoroastrian, than one of the seventy-two villainous sects who are tearing each other to pieces for the love of the Lord and hatred of each other." Even so, in the spring of 1824 at the Litchfield parsonage, news of that infidel Englishman's death brought with it more sadness. "My dear, Byron is dead—*gone*"; and on the following Sunday, in the meetinghouse on the green, the Reverend Dr. Beecher preached a funeral sermon on the text, *"The name of the just is as brightness, but the memory of the wicked shall rot,"* wherein he reviewed Lord Byron's career, evaluated the poet's writings, and, while conceding that some of his verses were as imperishable as brass, predicted that the impurities of others, for all their beautiful language, would condemn them to oblivion. A great writer had misused his gifts in the course of a wasted life. "Oh, I'm sorry that Byron is dead," that same minister had lamented to the second Mrs. Beecher just days before. "I did hope he would live to do something for Christ. What a harp he might have swept!" And if only the two had met: Dr. Beecher felt sure he could have cured the poet of his infidelism.

Two years after Byron's death—and after serving sixteen years as pastor at Litchfield—Lyman Beecher answered a call to the Hanover Street Church in Boston's North End. At the time he wrote to his eldest daughter of his satisfactions: "William, Edward, Mary, George and Harriet, all in their time and place, have come to be my most affectionate companions and fellow-helpers. If earthly good could fill the soul, mine might be running over; and, as it is, my consolations are neither few nor small." Past fifty then, Beecher assumed he would end his days serving this Boston congregation. Hanover Street Church had first approached a Dr. Payson of Portland, Maine, to be its pastor; and Dr. Payson, as Calvin Stowe wrote in retrospect, could "preach and pray as well as any man that ever lived; but as to laying out extensive plans of aggression beyond the limits of his own congregation"—that is, battling far and wide against tipplers, Sabbath breakers, and unbelievers—as well as "attending councils, making speeches at public meetings, writing essays and reviews, watching over theological discussions, taking care of all the young men he could drum up for the ministry, organizing the labor of others, setting everybody at work, in short wheeling any number of different heavily laden wheel-barrows all at one and the same time, this is what Dr. Payson could never have done; but this and more," Professor Stowe concluded in proud reference to the man who would become his father-in-law, "is what Dr. Beecher did during all the six years he labored in Boston."

At the end of which time, in 1832, having settled down in the city for good, Lyman Beecher was called to pack yet again, unexpectedly. With those family members who chose to come along he set out once more, the travelers singing in their stagecoach as it lumbered westward over country roads bound for Cincinnati. "I have responded to the call of Providence," the new president of Lane Theological Seminary, once arrived, explained in his inaugural address. "The great causes which are to decide the destinies of this nation are to be found in the West." On the eastern side of the mountains the struggle for political independence had been won; now an even more important struggle—for the saving of souls— was to be waged here on this side, among the great rivers, the exuberant soil, the teeming millions of people in a vast new territory.

But the years at Lane proved troubled ones. Early on, the issue of slavery—which young Theodore Weld's eloquence rendered keen—rent the seminary disastrously, as it would finally rend the nation. An Old School fellow minister, Dr. Joshua Wilson, leveled accusations of heresy against Dr. Beecher, who was obliged to endure the ordeal of an ecclesiastical trial, emotionally costly even though he won an acquittal. Soon after, the Presbyterian church, for which Lane was training seminarians, broke apart nationally into two quarreling factions. Never happy with the move from New England, Beecher's wife Harriet Porter died at mid-decade, in 1835, of consumption. Enrollment at the seminary remained low, so that its president was obliged to lease out parts of the campus to secure operating funds. Toward the end, President Beecher had found his mind growing less reliable in those final years of service—to an institution that after his departure would limp on through the nineteenth century and into the twentieth, its resources turned over at last, in 1932, to the McCormick Theological Seminary in Chicago. The final remnant of the Cincinnati campus was demolished in 1956, overtaken by a residential neighborhood.

A year after Harriet Porter's death, Lyman had married again, to Lydia Jackson, a widow nearing fifty, and together he and the third Mrs. Beecher moved at mid-century back east to Boston, bringing with them boxes of dated sermons and letters that the cleric had amassed over five decades. "He feels," his son Charles would write, "as if he could not die in peace & leave his life's works to lie waste. Hence he returns again & again to the hopeless task." Charles allows us one poignant glimpse of his father in those late years, spending "hours on hours in vain searching, and fruitless & painful shufflings & fumblings in manuscripts that *will* not come into order"—documents dead beyond resurrecting. Beecher's children, gathering at Hatty's Stone Cabin in Andover, helped all they could, but the task stretched on far into the decade of the 1850s, the old man's strength of mind continuing all the while to dwindle.

His daughter Harriet did her part, on hand to ask questions. H.B.S.: "Were there not some that held slaves then?" H.B.S.: "How did they live in those days? Tell us something about Aunt Benton's kitchen." And old Dr. Beecher would set off reminiscing a bit about his foster mother—"I can see her now as plain as I can see you"—until sinking into a distracted silence. Or until he had to suspend his labors in order to return to Boston, or his children were called away to their various enterprises.

For herself, Harriet kept as busy during these years as ever she did in her crowded life. Returned home from Europe, she was striving to spend as much time as she could with her own children: with the twins, now seventeen; Henry, sixteen; Fred, thirteen; Georgie, ten; and little Charley, just three. The girls were enrolled at the Abbot Academy there in Andover, the two older boys at school as well, Henry preparing to go off to Dartmouth next year. Mothering so active a brood took time. Professor Stowe remained absorbed in teaching at the Andover Seminary, pursuing his biblical studies, tending to his various ailments, and leaving his wife to provide what parental guidance was needed. Meanwhile, this busy mother was burdened with obligations that her English admirers had laid upon her to dispense their generosity back here in America in ways that would do the most good: investigating the feasibility of establishing normal schools to train African-American teachers, supporting antislavery lectureships, identifying further needs through correspondence with such abolitionist leaders as William Lloyd Garrison and Frederick Douglass. Also she wrote letters, newspaper columns, magazine articles, introductions, and forewords to antislavery books. And all the while she was working on another book of her own. For despite the enormous financial rewards of *Uncle Tom's Cabin* and *A Key*, the author's management of money had proved casual, her benefactions rather too generous, the family's outlays very large, and those beyond her immediate family in need of help grown suddenly numerous.

But any new book by Harriet Beecher Stowe would sell. This present, uncontroversial one, a travel guide in the form of her letters from Europe interspersed with segments of her brother Charles's journal describing their recent prodigious welcome overseas, appeared in 1854. She called it *Sunny Memories of Foreign Lands*; yet for all its sunshine, one or two shadows did fall over the pages. The author refers, for instance, to the passage this spring in the federal legislature at Washington of the "infamous Nebraska bill." That dark piece of congressional faithlessness overruled a long-standing exclusion of the South's peculiar institution from territories north of latitude 36°30'. By a shameful act of Congress, what before 1854 had been free soil west of the Mississippi was abruptly, ominously opened to slavery, with the southern planter oligarchy—the "Lords of the Lash," as the abolitionist Charles Sumner called them—bent yet again on extending thralldom into lands that were previously free.

14

RETURN TO EUROPE

The 1850s were arguably as bitter as any decade in our history, with the single exception of the five years that followed, during which 600,000 Americans killed each other in a civil war. Setting aside that bloody lustrum, when we revisit the period—ostensibly a time of peace—from 1850 to 1860, the vitriol of its public discourse even now sears more intensely than anything the longest-lived among us, from veterans of blue states versus red states back through survivors of Vietnam to children of the fractious New Deal, will have encountered elsewhere. Not even scurrilities that were hurled by Federalists and Democrat-Republicans across the beginning of the nineteenth century exceed in vehemence the political detestation expressed in both North and South during the ten years of the 1850s.

Outrage had erupted at the very start of the decade, with the passage of a federal law in 1850 letting lackeys of the Slavepower chase and snatch back into bondage blacks who had succeeded in fleeing to free states of the North. As noted, that Fugitive Slave Act, compelling northerners on penalty of fine and imprisonment to help in such renditions, provoked a housewife in Maine to write *Uncle Tom's Cabin.* Her protest was published in book form in the spring of 1852, to pained remonstrance in the South and loud acclaim elsewhere. In the North, the hated legislative act and the supremely popular novel by themselves altered the balance of public opinion, from an earlier wariness of abolitionists as shrill, canting zealots to a widespread sympathy for the reformers' humanitarian aims. Finally the bulk of northern sentiment was roused against any further advances of slavery, all the more resolutely after the passage, in 1854, of the Kansas-Nebraska Act, which revoked the provisions of the Missouri Compromise, thirty-four years earlier, that had excluded slavery from upper territories of the Louisiana Purchase. Now, by means of a "popular sovereignty" that the new act sanctioned, a simple majority of residents in each territory, at whatever latitude, were to determine for or against slavery; and voters' ranks could be swelled by partisans hurrying to the site and adding their angry voices to help choose whether land formerly free might enter the Union as soil for slaves to till.

Like most other northerners, Harriet Beecher Stowe was appalled by this new law. Even while Congress was debating its terms, she expressed her feelings in a widely read "Appeal to the Women of the Free States," in February 1854. "I do not think," she wrote then, "there is a wife who would think it right *her* husband should be sold to a trader, and worked all his life without rights and without wages. I do not believe there is a husband who would think it right that *his* wife should be considered, by law, the property of another man, and not his own. I do not think there is a father or mother who would believe it right, were they forbidden by law to teach their children to read. I do not believe there is a brother who would think it right to have his sister held as property, with no legal defense for her personal honor, by any man living." But all this—which the Nebraska bill was threatening to extend—"is inherent in slavery. It is not the abuse of slavery, but the legal nature of it. And there is not a woman in the United States, when the question is fairly put before her, who thinks these things are right."

Stowe's views of the South's paternal institution were growing more bellicose. After the Kansas-Nebraska Bill became law, she would set to work on a new novel—*Dred: A Tale of the Great Dismal Swamp*—that reflected her change of feelings. While writing *Uncle Tom's Cabin*, she had remained hopeful that she might awaken the better nature of southerners. Now, at mid-decade, amid the rancor that her first novel had provoked in the South, Stowe approached the odious subject once more, explaining in a preface to *Dred* that, like her first, this second novel would depict slavery, for two reasons. One was romantic: "there is no ground, ancient or modern," she wrote, "whose vivid lights, gloomy shadows, and grotesque groupings, afford to the novelist so wide a scope for the exercise of his powers." Here, close at hand in this matter-of-fact modern world, "exist institutions which carry us back to the twilight of the feudal ages, with all their exciting possibilities of incident." Those institutions, of plantation and slave life in the South, provided a writer of fiction with "every possible combination of romance."

For subject matter, *Uncle Tom's Cabin* had discovered this new vein of American fiction; nothing would be served by its author's forsaking a mine so rich in ore. But the other reason for again dealing fictionally with slavery was moral. "Never has there been," Stowe asserts in her preface, "a crisis in the history of this nation so momentous as the present. If ever a nation was raised up by Divine Providence, and led forth upon a conspicuous stage, as if for the express purpose of solving a great moral problem in the sight of all mankind, it is this nation." The question being put to Americans was clear: is slavery as an economic system so profitable "that you will directly establish it over broad regions, where till now, you have solemnly forbidden it to enter?" That question would soon be answered before the world. "Under such circumstances the writer felt that no apology was needed for once more endeavoring to do something towards revealing to the people the true character of that system. If the people are to establish such a system" as slavery in territory that had been free, "let them do it with their eyes open, with all the dreadful realities before them."

Stowe's second novel, which appeared in 1856, differs from its predecessor of four years earlier in crucial ways. *Uncle Tom's Cabin* had addressed readers of goodwill in North and South and, in so doing, had avoided criticism of southerners as people, deploring rather the inhuman institution under which they were forced to live. *Dred* is less indulgent. Through this advancing decade, the soul-wrenching research its author conducted in preparing *A Key to Uncle Tom's Cabin* and her familiarity with the ordeals experienced under slavery by such black leaders as Frederick Douglass and Sojourner Truth (both of whom visited her in Andover) had combined with southerners' increasingly defiant recalcitrance to weaken Stowe's confidence in the region's inherent goodwill. Now, instead of a noble black slave for its principal character—patient, long-suffering, forbearing—the eponymous protagonist of her new novel, although as pious as Tom, exhibits not love but wrath. Dred is a powerful black runaway who has fled with a band of insurgents into the Dismal Swamp of eastern North Carolina, from where he defies southern custom and national law. Endowed with great natural gifts, Dred succors those who have suffered from cruelty inflicted by whites, and he plots vengeance for the injustices perpetrated against his race, in the spirit of such historical slave insurrectionists as Denmark Vesey (represented here as the fictional Dred's father) in Charleston in 1822 and the more effective Nat Turner in Southampton County, Virginia, in 1831. Only near the end of the novel are Dred's plans foiled, when he is shot by a "drunken, swearing, ferocious set" of white men beating the swamps in search of a black who is fleeing toward the insurrectionist's sanctuary. After making his own way back to his enclosure deep in the wilds, the wounded Dred dies amid the grief of those, black and white, whom he has helped, while "the birds sang on as they ever sing, unterrified by the great wail of human sorrow" arising from the ground beneath the boughs.

Like its predecessor, this new novel can be faulted. It is too long for what it accomplishes. It was written too fast, in three months instead of the year and more that Stowe devoted to writing *Uncle Tom's Cabin*. There is too much sermonizing in it, and Dred's histrionic voice, biblical in the manner of the prophets—"a wild jargon of hebraistic phrases, names, and allusions"—soon becomes no more than an unconvincing pastiche of Old Testament prognostications, so that one finds oneself skimming the black man's page-long jeremiads quite unmoved.

Moreover, the structure of *Dred* falls into two parts that hardly cohere: a love story among whites on a plantation in the first half differs in tone from the fugitive's dark saga of resistance in the second. Indeed, the protagonist, unforeshadowed, makes his first appearance 200 pages into the book. Yet even so, even in Dred's absence, the initial portions of the novel have their appeal. The beginning, with the giddy young southern belle Nina Gordon debating which of three suitors most pleases her, anticipates the opening fiddle-de-dee spirit of *Gone with the Wind*. One of the suitors whom Nina has promised to marry is Edward Clayton ("his eyes have a desperate sort of sad look, sometimes—quite Byronic"); and the developing relationship between Clayton and Miss Nina does hold our interest, its themes growing consequential as they undertake the exploration of racial issues. The plantation atmosphere is vividly rendered, and the characters are believable and varied. But Nina, who becomes more substantial and hence more engaging as her responsibilities on the plantation increase, dies in a cholera epidemic halfway through, and the novel changes course, entering the Dismal Swamp to reveal the somber, tangled plight into which slavery has led the nation.

What accounted for the change of direction was a public event that, even as Stowe was writing, followed upon a speech delivered in Congress by the abolitionist Senator Charles Sumner of Massachusetts, whom the author admired and with whom she had been in correspondence. ("My dear Mrs. Stowe,—I am rejoiced to learn, from your excellent sister here, that you are occupied with another tale exposing slavery. I feel that it will act directly upon pending questions, and help us in our struggle for Kansas.") Soon after writing privately thus, Sumner rose in the Senate over two days in mid-May 1856 to deliver himself publicly of a scathing attack on "The Crime against Kansas," a territory now bleeding with internal strife as it made ready to join the Union. Would its brawling settlers vote to make it a slave state or a free state? In the course of his speech, Sumner singled out for particular scorn South Carolina's silver-haired Andrew Pickens Butler. When Senator Butler spoke— and he had spoken recently on the Senate floor against the free-soil settlers of Kansas—he had the misfortune to discharge spittle. Now Sumner alluded to that failing, along with the southern gentleman's pretensions to courtliness. Of course so chivalrous a knight, Don Quixote–like, "has chosen a mistress to whom he has made his vows, and who, though ugly to others, is always lovely to him, though polluted in the sight of the world, is chaste in his sight. I mean," Sumner specified, "the harlot Slavery. For her, his tongue is always profuse in words." Addressing this very assembly, for instance, the senator from South Carolina, "omnipresent in this debate, overflows with rage at the simple suggestion that Kansas has applied for admission as a State, and, with incoherent phrase, discharges the loose expectoration of his speech, now upon her representative, and then upon her people. There was no extravagance of the ancient Parliamentary debate which he did not repeat; nor was there any possible deviation from truth which he did not make,—with so much of passion, I gladly add, as to save him from the suspicion of intentional aberration. But the Senator touches nothing which he does not disfigure."

Two days later, as Sumner sat working at his desk in the Senate chamber, he was approached by a cousin of Butler's, Congressman Preston Brooks, also of South Carolina, who proceeded to beat the Massachusetts legislator senseless, shattering a gutta-percha cane over his head and shoulders and wounding the Yankee so severely that he was unable to perform his public duties for the next three years. Southerners gloried in the chastisement, sending Congressman Brooks an assortment of canes to replace the one he had broken. But the North was horrified. And in her novel *Dred*, Mrs. Stowe has the repulsive Tom Gordon, Nina's reprobate brother, break his own gutta-percha cane over the worthy Edward Clayton, in administering a thrashing that outrages the reader's sensibilities as it demonstrates (the author editorializes sardonically) the scoundrel's "eligibility for Congress by beating his defenceless acquaintance on the head, after the fashion of the chivalry of South Carolina."

Despite all that, Stowe's second novel appears less satisfying emotionally than *Uncle Tom's Cabin*, even if in some respects it seems superior artistically. Indeed, some readers of sound critical judgment at the time expressed their preference for *Dred* over the earlier work. Here, for instance, is George Eliot's opinion, given in the *Westminster Review* in October 1856: "At length we have Mrs. Stowe's new novel, and for the last three weeks there have been men, women, and children reading it with rapt attention—laughing and sobbing over it—lingering with delight over its exquisite landscapes, its scenes of humour, and tenderness, and rude heroism—and glowing with indignation at its terrible representation of chartered barbarities. Such a book is an uncontrollable power, and critics who follow it with their objections and reservations—who complain that Mrs. Stowe's plot is defective, that she has repeated herself, that her book is too long and too full of hymns and religious dialogue, and that it creates an unfair bias—are something like men pursuing a prairie fire with desultory water-cans. In the meantime, 'Dred' will be devoured by the million, who carry no critical talisman against the enchantments of genius." For this second of the author's narratives *is* a work of genius. As for her repeating herself, Mrs. Stowe "has *invented* the Negro novel, and is right to stay with it, as Scott stayed with Scottish history." In sum, no less a voice than George Eliot's concludes her review of *Dred* by rendering "our tribute to it as a great novel, leaving to others the task of weighing it in the political balance."

The British queen also preferred *Dred* to the earlier work. Like others in her realm, her majesty had loved *Uncle Tom's Cabin*, but she let it be known that she loved *Dred* more. A royal copy was given to Victoria in Mrs. Stowe's presence in the late summer of 1856, in the course of the writer's second trip abroad. On this occasion Harriet was setting foot on English soil before an overseas edition of her new novel was published, in order to gain for it the protection of a recently enacted international copyright; that way, profits from *Dred,* unlike those that had eluded her from the enormous, unprotected sales in Europe of *Uncle Tom's Cabin,* would fall—or at least some would fall—where they should, into the author's hands.

And *Dred* was profitable, although hardly to the degree of its predecessor—what other book could have been?—or to the extent of Stowe's own overoptimistic calculations. *Dred* gratified her by selling 100,000 copies in four weeks. "After that who cares what critics say? Its success in England," the author reported complacently from the scene, "has been complete, so far as sale is concerned"—even though the book "is very bitterly attacked, both from a literary and a religious point of view." But Mrs. Stowe had grown used to being attacked bitterly and would let such attacks trouble her hardly at all. As for meeting the queen, that could not, of course, have been done officially; officially Britain must remain neutral concerning America's internal quarrel over slavery. Thus, instead of a formal meeting there had occurred "an accidental, done-on-purpose meeting at a railway station, while on our way to Scotland," soon after the Stowes' arrival from America. A first-class waiting room had been cleared for the event. Calvin, one of the traveling party, is reporting to a friend back home: "The Queen seemed really delighted to see my wife, and remarkably glad to see me for her sake. She pointed us out to Prince Albert, who made two most gracious bows to my wife and two to me, while the four royal children stared their big blue eyes almost out looking at the little authoress of 'Uncle Tom's Cabin.' Colonel Grey handed the Queen, with my wife's compliments, a copy of the new book. She took one volume herself and handed the other to Prince Albert, and they were soon both very busy reading. She is a real nice little body with exceedingly pleasant, kindly manners."

Besides George Eliot and Victoria, a third reader who preferred *Dred* to *Uncle Tom's Cabin* was Harriet Martineau. That well-known English journalist—ailing, though destined to live twenty years longer—had traveled in America two decades before and written a famous book about it. "Did I see you (in white frock and black silk apron) when I was in Ohio in 1835?" Miss Martineau now inquired of Mrs. Stowe during the latter's present visit to England. "Your sister I knew well, and I have a clear recollection of your father. I believe and hope you were the young lady in the black silk apron." Be that as may, the journalist meant to speak her mind. "Do you know I rather dreaded reading your book! Sick people *are* weak: and one of my chief weaknesses is dislike of novels." But she might have spared herself the fretting: "oh! the delight I have had in 'Dred!'" this plainspoken Englishwoman reported. "The genius carries all before it, and drowns everything in glorious pleasure." Many of course will disagree, having made up their minds already, "and because it is so rare a thing for a prodigious fame to be sustained by a second book." But Martineau was categorical: "I am entirely convinced that the second book is by far the best. Such faults as you have are in the artistic department, and there is less defect in 'Dred' than in 'Uncle Tom,' and the whole material and treatment seem to me richer and more substantial."

One other reader's opinion Harriet waited eagerly to hear. It reached her in Scotland. Byron's widow wrote to say of *Dred* "that one perusal is not enough. It is a 'mine,' to use your own simile. If there is truth in what I heard Lord Byron say, that works of fiction *lived* only by the amount of *truth* which they contained, your story is sure of long life." That was most gratifying, as was what followed: "I know now, more than before," her noble reader concluded, "how to value communion with you." The letter was signed, with "kind regards to your family, Yours affectionately, A. T. Noel Byron."

Those of Mrs. Stowe's family whom Lady Byron thus graciously remembered were in Scotland traveling with the author; their party had disembarked at Liverpool in early August. Calvin was along again, and three of the children—the twin girls and Henry—together with Harriet's sister Mary Perkins, the conven-

warning." Yet in the four years since that sage counsel, familial and other applicants for Mrs. Stowe's help had shown no slackening as they laid before her their always worthy needs.

More distressing still than the burdens of fame and the slipperiness of finances had been the behavior of the Stowes' middle son, Fred. A student at Phillips Academy there in Andover, Fred at sixteen ("full of all manner of fun & mischief," according to his mother) had fallen in with some dashing young scholars up from the South—a group enamored of pistols and "cigars"—and had developed an alarming dependence on what his parents self-protectively called tobacco. Fred at a young age had become, in plain words, an alcoholic, whom a worried father in his mother's absence had sent off to a watercure in Elmira, New York. There the local pastor, Harriet's half brother Tom Beecher (a remarkable man in his own right), was helping to wring the boy out and look after him.

And about their eldest son, Henry, the nineteen-year-old at Dartmouth, Calvin found cause to brood as well. To his father, Henry seemed "indolent and self indulgent," although the boy's mother thought otherwise. That child was her favorite, the one on whom she had set her hopes highest. In England last summer Harriet had been unwilling that Henry leave her until the latest possible moment. Even after Calvin, who "gave out" early on, had sailed for home, the lad remained at his mother's side, as the Stowe party continued touring at Dunrobin, in Durham, in York. The late teens are difficult, neither boyhood nor quite yet manhood, and—as Harriet recognized in Henry's case—with "a blind desire to go contrary to everything that is commonly received among older people." Such a one "disparages the minister, quizzes the deacon, thinks the schoolmaster an ass, and doesn't believe in the Bible, and seems to be rather pleased than otherwise with the shock and flutter that all these announcements create." Still, Henry was trying. She had noticed approvingly that to toasts offered on public occasions in England he had raised a water glass; and after returning home to take his place as a freshman at Dartmouth, the youth made a vow: "I may not be what the world calls a Christian, but I will live such a life as a Christian ought to live, such a life as every true man ought to live." Surely so noble a resolve would soon bring him into the fold.

Having returned to America and upon making their way in mid-June 1857 back to the Stone Cabin at Andover, Mrs. Stowe and her sister Mary Perkins had been greeted not only by Calvin, Georgie, and little Charley, but also by Mary's neighbor in Hartford: her and Harriet's half sister Isabella Beecher Hooker, daughter of Lyman's second wife, Harriet Porter. At Belle's urging and after only a few days of recuperation, Harriet set off again—inveterate traveler that she was—to return with Mary to Hartford, which relatives down there were urging the famous author to make her permanent home. From Hartford she rode out by train to Elmira to see Fred, whose condition was improving, although not yet to the point where he felt he could leave his uncle's care. From Elmira, Harriet then traveled to Brooklyn to call on yet another brother; and it was while she was in his company, visiting in a neighbor's home in Brooklyn Heights at ten on a July evening, that a telegram reached her with dreadful news.

The news concerned Mrs. Stowe's favorite child. Her eldest son, Henry, was dead. Swimming that morning with classmates in the Connecticut River, near the campus, he had been caught in a current and drowned. The date was Thursday, July 9, 1857. Learning of the death hours later, his mother, horror-struck, thought at once of others. She wrote a brief note on the instant to her son Fred in Elmira, and another to Lyman Beecher: "My dearest Father, Lest your kind heart should be too much distressed for me I write one word." This present ordeal, she reassured him, "comes from One nearer & dearer than all earthly friends who loves us far better than we love ourselves." And she added: "In regard to Henry's eternal estate I have good hope."

But that, precisely, would become the issue: Henry Ellis Stowe's eternal state. "I may not be what the world calls a Christian . . ." Now, in addition to all the human, temporal grief during this most shatteringly grievous time in her entire life, Stowe was obliged to cope with a fear for her dead son Henry's soul. These Beechers were Calvinists, and the reality of Hell remained vivid to them— damnation forever and ever—as Heaven was a vivid place, one where Lady Byron, for instance, upon succumbing to her ossified lungs and diseased heart might arrive before Harriet to find departed loved ones waiting. Moreover, a New England mother's grief over her eldest son's drowning hurt even more than the pain she had felt after her Charley's death in Cincinnati eight years earlier. Charley had been scarcely more than an infant, a one-year-old; so that, as Calvin remarked at the time, he had not grown old enough to disobey God—"he knew no sin—he was innocent and pure. If he had lived he would have been a sinner, and felt the agonies of remorse and perhaps died unconverted." That early, the other Stowe children were already grown into just such sinners. If, instead of Charley, one of them had died, "could we," their father wondered back then, "have been comforted with the same confidence of hope?"

Now a sinning child *had* died—unconverted, unregenerate. They were Calvinists, these Beechers. We who are not must try to understand their beliefs even as we acknowledge the very real anguish arising in them from such all-important matters as depravity, conversion, election, and irresistible grace. As far back (to take one example) as 1696, more than 160 years before, on a January evening in Boston, "When I came in, past 7. at night," the Calvinist jurist Samuel Sewall wrote in his diary, "my wife met me in the Entry and told me Betty had surprised them." The Sewalls' daughter Betty, fifteen, "had given some signs of dejection and sorrow; but a little after dinner she burst out into an amazing cry, which caus'd all the family to cry too. Her Mother ask'd the reason; she gave none; at last said she was afraid she should goe to Hell, her Sins were not pardon'd. She was first wounded by my reading a Sermon of Mr. Norton's, about the 5th of Jan." Words read then from John 7:34—*"Ye shall seek me and shall not find me"*—had "terrified her greatly." The girl had prayed but feared her prayers weren't heard "because her Sins not pardon'd." Throughout that winter and spring in a Boston home toward the end of the seventeenth century, Betty suffered horribly, and her Puritan, Calvinist family suffered with her: weeping, praying, crying out in their affliction.

Their pain was very real. A century and more afterward (and all the suffering children in between!), another New England household temporarily emerged from its own anguish over similar uncertainties. "We have been," Lyman Beecher of Litchfield wrote on Tuesday, November 1, 1825, "this three weeks in a state of deep sympathy for George"—then age sixteen—"whose distress precluded sleep, almost, for many nights, and his voice of supplication could be heard night and day. But today, and especially this evening, he seems to be very happy, and, so far as I can judge by conversation, on good grounds. He is now with the girls, singing louder than he prayed. What shall we render to the Lord! Mary and

Harriet communed today for the first time, and it has been a powerful and delightful day."

Young George's distress had arisen from this matter of regeneration. The doctrine would trouble all of Lyman Beecher's children one by one, piercing their often happy youth with intervals of intense mental pain while they struggled toward achieving grace.

"It is a mark of a shallow mind," wrote Harriet Beecher Stowe, "to scorn these theological wrestlings and surgings." But imagine being a child growing up amid such beliefs! Never did Calvinists doubt the infinity of God's perfection, or the fact that beneath that dazzling impeccability all of us appear as the darkest of sinners. There is nothing for it but to awaken to our depravity, feel in our very bones our loathsomeness. Not one thing about us is holy: wake in all humility to that bleak truth. Thus awakened, we must surrender utterly to God, who alone can redeem us, and to Him we must entirely, disinterestedly submit in order that we may receive the gift of the Holy Spirit. We *may*, although we don't deserve that precious gift of salvation and very likely won't be granted it—and thus won't be elected. Most assuredly we won't without the rebirth that follows upon our awakening to a realization of God's rightful abhorrence, in His faultless sovereignty, as He looks upon such vileness as characterizes even the toadlike best of Adam's children, filthy, guilty, odious, abominable as all of us are.

Of course the ways of an omniscient God are far beyond our understanding, but His beneficence assures us that those ways are just. Our way is but to submit to His will. Thus in the Beecher household, as far back as 1822, when Harriet was ten, her eldest sibling, her sister Catharine, was urged to submit to a heavy loss much like the one that had now, thirty-five years later, befallen the grieving Stowes in July 1857. The drowning at Dartmouth of young Henry Ellis Stowe had been eerily anticipated at that earlier time, in a parsonage at Litchfield shaken in turn by a grief of its own. For then the twenty-two-year-old Catharine had been affianced to a man of great promise, a veritable paragon of virtue, Alexander Fisher, a brilliant young professor of mathematics at Yale. Friends and family had exulted in the match. As soon as the gifted Dr. Fisher returned from a professional voyage to Europe, the young people would join their lives together. He sailed away. His ship neared the coast of Ireland, off Kinsale, and there on rocks in a storm it foundered, and the young man drowned. Years later, aboard the *Canada* on their way to Mrs. Stowe's triumphal reception in Britain after she had written *Uncle Tom's Cabin,* Harriet and her brother Charles saw the site. "We are about passing Kinsale point with its lighthouse," Charles wrote in his journal then. "There is the very spot where the *Albion* was wrecked and Prof. Fisher met his untimely death." Even in sunlight the bluff looked grim and frowning. "We feel sad in passing this point. I was but a child when the news came," writes Charles, "but I well remember the impression made on me. I saw sister Catharine lying in bed in the room at Litchfield over the front door . . . pale and weeping. I shall never forget it."

Then, as now, an awareness that a young man, despite all his manifold gifts, had died unregenerate had achingly intensified the mourners' grief. The pious Fisher had struggled, but these matters are not to be feigned. He had failed in his soul to experience the sense of utter depravity that would have led him to give himself in total submission to his Creator. When the news arrived that Fisher had drowned, Catharine in desperation wrote to and received letters from her consoling father; and for all Lyman's tenderness with a daughter in the throes of such grief, what strikes the modern reader most forcefully about the exchange is a Calvinist parent's unwavering rigor. Facts are facts; Lyman will not equivocate to ease her pain. The most that can be offered by way of consolation is that the storm at sea had allowed time "for submission, and powerful means to a mind already furnished with knowledge, and not unacquainted with the strivings of the Spirit." Perhaps at the very last Fisher had felt the joy and serenity of utter subjection, but over this momentous subject God has thrown a veil that we cannot lift. "And now, my dear child," her father wrote, "what will you do? Will you turn at length to God and set your affections on things above, or cling to the shipwrecked hopes of earthly good?"

Catharine's brother Charles provides us with the aftermath, recording it in his journal years later off the coast of Ireland where Fisher had gone down. Catharine never married. She was destined to become a famous educator and a prolific writer on domestic economy, women's issues, religion, and reform. "And now when I see sister Cate without fixed home," wrote Charles in 1853, three decades after her fiancé's death, "with a mind too strong for her frail body and driving it as an engine drives a shattered boat, and then think how different her lot might have been but for the hand of God here so heavily laid on her. My heart is moved with mingled admiration and compassion. Admiration at the indomitable energy, resolution, benevolence, and hopefulness; compassion at her infirmity of body and nervous system, which so impair her usefulness."

God's ways are not for us to know, but of His goodness we must never doubt. Here meanwhile, four years later, in 1857, it had fallen to Harriet yet again, in her new grief, to ponder such mysteries. On her return from Europe, she who had never seen Dartmouth College had wanted to visit her son Henry in New Hampshire, but the young man had been in the midst of exams and would be home in the Stone Cabin at Andover "in a week or two" in any case. Thus Harriet had traveled instead to Hartford, Elmira, and Brooklyn. Now she was returning from Brooklyn with a broken heart, stopping again at her sisters' in Hartford, proceeding from there on home to Andover. The house when she arrived was full of Henry's classmates, who had come down to share his mother's sorrow. The dead son in his coffin was with them. "There he lay so calm, so placid, so peaceful," Harriet wrote, "that I could not believe that he would not smile upon me, and that my voice which always had such power over him could not recall him." From his friends she was to learn of Henry's having risen from the breakfast table at his boardinghouse on the last day of his life, someone noticing the ring he wore and remarking how handsome it was. "Yes, he said, and best of all, it was my mother's gift to me." Later the friends removed the ring from his lifeless finger and delivered it to Mrs. Stowe.

The family would bury Henry in Andover. The funeral took place on Saturday, July 11, and on the following Monday Harriet and Calvin journeyed to Hanover to see their son's college for the first time, see his room as he had left it: the Sutherland plaid that he had brought back from Scotland there on the wall; his books; other memorials of his European trip and of his famous mother, whose achievements had filled him with such pride. Henry's friends came into the room, as Harriet later wrote to his twin sisters at their boarding school in Paris, and related "one thing and another that they remembered of him. 'He was always talking of his home and his sisters,' said one. The very day he died he was so happy because I had returned, and he was expecting soon to go home and meet me. He died with that dear thought in his heart." The grieving mother and father descended the lane that led to the glen by the river where Henry had drowned. He had been returning from a swim across to the Vermont shore when he had called for help; two of his classmates leaped in but couldn't save him. The body had been recovered a quarter of an hour later.

"In the evening," wrote Harriet of her visit, "we went down to see the boating club of which he was a member. He was so happy in this boating club. They had a beautiful boat called the Una, and a uniform, and he enjoyed it so much." In the late light all the college crews were on the water. Henry's boat had its flag furled and tied with black crape.

Thus in grief they visited their son's college world, and then they buried him. "It seems selfish that I should yearn to lie down by his side," his mother wrote, "but I never knew how much I loved him till now." Harriet planted flowers beside the young man's grave: pansies, verbenas, petunias, white immortelles. She longed for one word, one look, a last embrace. "Papa walks there every day," she wrote, "often twice or three times."

Together the dazed parents planned a journey to Brunswick, to friends back in Bowdoin and ocean air, "for I am so miserable," Harriet wrote, "so weak—the least exertion fatigues me, and much of my time I feel a heavy languor, indifferent to everything. I know nothing is so likely to bring me up as the air of the seaside."

But more than sea air would be needed to assuage this pain. They did make their journey of two weeks to Maine in September 1857. Yet long after that, as far in the future as February 1859, Harriet was still enfeebled with grief. Eighteen months further along she would have to force herself to perform as simple a task as answering a letter from her daughter Georgiana, now fifteen: "My dear Georgie,—Why haven't I written? Because, dear Georgie, I am like the dry, dead, leafless tree, and have only cold, dead, slumbering buds of hope on the end of stiff, hard, frozen twigs of thought, but no leaves, no blossoms; nothing to send to a little girl who doesn't know what to do with herself any more than a kitten. I am cold, weary, dead; everything is a burden to me."

In fact, so disconsolate had this horticulturally devoted woman of vast energy become that she let her very plants die—"by inches before my eyes, and do not water them, and I dread everything I do, and wish it was not to be done, and so when I get a letter from my little girl I smile and say, 'Dear little puss, I will answer it;' and I sit hour after hour with folded hands, looking at the inkstand and dreading to begin."

She confessed to her daughter, "mamma is tired." More than tired: exhausted. Sometimes the bereaved mother would glimpse her dead son's sweet, fair face—so she wrote to Georgie—gazing down from out of a cloud, "and I feel again all the bitterness of the eternal 'No' which says I must never, never, in this life, see that face, lean on that arm, hear that voice."

But what Harriet went on to reveal in this intimate letter discloses, remarkably, the strength—alongside its oft-noted exactions—that Calvinism provided her. For "Not that my faith in God in the least fails," she hastened to make clear, "and that I do not believe that all this is for good. I do, and though not happy, I am blessed. Weak, weary as I am, I rest on Jesus in the innermost depth of my soul, and am quite sure that there is coming an inconceivable hour of beauty and glory when I shall regain Jesus, and he will give me back my beloved one, whom he is educating in a far higher sphere than I proposed. So do not mistake me,—only know that mamma is sitting weary by the wayside, feeling weak and worn, but in no sense discouraged."

16

THE MINISTER'S WOOING

*F*ar from feeling discouraged, Stowe—despite her weariness and out of her great grief—would soon begin composing yet another novel, which after *Uncle Tom's Cabin* proved to be perhaps the richest she ever wrote. In working on this present fictional narrative the author was tilling new ground, departing from the national travails of slavery in order to cultivate a different subject entirely, in a field so fertile that from it in years ahead she would harvest three additional novels, each one a memorably original achievement. The four together describe, more revealingly than does any other fiction in the whole range of American literature, the seminal world that was postrevolutionary New England. Out of that Calvinist world, Yankee settlers streaming westward in the late eighteenth century and the nineteenth (as streamed the Beechers themselves, singing in their stagecoach) would spread across the American continent evangelical values that, for better or worse, continue to distinguish the United States sharply from the more secular European nations of our time.

The four novels—*The Minister's Wooing* (1859), *The Pearl of Orr's Island* (1862), *Oldtown Folks* (1869), and *Poganuc People* (1878)— all do exhibit the faults "in the artistic department" that Harriet Martineau discovered in *Dred*. Stowe was not a litterateur. She was a sophisticated observer who read widely and intelligently, but not as an aesthete. Rather, she was a moralist possessed by chance of a great gift for telling a story. Her ability to create believable characters, give them distinctive voices, place them in vivid settings, assign psychologically penetrating motivations to prod them into action, and with sharp nouns and wonderfully vigorous verbs keep them moving mark her as a natural storyteller; so that in these four New England novels, as in their two predecessors about slavery, things are constantly happening to hold the reader's attention— interesting things, stimulating things, significant things.

For all that, she wrote to make money, because people would pay her well to write; and, in focusing as much on an afterlife as on this present one, she was careless enough with the money she made as always to be needing more. A new magazine, the *Atlantic Monthly,* had been proposed in the fall of 1857, and its founders journeyed to Andover to solicit a contribution from the vastly popular Mrs. Stowe. Off and on since finishing *Uncle Tom's Cabin* the author had worked on a novel set in Maine; perhaps she could finish that and give it to them. But instead, in the summer of 1858, back in her beloved New England for good, with her aged father and his jumbled memories taking their ease in the sun in her Stone Cabin garden, and with a biography in her hands of the eighteenth-century divine Samuel Hopkins written by a neighbor and head of Andover Theological Seminary, she changed her mind. She would write a story about Hopkins, a grave, worthy disciple of the great Jonathan Edwards and an early foe of slavery. Stowe's story would be set in Newport, Rhode Island, very late in the eighteenth century, at a time when Lyman Beecher had been young and a student at Yale. "How did they live in those days?" she had queried her father earlier, as the old man sat reminiscing in her parlor. "Tell us something about Aunt Benton's kitchen." Thus Chapter 2 of this new novel, which the *Atlantic Monthly* started publishing in December 1858, was entitled "The Kitchen," wherein was described with warmth and precision of detail the huge ancient fireplace with its great jolly fire crackling, the snowy floorboards "sanded with whitest sand," the shining pewter plates and dishes, the commodious wooden settee for the repose of "people too little accustomed to luxury to ask for a cushion."

For Newport of the 1790s was an austere world, as was Calvinist New England in general. Yet there was Yankee humor in those earlier ways, and integrity, and much about that simpler time for an increasingly materialistic, consumeristic America of the 1850s to admire. Stowe wrote for money, but she wrote also with an acute awareness of the possibilities of fiction as a moral force. Who could better comprehend the power of stories to affect a populace than she who had gazed at crowds of people putting down their labors to stand alongside the road waving and bowing as the author of *Uncle Tom's Cabin* passed by? Whatever she wrote would be for their good as well as their entertainment, even as she acknowledged the impossibility of composing a story about manners in Calvinist New England that would appeal to "a thoughtless, shallow-minded person. If," she explained in this new novel, *The Minister's Wooing,* "we represent things as they are, their intensity, their depth, their unworldly gravity and earnestness must inevitably repel lighter spirits, as the reverse pole of the magnet drives off sticks and straws." Nevertheless, she would write of such things, because she wrote as she thought, not as genteel fashion dictated; because she cared about and had a rare understanding of her New England ancestors; and because, in her abiding grief for her drowned son and as the sectional storms of the late 1850s grew darker and ever more thunderous, she would willingly turn to an earlier era of disciplined living, honest physical labor, and dogged seeking after spiritual truths from Calvinist ministers who, without condescension or compromise, expatiated in their plain meetinghouses on the mystical verses of the King James Bible.

Yet for all their questing after God, people had no easier time of it in those postcolonial days than in this contentious antebellum present. Harriet herself knew firsthand the rigors of Calvinism, having long struggled with the obligations of its dogma. When she was fourteen and pining for rebirth, she had once even fancied herself regenerated, attending a communion service in her father's church at Litchfield and hearing him preach on Jesus's declaration in the Gospel of John: *"Behold, I call you no longer servants, but friends."* The child had left the meetinghouse in ecstasy; nature itself—as she recalled—was hushed to hear with her the music of Heaven. "Father, I have given myself to Jesus, and He has taken me," she reported as soon as Dr. Beecher was settled into his study at home. And "'Is it so?' he said, holding me silently to his heart, as I felt the hot tears fall on my head. 'Then has a new flower blossomed in the kingdom this day.'"

But it was not so. Regeneration didn't come so easily, and we recollect that in later months and years of her adolescence Hatty Beecher wrote of her life miserably as "one continued struggle: I do nothing right. I yield to temptation almost as soon as it assails me." Beset from all sides, this (as she saw herself) sinful child of the 1820s felt robbed of every happiness; and "that which most constantly besets me is pride—I can trace almost all my sins back to it."

Her brother George had suffered similarly in adolescence; all her brothers and sisters had. Good Calvinists did, struggling in youth to experience fully the depravity of their nature as a first step toward submitting themselves humbly and wholly to their Heavenly Father. In Harriet's case, such submission came only much later, in 1843, when she was in her early thirties and overwhelmed by the void that followed upon that same brother George's returning on a summer morning from market in Chillicothe—his family about to sit down to breakfast—and stepping outside to his garden with a shotgun to chase off the birds. Once there, he had pointed the muzzle at his cheek and pulled the trigger. Her brother's suicide left Harriet desolate, seeking consolation in what abruptly appeared to be "the entire emptiness of this world." Any one of her siblings' homes—"living, cheerful, strong & full of life"—in whose repose she had dwelt in hope and love as in green comfort, might as suddenly as George's wither into a desert. "I fear," she wrote at the time, trying to steel herself, "we have too much in this world to love—and that we love it too well—How precious have been the gifts of the Lord unto us"—and among those great gifts "what a father!—and he still lives." But in her anguish she trembled, recalling the many pleasant hours spent in the homes of her siblings: Edward, Mary, Henry, Isabella. Were those any more secure than the home that had been swept away?

During the bleak season immediately after George's suicide, Harriet had given birth to a sickly daughter, whom she herself was too ill to nurse. The nurse who was hired was unstable, and the other four Stowe children were bumptious. Calvin, when not ill, was away attempting to raise funds for Lane Seminary, his modest teaching salary paid only in inadequate part. Day and night Harriet was, as she said, "haunted & pursued by care that seemed to drink my life blood." And at that very time, when she had approached despair, "then *came* the long-expected and wished help." All at once she had felt "calm, but full"; her heart, which had run with a strong current toward worldly things, turned suddenly and ran the opposite way. Helpless, she yielded herself to God, trusted in Him, and felt flow through her the serenity of total surrender.

The change had sustained her through fourteen years—through the move to Maine, the writing of *Uncle Tom's Cabin* and *Dred,* the triumphs in Europe—until Henry's drowning in the summer of 1857. Then she was to be tested again, severely. "If ever I was conscious of an attack of the Devil trying to separate me from the love of Christ," she wrote, "it was for some days after the terrible news came." Satan had appeared to taunt her: "You trusted in God, did you? You believed that He loved you! You had perfect confidence that he would never take your child till the work of grace was mature! Now He has hurried him into eternity without a moment's warning, without preparation, and where is he?"

The Minister's Wooing addresses that torment. Newport in the 1790s lives off trade; and one of its bold young men, James Marvyn, is about to set sail as first mate of the *Monsoon* on a three-year voyage. Before sailing, James surprises alone a longtime friend and relative, Mary Scudder, and confesses his love for her, even while knowing that he is unworthy of such ideal goodness; for Mary is one of Stowe's model heroines: unassuming, duteous, pure, quietly pious, and beautiful. (Such people do exist, of course, the more frequently in the romantic age of antebellum America.) "But do you remember you told me once," James writes in a letter delivered to Mary after his departure, "that, when the snow first fell and lay so dazzling and pure and soft, all about, you always felt as if the spreads and window curtains that seemed white before were not clean? Well, it's just like that with me." Alongside Mary, James feels low and unworthy—as indeed in a Calvinist world, on a global scale, even the most blameless of us would feel in the presence of God's perfection. But by no means is James a bad person, even if spirited and irreligious, even if, as he admits to Mary in their interview, he doesn't get "the hang of predestination, and moral ability, and natural ability, and God's efficiency, and man's agency, which Dr. Hopkins is so engaged about; but I can understand *you*"—he tells her—"*you* can do me good!"

James's declaration of love stirs Mary deeply. Her mother, however, sensing danger, is opposed even to the young people's friendship. Mrs. Scudder has hopes that her daughter will marry the boarder in their household, the middle-aged Reverend Dr. Samuel

Hopkins whom James has spoken of, an esteemed scholar and Newport's otherworldly pastor. Encouraged by Mrs. Scudder, and despite his bookish abstractedness, Dr. Hopkins learns through the months ahead to find cheer in the beautiful Mary's quiet presence, to the point of daring at last to imagine her as a helpmeet for his declining years.

None of these people is evil, or even self-seeking. Mrs. Scudder genuinely believes that young James, a flighty infidel, would be grievously miscast as her devout daughter's husband. The widow even knows just the girl in Newport who would suit James; and meanwhile, her Mary's opportunities for benevolence as the wife of Dr. Hopkins—the noblest man in the village—would answer a mother's most ardent prayers. The reverend doctor is himself aware of Mary's piety and has seen her enraptured gaze upon him as he preaches the gospel in the meetinghouse. And all the while, quiet Mary during these same months has come to realize how much she loves her absent friend James Marvyn, for his spirit, for his warmth of feeling, and for his parting resolve—with the gift of her pocket Bible in his hand—to strive sincerely for grace.

But, as came to Harriet Beecher Stowe in Brooklyn one terrible summer evening, so to Newport comes a day that brings word of the first mate's death at sea. It has been God's will that James Marvyn perish as Henry Stowe had perished, unregenerate, unconverted. Mary, heartbroken, hides her grief while carrying on with the relentless household duties of those demanding times. "There is no healing for such troubles," her minister advises her gently, "except in unconditional submission to Infinite Wisdom and Goodness. The Lord reigneth, and will at last bring infinite good out of evil, whether *our* small portion of existence be included or not."

In time Mary does accede to her mother's and Dr. Hopkins's wishes by agreeing to marry the worthy cleric. The dead James's own grieving mother, meanwhile, cannot reconcile herself to the idea that her unregenerate son is doomed to suffer eternal torment. In a brilliant chapter, "Views of Divine Government," the author has Mrs. Marvyn express her anguish in the face of Calvinist doctrine: "Mary, I cannot, will not, be resigned!—it is all hard, unjust, cruel!—to all eternity I will say so! To me there is no goodness, no justice, no mercy in anything! Life seems to me the most tremendous doom that can be inflicted on a helpless being!" Only the merest few will be saved;

all the others—those warm, generous hearts, those splendid natures and noble minds all doomed by the thousands and tens of thousands! Mrs. Marvyn cries out: "it isn't *my* sorrow only! What right have I to mourn? Is *my* son any better than any other mother's son? Thousands of thousands, whose mothers loved them as I love mine, are gone there!"—to suffer forever. "Oh, my wedding-day! Why did they rejoice? Brides should wear mourning,—the bells should toll for every wedding; every new family is built over this awful pit of despair, and only one in a thousand escapes!"

As often in Stowe's narratives, Mrs. Marvyn provides the deeply realized opposing point of view, fully understood and memorably expressed. Of course her heart-wrenching sentiments are those of the author herself, in certain moods after Henry's death. But one admirable aspect of the best of Stowe's fiction arises from her ability to express all sides of an issue dramatically, through credible characterizations and apt dialogue. The historical Samuel Hopkins, for instance, the disciple of Jonathan Edwards, is here contrasted with Edwards's historical grandson Aaron Burr, another character in the novel, who was born—as was Hopkins—into Calvinism and who, like Lord Byron, rejected it in the course of his young manhood. Indeed, Burr is Byronic in many ways: handsome, nonchalant, cynical, self-absorbed, indiscriminately licentious. And the wonder is how skillfully Stowe captures such an unclerical figure and renders convincingly his cultivation, the assurance of his worldly voice, his baleful influence over women.

There are other wonders in this long novel (people of the mid-nineteenth century, hobbling along without such distractions as television, welcomed long novels as whole worlds wherein to roam at leisure). *The Minister's Wooing* considers profound questions: What sort of universe do we live in? How is it governed? How best should we lead our lives? What constitutes our proper duty? Such concerns it vivifies through a story that never lacks for interest, in part because, as often in Stowe's fiction, the imagery is fresh and evocative, the analogies are frequent and apposite, and the author's broad wisdom—about life, death, grief, and mourning; about the quirks and crotchets of living; about what delights and what consoles—is almost unfailingly sound.

Still, the book displays some familiar faults. Bent not only on entertaining but on doing good, Stowe sermonizes rather too much for our taste, even if we allow for her theological subject matter. Victorian sentimentality wafts in and out in ways that displease, and melodrama sets the plot creaking. James, we learn, isn't dead after all. He arrives back in Newport regenerate, and as rich as Captain Wentworth in Austen's *Persuasion*. But by then Mary has plighted her troth to the worthy Dr. Hopkins and is honor-bound not to go back on her word or even mention her feelings about James. The nuptials loom. But just in time, three days before the wedding, the minister learns by chance of his fiancée's love for the young sailor. He promptly releases Mary from her commitment, freeing the lovers to wed. The Reverend Dr. Hopkins himself officiates at the ceremony, after which husband and wife settle down in a very nice home—not so foolish an ending when one considers the high value mid-nineteenth-century America was learning to place on the home as the moral counterweight of an amoral workplace.

But in Stowe, the plot matters less than other fictional values: the vividness with which she has caught and held a dense, rich, seminal way of life and the memorable characters she creates to exemplify that life in its great variety—all those different voices, those evanescent gestures, the vanished customs preserved. That plus the rich themes. Her beautiful descriptive passages. Her humor. And Stowe's witty, wise irony. About, for instance, an early foe of slavery: "Nobody had ever instructed him that a slave-ship, with a procession of expectant sharks in its wake, is a missionary institution, by which closely-packed heathens are brought over to enjoy the light of the gospel." Or about a certain brassbound Newport insensate: "He was one of that class of people who, of a freezing day, will plant themselves directly between you and the fire, and there stand and argue to prove that selfishness is the root of all moral evil." Or about the comfortably placed Mrs. Brown, who nevertheless, "like all other human beings, resented the implication of not having as many trials in life as her neighbors." Or about the then reputable Newport slave trade: "Large fortunes were constantly being turned out in it, and what better providential witness of its justice could most people require?" Such clear, bright shafts of wit furnish not the least of the pleasures of *The Minister's Wooing*.

17

CIVIL WAR

*I*n order to secure an international copyright and consequent profits for her latest novel, Harriet made a third, final voyage to Europe, this time bringing with her all her family but the youngest,
Charley. As passengers on the steamer *Asia*, the Stowes landed at
Liverpool Sunday morning, August 14, 1859. Not three months
earlier, Lady Byron in England had written to the author about her
reading the serialized *Minister's Wooing* with "intense interest"; it
displayed more power, Lady Byron said, than either of Mrs. Stowe's
earlier novels, "at least to my own mind"—more power even than
Adam Bede ("*the* book of the season," her ladyship reported from
London). Of course Harriet, once arrived, would call on Lady Byron,
though when she did, she found her friend quite unwell, "in a state
of utter prostration." Later, in a second interview, Byron's long-
suffering widow was fortunately much improved, enjoying "one of
those bright intervals of freedom from pain and languor" that let
her appear at her best. Thus the two friends could share a quiet
summer afternoon together, strolling and lounging contentedly in
Lady Byron's garden. On departing, the invalid even felt up to accompanying her American visitor in her carriage to the station,
kindly removing her gloves—"Take mine if they will serve you"—
to replace the ones Mrs. Stowe discovered she had left behind.

There were other happy reunions with old friends in England,
before the Stowes set off for an extended vacation on the continent.
The twins, Hattie and Eliza, were to linger in Paris among familiar
surroundings; and after Switzerland, Calvin and daughter Georgie
would return to America. But young Fred, nineteen, planned to set

off on a walking tour in Italy with a chum from home, hopeful that the Tuscan countryside would cure him of his persisting, shameful addiction to alcohol. Perhaps when he got back to Massachusetts he might take hold and study medicine; that was Calvin's idea. However, "if this trip which I am on makes me well," Fred fretted in a letter to his father from Florence in December 1859, "is there not danger that the intence application that I should have to give to the study before I could do anything for my self would not break me down again and I would be helpless on your hands a worse clog than before"? By his own account, for nearly four years the youth, with his penchant, had been able to do very little—a burden to everyone—even though, poignantly, "I have tried every thing and instead of getting better have rather got worse."

Now Fred would attempt to walk his way to health over the Italian hills. Harriet was in Italy as well, in Florence with her son (that "smart bright lively boy," as she had described Fred earlier, with his "warm affectionate heart"). In addition, she would spend several months in Rome, joining the expatriate American and English community there. Those days proved to be a magic time for her; through the spring of 1860 she was in the company of such stimulating people as the Brownings, the Storeys, and the Fieldses. Annie Fields became a close friend of Harriet's from this point on; their meeting in Florence led Mrs. Stowe to join that young, second wife of the great publisher James T. Fields—she was twenty-six—aboard the *Europa*, on which Mr. and Mrs. Fields had booked passage, when it sailed from Liverpool Boston-bound that same summer, in June 1860.

By then—exactly a month before, on May 16—the ailing Lady Byron had succumbed at last, at sixty-eight, while her American friend was still traveling on the continent; so that the gift in the carriage of her gloves at their final encounter would become all the more precious for memorializing the generosity of one safe now among eternal friends. Both women—Annabella Noel Byron and Harriet Beecher Stowe—were sure of that: three years earlier, "if you see morning in our Father's house before I do," the one had confidently written to the other, now deceased, "carry my love to those that wait for me."

Among earthly friends meanwhile, at sea aboard the *Europa*, in addition to the publisher Fields and his charming young wife,

was Nathaniel Hawthorne, the most esteemed member of the pan-
theon of authors published by Ticknor & Fields of Boston. For his
publishing house Fields had assembled an impressive literary list that
Mrs. Stowe meant to join in the course of this voyage—"a delightful
voyage in every sense," as Annie Fields recalled years later, "a good
fourteen days of sitting together on deck in pleasant weather." For
the most part, the exceptionally reserved Hawthorne, then in his
mid-fifties, kept to his cabin or leaned at the stern in his felt hat
gazing alone at the horizon; but the ladies chatted on deck and
became warm friends: Sophia Hawthorne, Annie Fields, and Harriet
Beecher Stowe, whom Mrs. Hawthorne would describe as looking
"tired far into the future." Or was that merely Mrs. Stowe's characteristic abstractedness, which everyone spoke of: her "far-away
dreaming eyes," as Annie recalled, "and her way of becoming occupied in what interested her until she forgot everything else for
the time"? For their part, the Hawthornes were on their way home
to Concord, Massachusetts, the author of *The Scarlet Letter* having concluded his service as United States consul at Liverpool,
following it with extended travels in Italy and back in England. The
fruit of all that wandering was *The Marble Faun,* Hawthorne's new
novel, his first in eight years and with an Italian setting, which
Ticknor & Fields was in the process of publishing to great acclaim.

Harriet, too, had an Italian novel in progress. Accordingly, after landing and returning to Andover, she would be negotiating with
Mr. Fields, who was now also editor of the *Atlantic Monthly,* to
furnish his magazine with her Mediterranean story as a serial that,
when completed, would appear in book form under the Ticknor &
Fields imprint. But the dynamic young Theodore Tilton, a close friend
of Harriet's brother Henry Ward Beecher and editor of the influential *New York Independent*—for which Mrs. Stowe had written columns of opinion—was after her for a more substantial contribution;
so, in a weak moment, ever needful of money, she committed herself to providing Mr. Tilton with that Maine novel to which she had
been returning off and on since finishing *Uncle Tom's Cabin* in her
days at Brunswick. Two novels, then—*The Pearl of Orr's Island* and
Agnes of Sorrento—she worked on simultaneously into 1861, with two
editors, one in Boston, one in New York, much interested in her
auctorial prowess, cause enough for Stowe's looking "tired into the
future," however she may have appeared in times past.

This new year, meanwhile, was proving one of extraordinary significance to the nation. An Illinois lawyer, a sectional candidate, had been elected last November to the presidency, leading irate southern states to withdraw from the Union late in 1860 and as 1861 advanced through the winter toward spring. Like everyone else, the Stowes in Andover were absorbed in the unfolding national drama. How get on at such a time with writing even one novel, let alone two? Although Mr. Lincoln had made clear that he would enforce the Fugitive Slave Law and would not interfere with slavery in the southern states, his Republican Party was committed to arresting the institution's farther spread in the territories. That was as much as the South had needed to hear. In early February six seceding states met in Montgomery, Alabama, to proclaim an independent Confederacy. Lincoln came east and assumed the presidency of the United States in March: "In *your* hands, my dissatisfied fellow countrymen, and not in *mine*, is the momentous issue of civil war." And in early April rebel troops under General Beauregard fired on the Union flag at Fort Sumter.

The president called for volunteers to put down the rebellion; and Fred Stowe, back home now and struggling at the start of his medical studies, was among the earliest to answer that summons to arms. He joined Company A of the First Massachusetts Volunteers; and in June his mother, in Brooklyn visiting her brother Henry, got word that Fred's regiment was in transit toward a nearby port. With Henry's wife, Eunice, Mrs. Stowe set forth at once in a carriage to the Fulton ferry, from there steaming across the bay to Jersey City, to find the troops already landed and at a makeshift meal in the immense depot. A surrounding gallery had filled with civilian crowds pressing against cast-iron gratings through which the soldiers could be seen, "eating, drinking, smoking, talking, singing, and laughing. Company A was reported to be here, there, and everywhere." Finally Mrs. Stowe's party was admitted through the doors, and in time they located Fred, "a blue-overcoated figure bristling with knapsack and haversack," hurrying toward them overjoyed. "I gave him my handkerchief and Eunice gave him hers," and the women filled their soldier's haversack with oranges for a treat, while people in the gallery went on waving and cheering, and the band played, and men sang, and the companies drilled—everyone, as Harriet reported, appearing "to be having a general jollification."

Jollity would be short-lived. The following month young Fred's company took part in the Union disaster at Bull Run, and Mr. Lincoln's war turned into a long, bloody conflict. The gangly politician had not been this mother's candidate in any case; Mrs. Stowe, whose experiences in England had taught her what rulers should look like, had last year supported for chief executive the presidentially handsome Salmon P. Chase, a friend of her young womanhood, former member of Cincinnati's Semi-Colon Club, antislavery lawyer, governor of Ohio, senator, and at the present moment a member of Lincoln's cabinet. In the grim months ahead Calvin Stowe would find occasion to write to his old acquaintance Chase; for in August 1861, General Frémont issued an order emancipating the slaves of Missouri, an action that led Harriet to exclaim publicly, jubilantly: "at last a blow has been struck which finds an echo in the heart of a whole nation. The hour has come, and the man!" But in Washington President Lincoln countermanded the order as exceeding Frémont's authority and relieved the general of command. The Stowes were enraged. "Our Government gives rewards to defeat and shame, and punishes success and honor," Calvin wrote in a furious protest to Lincoln's secretary of the treasury. "Imbecility and treachery are sure of favor; fidelity and energy are equally sure of hostility and disgrace." He signed that scorching missive to his old friend Chase, "Very truly and sadly yours, C. E. STOWE."

To Professor Stowe and his fervent wife, the purpose driving this millennial conflict was unequivocal: the war was a reckoning for sins of both the South and the North, sins that could be atoned for only when the awful curse of slavery had been lifted. Yet a year later, amid a succession of Federal losses in the dark summer of 1862, Mr. Lincoln, sensitive to the imperative of retaining the loyalty of the border states, declared publicly that all these bloody battles were being fought only to save the Union. Just that. "If I could save the Union without freeing *any* slave I would do it, and if I could save it by freeing *all* the slaves I would do it; and if I could do it by freeing some and leaving others alone I would also do that." But what would Jesus do? Jesus's object would be, as Harriet explained in a bitter parody in the columns of the *Independent*, "to set at liberty them that are bruised, and *not* either to save or destroy the Union. What I do in favor of the Union," she imagined her Savior declaring, "I do because it helps to free the oppressed; what I forbear, I forbear because it does not help to free the oppressed."

This northern observer had, in short, grave doubts about an inexperienced Illinois politician charged with conducting a great religious crusade. And during those desperate months of 1862, when Union fortunes were at their lowest ebb, she was also feeling hot anger toward the English people. British crowds welcoming her presence among them a decade earlier had given such vehement support to the antislavery cause! Now, though, with the South victorious in the Shenandoah Valley, at Cedar Mountain, at Second Bull Run, at Harpers Ferry, the English were behaving as neutrals, and even so in name only. British public opinion viewed the humbling of an American rival with equanimity, rather heartened than otherwise by the sight of a single continental power breaking in two. Confederate warships were being built in English shipyards, launched from English ports, and manned with English sailors. British merchants decried northern blockades that interrupted the cotton trade on which their textile mills depended; and British politicians were urging the bellicose North to desist, to let their southern sisters go in peace. Just recently, Gladstone had proclaimed in a much noted speech that the South was already doubtless a nation, sure of success in its bid for independence.

What had become of Britain's antislavery spirit of nine years earlier, when the author of *Uncle Tom's Cabin* had arrived on English shores to loud acclaim and received the vellum gift of an "Affectionate and Christian Address of Many Thousands of Women of Great Britain and Ireland to Their Sisters the Women of the United States of America," supported by the twenty-six fat folio volumes of well over half a million signatures? As Stowe in dismay contrasted the humane spirit that had informed Britain then with its mean expediencies now, she determined to answer the "Affectionate Address." In September of 1862, following upon the battle of Antietam—if hardly an unalloyed northern triumph, at least not a defeat—President Lincoln announced his intention of issuing at year's end a proclamation of emancipation, freeing the slaves of all rebel belligerents. Stowe seized upon that news to compose a reply to her British sisters, reminding them of England's current biases, that "the party which makes Slavery the chief corner-stone of its edifice finds in England its strongest defenders." Why should that be? But because it is so, British women must not think their American sisters "strange, if we bring back the words of your letter, not in bitterness, but in deepest sadness, and lay them down at your door"— those eloquent words that nine years earlier had urged the women of America to unite in ridding their land of slavery's barbarousness. We heard your plea and now are sacrificing the blood of our husbands, brothers, and sons toward that glorious end. But sisters, the author wrote in her anguish, "what have *you* done? And what do you mean to do?"

Before finishing her reply and sending it off to the *Atlantic* for publication, Mrs. Stowe intended to speak with President Lincoln himself, having been invited to Washington in any case, to attend a Thanksgiving banquet for some 1,000 slaves—fugitives from the South—that the war had already made free. To James T. Fields she explained that her trip was "to satisfy myself that I may refer to the Emancipation Proclamation as a reality & a substance not to fizzle out at the little end of the horn." Accordingly Stowe made her journey in mid-November 1862; attended the inspiring banquet of freedmen enjoying their first Thanksgiving out of slavery; visited yet again with her son Fred, now a lieutenant encamped nearby; called on Secretary Chase; and on November 25 spent an hour at the White House in private conference with President Lincoln.

No one knows what passed between those two, although it is from that interview that family legend reports the very tall president's greeting to the very short author: "So this is the little woman who wrote the book that made this big war!" Charley, who was then twelve years old and accompanied his mother without taking part in her private conversation, did at least meet Lincoln and wrote years later of the rustic flavor of the president's midwestern speech. Charley's sister Hattie, in her mid-twenties and also along on the trip, was not present at the interview. Hence, whatever was said between their mother and the statesman is conjectural, though Stowe must have left the White House assured that, unless the rebels abandoned their cause, the Emancipation Proclamation would be issued on the date specified.

And it was. In Boston at the start of a new year, on January 1, 1863, Harriet was in the gallery among crowds at the Music Hall, attending a jubilee program that featured an orchestral rendering of a Beethoven overture, Mr. Emerson's reading of a poem of his own composition, and a choral performance of Mendelssohn's *Hymn of Praise*. At the intermission, while the audience was milling about, an official of the hall appeared onstage and called for quiet. He shouted out an important announcement: from Washington, news just arrived by telegraph, president has signed the Emancipation Proclamation, text even now coming over the wires!

At the word "signed," the crowd in this antislavery city erupted. The diminutive Harriet, hidden among bulkier forms in the gallery, was as excited as anyone, her bonnet awry from the jostling, her shawl half off her shoulders. There was clapping and cheering and shouting, she cheering along with the rest; and then she heard from a distance what sounded like her name being called: "Mrs. Stowe. Mrs. Stowe." The call came up from below, growing in intensity, soon taken up by those near at hand. "Mrs. Stowe! Mrs. Stowe! Mrs. Stowe!" Knowing of her presence, the audience as one was summoning her from the crowd: "Mrs. Stowe! Mrs. Stowe!" People near her moved aside, pointed toward the railing. Hands gently ushered her forward. Thus at the gallery rail she stood to hear once more cheers of acclaim, a tiny woman up there in her bonnet askew, looking down at a multitude that was grinning, applauding, calling out—"Mrs. Stowe! Mrs. Stowe!" At this climactic instant of her life, here for a last time, smiling, tears streaming down her face, Harriet Beecher Stowe acknowledged yet another clamorous public recognition, this time for her crucial role in bringing about so epochal an outcome.

Her "Reply to the Women of Great Britain," fourteen pages in print, appeared that same January. Its persuasive eloquence moved even the reclusive Hawthorne, who detested writing letters, to respond. "I read with great pleasure your article in the last Atlantic," he wrote to Mrs. Stowe from Concord. "If anything would make John Bull blush, I should think it might be that, but he is a hardened and villainous hypocrite." This witness had spent five years living among the English, invariably treated with personal kindness but increasingly resentful of British condescension toward his countrymen. "I always felt," Hawthorne went on about John Bull, "that he cared nothing for or against slavery, except as it gave him a vantage-ground on which to parade his own virtue and sneer at our iniquity. With best regards," the former consul ended, "from Mrs. Hawthorne and myself to yourself and family, Sincerely Yours, Nath'l Hawthorne."

A few months earlier, Harriet had written to her daughters from Brooklyn: "I am going this afternoon to sit with my dear blessed Father." She meant her temporal father in this case, old Lyman Beecher, eighty-seven by then, living out his days near his son Henry in Brooklyn Heights. "He is always delighted to see me," the dutiful Harriet went on, "tho he knows not who I am. God bless his precious white head—it is white as silver snows and his poor trembling hands once so strong! I remember when the very touch of his hand seemed to put strength into me and his brisk joyful footstep at the door made me feel as if I had some one coming on whom I could lean all my cares." No longer; not for a long, long while. In this same January 1863, as the Emancipation Proclamation went into effect and Harriet's impressive "Reply to the Women of Great Britain" was published, old Dr. Beecher finally, peacefully died in mid-month at four o'clock one afternoon and, after an imposing funeral at the Plymouth Church of his son Henry Ward Beecher, was buried in his birthplace, New Haven.

The mourners' grief was muted of course, for one whose mind had drifted away years before the end of a life lived long and well, so Harriet and her daughters, returning from the funeral, could delay in Boston cheerfully enough and take care of some needed shopping. But in this wartime much sadness awaited them still. During the July ahead, the Stowes would receive the message that all the loved ones of soldiers were dreading—and have dreaded since the beginning of warfare. Mrs. Stowe's message, written on the evening of July 11, 1863, by a J. M. Crowell, came from Gettysburg, Pennsylvania: "Among the thousands of wounded and dying men on this war-scarred field, I have just met with your son, Captain Stowe." Fred had been struck by a shell fragment that penetrated his right ear. At the moment the captain was quiet and cheerful, though wanting his family to know of his fate. "I assured him that I would write at once; and, though I am wearied," Army Chaplain Crowell explained, "by a week's labor here among scenes of terrible suffering, I know that, to a mother's anxious heart, even a hasty scrawl about her boy will be more than welcome."

With that, effectively, Harriet's Civil War ended. After several months, Fred did get home and try to resume his medical studies, but the head wound was a long time healing. In fact, the young man never healed; during the coming months and years Fred Stowe became a familiar figure in local bars and staggering drunk around the streets of his parents' town. Through it all, Harriet herself kept occupied, writing three hours every morning, but almost never about the war. She wrote instead *House and Home Papers*, a series of newspaper articles on homemaking, about which she had learned something over the years. Designed to brighten the gloomy days of wartime, they were both popular and profitable, as was her series of essays about famous men: potboiler stuff, professional journalism to be turned into books, meant to make money to pay for mounting expenses.

But when her eighteen sketches of famous men were published in book form in 1868 as *Men of Our Times,* the longest among them—a hundred pages long and taking up more than a sixth of the volume—was the essay on that Illinois politician who had impressed her hardly at all at the start, one whom Harriet Beecher Stowe, like many others after coming to know Mr. Lincoln better, now judged to be "the greatest sign and marvel of our day."

18

POSTBELLUM

*I*n part she needed money to build and furnish a new home, in Hartford. Its site was alongside the Park River, where Harriet and her friend Georgiana May used to wander as schoolgirls, in a grove of oaks among which even so long ago she had dreamed of living someday. Now the author was making that dream come true. During the war Professor Stowe, at sixty, ailing as always and exhausted by the demands of the classroom, had submitted his resignation to the Andover Theological Seminary effective the following August, of 1863; thereupon his wife had set about making the move from a Massachusetts village rather out of the way to the more conveniently located town in central Connecticut where her sisters Mary Beecher Perkins and Isabella Beecher Hooker had often welcomed her into their homes. Wartime, with builders scarce and prices inflated, was not the best time for launching such a project; and Calvin fretted: at the spiraling costs, at the thought of moving at all. But the bother entailed in home construction was much to his wife's creative tastes. "Tell Mrs. Fields," Harriet wrote to her publisher in late 1863, "that my house with *eight* gables"—one more than Hawthorne's seven—"is growing wonderfully and that I go every day to see it—I am busy with drains sewers sinks digging trenching—& above all with manure!—You should see the joy with which I gaze on manure heaps to which the eye of faith sees Deleware grapes & D'Angouleme pears & all sorts of roses & posies."

It was to be a huge place, this Oakholm, the only such construction that Harriet ever oversaw from the ground up—and with tireless zest: an Italianate Victorian Gothic villa almost big enough for all the Beechers, of brownstone and brick with hooded windows and battlemented chimneys, with a glass conservatory two stories high that featured a bubbling fountain and an ornamental gallery, and with rooms lighted by large bay windows and paneled in oak available in such abundance from the surrounding acreage that even with construction done, the lawns of the place remained well shaded. "The confusion at present grows wilder every day," the homemaker wrote from the site in April 1864, "but it is the confusion of activity & I am driving at every body's heels." Her family's many belongings, including accumulations from three trips to Europe, were transported down from Andover toward the end of that month, so Harriet could write Fields on the first of May: "I came here a month ago to hurry on the preparations for our house, in which I am now writing, in the high bow-window of Mr. Stowe's study, overlooking the wood and river. We are not moved in yet, only our things, and the house presents a scene of the wildest chaos, the furniture having been tumbled in and lying boxed and promiscuous."

During the months ahead, wild chaos was badgered into order, and in the absence of Calvin's $2,000 annual salary from Andover, Harriet got busy paying for it all. Indeed, henceforth she would remain the family's essential support far into the future: the support of the twins (now in their late twenties and well settled into spinsterhood), of teenage Charley, of poor Fred, and—at least for the time being—of pretty Georgiana, in her early twenties, as well as of Stowe's husband Calvin, her sister Catharine, her brother Charles and his family, and others to a greater or lesser extent of the numerous Beecher clan.

Toward the end of making and generously spending money on her own and their behalf, Harriet worked prodigiously. But she had always worked; working was a part of her Puritan heritage. God has given you gifts, and whatever they are, you use them to illustrate His glory and fill His realms with praise. Throughout her lifetime this disciplined author wrote ten novels, four collections of tales and sketches, three large volumes of biographical profiles, two book-length children's stories, a volume of religious verse, a couple of fat volumes of polemics, two travel books, a geography text, a hugely popular homemaker's manual, and hundreds of journalistic essays on all kinds of subjects for magazines and newspapers. As sheer industry directed toward serious ends and emerging out of a life already socially involved, well filled domestically, and tire-lessly peregrinating, it constitutes a stupefying achievement in quantity alone, even if much of that output is fugitive, rather too fluently written in order to make money and because a timely sub-ject engaged Stowe's interest and would—she knew with uncanny accuracy—interest her vast audience as well. We of a different era, with different issues and tastes, are perforce less partial to her journalistic prose, even as we pause in wonder at the bulk of it, the more wonderful for being produced in the midst of cease-less distractions.

Homebuilding and the war provided two such distractions from Stowe's writing; her son Fred as a disabled victim of the war per-sisted as another. At war's end, and with the new house in Hart-ford just barely in order at last, her daughter Georgiana became a fourth distraction, though in quite a more pleasant way, when, in June 1865, that liveliest of the Stowe children married a well-to-do Episcopal minister, Henry Allen of Stockbridge, Massachusetts. The wedding entertainment at the Stowes' new Hartford home was lavish, Harriet agitating beforehand that the grounds be as they should be, every plant in place and blooming. For a bridal gift the Fieldses gave the new Mrs. Allen a complete set, bound in white leather, of the works of Nathaniel Hawthorne, who had died the year before. So taken with the gift was the bride's mother that for special weddings thereafter Mrs. Stowe would have Fields's pub-lishing house present the couple with sets of her own works, simi-larly bound. This current young bride and groom meanwhile went off to live in Stockbridge, and Harriet took pleasure in adding that destination to the several others she often called at: Peekskill and her brother Henry's summer home; Brooklyn and her and Henry's friends the Howards' home; Boston and the Fieldses' home; her sisters' homes here in Hartford; and soon her own new winter home in Florida—yet another considerable expense—which she visited regularly from the years immediately ahead well on into the 1880s.

The Florida purchase came about this way. Her son Fred, still suffering from his head wound, had met a couple of Union veter-ans in a tavern in Hartford, young men who, having been discharged in Florida, remained there long enough to glimpse the potential of the place before bringing north glowing accounts that Fred passed on to his mother. She saw an opportunity to get her troubled son away from city saloons into fresh air and outdoor labor. Accordingly she underwrote a philanthropic business venture: Fred and his new friends would lease a cotton plantation at Laurel Grove, just south of Jacksonville, and employ free blacks to work it. The plan didn't come cheap. It ended by costing Mrs. Stowe over $10,000, which despite rosy predictions she never recovered, for Fred as an administrator proved feckless, as did his partners and the freedmen working under them. But early in the enterprise, in the late winter of 1867, Harriet sailed south to Charleston, farther on to Jacksonville, and then fifteen miles still farther south along the broad St. Johns River to have a look.

At Mandarin, across the river from Fred's plantation, she came upon a cottage on 200 acres for sale and ended by buying it, having promptly fallen in love with Florida's climate, its flora, its fauna: the delicious mild air of March on this high bluff overlooking a blue river five miles wide, the hanging moss, the rose garden in front, a fragrant big orange grove in back, date palms, hedges in bloom, olive trees, singing birds. The cottage nestled against a live oak twenty-five feet in girth; and the Stowes, who soon came to love the place extravagantly, set about adding rooms and gables and, across the front and around that massive live oak, a wide veranda where Calvin in his white beard and red skullcap could sit contentedly all day long beside a basket of books, reading black-letter volumes of physiology and philosophy in medieval German or biblical tomes in Greek and Hebrew. The scholar, considerably overweight by age sixty-seven, did consent to bestir himself to accompany his son, after the disastrous cotton venture had been abandoned and Fred was again staggering around Hartford—and after the inebriate had spent several months to no good effect at an asylum in Binghamton—on a sailing voyage to the Mediterranean in 1868, in yet one more vain effort to help the alcoholic recover. But Fred's illness held on, to the young man's own great shame and at a time when understanding and treatment were primitive, so that his family had to continue as best they could to nurse him and pity and agonize.

Calvin in retirement constituted one more distraction while his wife was endeavoring to write. Harriet sought to get her husband writing too, setting down on paper the rich products of his mind after all those years of study. For some time she was preoccupied with the challenge, dealing cunningly with her phlegmatic, temperamental scholar as well as with James T. Fields to coax forth a manuscript from the one and get the other to start setting it into type: *Origin and History of the Books of the New Testament, Both the Canonical and the Apocryphal.* It appeared finally (although not under Fields's imprint) in 1867. The volume sold an astonishing 50,000 copies and earned its dilatory author, besides much satisfaction, some $10,000 in royalties to contribute to his wife's multifarious enterprises.

She herself, in addition to her vast journalistic output, was all this while working on what she envisaged as her literary masterpiece. It had been on her mind a long time—a new novel that she thought about and thought about and that took her, when this usually facile author finally got down to writing it, four years to finish. With many interruptions and much revision, she exerted a care during composition that earlier efforts had never exacted of her. *Oldtown Folks* was to be Stowe's classic, worthy of setting beside those other classics of American literature—*Evangeline, The Scarlet Letter*—that the great Fields had been sedulously promoting; that is, alongside the exalted best of Hawthorne or Longfellow. By means of this novel the authoress intended to ascend steep slopes and finally enter Fields's lofty male bastion of immortals.

For subject matter, *Oldtown Folks* returned to an earlier New England that Stowe and her husband both remembered well, before textile mills and railroads, in a simpler agrarian age. Calvin Stowe, in fact, was the chief inspiration for the novel, and in fictionalized form as Horace Holyoke he serves as its narrator. The setting is Natick, Massachusetts, the Oldtown where Calvin was born; and his counterpart Horace is accompanied through childhood and into adulthood by the same apparitions that visited the professor, incorporeal creatures emerging from closets or peering out of gaps in bedroom walls. Moreover, much of the action of the story derives from anecdotes with which Professor Stowe had regaled his wife over the years, his resonant voice accurately reproducing the various rural dialects. The young people in Oldtown go off to school at the mountain village of Cloudland, which is Litchfield, Connecticut, as Harriet knew it in her youth; the village minister, Mr. Avery, is Lyman Beecher in all his consequential exuberance. Lively Tina is based on Harriet's sprightliest daughter, Georgiana, recently wed. And as in *The Minister's Wooing,* where Aaron Burr credibly fills the Byronic role of a suave skeptic, so in *Oldtown Folks* one Ellery Davenport—a fictional descendant of Jonathan Edwards (as Burr was in fact)—thrusts into the lives of these villagers the wit, allure, and danger of handsome, worldly, Byronic sophistication.

The novel is long, and the story rambles, its plot constructed out of whatever Victorian lumber lay at hand: orphans, a flight from tyrannical guardians, a haunted house, a kidnapping and a rescue, a seduction, an illegitimate child, a religious revival, a wedding. Here as elsewhere in her fiction, the author keeps things moving, but it is the still moments in *Oldtown Folks* that glow with an abiding charm. Stowe's sketch—to take a single example—of Sunday in a village meetinghouse in the time of President Washington preserves the very feel of that experience, so central to generations of our forebears: "Nobody thought of staying away,—and, for that matter, nobody wanted to stay away. Our weekly life was simple, monotonous, and laborious; and the chance of seeing the whole neighborhood together in their best clothes on Sunday was a thing which, in the dearth of all other sources of amusement, appealed to the idlest and most unspiritual of loafers. They who did not care for the sermon or the prayers wanted to see Major Broad's scarlet coat and laced ruffles, and his wife's brocade dress, and the new bonnet which Lady Lothrop had just had sent up from Boston. Whoever had not seen these would be out of society for a week to come, and not be able to converse understandingly on the topics of the day."

An earlier, simpler life, increasingly foreign to people thriving among the economic benefits bestowed on wartime and postwar America at the threshold of the Gilded Age, had for all its simplicity real values to impart to prospering descendants erecting their mansions and acquiring their bric-a-brac. Flinty ancestors had wrestled daily with profound issues of life and death; having heard sermons about such issues on Sunday, they had talked them over through the week while clearing and planting their fields, digging their wells, and laying out their stone walls. To those earlier New Englanders, the traits of their Calvinist God seemed everywhere apparent. Look around: "Now as Nature is, in many of her obvious aspects, notoriously uncompromising, harsh, and severe," the narrator of *Oldtime Folks* explains in one of several enlightening passages on Puritan faith, "the Calvinist who begins to talk to common-sense people has the advantage on his side,—that the things which he represents the Author of Nature as doing and being ready to do, are not very different from what the common-sense man sees that the Author of Nature is already in the habit of doing. The farmer who struggles with the hard soil, and with drouth and frost and caterpillars and fifty other insect plagues,—who finds his most persistent and well-calculated efforts constantly thwarted by laws whose workings he never can fully anticipate, and which never manifest either care for his good intentions or sympathy for his losses, is very apt to believe that the God who created nature may be a generally benevolent, but a severe and unsympathetic being, governing the world for some great, unknown purpose of his own, of which man's private improvement and happiness may or may not form a part."

In such a world, under such a God, people learned to do their duty, take life earnestly and without immoderate expectations (though—if possible—with Yankee humor), and pass their days in fitting reverence. Those values emerge from Stowe's narrative re-creation of New England in the 1790s; and the spirited authenticity of her depiction, along with its depth, has led some later readers to esteem *Oldtown Folks* very highly, as the brilliant "chronicle of a race," in Vernon Parrington's phrase; or as Perry Miller, a scholar of Puritanism, suggests, "fundamental for understanding American culture." To the discriminating Charles H. Foster, writing in 1954, Harriet Beecher Stowe's *Oldtown Folks* is no less than "one of the unquestionable, but still generally unacknowledged, masterpieces of New England, indeed of American, literature."

Just before publication, Stowe had told James T. Fields: "I have never put so much work upon anything before"; and many of her earliest readers, like some of her later ones, thoroughly approved of the result. George Eliot—by now a warm epistolary friend, although the two authors never met—wrote to Harriet in July 1869 about how much pleasure she had taken, while reading *Oldtown Folks*, "in that picture of an elder generation," both because of Eliot's love of provincial life—not so different in Old England from in New—and because of her acquaintance with Calvinist orthodoxy. "I think," Eliot wrote, "your way of presenting the religious convictions which are not your own, except by the way of indirect fellowship, is a triumph of insight and true tolerance."

But other readers were less kind. The authoritative *Edinburgh Review* was hard on Stowe's new novel; and in America the *Nation,* a magazine founded at the end of the war, in 1865, professed weariness with the author's subject matter. This new, stylish periodical (which, like the *Atlantic,* is still extant) protested that we have had enough of literary moping over old New England and its bygone ways—its upstanding deacons and cranky maiden aunts, its town meetings and Puritan schoolhouses, its donation parties and 'Lection cakes and ministers' woodspells. Mrs. Stowe's new book, "though it is called a novel, is better to be described as a series of pictures of life as seen from the kitchen, and best-room, and barnyard, and meadow, and wood-lot of a Massachusetts parsonage of the pre-locomotive days." As such, the effort is somewhat redeemed by its author's "vigorous writing—humorous, and kindhearted, and shrewd"; but she has made an "entirely needless mistake" in having the unconvincing Horace Holyoke tell the story, and the characters in general are so tediously familiar—says this reviewer—and the incidents so threadbare, that even a patient reader must "beg for fresh fields and new men and times." Enough of picturesque reminiscences about New England—this despite what coming literary history was to reveal: that Stowe's regional novels were not the end but rather the beginning of a whole fruitful genre of fiction by such superior local-colorists as Sarah Orne Jewett, who would gratefully acknowledge her own indebtedness to Harriet's achievement. Nevertheless, for the moment the querulous responses from the *Nation* and the *Edinburgh Review*—both male citadels and both of much influence—to what she regarded as her finest work put this one female author in a professionally dark frame of mind.

Nor was Stowe's mood improved when she became aware, this same year, of a book translated from the French and published anonymously by Richard Bentley of London, entitled *My Recollections of Lord Byron; and Those of Eye-Witnesses of His Life.* On opening the first of the two marbled volumes, she would have read on a full page of front matter: "ADVERTISEMENT BY THE ENGLISH PUBLISHER. The Publisher of this Translation feels authorized to state, that it is the production of the celebrated COUNTESS GUICCIOLI. RICHARD BENTLEY. October, 1868."

La Guiccioli. When Byron and his wife had separated those many years ago, in the spring of 1816, and the poet went into exile, he had made his way to Venice, where in time, at a *conversazione* at the Countess Benzoni's, he had been introduced to a young woman—auburn-haired, petite, beautifully formed, the lovely third wife of an Italian nobleman. From Ravenna three months after that meeting, Byron wrote to his half sister Augusta in England: "I came here on account of a Countess Guiccioli—a Girl of Twenty married to a very rich old man of Sixty—about a year ago;—with her last Winter"—in fact, in April 1819—"I had a *liaison* according to the good old Italian custom— . . . She is pretty—a great Coquette—extremely vain—excessively affected—clever enough—without the smallest principle—with a good deal of imagination and some passion." The young countess and the dissolute English poet (then thirty-one) were engaging all this while in a love affair that would last four years, until Byron's departure for Greece and his death there in 1824. Now that same woman, that antiquated Italian adulteress nearing seventy, had presumed in her decrepitude to write of a long dead lover, of "His Religious Opinions," of "His Friendships," of "Lord Byron considered as a Father, as a Brother, and as a Son—His goodness shown by the strength of his distinctive affections," of "Qualities of Lord Byron's Heart," of "His Benevolence and Kindness," of "Lord Byron's Qualities and Virtues of Soul," of "Lord Byron's Constancy," of "His Courage and Fortitude," of "His Modesty," of "His Generosity elevated into Heroism."

Those infatuated chapters were repellant enough; but there was another, in Volume 2, commencing at page 220, called "Lord Byron's Marriage and its Consequences." And who was this superannuated courtesan to speak on such a subject? Byron's former mistress was here proceeding to explain in unambiguous terms what had gone wrong back in 1816 with the poet's marriage, a subject about which Harriet Beecher Stowe's later friendship with his widow had taught her a great deal. From the countess's pages the knowledgeable American was now to learn that such a one as Byron "would have required to meet with kindness, indulgence, and peace at home; thus supported, his heart would have endured everything. Instead of that, what did he find? A woman whose jealousy was extreme, who had her own settled way of living, and was unflinching in her ideas; who united a conviction of her own wisdom to perfect ignorance of the human heart, all the while fancying that she knew it so well"—*this* was *Lady Byron*? this ignorant distortion, this gross slander!—"who, far from consenting to modify her habits, would fain have imposed them on others. In short, a woman who had nothing in common with him, who was unable to understand him, or to find the road to his heart or mind; finally, one to whom forgiveness seemed a weakness, instead of a virtue."

The countess would have us understand the "inexplicable conduct" that Byron's wife displayed those long years ago. Her readers should recall that "Lady Byron was an only and a spoilt child, a slave to rule, to habits and ideas as unchanging and inflexible as the figures she loved to study." For milady was a coldly competent mathematician; no one disputed that. But she was also pampered, petted, and surrounded by luxury. Thus "it was no easy matter to satisfy all her tastes with mathematical regularity, to let her keep up all her habits, and, above all, to make Lord Byron share them in their married life." The more so because Byron himself was un-English: he slept late, worked all night, ate ascetically—breakfast for him was green tea without sugar and the yolk of an egg swallowed standing—didn't like dining or seeing women eat. And as for his consort? "Being *extremely jealous*, she became the easy dupe of malicious persons" under whose influence she "allowed herself to be persuaded that her husband committed grave faults, though in reality they were but slight or even imaginary ones. She forced open his writing-desk, and found in it several proofs of intrigues that had taken place *previous* to his marriage. In the frenzy of her jealousy, Lady Byron sent these letters to the husband of the lady compromised, but he had the good sense to take no notice of them. Such a revolting proceeding on the part of Lady Byron requires no commentary," the moralizing paramour scoffs dismissively: "it cannot be justified."

But indeed it *does* require commentary. And in Hartford, seething, Harriet waited impatiently for all those English friends of the late, saintly Lady Byron to leap to the dead woman's defense.

19

A VINDICATION

No one did. The Countess Guiccioli's outrageously hostile portrait of a friend whom Stowe had known and idolized for her kindness, her charity, her wisdom, her greatness of heart was allowed to stand unchallenged as the weeks passed. Moreover, an edition of the Italian woman's book about Byron soon appeared in America under the respectable imprint of Harper & Brothers, spreading a courtesan's lies ever more widely. That business, for instance, about prying open the poet's desk and ferreting out his love letters: absurd! That was a palpable falsehood, propagated by the notoriously unreliable Thomas Medwin with little evidence elsewhere to substantiate it: no mention of such behavior by Byron's friend Moore in his authorized biography that appeared six years after the poet's death, no reference to such rifling of letters by the many other loquacious confidants to whom the poet had expressed his reflections on his wife—and, most assuredly, absolutely nothing in the ethical bearing of Lady Byron herself to warrant the leveling of such a ridiculous charge against her.

Mrs. Stowe waited, and still not a word appeared from overseas in defense of her deceased friend. She would have to conduct the defense herself. Calvin opposed the idea, sure that it would create a furor; but Harriet was a Beecher and did as she thought right, regardless of consequences. Accordingly, in the late spring of 1869 she submitted an article on Lady Byron's marriage to the *Atlantic Monthly*. At the time Fields, editor of the periodical, was in Europe with his wife on yet another extended trip, part business, part pleasure, leaving his assistant editor, William Dean Howells, in charge at home. Howells would write to his superior that he had seen Mrs. Stowe's essay only after it was set in type; but he was in his early thirties and rather new at the job, so would have been unlikely to raise objections anyway to anything that the most popular and successful author in America chose to submit. In fact, Howells felt that this particular article deserved to be read. "The world needed to know," he wrote at the time to his father, in Ohio, "just how base, filthy and mean Byron was, in order that all glamor should be forever removed from his literature, and the taint of it should be communicated only to those who love sensual things, and no more pure young souls should suffer from him through their sympathy with the supposed generous and noble traits in his character."

The Guiccioli woman had referred to Lady Byron's allowing advisers to dupe her, shortly before the notorious separation, into thinking "that her husband committed grave faults, though in reality they were but slight or even imaginary ones." Byron's marital faults *slight? Imaginary?* These many years later, his widow's friend in Hartford knew better, as did a few others in England—although apparently only she would step forth to tell the truth. And wasn't it her duty to do so? Thus through nineteen double-column pages in the *Atlantic Monthly* of September 1869 appeared the fulfillment of that duty: Harriet Beecher Stowe's "The True Story of Lady Byron's Life."

The magazine's September issue was an impressive one, as assistant editor Howells proudly informed James Fields during his absence overseas, "though Mrs. Stowe's sensation of course benumbs the public to everything else in it." Her essay starts with a summary of Countess Guiccioli's charges: that Lord Byron, a hero possessed (in Stowe's ironic paraphrase) of "every natural charm, gift, and grace," was guilty of only one misstep, by making an unsuitable marriage that wrecked his life. Through ill luck, Byron had allied himself to a "narrow-minded, cold-hearted precisian, without sufficient intellect to comprehend his genius, or heart to feel for his temptations." This was, to be sure, "one of those mere worldly marriages common in high life"; and Lady Byron, finding that she could not reduce her husband "to the mathematical proprieties and conventional rules of her own mode of life, suddenly, and without warning, abandoned him in the most cruel and inexplicable manner." Worse, according to the countess's charge as Stowe relates it, the wife left her husband "in apparent affection and good-humor, wrote him a playful, confiding letter upon the way" to her family's country estate, "but, after reaching her mother's house, suddenly, and without explanation, announced to him that she would never see him again." Of course this behavior brought down on the abandoned spouse's head all manner of vilifying conjectures, as society set about gossiping: what had the rakish celebrity poet done to make his young wife flee from him thus?

Indeed, the rupture bestirred international wonderment. "It is within the writer's recollection," Stowe interrupts her summary to speak in her own voice, "how, in the obscure mountain-town where she spent her early days, Lord Byron's separation from his wife was, for a season, the all-engrossing topic"—that far away, in the far-off village of Litchfield, Connecticut. "She remembers hearing her father recount at the breakfast-table the facts as they were given in the public papers, together with his own suppositions and theories of the causes." For Lady Byron did not return to her husband, and her "sudden abandonment drew down upon him a perfect storm of scandalous stories, which his wife never contradicted." In fact, in the Countess Guiccioli's telling, "she never in any way or shape stated what the exact reasons for her departure had been, and thus silently gave scope to all the malice of thousands of enemies. The sensitive victim"—Byron himself—"was actually driven from England, his home broken up, and he doomed to be a lonely wanderer on foreign shores."

What followed was a period of which the world had been informed in all too glaring detail—through the poet's letters at the time, through accounts of both friends and foes, and through the biography written soon after his death by Thomas Moore—of shameless, dissolute behavior, now to be understood as Byron's wallowing in depravity in the wake of his wife's cruel forsaking of him, their infant daughter in her arms. In Venice the poet plunged "into every kind of vice and excess, pleading his shattered domestic joys, and his wife's obdurate heart, as the apology and the impelling cause." Until—and the story finally turns toward its happy ending—there in Italy, "under bluer skies, and among a gentler people, with more tolerant modes of judgment," the tortured Byron achieves peace. "A lovely young Italian countess falls in love with him, and, breaking her family ties for his sake, devotes herself to

him; and, in blissful retirement with her, he finds at last that domestic life for which he was so fitted." Soothed and calm, he writes
Don Juan (a work, in Stowe's opinion, full of indecency and vulgar
tastelessness, "which the world is at this late hour informed was a
poem with a high moral purpose"). Moreover, in love's elevating
influences Byron resolves to devote his life to noble public ends.
With that, and on the point of becoming the savior of Greece, he
dies an untimely death at Missolonghi, in the spring of 1824.

But these forty-five years later, the time has come to set the
record straight. "All the actors in the scene," Stowe notes, "have
disappeared from the stage of mortal existence, and passed, let us
have faith to hope, into a world where they would desire to expiate
their faults by a late publication of the truth." Here, then, is the
truth. As the brooding Byronic hero in various poetic guises invariably harbors a "secret woe," so the creator of those enormously
popular narratives—*The Corsair* and *Lara* and the others—had been
shielding his own secret, a "deadly secret that lay cold at the bot-
tom of his heart." For young Byron had engaged in a "secret adulterous intrigue with a blood relation, so near in consanguinity, that
discovery must have been utter ruin, and expulsion from civilized
society." Stowe names no names, but few of her readers, versed in
details of both the public and the titillating private life of England's
great poet-luminary, would have felt taxed in identifying Byron's
partner in shame: it could only have been Mrs. Leigh, his father's
daughter by a previous marriage, Byron's sole sibling, his half sister, Augusta.

As for the poet's wife—that "cold, correct, narrow-minded
woman," that "moral Clytemnestra"—hers had hardly been the
villainous role in which Byron's mistress would later cast her. See
the situation, rather, from Lady Byron's point of view. At nineteen
and much sought after, she (like the rest of England) had fallen in
love with the dashing young author of *Childe Harold's Pilgrimage*;
yet when the gifted, handsome Byron first proposed to her, she selflessly turned him down. After that rejection, he entered into incestuous relations with his half sister, who was a wife and the
mother of four children. Fearful of discovery, Byron, on the advice
of friends, later set about regularizing his behavior, impulsively
proposing marriage, in writing, to two eligible women at the same
time. One declined his offer. The other, the innocent heiress Miss

Milbanke, moved by love on this second occasion and to the poet's confusion, accepted.

But the marriage, which was entered into in January 1815, was a disaster. Proper enough in public, and despite intervals when even in private he behaved toward his wife with consideration and affection, Byron too often conducted himself atrociously, and from the very start. As Stowe explains of Lady Byron's marriage: "There were summer hours in her stormy life, the memory of which never left her, when Byron was as gentle and tender as he was beautiful; when he seemed to be possessed by a good angel." But as early as the wedding afternoon and during the horrid honeymoon that followed, the sullen groom repeatedly made clear how much he despised the married state and how misguided his bride had been to marry with the thought of reforming him. Soon he set out to corrupt her, seeking through sophistry to destroy her faith and insisting that the only way Lady Byron could enjoy peaceful days was to give him the latitude that he was more than willing to allow her, so that the resulting "good-humored marriage" might serve each by cloaking the other's infidelities. To that his lady replied simply: "I am too truly your friend to do this."

In time there came "an hour of revelation,—an hour when, in a manner which left no kind of room for doubt, Lady Byron saw the full depth of the abyss of infamy which her marriage was expected to cover." Her condition was delicate; the couple's only child, a daughter, would be born before the year's end. During that sensitive period her husband, exasperated, often drunk, treated her with a cruelty so brutal that she was driven to suspect insanity as the only explanation. On January 6, 1816, not long after her confinement, Lord Byron instructed his wife in writing that "as soon as she was able to travel she must go,—that he could not and would not longer have her about him." On January 16, with her infant, she set out from London for her parents' home at Kirkby Mallory and from there sought knowledgeable counsel with advisers; they forbade her to have anything further to do with the poet. Soon afterward, Byron left England to pursue on the continent the course of shame that Thomas Moore's biography describes. Lady Byron, for her part, through the rest of her life would rear her and the poet's daughter to become an estimable lady, would provide for the troubled child born of Byron's illicit connection with his sister, would even befriend that grateful sister to spare her name and reputation, and would devote time and fortune all the while to numberless works of charity.

Of course Lady Byron kept silent throughout those years; to disclose the appalling truth about her husband would have injured many innocent people. But now the time had come to speak for one no longer able to speak for herself. Harriet did, and the reaction to her article in the *Atlantic* was swift and cataclysmic, far beyond anything the author had expected.

Nobody, in fact, was prepared for such a nearly universal cry of outrage. As early as August 21, 1869, with the September issue scarcely distributed, Fields's assistant reported: "So far her story has been received with howls of rejection from almost every side where a critical dog is kept." Fifteen thousand readers—more than a third of the total—canceled their subscriptions to the *Atlantic*; and Stowe's friend Oliver Wendell Holmes, who had seen the essay in proof, was writing to a correspondent in England before the end of September: "About the Byron article I confess that, great as I expected the excitement to be, it far exceeded anything I had anticipated. . . . The general opinion," Holmes summarized, "was strongly adverse to the action of Mrs. Stowe," though the poor woman had only done "what she thought an act of supreme justice." For that she was being abused as a ghoul digging up corpses, as a hyena feasting on dead flesh.

Harriet made a point of not reading the infuriated reception to her article. But from others she learned the gist of the public's objections: that what she said about Byron wasn't true; that she had no evidence to support her slander; that his aging, infirm widow had doubtless been of unsound mind when she spoke, or that Lady Byron had hallucinated or imagined the whole thing; that she would never have befriended her husband's sister or agreed to name their daughter Augusta Ada after that sister if what Stowe wrote were fact; that it was a scurvy thing to write in any case, and poorly written, too, about a great poet long dead and his late sister, who could no longer defend themselves against charges affecting Mrs. Leigh's living children and Lady Byron's own living, humiliated grandchildren.

Aware of the outcry, Harriet did what she had done once before, after the clamor that followed upon publication of *Uncle Tom's*

Cabin. Then, uncowed, she had leaped to her own defense by re-searching and writing her *Key to Uncle Tom's Cabin.* Now, again, she set about preparing a lengthy defense of her essay on Byron, which had in any case been written less to besmirch the poet than to exculpate his wife. As the reaction in the South against *Uncle Tom's Cabin* had astonished her (the novel, we recall, condemns not southerners but the inhuman system under which they were forced to live), so here she was surprised by a tumult even more rancorous in postbellum 1869 than in the embittered antebellum America of 1852. Once again Harriet Beecher Stowe was at the center of thunderous controversy; and again she was undeterred, publishing in 1870, under Fields's prestigious imprint, *Lady Byron Vindicated: A History of the Byron Controversy from Its Beginning in 1816 to the Present Time.*

Her book-length vindication is in three parts. Part One reca-pitulates the facts of the case; Part Two presents Lady Byron as Stowe knew her, recounting their meetings and furnishing speci-mens of their correspondence; Part Three provides as appendixes appropriate documentation, including the essay in the *Atlantic* that had prompted this recent interval "of stormy discussion and of much invective." And at the start Mrs. Stowe concedes that she has no reason to congratulate herself on her essay as a literary effort. But are "the cries of the oppressed," she wonders, "the gasps of the dying, the last prayers of mothers,—are *any* words wrung like drops of blood from the human heart to be judged as literary efforts?" What purpose would rhetoric have served? And what interest, she asks her readers, "have you or I, my brother and my sister, in this short life of ours, to utter anything but the truth?" Truth, not lit-erary showmanship, is what her essay was about. A flagrant at-tack on her friend's memory had appeared in Britain's influential *Blackwood's* magazine of July 1869, "branding Lady Byron as the vilest of criminals"—frigid, unfeeling, forsaker of her husband, destroyer of his happiness—"and recommending the Guiccioli book to a Christian public as interesting from the very fact that it was the avowed production of Lord Byron's mistress. No efficient pro-test was made against the outrage in England, and Littell's Living Age"—here in the United States—"reprinted the Blackwood article, and the Harpers, the largest publishing house in America, perhaps in the world, re-published the book." Those were the provocations that had moved Stowe to speak, and not at all gratuitously: she wrote "in defence of a beloved, revered friend, whose memory stood forth in the eyes of the civilized world charged with most repulsive crimes, of which I *certainly* knew her innocent."

She knew because Lady Byron had told her all about the marriage. Readers were invited to form their own impression of who that lady was: her founding of training schools for the poor, her succoring of the outcast and helpless, her befriending of former slaves including William and Ellen Craft of Boston, her reclaiming of fallen women, her tireless generosities. According to Harriet Martineau, Lady Byron was known to have done more good than anybody else in England. For that matter, Stowe judged Byron's widow the most remarkable Englishwoman of the century. Read these letters to her American friend, from soon after their meeting in 1853 through the seven reunions that followed right up to 1860, the year of Lady Byron's death. They show no sign of mental impairment. Lady Byron's mind to the last was sharp and comprehensive; she could speak with equal penetration on literature, philosophy, mathematics, religion, current affairs—and penetratingly, too, on her own marriage.

Lady Byron did *not* abandon her husband. *He* dismissed *her,* driving her out of 13 Piccadilly Terrace, London, in the dead of winter.

Stowe recapitulates. "At what precise time the idea of an improper connection between her husband and his sister was forced upon her, she did not say; but she told me *how* it was done. She said that one night, in her presence, he treated his sister with a liberty which both shocked and astonished her. Seeing her amazement and alarm, he came up to her, and said, in a sneering tone, 'I suppose you perceive *you* are not wanted here. Go to your own room, and leave us alone. We can amuse ourselves better without you.'" Yet even so, after her brother's marriage Augusta, to her credit, had refused to permit the resumption of their premarital relations; and her refusal put the poet in a surly mood. Later, before departing for her parents' home, Lady Byron consulted a doctor about Byron's mental state. Dr. Baillie recommended that she do nothing to aggravate the man—write him "a few lines in the usual form without any notice of serious subjects"; hence the famous playful letter—otherwise inexplicable—to her "Dearest Duck" sent back from Kirkby Mallory.

Nor was Byron run out of England; he chose of his own accord to go into exile. On the continent, the poet was free to propagate his version of events with a wit and verve that carried the distortion around the world, most notably by means of the mischievously riotous portrait in *Don Juan* of Donna Inez—obviously the mathematically inclined Lady Byron, "a walking calculation," "perfect past all parallel," although:

> 'Tis pity learned virgins ever wed
> With persons of no sort of education,
> Or gentlemen, who, though well-born and bred,
> Grow tired of scientific conversation:
> I don't choose to say much upon this head,
> I'm a plain man, and in a single station,
> But—Oh! ye lords of ladies intellectual,
> Inform us truly, have they not henpeck'd you all?
>
> Don Jóse and his lady quarrelled—*why*,
> Not any of the many could divine,
> Though several thousand people chose to try.
> 'Twas surely no concern of theirs nor mine. . . .

And this husband's published version of the marital breakup, of a wife without imagination, warmth, or compassion, would remain uncontradicted; for if Lady Byron had spoken, the first casualty would have been Augusta, Byron's beloved sister, she and her family instantly, utterly ruined. As it was, "Mrs. Leigh never lost position. Lady Byron never so varied in her manner toward her" as to awaken the least confirmation of malicious suspicion or gossip.

All this was the simple truth. Mrs. Stowe had learned it in a confidential interview conducted at Lady Byron's request, west of London at Ham Common, where the widow was living in the fall of 1856, during Stowe's visit to England to secure a copyright for *Dred.* Throughout an entire November afternoon Lady Byron and her American friend had conferred in private. Byron's widow was unwell; her doctors held out scant hope for her remaining long among the living (though she was to survive another four years). She had a secret; should she take it with her to the grave? That was the question put to Mrs. Stowe, as someone of sensibility and understanding who might judge matters unentangled, objectively, as from a distance. Lady Byron sought Mrs. Stowe's advice, and the advice proffered was to say nothing. Entrust the shocking story to a few close friends who might in future years, when all the principals had passed away, choose whether to reveal what was hidden or let it slide into oblivion.

But these recent defamations from La Guiccioli demanded a response. "I have been blamed for speaking on this subject without consulting Lady Byron's friends, trustees, and family," Stowe now wrote. "More than ten years had elapsed since I had had any intercourse with England, and I knew none of them." Indeed, she had been surprised to learn from solicitors' letters after the appearance of her essay in the *Atlantic* that there were trustees at all, "who held in their hands all Lady Byron's carefully-prepared proofs and documents, by which this falsehood might immediately have been refuted."

The trustees didn't refute it, because what Stowe charged was no falsehood. The solicitors "try to cast discredit on me for speaking; but they do not say that I have spoken falsely, or that the story is not true." Lady Byron's words still rang in her dear friend's ears: "Mrs. Stowe, he was guilty of incest with his sister!" And wasn't testimony to that effect now owed to truth and justice? "Had the world no right to true history? Had she who possessed the truth"— off here in Hartford after so many years—"no responsibility to the world? Was not a final silence a confirmation of a lie with all its consequences?"

woman with no manner of evidence to sustain or excuse it, but the incoherent recollection of an unsupported statement made a dozen years ago, by a woman broken in health and morbid in mind, and who, being now herself in the grave, cannot sustain, or qualify, or withdraw her accusation."

Mrs. Stowe's writing about Byron contained, in the view of the *New York Herald*, "the most infamous and malignant libels in the history of the living or the dead." The *New York World* could find "no good reason why she, or any body else, should be permitted to needlessly poison the public mind, and deprave the public morals" with such a "deluge of nastiness." In Scotland, the Reverend George Gilfillan referred to Stowe as a "female executioner to a man whom, with all his faults, I pronounce ineffably greater and nobler than her small, sanctimonious, but viperous, Yankee self." Back home, a certain Emerson Bennett took to public print to remind readers that, at Byron's death forty-five years earlier, it was presumed "that every lying scandal which human ingenuity could invent, had been heaped upon his devoted head; till at last, being dead, even the harpies were disposed to let him rest in peace; but it seems it was reserved for a far-off woman, in a country that he loved—a woman then in tender years—a woman he had never wronged in deed or thought—to voluntarily come forward, with a mercilessness almost unparalleled," in order to "violate the sanctity of the tomb, and blacken the unprotected dust of himself and his beloved sister with an accusation shocking to all the finer and nobler feelings of humanity." And from below the Mason-Dixon Line, the *Charleston Daily Courier* was led to inquire: "Where are Mrs. Harriet Beecher Stowe's friends? By *Uncle Tom's Cabin* she earned the hostility of the South, and now in equal proportion is receiving the disapprobation of the men and women of the North." According to the *Courier*, the author's name would be associated from this time forward with the "perpetration of as heinous a piece of bawdy as the literature of licentiousness in this country presents."

A few did defend the author. Among them, George William Curtis, editor of *Harper's* magazine, made clear to his numerous readers that "Lady Byron's assertion is not answered by accusing her of unspeakable malice, and by denouncing her story as an outrage upon the dead in their graves." That influential observer saw no reason to doubt that Mrs. Stowe reported what Byron's widow honestly believed; "nor until we have some evidence of the decay of her faculties have we any right to question upon that ground the truth of Lady Byron's story." Out in western New York, meanwhile, the *Buffalo Express* was wondering, in an unsigned editorial, why a charge of incest should be dismissed out of hand. Do we suppose such a foul crime cannot be committed? "But it has been committed, time and again. History furnishes examples enough, to say nothing of the current experience of society, and it is quite as possible that Byron may have added one to the horrid examples of unnatural vice in history as it is undoubted that other men of noted name and distinguished position did so before him." A combination of poetical imagination and subtle intellect with gross sensuality is "no uncommon thing," according to this commentator, who could sooner believe that "Lord Byron was in one act of his vicious life a licentious beast, than we can believe that Lady Byron either malignantly lied, or recklessly, at the end of forty years' concealment, permitted the revelation of so monstrous a thing without knowing it to be true." And if it was true, Mrs. Stowe, under the circumstances, was duty-bound to write what she did, although she might have obliged us by expressing herself more artfully.

The editor of that Buffalo newspaper at the time was Mark Twain, who had taken on the responsibility ten days earlier. And young William Dean Howells, we recall, was yet another who supported Mrs. Stowe, if privately. Howells of the *Atlantic* had written to his father that the world ought to know "just how base, filthy and mean Byron was, in order that all glamor should be forever removed from his literature," thus sparing pliable youth from being subjected to such baneful verbal influences.

Like Howells, Mrs. Stowe was concerned about Byron's grip on the hearts of the young, and she had composed her "True Story" and her *Lady Byron Vindicated* in part to loosen that grip. The situation is filled with ironies. About *Don Juan,* for instance, the poet himself had insisted "that it is the most moral of poems—but if people won't discover the moral that is their fault, not mine." Yet Mrs. Stowe could find no trace of a moral in its rollicking pages; to her, Byron's epic was simply an outrage. Like many others of her time she took offense at flippancies in the narrative, at its voluptuousness, at its irreverence, at precisely the poet's *refusal* to moralize—the very traits that recommend to our own, different literary appetites such a well-spiced, savory, nourishing masterpiece. How tastes do shift about! *Don Juan,* that coruscating product of laxer social values, gratified the most discriminating of its earliest liberal readers even as it displeased an increasingly conservative Georgian England, as it later shocked the sensibilities of straitlaced Victorians, and as it now delights our own era, far beyond the soberer posturings of *Childe Harold's Pilgrimage,* which with the love lyrics carried Byron's fame through much of the nineteenth century.

But as for that, his initial fame was already in decline when Stowe leveled her sensational accusations, in 1869 and 1870. Partly, that good Christian wrote to demolish the few pillars left standing among the ruins of Lord Byron's former glory, in hopes that the young might forsake the Englishman's literary shrine altogether. And thus another irony: one effect of Stowe's *Atlantic* article and of *Lady Byron Vindicated* was to reawaken interest in a poet recently neglected; so that from then on editions of Byron's verse multiplied, and his reputation rose in esteem even as Harriet Beecher Stowe's plummeted. The Hartford author never recovered from the Byron outcry. In 1869 the most famous, most influential, best-selling writer in America—and America's most celebrated woman—Stowe a year later would tumble from her exalted position after the publication of *The Innocents Abroad* caused the literary reputation of that editor out in Buffalo abruptly to soar. Thereafter for two decades the westerner Mark Twain was the nation's favorite author, while only diehard fans persisted in taking the New Englander Stowe seriously as a major literary figure.

It is true that part of Stowe's eclipse arose from non-Byronic agencies: for example, from a postbellum literary establishment bent, consciously or unconsciously, on promoting classic American male authors, bellelettrist reviewers in male-dominated periodicals setting about to define our literary canon in ways that excluded such artless, popular female practitioners—however meritorious in other respects—as Harriet Beecher Stowe. And all the while in Reconstruction America the growing agitation for women's rights was bestirring a new, patriarchal impatience with authoresses generally. But Stowe meanwhile went on writing—four more novels as well as much else during the 1870s—and making money, and getting herself talked about, even as increasingly her work was belittled or, worse, ignored.

"As to 'Don Juan,'" Byron had written long before to a friend in England—to one of the poet's many friends—in a characteristically exuberant tone that helps account for the lasting strength of those friendships, as it conveys his lordship's outrageous charm across the chasm separating his decades from ours: "As to 'Don Juan'— confess—confess—you dog—and be candid—that it is the sublime of *that there* sort of writing—it may be bawdy—but is it not good English?—it may be profligate—but is it not *life*, is it not *the thing*?—Could any man have written it—who has not lived in the world?—and tooled in a post-chaise? in a hackney coach? in a Gondola? against a wall? in a court carriage? in a vis à vis?—on a table?—and under it?"

The image of young Byron at his various Georgian toolings belongs to a realm far removed from that of Harriet Beecher Stowe of Mandarin, Florida, and Hartford, Connecticut, who as an American institution in her late fifties, by 1870, had grown increasingly conformist. And the ironies continue. No serious scholar of Byron now questions the truth of what Mrs. Stowe revealed to a shocked and generally disbelieving Victorian public about the poet's incestuous relations with his half sister. On the contrary, in its candor modern scholarship elaborates transgressions that would have further appalled Stowe's innocent contemporaries. Among the melting love lyrics of this Regency poet are some discreetly addressed to boys and young men, and the hundreds of Venetian copulations about which Byron wrote home are now understood to include males as well as females, incriminating personal pronouns suppressed in the telling. Byron's very taste in women inclined to the boyish: Stowe describes Lady Byron's physical appearance as almost infantine; La Guiccioli was petite; and Lady Caroline Lamb could famously disguise herself as a male page to gain entrance into the poet's chambers. That Byron was bisexual is no longer disputed; modern scholarship has further suggested that his offenses against his wife pertained as much to sodomy as to incest—at a time when sodomy was a felony in an England intensely homophobic: six unfortunates were put in the pillory in 1811, in the decade of Lord and Lady Byron's marriage and scandalous separation, locked there in Haymarket where Dickens later jokingly thought Mrs. Stowe herself should be displayed. Thus had the true causes that led to the breakup of his marriage become public, Byron would have been disgraced for a certainty, might—like Wilde at the end of the century—have found himself in prison, might have found himself publicly exhibited, offal-besmeared.

Accordingly, in the spring of 1816, the poet hurried into exile, bound, he thought, for Greece and like places in the eastern Mediterranean, where during earlier travels Childe Harold's creator had met with an indulgence of irregular sexual preferences among obliging catamites. Byron lingered at Geneva, reached Venice, and there, in 1819, was introduced to the Countess Guiccioli. Yet further ironies. After the poet's death in 1824, Teresa Guiccioli remarried her elderly husband, whom she had divorced; later still, she took two men successively as lovers before finally, in 1847, marrying the marquis de Boissy. All the while she maintained that her relations with the great English poet had been platonic, a union of souls. Yet her own letters and those of Byron's give the lie to that. Their letters tell of a relationship filled with passion; and, moreover, her *Vie de Lord Byron en Italie,* which remained in manuscript from the countess's death in 1873 until our own times, discloses—in the nearly 700 pages of its English translation—a woman of great attractiveness. Mrs. Stowe, of course, would never have thought so. Drawing on what evidence she had at hand, Stowe didn't like anything about Byron's mistress—detested her, in fact, as (while continuing—this fellow foe of slavery—to admire the poet as a fighter for freedom) she loathed the man Byron as well, for his cruelty to his wife and for his making light, as throughout *Don Juan* he appeared to make light, of such matters as educated females, adultery, cannibalism, drunkenness, and canting religion.

To Stowe, that last was no more a laughing matter than were the others. Her own novels might deplore the apathies and hypocrisies of a Protestant church that had long and fatefully tolerated slavery's horrors; but Byron's glamorization of godlessness and carousing was too much to be endured. Always close by, poor Fred—Captain Stowe, Grand Army of the Republic—was staggering about, Harriet's son returned now from a Mediterranean cruise with his father and not a whit improved. "I cannot live on shore," Fred the drunkard—the much loved son—concluded. "I am willing to serve seven ten or twenty years or even the rest of my life in the navy rather than to live on shore subject to the continual torment and fear of falling into a sin I hate and despise but before which I seem to be powerless." And impressionable young people all this while are to be entertaining themselves with the debaucheries in Lord Byron's seductive poems?

Stowe professed never to have regretted writing "The True Story of Lady Byron's Life" or *Lady Byron Vindicated*. We in our turn must admire her courage, her selflessness, her sincerity, and her loyalty to a friend as she entered into and fought her way through the Byron controversy. At the time she explained to Annie Fields how she was dealing with the uproar that those productions had set off around the English-speaking world. That very year Stowe's daughter Georgiana Stowe Allen gave birth to a son, and "I am doing just what you say," the young mother's mother wrote to her friend, "being first lady-in-waiting to his new majesty . . . getting to be an old fool of a grandma, and to think there is no bliss under heaven to compare with a baby."

But during this summer, in Florida in June of 1870, Georgie's troubled brother, Harriet and Calvin's son, signed on board a sailing vessel bound via Cape Horn for Chile and California. The vessel got under way. Once it had arrived at its destination, Fred Stowe went ashore in San Francisco with shipboard friends. The group checked into a rooming house, where Fred soon eluded the others. That was as much as could be learned of young Stowe's latest movements. On the far side of the continent the thirty-year-old disappeared and was never heard from again.

HENRY

"I have had such a delightful visit with Henry this summer such warm full confiding outpouring of soul to soul—I love him so much—you dont know how much—it really makes me cry to think of it— Oh this love—if we only could have enough of it—."

Harriet Beecher Stowe to Calvin,
of Henry Ward Beecher, 1844

HENRY WARD BEECHER, C. 1840
engraved portrait by A. H. Ritchie and printed by A. H. Dunnell,
Harriet Beecher Stowe Center, Hartford, Connecticut.

21

THE BEECHERS

*T*hey constitute one of America's great families, but unlike other such families—the Rockefellers, say, or the Kennedys—these two generations of Beechers built their achievements without the aid of a patriarch's fortune from oil or whiskey or anything else material. Lyman Beecher remained poor all his life. So for that matter did John Adams—patriarch of yet a fourth great American family—remain a man of modest means. The influence of the Adamses, the Rockefellers, the Tafts, the Kennedys, the Bushes, and the Beechers has been widespread, but the children of only two of those celebrated dynasties came into adulthood making their way without wealth, and the Beecher children who did stumble into money let much of it slip through their fingers. Moreover, unlike the proud, fiscally unobtrusive Adamses—presidents, ambassadors, statesmen—or the various later, more opulent dynasties of the twentieth century, the Beechers acquired their fame from sources other than politics. Rather, they were for the most part, with a quite astonishing consistency, moralists. The Beechers told other people how to lead their lives, and in doing so the family stirred up resentment. Thus when Harriet Beecher Stowe spoke out indignantly in 1869 and 1870 on behalf of the late widow of the poet Lord Byron, numbers of her fellow citizens gloated to hear the outcry that erupted.

The South, of course, had long borne grievances against Mrs. Beecher Stowe. Those had not abated as of March 10, 1872, when the *Daily Picayune* set a news item before its readers. "SORRY: Mrs. Harriet Beecher Stowe recently met with a very serious accident at her residence at Mandarin, Florida. She fell with violence, striking the base of her brain against the sharp edge of a bedstead, while her back fell squarely upon a bath tub. She was picked up insensible. Everything was done which could be suggested, and the following morning Mrs. Stowe was without much pain in the head, but suffered much in the back." Distress in the life of a figure so prominent merited comment, and the *Picayune* chose to respond with labored commiseration. The editors there in New Orleans felt tempted to urge the passage—after the recent passage of the Fifteenth Amendment to the Constitution, which gave African-Americans the vote in the wake of the Civil War—of a sixteenth, "prohibiting Southern bedsteads and bath tubs from being impertinently in the way, and knocking the author of 'Uncle Tom's Cabin' insensible." Clearly the soft-brained lady's head and back were tender parts. However, had the blow gone straight to the heart, "it would have been painless to her," damaging only the furniture, "as either tin or wood is apt to be damaged in an encounter with stone." But "this is too fast," the jocular editors persist: hold on. Mrs. Stowe has no heart. "She sold that viscus, the supposed organ of emotion in normal humanity, to a museum of natural history, department of petrifactions, when she polluted literature with a defamation of poor Byron's memory."

We hear nothing further of the author's mishap at Mandarin, but ill will was lurking out there against her, and against many of her siblings as well. Those Beechers seemed so sanctimoniously ubiquitous, so meddlesomely self-assured. Their moralizing arose from their father, of course, that successful evangelical committed to saving other people's souls. *"Go, therefore,"* Christ had commanded, *"and make disciples of all nations"*; tell them to change their ways, for *"the kingdom of heaven is at hand."* *"Let your light shine before men,"* Jesus directed his followers, *"so that they may see the good you do and give glory to your Father in heaven."* In pursuing those instructions, Lyman Beecher spent his adult life setting an example for his family. The inclination of his offspring to tell others how to behave came from their mother, too, from Roxana Beecher, Lyman's peerless first wife, who on her deathbed ardently prayed that "her children might be trained up for God." Accordingly, all the boys in the family—the seven who grew to maturity, out of eight—did, in fact, become ministers of the gospel.

The female children became ministers of a sort as well—three of the four girls who reached adulthood (a daughter of Roxana Foote and a son of Harriet Porter having died as infants). Only one of the adult children, Mary, kept out of the public eye, marrying a Hartford lawyer and living her long life without sermonizing, as a wife and mother, until her death in her mid-nineties, in 1900. But the other three female Beechers became celebrities. Nineteenth-century America heard much of Harriet, and of her sister Catharine, and of her half sister Isabella. Isabella Beecher Hooker came into her own as a public figure only in this present decade of the 1870s; but Catharine—eldest of the Beechers, whose fiancé had drowned off the coast of Ireland half a century earlier—had long been known for her authorship of such instructive texts as *An Essay on Slavery and Abolitionism, with Reference to the Duty of American Females;* and *The Moral Instructor, Containing Lessons on the Duties of Life;* and *Principles of Domestic Science, as Applied to the Duties and Pleasures of the Home.* Moreover, the spinster Catharine had built a reputation nationally as a leader in education, founding academies in Hartford, Cincinnati, and Milwaukee; and she enlarged that reputation not only through her many instructive writings on a wide variety of subjects (religion, women's rights, home decorating, cookery, gymnastics) but also through her devotion east and west—as far east as Maine, as far west as Wisconsin—to the cause of female education in particular. Catharine extolled the virtues of women as teachers of the young, a progressive idea that became commonplace during her lifetime. In the 1840s she founded the National Board of Popular Education to place women teachers from the East in western communities, toward that end recruiting females away from factories and farmwork into this new opportunity for their sex that was of broad, humanizing public benefit. Catharine Beecher was not always an easy person to get along with—imperious, abrasive, oversensitive—but she was an influential force who made her many views known and respected: with Emma Willard and Mary Lyon, one of the three great nineteenth-century American women reformers dedicated to educating a neglected half of the country's white population.

Catharine had, obligingly, been born in 1800, making her age calculable at once at any year during her lifetime. Her brothers, those seven ordained ministers, included among them similarly formidable personalities. Two, to be sure, pursued their calling in ways that would have hardly marked them out except that their last name was Beecher. William, the oldest boy, two years younger than Catharine and the only male not to go to college—only male Beechers went to college—never made much of himself, though like Catharine, Mary, and most of the others in the family, he lived a long life. (Mary, as noted, died at ninety-five; Catharine was seventy-eight at her death; William was eighty-seven; Edward ninety-two; Harriet eighty-five; Henry seventy-four; Charles eighty-five; Isabella eighty-five; Thomas seventy-six.) This second oldest, William, had married at thirty and had six children—the Beechers, in addition to being long-lived, were fruitful and multiplied: Lyman with thirteen children, William with his six, Edward with eleven, Mary with four, Harriet with seven, Henry Ward with nine, Charles with six. However, William seemed not as gifted as his siblings, struggling to win and hold the loyalty of the several congregations whose spiritual welfare he was charged successively with promoting, ending his affiliation with this church or that—in Newport, in Middletown, Connecticut, in Putnam, Ohio, in Batavia, New York, in Toledo, in Reading, Pennsylvania, in North Brookfield, Massachusetts—often under clouds variously shaped and of varying densities. Perpetually in debt, William retired from his barely satisfactory labors at his wife's death in 1870 and lived out the remainder of his days quietly with his daughters in Chicago.

James, the youngest, handsomest Beecher, one of the three children of Harriet Porter (with Isabella and Tom), was yet another reluctant and scarcely successful minister, coming to his calling late and finding alternatives to conventional pastoral duties once he arrived there. Suspended from Dartmouth, awarded a degree more out of deference to his father than for his own accomplishments, James went to sea and spent five years in the China trade before returning home to be ordained and take up misssionary work—again in the Far East, in seamen's bethels in Canton and Hong Kong. He had married an older widow who became an alcoholic; poor Annie died after causing her husband and other Beechers much grief, freeing James to marry more happily. Back home, he served with distinction in the Civil War, reaching the rank of brevet brigadier general. As devout as any Beecher, James was as selfless, devoting his late years to helping the poor and dispossessed. Finally he retreated to the backwoods of upper New York state, where, grown mentally troubled and paranoid, he suffered through four tormented years in various asylums before ending his days a suicide, in 1886.

The other Beecher who had died by his own hand, four decades earlier, in 1843—William's half brother George—had been considered one of the most gifted members of the family. We encountered him first as a young man singing on the roof of the stagecoach heading west with his family in Pennsylvania, and we recall his earlier anguish as an adolescent seeking spiritual rebirth in Litchfield. In his mid-thirties George in his garden in Chillicothe on a Friday morning before breakfast shattered his brain with a rifle blast—an accident, in the hopeful opinion of the coroner and the grieving family, although George Beecher's pronounced mood swings, his having spoken not long before of his imminent demise, and his aspirations for a perfection toward which he judged himself to have fallen far short all strongly encourage the different, bleaker supposition.

Of the remaining Beechers, Edward, like George, was brilliant; and like George and William, Edward was early on a foe of slavery, close friend of the martyred abolitionist Elijah Lovejoy. For some years this elder Beecher served as first president of (still thriving) Illinois College in Jacksonville, Illinois, the earliest of the family to make his way west, in 1830. We met him and his wife back east two decades later, amid the tumult of 1850, after he had returned to Boston as minister of the Salem Street Church. In Boston Edward offered his sister Harriet hospitality during her travels from Cincinnati to Brunswick; it was his wife who wrote to Harriet after her arrival in Maine urging her to compose something that would strike a blow against slavery. And we have encountered another brother, Charles, a year after Harriet's book against slavery was published and while that younger Beecher—like George, musical, like George, William, and Edward, a committed foe of the South's patriarchal institution—was accompanying his suddenly famous sister on her triumphal tour of England in 1853. Charles, like many of the other children, had been slow to come to his calling; and like his father, he would later be tried for heresy. Lyman had been exonerated; Charles was not, but his congregation stayed with him nevertheless, preferring their lovable pastor's heterodox ways to the rectitudes of orthodoxy. "So it seems you never saw my brother

Charlie before," Harriet found occasion to write a close friend during the 1870s. "He is just the loveliest sweetest most perfect old gentleman you ever saw"—Charles was sixty-two by then—"and I wish you could hear him play on the violin and sing. He has passed through bitter sorrows," including the drowning of two daughters in a boating accident, "and come out purified like gold."

In addition, there was Tom Beecher, like James a half brother of Harriet's, son of Lyman's second wife. No more than James or Charles did Tom aspire to the ministry, but a strong-willed father urged him into it, away from his inclination to work as an artisan with his very clever hands. Tom spent most of his life as an eccentric, much loved clergyman in Elmira, New York, where he ministered to the spiritual needs of Olivia Langdon, among others, and—with the Reverend Joseph Twichell of Hartford, Connecticut— performed the service at the wedding in 1870 of that well-to-do young lady and Mark Twain. The affluent community of Elmira paid their beloved minister generously, but Tom gave the bulk of his pay to charity. With special fervor he served life's wounded—such people as Fred Stowe and James Beecher—providing succor to the troubled, taking in prostitutes and fallen women, innovatively furnishing his church with a gymnasium and a dancing room, all the while further defying convention by sometimes preaching outdoors or in the local opera house. Tom was never able to share his father's buoyant optimism. "This is a gloomy world," Lyman's sixth son wrote in his early forties, in 1866, shortly after the Civil War and on the occasion of a nephew's dying young. "I give it up. I have no part in it. I wont plan—I wont hope—I wont fear. I will only endeavor to keep from its evil, bind up its gashes, shine into its darkness, prophesy heaven and wait—wait—singing songs in the night."

Those were the Beechers, then, close to each other though widely scattered; from early on staying in touch through circular letters; highly opinionated yet never (whatever their disagreements might be in private) quarreling publicly except on one occasion ahead, in this present decade of the 1870s. All the while they kept exerting their apostolic influence throughout the northern states from Brunswick in Maine to Brooklyn and Elmira in New York, from Hartford in Connecticut to Jacksonville in Illinois, from Cincinnati to Fort Wayne to Indianapolis and on to Milwaukee in Wisconsin. A quite remarkable family in truth: in the 1850s one

celebrated divine, the Reverend Leonard Bacon, divided his countrymen into saints, sinners, and Beechers; and around that time
Lyman Beecher was identified as the father of more brains than
anyone else in America. Of his children, five are even now included
among the notables in *American National Biography* (1999), a multi-
volume compendium of life stories of significant Americans from
as far back as the seventeenth century: "people from all eras," as
ANB's promotional material explains, "who have influenced and
shaped American history and culture."

Also to be included among the Beechers thus memorialized
this far along is Henry. Henry Ward Beecher was the seventh of
Lyman's progeny to live past infancy, next after Harriet and closest to her in age; those two, in fact, would become by far the most
famous of all the family, more famous than Isabella, Edward,
Catharine, or their illustrious father, the evangelist Lyman. Henry
had been born in Litchfield in June 1813, two years to the month
after Harriet, and he and his sister Hatty grew up hand in hand.
In such a large family, with a father busy with pastoral labors,
brothers off at college, older sisters preoccupied with teaching
and courting, and a stepmother tending the younger children,
"except here and there, I hardly came under the parental hand at
all"—so Henry remembered, looking back on his childhood. Middle
children, particularly in large, poor families, must take care of
themselves. "In those days," moreover, as Harriet recalled in the
1860s, "none of the attentions were paid to children that are now
usual. The community did not recognize them. There was no
child's literature; there were no children's books. The Sunday
school was yet an experiment, in a fluctuating, uncertain state of
trial. There were no children's days of presents and *fêtes*—no
Christmas or New Year's festivals." Henry's childhood in Litchfield
"was unmarked," writes Harriet, who shared it with him, "by the
possession of a single child's toy as a gift from any older person."
Nor were there any concessions to children at church, where they
were obliged to sit up straight through the unalleviated terrors of
unabridged Calvinist sermons; hence, as we remember, four-year-
old Calvin Stowe in nearby Natick could lie awake at night star-
ing horrified at swirling dark clouds arising from a Hell far below
his bed that replicated what he had heard the minister vividly
describing on Sundays at the meetinghouse.

Roxana Beecher, Henry's mother, had died when he was three, when he was still too young to attend her funeral. Of that day, "I can see his golden curls and little black frock," wrote Harriet much later, casting her mind back to 1816, "as he frolicked in the sun like a kitten, full of ignorant joy." And of that same sad September day in Litchfield she recollected "the mourning dresses, the tears of the older children, the walking to the burial-ground, and somebody's speaking at the grave. Then all was closed, and we little ones, to whom it was so confused, asked where she was gone and would she never come back." Soon after, the child Henry was discovered digging a hole in the yard in search of his mother, having learned that she was laid in the ground and had gone to Heaven. He would try to find her. And for the rest of his life Henry Ward Beecher idealized that paragon whom he could hardly remember, a human perfection that inspired him (so he insisted) day by day as the Virgin Mary inspires the devoutest Catholic.

Back then, very early in life a lad was assigned chores to perform: piling wood, weeding the garden, tending the cows and pigs. And in addition Henry acquired some rudimentary schooling, "this bashful, dazed-looking boy," as his sister recalled, pattering "barefoot to and from the little unpainted school-house, with a brown towel or a blue checked apron to hem during the intervals between his spelling and reading lessons." By no means was the seventh Beecher child an able scholar. "No very striking early results were the outcome of this teaching," Harriet remembered drily. "Henry Ward was not marked out by the prophecies of partial friends for any brilliant future." Indeed, unlike her, he seemed slow, his memory feeble (as it would remain through his lifetime), his speech impeded by shyness and what was variously termed an oversize palate or tonsils. Whatever the cause, "When Henry is sent to me with a message," the child's kindly Aunt Esther complained innocently, "I always have to make him say it three times. The first time I have no manner of an idea more than if he spoke Choctaw; the second, I catch now and then a word; by the third time I begin to understand."

"Nobody thought much of his future," Harriet tells us, "further than to see that he was safe and healthy, or even troubled themselves to inquire what might be going on in his life." The boy was entering his teens when the family moved from Litchfield to Boston. Henry's childhood had left him feeling neglected, unloved, and now, even more so on Boston's uncongenial urban streets instead of among the comforts of woods and meadows, what Harriet calls the "era of fermentation and development was upon him, and the melancholy that brooded over his childhood waxed more turbulent and formidable. He grew gloomy and moody, restless and irritable."

Such moods seemed hardly to anticipate the dazzling, ebullient success for which this young man was destined; but then Henry's adolescence may have been not unlike that of some of his brothers. All had had trials growing up, their father fretting over the welfare of each one of them. As for example in 1819, when Lyman had found himself writing to his eldest son: "my heart sinks within me at the thought that every one of my own dear children are without God in the world, and without Christ, and without hope. I have no child prepared to die; and however cheering their prospects for time may be, how can I but weep in secret places"—as a minister each one of whose children was apparently bound for Hell—"when I realize that their whole eternal existence is every moment liable to become an existence of unchangeable sinfulness and woe."

22

RELIGION

*W*hat distressed that devout parent concerned the matter of regeneration. *Except a man be born again, he cannot see the kingdom of God. Except a man be born of water and of the Spirit, he cannot enter into the kingdom of God.* And as of 1819, when William, the eldest boy, was seventeen, not one of the numerous Beecher children had been regenerated, converted, reborn.

Always in those times when death was ever near, the imperative question for such a family as the Beechers was this: are you ready to die? *In the midst of life we are in death*—death of the elderly, of people in their prime, of young men and women, of Roxana Beecher's infant daughter and Harriet Porter Beecher's infant son, and even more so then, with many more deaths among young people then than now. Nor did those deaths take place off in hospitals; they happened upstairs or downstairs in the back parlor converted into a sickroom: most people, old or young, died at home.

The professor of biblical literature whom one of the Beecher daughters was to marry years later in Cincinnati had been christened Calvin, after the great Protestant reformer of the sixteenth century. John Calvin (1509–1564) thought and wrote much about such critical matters as are contained in the Catholic "Four Last Things": death, judgment, Heaven, and Hell (here capitalized because they were places then, like Boston and Brunswick). A lawyer and logician, Calvin had pursued the logic that God as perfection must be all-knowing, and if all-knowing He cannot be surprised. As in an Einsteinian universe, so with Omniscience: past, present, and future are simultaneous. So an ominiscient God must know everyone's fate from the beginning, because He knows everything that has been or will come to pass. In other words, the working out of the divine plan has, logically, to be foreordained; otherwise, not knowing future outcomes, a continually surprised God would be imperfect. And by the same token, nothing you may do in the course of your brief life can alter your fate, which is already established irrevocably in God's knowledge.

Foreordination—predestination—constitutes a signal certainty of Calvinism. During the sixteenth century, religious persecutions had caused Protestants from other nations of Europe to flee to John Calvin's Geneva; and from that sanctuary those Protestants returned to their homelands when they could, thereby spreading the influence of Calvinist doctrines. One significant bearer of such an influence was the Puritan group from England that journeyed to the New World and landed at Massachusetts Bay in the early seventeenth century. There John Winthrop and his adherents, purified of the corruptions of Anglicanism and merging their religious thought with that of Dissenters in nearby Plymouth (who had arrived earlier aboard the *Mayflower,* bringing Calvinist influences from the Netherlands), established a theocracy out of which arose the Congregational churches that dominated New England in the century that followed. And in that later, eighteenth century, by far the greatest of the Calvinist theologians in America—and one of the greatest metaphysicians ever to draw breath in the New World—was Jonathan Edwards (1703–1758), minister for a quarter century in the western Massachusetts village of Northampton.

Like every good Calvinist clergyman, Edwards often preached to his congregation on the horrors of Hell, evoking as vividly as he could its eternal pain and everlasting burnings. "The devil thirsts for the blood of souls," he would preach before old and young, "and 'tis only because God restrains him that he don't lay hold of the soul before death; but as soon as ever the man is dead, God restrains him no more, but then these hell hounds fly upon their prey, these roaring lions dare then lay hold as it were with open mouths." Describing such ghastliness, the Reverend Mr. Edwards would speak without gesticulations, without raising his voice beyond what was needed to be heard; but his dreadful images—in such sermons as this of "The Warnings of Future Punishment Don't Seem Real to the Wicked"—so successfully evoked the fearsome literalness of agonies that lay ahead that his congregation in their pews would wail and faint and cry out in terror on hearing him.

Compassion forced the minister to speak thus. Edwards would have been inhumanly remiss not to warn his listeners about Hell, to awaken them fully and fearfully to their danger. Yet a paradox of Calvinism lies in the fact that those listeners, made conscious of Hell, could do nothing to save themselves from its horrors. For Calvinists read the Bible literally and as the supreme authority, and the Bible says, *"by grace are ye saved through faith; and that not of yourselves: it is the gift of God: Not of works."* The Bible says, *"Not by works of righteousness which we have done, but according to His mercy He saved us, by the washing of regeneration, and renewing of the Holy Ghost."* Nor will God's saving mercy extend to all. He will save from Hell only a few, the elect. The Bible says so, and God's natural world confirms as much: "of so vast and innumerable a multitude of blossoms that appear on a tree," Edwards observed, "so few come to ripe fruit"—just so, "how few are saved out of the mass of mankind." Moreover, no one but God knows which few among the mass of humanity will come to salvation, while the rest of us upon dying—the beautiful with the ugly, the good and the wicked—are falling into Hell as unfruitful blossoms fall multitudinously to the ground.

But why should an enlightened twenty-first century care about all that grim Calvinist eschatology, those antiquated agonizings over last things? Calvinism may retain some interest because of a shared humanity: generation after generation of Americans from the seventeenth century well into the nineteenth believed in those doctrines as the essentials of life, bewailing their own mortal odiousness while fervently seeking signs of membership among the blissful few elected for salvation. Calvinism might interest us as well because (as mentioned earlier) many of its adherents, setting out from New England to richer soils, spread their beliefs broadly over what would become a continental nation. Through successive waves of religious awakenings among settlers in the expanding West, itinerants preached the gospel according to Calvin or Edwards or—more inclusively—the Methodist Wesley at revivalist camp meetings in Tennessee and Indiana, up and down the Mississippi, farther westward into villages of the plains and on into the Oregon Territory. As one consequence, evangelical America survives sturdily into the twenty-first century. And we of that century who are considering these present pages should, in particular, have an interest in Calvinism because it formed the bedrock of Beecher family life, providing the theme of every day and evening, filling their frequent prayers, and molding their youth in Litchfield as a torment and an aspiration.

Harriet Beecher Stowe in adulthood thought long about her Calvinist ancestors who had forsaken Europe to found colonies nearby expressly to focus their lives on religious truths, on the *whence* and the *why* and the *whither* of humankind. In *Oldtown Folks* (1869)—the novel she struggled hardest to write, completing it shortly before the Byron controversy and judging it to be her masterpiece—she describes those New England ancestors, who had "set themselves grimly and determinately to study the severest problems of the unknowable and the insoluble. Just as resolutely as they made their farms by blasting rocks and clearing land of ledges of stone, and founded thrifty cities and thriving money-getting communities in places which one would think might more properly have been left to the white bears, so resolutely they pursued their investigations amid the grim mysteries of human existence, determined to see and touch and handle everything for themselves, and to get at the absolute truth if absolute truth could be got at." And the truth that those earlier New Englanders had settled on regarding our ultimate purpose acknowledged natural laws governing equally the fall of an apple and the planets in their orbits—governing us, too, in a harsh universe under a stern patriarchal God who in His omniscience was strictly just. Reasonably, sin angered such perfection; and thus for Adam's sin, as Genesis reveals it, a consequently depraved humanity justly suffers.

Yet that benevolent moral governor of the universe has been merciful too, sending his son to make the exacting atonement that justice demanded for those sins. *"For God sent not his Son into the world to condemn the world; but that the world through him might be saved."* Through that act God expressed His love for us, a love that in an eighteenth-century, Edwardsean deity took a preromantic form: a classical, unsentimental love, in those years before there were childhoods and gifts for children, when children were considered miniature adults and were set early to doing chores and made to sit upright through unmitigated Calvinist sermons on

Sundays. Romanticism would change all that, but in the preromantic 1700s, religious love was of a sober, uneffusive sort. In fact, God had created the universe precisely to extend the love that existed among Father, Son, and Holy Spirit; and "in heaven," as Edwards preached, "this fountain of love, this eternal three in one, is set open without any obstacle to hinder access to it." For humans then, in the hierarchical eighteenth century, love here on earth denoted adoring what God adores and despising what He despises: despising, that is, all that rebels against the divine.

There was rebellion enough against so stern a creed; wickedness was everywhere in the 1700s. The devout might agonize over the strictures of their faith, but many nominal believers were (as always) apathetic, and many other people in that rational century of Voltaire, Hume, and Thomas Paine rejected such harsh doctrines altogether. After Jonathan Edwards's death in 1758, political disruption distracted the attention of succeeding generations from religious to secular concerns; Lyman Beecher, Edwards's disciple, was born, in fact, in the year of gunfire at Concord and Bunker Hill, when political friction flared at last into the open warfare of the American Revolution. With that revolution won, near the century's end after the French Revolution had raged in its turn in Europe, Lyman at Yale College was coming under the influence of Jonathan Edwards's grandson, the Reverend Timothy Dwight— "Oh, how I loved him! I loved him as my own soul, and he loved me as a son." Thereafter, this young votary would dedicate his life to fighting foes of Calvinism as they grew in number in a new, expanding nation: not only freethinkers but also Deists, Unitarians, Methodists, Episcopalians, and immigrant Roman Catholics.

Thus the Reverend Dr. Beecher in upholding the old faith carried dogmas from a colonial, hierarchical past into an increasingly democratic, egalitarian new republic. But to self-reliant Americans Beecher found himself preaching a faith that had strayed from orthodox Calvinism, particularly in regard to the issue of free agency. *Was* everything predestined, so that there was little point in striving through life—and no blame could be justly attached to sins committed—or were people free to affect their own fate after all? Pioneers building a nation insisted that people were free, and the progressive Calvinist Beecher preached to them what they and he wanted to believe: that "men are free agents, in possession of such faculties, and placed in such circumstances, as render it practicable for them to do whatever God requires." Thus God gives us choice (even if He knows how we will choose). Nor does He tempt us with sins that it is predetermined we must commit. We *choose* to sin. On this liberalized point of free agency, Dr. Beecher would be tried for heresy in Ohio and would emerge exonerated, even as Old School Calvinists clung to the orthodox view that the elect found salvation through nothing at all that they did or avoided doing, but rather by God's inexplicable, irresistible grace alone.

Such theological controversies, then so full of warmth, may make for cold reading now. And the same doctrinal niceties—about free agency, imputation, inability, limited atonement, total depravity—that preoccupied his father and the other reverend Congregational and Presbyterian divines of the time held little to attract the interest of Beecher's son Henry, emerging from a mischievous childhood as Litchfield's former pastor was taking up a new charge at Boston's Hanover Street Church in the spring of 1826. "I was reared in the household of faith," Henry Ward Beecher recalled long after; "I knew the Catechism as it was taught; I was instructed in the Scriptures as they were expounded from the pulpit and read by men; and yet, till after I was twenty-one years old, I groped without the knowledge of God in Jesus Christ." The God the boy did learn about he disliked and feared: the wrathful deity of whom Jonathan Edwards had preached his most famous sermon, the angry Calvinist God whose hands hold us sinners by the slenderest of threads over the flames of Hell. And twelve-year-old Henry, angry himself, settled only skeptically into life in Boston, according to his sister's recollection, "gloomy and moody, restless and irritable," perhaps not unlike others in early adolescence before and since.

In that port city, with sailing vessels constantly loading and unloading cargo at docks nearby, Henry, entering his teens, hit upon a plan to go to sea. That was a standard recourse for restless young people in an America facing eastward in the 1820s, with the West scarcely known and our Far West still a part of Mexico. Henry would go to sea the way Melville did a decade later; the way Henry's half brother James went to sea to China in the early 1850s; the way Henry's unfortunate nephew Fred Stowe, at a still later time, after the Civil War, went to sea to escape his demons ashore.

Young Beecher's father learned of the plan.

"To sea!" Lyman is recorded as having said. "Of all things! Well, well! After all," that sage parent concluded, "why not? Of course you don't want to be a common sailor. You want to get into the Navy?"

"Yes, sir, that's what I want."

"But not merely as a common sailor, I suppose?"

"No, sir; I want to be a midshipman, and after that a commodore."

The Reverend Dr. Beecher raised no objection, but he did offer advice. To be a midshipman, the boy would need to study mathematics and navigation. Was that agreed?

"Yes, sir, I'm ready."

"Well, then, I will send you up to Amherst next week, to Mt. Pleasant, and then you'll begin your preparatory studies, and if you are well prepared I presume I can make interest to get you an appointment."

Accordingly, from 1828 to 1830, Henry Ward Beecher attended the Mount Pleasant Classical Institute in western Massachusetts, and in the course of those two happy years inland he lost interest in the sea. Not that he became a scholar, but the youth did prosper as a social being away from his formidable father and among people his own age. And he mastered lessons in elocution—drilling each day on gestures, posture, projection, articulation—until whatever oversize tonsils or palate he was born with no longer impeded his speech. From Mount Pleasant Henry went on to Amherst College, founded nine years earlier. His father had frankly doubted that this fourth son had the intellect to take on Yale, which Lyman and his son George had attended and where Henry's brilliant older brother Edward had been valedictorian. Anyway, Amherst was cheaper than Yale. And once there, if Henry Ward Beecher achieved no more than a middling academic record, he did show himself during four years to be energetic, responsible, and popular with his classmates. In particular, young Beecher flourished as a football kicker and in the school debating society, where soon he was recognized as the best orator in the class.

Among his many school friends was Ebenezer Bullard. Over a spring vacation early in their college years Henry and Ebenezer walked the fifty miles to the Bullard home in West Sutton, Massachusetts, due north of the Connecticut–Rhode Island line. The Bullards were a large, comfortable farm family that included

Ebenezer's sister Eunice, a year older than their house guest, who was seventeen. In the course of his visit she and this guest fell in love. Learning of it, Eunice's parents protested; they were both too young, mere babies. And indeed, seven years would pass before Henry Ward Beecher and Eunice Bullard finally married. Meanwhile, the young man must finish college and decide what he meant to do with the rest of his life.

He would be a missionary out west; he and Eunice talked about that. Some of the Beechers were moving to Cincinnati, riding in their great chartered stagecoach over the country roads of Pennsylvania in the autumn of 1832; and Henry, at Amherst, longed to go with them. In fact, he was ecstatic about the family's resettling in a region so full of possibilities. "Father's removal to THE WEST is my 'hearts desire,'" he had written his sister Harriet jubilantly that March, at the time of Lyman's exploratory trip to Walnut Hills. Thereafter the college student in love chafed at delays that kept him from joining his family resettled in a rising new land.

Two years later, in 1834, Harriet, as yet unmarried and just turned twenty-three, set forth from Cincinnati on the arduous journey back east, principally to attend her younger brother's commencement exercises at Amherst. Now, with college behind him, the graduate must make some decisions. He might well have become a journalist: displaying the Beecher facility with words, Henry Ward in the years ahead would amply demonstrate his sound editorial gifts. And even now, after graduating and making his way to Ohio, he edited and wrote for the *Cincinnati Journal,* a weekly newspaper hospitable to the Beecher family's prose. As editor, Henry involved himself in local issues concerning mob violence and racism along the Ohio River, standing staunchly on the side of law and order. In addition, this young Beecher, new on the scene, was studying at Lane Seminary, preparing for the missionary work that he and the faithful Eunice had agreed he should undertake.

But while he was pursuing his studies at Lane, a great change occurred in Henry's life. Alone one spring day walking alongside the campus in Walnut Hills, "working over a lesson that I was to hear recited," Henry Ward Beecher abruptly, finally experienced a regeneration of his own. This particular religious conversion would be spared the anguish that had accompanied such visitations in the lives of Henry's older brothers. There was nothing of Calvinist self-loathing about it, and no dark fear of God's wrath, though young Beecher's cloudless rebirth was hardly less life-changing for that. Reconsidering it in full maturity, he would doubt that anything else he had ever lived through could compare to that moment, which was the "brightest thing I shall look back upon" even after death, he thought, even when standing in Zion before the Most High. A "blessed morning of May," he described the occasion in generalized recollection, "when it pleased God to reveal to my wandering soul the idea that it was his nature to love a man in his sins for the sake of helping him out of them." Suddenly to this seminarian had come a revelation that our sins moved God not to anger but to sorrow, "that he was not furious with wrath toward the sinner, but pitied him—in short that he felt toward me as my mother felt toward me, to whose eyes my wrong-doing brought tears, who never pressed me so close to her as when I had done wrong, and who would fain with her yearning love lift me out of trouble." With that crucial realization, "I felt," writes Beecher, "that I had found a God. I shall never forget the feelings with which I walked forth that May morning." The very grass underfoot assumed an otherworldly texture, while birdsong in the trees overhead—"for I roamed in the woods"—sounded almost dissonant compared with "the sweet music of my thoughts; and there were no forms in the universe which seemed to me graceful enough to represent the Being, a conception of whose character had just dawned on my mind." At that intense instant, as he wrote in yet another account of it, "the clouds rose and the whole heaven was radiant, and I exclaimed 'I have found God.'" Upon so joyful a discovery, he recalls, "I went like one crazed up and down through the fields, half crying, half laughing, singing and praying and shouting like a good Methodist."

Our sins don't make God *angry;* they make Him *sorrowful.* That single, sudden insight would stay with Beecher from a May morning in Walnut Hills through the rest of his life, an ineffaceable corrective yielding a deity far removed from the glacial, ungenial God of Jonathan Edwards.

23

BROOKLYN

*T*he God of this Beecher would be of the New Testament more than the Old, realizable far more clearly through the Son than through the Father. "A dim and shadowy effluence rises from Christ," Henry Ward later explained, "and that I am taught to call the Father. A yet more tenuous and invisible film of thought arises, and that is the Holy Spirit. But neither are to me aught tangible, restful, accessible. They are to be revealed to my knowledge hereafter, but now only to my faith. But Christ stands my *manifest* God. All that I know is of him, and in him. I put my soul into his arms, as, when I was born, my father put me into my mother's arms. I draw all my life from him. I bear him in my thoughts hourly, as I humbly believe that he also bears me. For I do truly believe that we love each other!—I, a speck, a particle, a nothing, only a mere beginning of something that is gloriously yet to be when the warmth of God's bosom shall have been a summer for my growth."

Called in 1837 to be the pastor of Lawrenceburgh, twenty miles downriver from Cincinnati, Henry, afire with the conviction of his God as love, wrote to Eunice back in Massachusetts urging that they marry within weeks; then he set out east to plead his suit in person. He reached West Sutton the same day as his letter, swept all before him in his eagerness, and wed Eunice peremptorily, that very August, almost as soon as the two together could bake their wedding cake. The bride and groom were to enter their new lives with eighteen cents between them. Straightaway, Mr. and Mrs. Beecher established themselves in two rooms over a warehouse near the wharf of an Indiana village. The couple's furniture consisted of hand-me-downs from relatives in Walnut Hills. The minister's salary would be a paltry $150 annually, irregularly paid, supplemented by a less than munificent $250 from the American Home Missionary Society. This new Reverend Mr. Beecher of Lawrenceburgh, Indiana, would have to act as his own janitor, dusting, sweeping the floor, lugging in firewood, filling and lighting church lamps that he had been obliged to purchase himself, unlocking the front door for services and locking it in the evenings. "I did not ring the bell," he remembers, "because there was none to ring." Henry's flock in the wilderness numbered twenty people: nineteen women and a single negligible male.

It was the humblest of beginnings, yet the young cleric took up his pastoral responsibilities with vigor. Within two years a summons came from a somewhat larger, more established congregation in the state capital; and there, at the Second Presbyterian Church in Indianapolis, Henry Ward Beecher would remain eight years longer, a decade in all in Indiana. And in Indianapolis he began making a name for himself statewide.

The man seemed tireless, and interested in everything. He conducted weekly prayer meetings, supervised Sabbath school classes, and directed the choir (until his brother Charles arrived to help with that last). Henry preached two sermons each Sunday. He took part in revivals at his own church and at churches all over the state. Of course as a minister he performed weddings and funerals and made pastoral calls on the sick and the faltering; but in addition, in those lecture-happy times, he spoke in town frequently on secular subjects, being much in demand. He encouraged the Ladies' Sewing Society. Since childhood Henry had gardened, and here in Indianapolis his horticultural gifts fairly blossomed, his earth yielding prizewinning flowers and vegetables. Accordingly, the Reverend Mr. Beecher became editor of the bimonthly *Indiana Farmer and Gardener,* a demanding labor that he performed to that journal's great benefit. He joined civic organizations: the Indianapolis Benevolent Society, the Indiana Historical Society. He spoke before the Union Literary Society. He worked with others to set up a school for the deaf and dumb, and another for the blind. He was a member of a volunteer fire company. And like his father, this Beecher was ardently and evermore espousing a favorite cause—temperance.

His fame grew. His half sister Isabella, then in her early twenties, visited from Walnut Hills and gave her opinion promptly: "I think he is going somewhat in father's track and will perhaps one day come somewhere near his eminence." Others visiting the capital began making their way to the Second Presbyterian Church to hear this gifted young preacher who spoke so colorfully, so vividly, and so well. His *Seven Lectures to Young Men*—on various forms of immorality to be avoided (idleness, cynicism, gambling, strange women, popular amusements), each dramatically evoked—was published in 1843 and widely read and admired. The following summer Henry's sister Hatty, now Mrs. Stowe and the mother of five, came from the travails of Walnut Hills and had a grand time visiting her favorite brother: no children of her own underfoot, no boarders to attend to as at home, Henry and Eunice's cottage so quiet that she could blessedly hear the clock tick. The siblings played at mesmerism: "The first session," Harriet wrote to Calvin, "he succeeded in almost throwing me into convulsions—spasms & shocks of heat & prickly sensation ran all over me." And having returned to the familiar impoverishments of Walnut Hills—to her tireless children and to the lodgers whose rent had been needed to supplement the Stowes' dwindled income—Harriet remembered her stay in Indianapolis wistfully: "I have had such a delightful visit with Henry this summer," she wrote to her absent husband, Henry's good friend from their days together at Lane, "such warm full confiding outpouring of soul to soul—I love him so much—you dont know how much—it really makes me cry to think of it—Oh this love—if we only could have enough of it—."

Others even farther afield than Cincinnati were hearing—and feeling the attraction—of this phenomenon out west. Back east, across from Manhattan, a swelling population of Congregationalists in Brooklyn had needed a second church to accommodate so many. One founder of the new and well-funded Plymouth Church, traveling west, made a point of attending the preaching of the celebrated Lyman Beecher's son in Indianapolis. Soon a liberal offer arrived from Brooklyn Heights: a new Congregational church there was prepared to guarantee the Reverend Henry Ward Beecher a salary of up to $2,000 a year with assurances of further raises. However fulfilled Henry felt in Indianapolis, such princely remuneration as the Brooklynites were offering tempted him, even though President Beecher of Lane Seminary discouraged the move. In the West lay America's future, and the West was where the most good could be done. Brooklyn, persistent, wrote back in February of 1847: "You can probably do as much or more for the West by living here," a church spokesman argued; "you could *publish* much to benefit the world. Your influence would be felt *beyond* the Atlantic as well as *West* of the Alleghenys."

Moreover, Eunice's condition urged their leaving. Indiana had never agreed with Henry's wife, who had been sorely tried by the Beechers' earliest, impoverished years in the West, wrenched as she was from her family and friends in Massachusetts to set up housekeeping without help among uncouth folk amid frontier squalor. Worse, some of those countrypeople earned more money than their ill-paid minister, to whose proud wife they accordingly condescended as to a charity case. Eunice's health had suffered in such an atmosphere; one infant had died; another she had even half-hoped in her despondency would be stillborn. As for Indianapolis, she would never forgive the town for having extended an invitation to the Reverend Mr. Beecher and his family without warning of the malaria rampant in its environs. As recently as this past December of 1846, Eunice, malarial herself, had been writing that her sister-in-law Harriet would hardly recognize her now, only a couple of years after the prolonged summer visit from Walnut Hills, Henry's wife at thirty-four already turned into a "thin faced—grey headed—toothless old woman."

Meanwhile, letters kept arriving from Brooklyn, thirty in all. During the summer of 1847, in July, Henry Bowen, one of the founders of Plymouth Church, implored the Reverend Mr. Beecher: "the truth is we are *willing* to do more for you than you ever *dreamed* of." Church officers just then were in the position of "any loving wife like yours or mine, willing to do just what 'you say,' for you have 'stolen our hearts.'" They set up a fund to help Mr. Beecher out west with moving expenses and to pay any debts that might have accrued. "We want you," Bowen pleaded; "come! you must come!"

Advancing his wife's poor health as his reason, Henry Ward Beecher did sever ties with Indianapolis and make the move back east in that summer of 1847. When his letter of acceptance reached Plymouth Church, the merchant Bowen shared its happy contents with another member of the search committee, who later recalled that the news so affected them both that they fell "in each other's arms, crying and laughing and capering about like a couple of school-boys." Nor was such artless enthusiasm unwarranted. Almost immediately upon his arrival, the new preacher proved a colossal success. Within three years, when Harriet—on her way from Cincinnati to Brunswick, in 1850—visited Henry Ward and his family in their eastern surroundings, she could report to her husband, her less thriving Calvin, that this younger brother's Plymouth Church congregation was "more than ever in love with him, having already raised his salary to $3,300," besides giving Henry "a beautiful horse and carriage worth $600."

A minister's skills as performer mattered more then than now—or than earlier, in Jonathan Edwards's hard and devoted world of the eighteenth century. Churchgoing by the mid-nineteenth century survived as one of the few respectable communal pastimes available during the years before *Uncle Tom's Cabin*—in the form of a highly moral play—transformed the theater into appropriate public entertainment for the family. By the 1860s, for instance, President Lincoln would relish evenings at the theater; but in these 1840s—and even into the 1850s—proper people avoided the waywardness of the public stage, assembling instead at more sedate lyceum lectures or at their churches, at the latter not only for Sunday services but also for Bible study classes, Friday evening discussion groups, and various other uplifting occasions that were as much social as religious. Under such circumstances, the entertainment value of its minister could count for more than doctrinal purity in maintaining a church's standing among the populace.

Henry Ward Beecher's value as an entertainer was very high. To start with, he looked not at all like a solemn ecclesiastic. He wore no clerical collar, favoring instead a black bombazine stock, a soft felt hat, rusty ill-fitting clothes, and boots still muddy from the garden. One who saw him deliver an initiatory sermon at Plymouth Church recalled the man as youthful-looking (then in his mid-thirties), with blue eyes, fine teeth, and long thick hair. Alongside polished, glossy clergymen, Henry appeared, in fact, a bit like a hayseed, at least in those early years back east. In preaching he lurched about, shunning any studied grace of movement; and his words, though carefully rehearsed, seemed to lurch as well, as though spontaneously plunging from this image to that anecdote to yet another agreeable insight. To Jesus he prayed as to an intimate friend; and his rich, carrying voice (which many, many thousands of contemporaries were privileged to hear) he put to use achieving astonishing verbal effects through an amazing range of feeling.

And he avoided pomp; seldom did Beecher even venture into Plymouth Church's olivewood pulpit. Rather, the organist would play as the minister, bearing his hat and hymnbook, entered unobtrusively through a rear door, taking his place before his audience on an unpretentious, flower-bedecked platform only a bit above the floor. On the platform were an armchair, where he sat, and a small table on which he set his hat down. When he rose and spoke, it was to utter in intimacy what, for the most part, his listeners wanted to hear, related in a way that transfixed them. *Harper's Weekly* reported on Beecher's "fresh feeling, his exuberant and rollicking humor, his genuine love" of humanity. And indeed there was much humor in what this cleric shared, and much love. But he could also pound his fist and stomp with the best of them, then, having reached a crescendo, turn abruptly, soothingly tender, his rich whisper carrying to the farthest corners of the room. Moreover, he spoke with his whole body. When—a famous instance—Beecher described a fisherman, he cast his imaginary line and reeled in the catch with such verisimilitude that one among the audience is said to have called out impetuously: "By God, he's got him." Beecher imitating an old tarheel took from his jaws a nonexistent quid of tobacco and threw it to the platform, not forgetting to wipe unsoiled fingers on the back of his coat. Now he was a blacksmith sweating at his forge, now a young girl flirting, now a drunk wheedling before a judge. His listeners craned forward riveted, as their minister's voice variously cajoled, amused, ranted, beguiled, mimicked, and enlightened, always with vivid, homely imagery, pertinent analogy, and inexhaustible life.

Beecher was able to draw those assembled before him into his confidence, bringing them to laughter and tears while laughing and crying along with them. His sister Hatty heard him preach numerous times, recording the effect on her "in one of his happiest moods," as she said: "Some times a thought would seem so beautiful so comforting so tenderly and nobly expressed I would say, I will remember that, and write it to the girls"—to the twins in Hartford—

"but it was just as it was on the sea beaches; one long bright wave effaced the last and so one after another, each bright and making room for another." Lest that seem like partial testimony, further evidence of Beecher's success was everywhere apparent. Plymouth Church burned in 1849, and a replacement structure arose those couple of years into his tenure. Within the new church were more than 2,000 red upholstered seats in semicircular rows, as well as several hundred stools and folding chairs for use in aisles and vestibule, all to accommodate what was already the largest congregation in America. The extra seats were often needed. Ferries from Manhattan bound for Brooklyn on Sundays were nicknamed "Beecher's Boats," so crowded were they with congregants and the curious headed toward enlightenment within the spacious pink-and-white interior of the now famous redbrick sanctuary on Orange Street. And every sermon of Plymouth Church's minister, filled with the good news of a God of love, could be counted on not only to divert, but also to inspire and reassure.

For Beecher's thoughts stayed in the mainstream, vigorously opposed as he was to the Fugitive Slave Act of 1850, vowing not to obey it, but opposed as well to the strident cant of abolitionists. The way to deal with the South and its peculiar institution was, he preached back then, through moral suasion, as Christian brother to brother. Yet as the decade advanced, Henry's opposition to slavery, like the North's in general, hardened. When Kansas burst into flames in mid-decade, his earlier moral suasion took a more tangible shape, the shape of Sharps rifles, which his congregation helped purchase to send to free-soil settlers of that tormented territory; "Beecher's Bibles" was the ironic name applied to the crates of weaponry bound west to defend Kansas in its struggle for freedom. Back in Brooklyn, meanwhile, the flamboyant preacher held auctions in church to buy the liberty of those out of bondage whom slavecatchers had recaptured or of slaves down South for sale, Henry's voice taking on the harsh nasal whine of the auctioneer: "How much will you give . . . ?" while the slave girl (often a girl, usually pale of skin and Caucasian-featured) whose purchase price was sought sat pitifully on the platform before a vast, excited audience tumbling money, watches, and jewelry into the collection trays.

Beecher remained active, moreover, as a lyceum lecturer, a journalist, and an editor. Church officials had promised that if he came to New York, he could extend his influence through publishing far beyond Brooklyn, out west and across the Atlantic as well. So it proved. The minister was soon writing well-received secular articles for such mainstream newspapers as Robert Bonner's *New York Ledger* and Greeley's *Tribune*. These would be subsequently collected into popular volumes of prose essays, as were his columns—ruminations on rainfalls, frost at the window, October days, graveyards—for various religious newspapers of hefty circulation, including the *Independent*, for which he served as contributing editor over two decades. In addition, Beecher was later the driving force behind the widely read *Christian Union*, a weekly that featured not only his but his sister Harriet's coveted productions. And as early as 1855, during the troubles in Kansas, he was giving as many as fifty public lectures a year, a figure that increased to an average of 100 lectures annually; and these, and his newspaper columns, and his sermons, and his famous prayers were all collected as volumes to be distributed across the land, so that a year seldom passed without the appearance of a new title by Henry Ward Beecher.

He grew wealthy, purchasing oriental rugs and precious gems—samplings of beauty, as he saw them, that provided glimpses into the ultimate beauty of Heaven. And his congregation could only adore the man, indulging his love of fast horses along with the numerous extracurricular claims on his time, providing the means for him to acquire—and enjoy restorative interludes at—a country home in New York state, happily furnishing him with a couple of paid months off in the mid-1850s to campaign for a personal acquaintance, the first presidential candidate of the new Republican Party, John Charles Frémont.

Frémont didn't win that election; the Democrat Buchanan did—and as president proved feeble and bumbling. Thus four years later, the Republicans were poised to take the prize. Senator Seward of New York would likely be the party's standard-bearer; but in February 1860 a former member of the House of Representatives, now a lawyer for the Illinois Central Railroad, came east to let New Yorkers have a look at him. On that occasion, Abraham Lincoln was scheduled to address an audience in Brooklyn's spacious Plymouth Church, but at the last moment inclement weather moved the lecture to Manhattan, to the Great Hall at Cooper Institute on Astor Place; and there on the evening of February 27, the westerner made so favorable an impression on skeptical observers as to launch his campaign for the White House. "Neither let us be slandered from our duty by false accusations against us," Mr. Lincoln concluded his remarks before a crowd entirely won over, "nor frightened from it by menaces of destruction to the Government nor of dungeons to ourselves. LET US HAVE FAITH THAT RIGHT MAKES MIGHT, AND IN THAT FAITH, LET US, TO THE END, DARE TO DO OUR DUTY AS WE UNDERSTAND IT."

Those words were spoken on a memorable Monday evening early in a new year. The previous morning Lincoln had joined passengers ferried on Beecher's Boats across the East River to hear another impressive speaker, the minister of Plymouth Church, preach his Sunday sermon. Thereafter the visitor from the West, returned to Illinois, would go on during the spring to secure the Republican nomination; and upon Lincoln's election to the presidency in November, the Union began to crumble. The following year, on April 12, 1861, Fort Sumter in Charleston Harbor was fired upon, its commander, Major Robert Anderson, forced two days later to lower the Union flag and evacuate the premises, allowing troops of Confederate general Beauregard to raise over Sumter's ramparts the banner of rebellion.

Four years of fratricidal conflict followed. At the war's end, from among all the northern orators well skilled by then in patriotic utterance, President Lincoln chose the minister of Brooklyn's Plymouth Church to deliver a key address at a crucial time in the heart of the conquered South. The steamer *Arago* brought the Reverend Mr. Beecher and other notables—the abolitionist William Lloyd Garrison, the brilliant young editor Theodore Tilton—from New York to a South Carolina at peace at last. There in Charleston harbor, at Fort Sumter, at noon of an April day as 100 guns boomed forth their imposing salute, the same Old Glory that Major Anderson had taken with him when his troops evacuated four years earlier rose to flutter once more over the ruined battlements. Sumter's former commander, now a brevet major general, himself performed the victorious flag raising, then joined the other dignitaries attending as the Reverend Henry Ward Beecher, spokesman for America, addressed the assembled celebrants on behalf of the *United* States as a nation restored.

That triumphal ceremony, following four years to the day after Confederates had occupied the Union fort, took place on Good

Friday, April 14, 1865. Around 10:30 on the same evening, farther
north in the federal capital of Washington, on Tenth Street in a
box at Ford's Theater, a derringer pistol in the hands of a real-life
Byronic villain (handsome, gifted, adored by women, aflame with
misguided idealism: *sic semper tyrannis*) was fired from inches behind the head of one member in the audience, seated in his rock-
ing chair smiling over the foolery onstage. "You sockdologizing old
mantrap," the actor down there had been pronouncing the instant
before a lead bullet pierced President Lincoln's brain, entering
behind his left ear, coming to rest behind his right eye, and bringing crashing to an end a tortured, heroic era of American history.

24

CHANGING AMERICA

*T*he era that followed—of Reconstruction and the Gilded Age—
was meaner by almost every measure, less noble. Despite general suffering during the Civil War, some people had made a great
deal of money out of the conflict, the North completing its transfor-
mation from a predominantly agrarian economy to a highly profitable industrial one, and all that new prosperity went on flourishing
into the peace that followed. With prosperity in peacetime came increasingly ostentatious consumption, widespread corruption, and—
among bribable public servants—scandal in high places. All the while,
the South in defeat struggled to adjust to a different reality: cities
and countryside despoiled, the federal Constitution amended, laws
enacted to establish a new social context, freedmen where slaves had
been before, and northern troops south of the Mason-Dixon Line
helping to enforce new rights for African-Americans.

Like everybody else, Henry Ward Beecher expressed opinions
on the various changes that had abruptly overwhelmed those re-
United States. In his speech at Fort Sumter, for example, on the
day of Lincoln's assassination, the Reverend Mr. Beecher uttered
fiery language hardly akin to his president's tempered prose at
Gettysburg or at the second inaugural a month ago. "I charge the
whole guilt of this war," Beecher had cried, "upon the ambitious,
educated, plotting political leaders of the South. They have shed
this ocean of blood. They have desolated the South. They have
poured poverty through all her towns and cities." Toward the mis-
led southern people *"let not a trace of animosity remain"*; the benighted multitudes are innocent. But rebel leaders from Jefferson

Davis on down must pay a condign price for their grotesque and traitorous folly. Within months, however, Brooklyn's influential minister was urging amnesty for many of those same traitors, and a welcome back into the halls of the federal legislature. "Refusing to admit loyal senators and representatives from the South to Congress will not help the freedmen," recently liberated. "It will not secure for them the vote. It will not protect them." What will help African-Americans in a new South, Beecher declared, was restoration of amity among white people South and North, with southern whites in defeat reclaiming their rightful place in the American commonwealth. "Whether we regard the whole nation or any section of it or class in it, the first demand of our time is entire reunion!" Blacks for their part must be accommodating. "Civilization is a growth," the preacher explained. "None can escape that forty years in the wilderness who travel from the Egypt of ignorance to the promised land of civilization. The freedmen must take their march. I have full faith in the results. If they have the stamina to undergo the hardships which every uncivilized people has undergone in its upward progress, they will in due time take their place among us."

Many whites agreed with the Reverend Mr. Beecher's complacent call for blacks to show patience until the arrival of that unspecified due time. And during the years of Reconstruction, from 1865 to the definitive betrayal of black people's rights and hopes in 1877, conservative opinion in the North sided with this Brooklyn minister on the vexed question of how best to deal with a defeated Confederacy. After four years of fratricidal slaughter, the North in its new prosperity had accumulated an abundance of guilt, along with an abiding and widespread aversion to the idea of African-Americans as social equals. Radicals, to be sure, felt otherwise. They wanted no easy amnesty for rebels, wanted them to serve a stiff term of probation, and wanted blacks meanwhile to enjoy their new rights at once—political, economic, social—enforced with federal arms where need be. Thaddeus Stevens and Charles Sumner were among the radicals in Congress who initially succeeded in imposing such sterner reshapings on a morose South, with Freedmen's Bureaus established in southern states to ensure voting rights for every male citizen, white or black. But all the while northern conservatives, whose outlook Lincoln's successor Andrew Johnson came to speak for, insisted that a gallant foe at war's end was owed magnanimity; or, as Beecher put it in his not invariably happy prose (more for the ear, perhaps, than the eye): "The moment their willing hand drops the musket and they return to their allegiance, then stretch out your own honest right hand to greet them"—color of both hands, joined thus in greeting and friendship, presumptively white.

Beecher was articulating views that many of his contemporaries shared. The optimistic preacher did speak expressively, with ebullience, humor, and richness of voice, and those traits help account for his extraordinary and ever-growing popularity. But what he said was as important as how he said it. Like many northerners at the immediate moment of victory, Henry Ward Beecher had clamored for vengeance against Jeff Davis's bloodstained cohort. But—again, like many other northerners—after a few months Henry had mellowed, his indignation giving way to a grudging sympathy for fellow Anglo-Saxons struggling south of the Mason-Dixon Line to recover from the war's devastations and put their world back together. The problem lay in what values were to be espoused down there: was the southern way of life to be reconstructed or simply restored? The easier option was effectively to restore the semblance of an antebellum world, while indefinitely postponing (that is, denying) rights newly granted to a vulnerable portion of the population. Beecher's views in effect supported the easier plan: restoring white supremacy.

Or consider his views on a second change of the times: postwar prosperity that made a conspicuous few very wealthy. In full sincerity Henry preached what most people in his vast flourishing congregation wanted to hear about their new Gilded Age. "The question," he posited, "is not what proportion of his wealth a Christian man may divert from benevolent channels for personal enjoyment through the element of the beautiful"—more simply: how much he may spend on himself. "For, if rightly viewed, and rightly used, his very elegances and luxuries will be a contribution to the public good." How so? Because, as Beecher explains, the rich man's tastes help educate the multitudes. "And the question becomes only this: How much of my wealth given to the public good shall be employed *directly* for the elevation of the ignorant, and how much *indirectly*?"—through buying fast horses, gems, oriental rugs, a summer home, and other such elements of the beautiful as please my tasteful self?

The point may become clearer through an analogy: think of a great elm tree. The elm gets to fretting—"creaking and groaning"—that its surpassing height and girth cast too wide a shadow, so that saplings are unable to sprout and grow in its shade. Scores of trees could thrive in this same space; but as it is, when the sun shines, "I take its whole glory on my head," the conscientious elm worries, "and nothing below can get a fair share, and my roots are drinking out of the ground an enormous supply of food and moisture."

But take heart. Whatever makes the huge tree healthy makes the village happy. "Hundreds sit down in your shadow," a wise observer reassures the anxious elm; "this house, of which you are a dendral guardian-angel, is blessed in your prosperity; weary laborers stop and rest under you; all the village is proud of your beauty; sick people look at you out of their windows and are comforted." Besides, insects live on your bounty, and birds that nest in your branches "disport themselves for our happiness. It is true that it takes a great deal to keep you, but you pay it all back a hundredfold in use and beauty."

Such reassurances may sound smugly self-serving. But those up-to-date postwar Americans (however prominent their flaws, however enduring the record of their tawdriness: their wallowing in luxuries, their hypocrisy, their corruption, their intimidations and betrayals—crosses aflame, lynchings, Tweed rings, Crédit Mobiliers, race riots, ten- or twelve-hour ill-paid workdays six days a week for the many, children laboring near the gaudy palaces of Newport and Fifth Avenue) saw much about their era that filled them with satisfaction. The rebellion was ended. North and South had put aside their differences. Swords were being beaten into profitable plowshares, as what recently had been munitions factories resumed the manufacture of sewing machines, threshing machines, tractors, kitchen ranges, parlor furniture. Science meanwhile continued making strides. "I remember, in my own day," a marveling Henry Ward Beecher had been able to write as early as 1859—the year of Darwin's *On the Origin of Species*—"very long sermons to prove that the cholera did not depend on natural agencies, but that God held it in his hand, and dropped it down upon the world." In this more enlightened era on the far side of wartime, such superstitious blindness appeared consigned forever to credulous antiquity.

For now, in sunlit peace, America—that very special place at a special moment; a city upon a hill for all the world to pattern itself after—was shining forth through progress upward toward a millennial goal. True, as far back as 1742 Jonathan Edwards had imagined millennial days arriving: promises in Revelation were about to be fulfilled globally from the New World by means of a religious renewal miraculously pouring out of one Massachusetts village. And even before the colonials gained their independence from royal tyranny, as early as January 1776 Thomas Paine could write in *Common Sense* of America's having the power "to begin the world over again." Europe and other lands around this weary globe were "overrun with oppression," but young America—alone among nations—could serve as freedom's home, "an asylum for mankind."

Now, finally, after Appomattox, such an aspiration seemed close to being achieved. "Oh, my friend, when I think," Harriet Beecher Stowe had written feelingly to an English correspondent at the end of the Civil War, "of what has been done these last few years, and of what is now doing, I am lost in amazement. I have just, by way of realizing it to myself, been reading 'Uncle Tom's Cabin' again, and when I read that book, scarred and seared and burned into with the memories of an anguish and horror that can never be forgotten, and think it is all over now, all past, and that now the questions debated are simply of more or less time before granting legal suffrage to those who so lately were held only as articles of merchandise,—when this comes over me I think no private or individual sorrow can ever make me wholly without comfort. If my faith in God's presence and real, living power in the affairs of men ever grow dim, this makes it impossible to doubt."

As for that, could a sensitive person doubt any longer that God—so obviously present in the affairs of men—favored our vast, rich land, this "last, best hope of earth," as Lincoln had described it? Into the 1870s, while the size of the congregation at Plymouth Church doubled, the popularity of Harriet's brother, the Reverend Henry Ward Beecher, continued to rise, because of how the minister spoke and for what he said—in no small part because of what he said about a loving God who was partial to America. Beecher would trouble his listeners with scarcely a word concerning the doctrinal differences that had so exercised his honored father. The Calvinist doctrine of total depravity, for instance, the younger man dismissed in a phrase (again in 1859): "one of the most unfortunate and misleading terms that ever afflicted theology." Original sin, infant damnation: where in all the Bible except for a few passages of Genesis is Adam's fall so much as even mentioned? Somber doctrine deriving from that fall the son rarely spoke of, doctrine that had earlier preoccupied Lyman Beecher, as he railed against watered-down faiths—Deists, Unitarians, Episcopalians, Catholics—and wielded the weapons of reason and logic against every departure from religious truth. Henry's weapons, by contrast—in this different, romantic era—were intuition and sympathy. Trust your feelings! And the younger Beecher spoke ecumenically, about truths that all the various religions shared, leaving their differences alone. People came to hear Lyman's son—and came in droves—not out of any fear of hellfire or to have their brains challenged with logic-chopping legalisms about depravity, free agency, and election. In a sentimental age Henry spoke rather to his listeners' hearts, and he spoke of love: of Jesus's love for the sinner and of affinities among us here on earth—between friends, between spouses—that helped to disclose that higher, spiritual love. He who in childhood had felt *un*loved, neglected, who as an adult frankly confessed that above all things he did love being loved, now could bask in the approbation of thousands gathering adoringly to hear his words, and could reflect as well on many additional thousands savoring Henry Ward Beecher's warm nature through the pages of his lectures, essays, and sermons abundantly in print.

The God who emerged from those pages was hardly a demanding God, any more than was the deity that Lyman's other children had by this time learned to worship. None of the second generation of Beechers—not one—had stayed loyal to their father's Calvinism, however much Lyman may have ameliorated its grimmest teachings in practice. The eldest child had turned away early, in her twenties, after the drowning of her fiancé off the coast of Ireland. Catharine refused to believe that a Most High could be so unjust as to condemn to eternal torment the exemplary Professor Fisher; as she said, that defied common sense. And a later drowning, in 1857 in the Connecticut River, of the beloved Dartmouth student Henry Stowe, led Catharine's sister Harriet to a similar renunciation. By 1860, the drowned student's mother had laid aside "the awful burden of think-ing that every person who does not believe certain things and is not regenerated in a certain way *in this life* is lost forever." Harriet could find no such doctrine in Scripture, though she did find "numerous passages which state that God has for all creatures He has made the feelings of a Father." Meanwhile, simple arithmetic disposes of the idea that regeneration provides the only path to heaven. If that were so, wrote Harriet, "all the human race up to our time, and about all in our time, are lost or going to be. Any map of the world will show you that the proportion which have even heard of Christ is the minority—and the minority of that the Protestant world—and in that, the majority are the utterly ignorant and uninstructed who, from their circumstances, are like Heathen, and of those who *do know* and have opportunity, a great proportion still even of good people do not believe orthodox doctrine, and of those (who do believe orthodox doctrine), how small the number who show any signs of such a regeneration as we believe in. So that, instead of Christ having brought a glorious gospel of salvation, He has only brought the news of damnation, and we learn the appalling fact that the whole human race, with some small exceptions, is made for everlasting misery, for the number who have been true saints is certainly, in comparison to the human race, only in the proportion of one in a million."

All that cannot be. If it were true, it would make a mockery of the gospel's reassurances that God feels for us the love of a father. "So *I* believe," Harriet concluded in her maturity, "the text so often repeated that 'His mercy endureth forever,' and do not think God is a loving father for sixteen or eighteen years of some person's life"—someone like Henry Stowe at the time of his drowning—"and an enemy ever after."

So far did Harriet's beliefs depart from the Calvinism of her youth that by the mid-1860s, not long after her father's death, she returned to the church her mother had been reared in, the more lenient Episcopalianism that the Foote side of the family embraced. That denomination's elaborate ritual appealed to Mrs. Stowe, as did the music and the language of the Episcopal *Book of Common Prayer*. Moreover, she who for all her faith in the eternal hereafter was ever entranced by fads of the moment—such fads as mesmer-ism, electrical treatments, and watercures—had been dabbling in yet one more current fad, spiritualism.

More precisely, spiritualism as then practiced was less a fad than a variant religion. Nor should we imagine it then quite as we think of it now. Now the word conjures forth a charlatan's darkened séance, fake ectoplasm wavering overhead while a hidden confederate raps behind the wall or sounds a gong out of sight: the very image of fraud meeting gullibility over a tilting table. "Is it absurd," however, "to suppose that some peculiarity in the nervous system, in the connecting link between soul and body, may bring some more than others, into an almost abnormal contact with the spirit-World"? The questioner is the erudite Calvin Stowe, who knew something about paranormal manifestations, having lived all his life with his visions. Writing to George Eliot, Professor Stowe thought to add: "and that, too, without correcting their faults, or making them morally better than others?" Some people, neither better nor worse than you and I, may simply be able to experience visions that we don't see; some, like the otherwise quite ordinary Fox sisters of Hydesville, New York (in the upstate region out of which had arisen, in the late 1820s, the paranormality that led to Mormonism)—some few among the living may be inexplicably gifted with psychic proclivities, including the knack of channeling communications from the dead to those alive less sensitively attuned.

Mediums, as it turns out, were almost always female. And early in the second half of the nineteenth century, before an overabundance of mediums and rivalries among them and an overfamiliarity with their methods had urged ever more preposterous demonstrations of the dead reappearing—extravaganzas that led at last to exposable fraud and to respectable people's disenchantment with channeling—many believed in and took comfort from communing with the dead. For those early believers, death appeared to be no more than an extension of life, the bud opening into a flower, with the soul after death continuing its moral growth toward perfection. A person not regenerated *in this life,* as Harriet had written, would find regeneration in the life to come; Lord Byron's departed soul, for one, was presumably being purified as it evolved toward a Heaven that—to Lyman Beecher, as to his children and many others— figured as a real and splendid place from which the likes of the blessed Roxana Beecher, wife and mother, looked down. There with her, in supernal beauty, the glorious dead (Lady Byron and the evolved Henry Stowe among them) retained their earthly characteristics in transmogrified but still recognizable form: although *"worms destroy this body, yet in my flesh shall I see God,"* as the Bible affirms. That being so, why should our dead not evolve to where they may speak to us? And why might the veil hiding those who have gone before not be permeable to at least a few among the living?

The supply of people in need of such comfort has always been massive—including, just now, many who had lost husbands, brothers, and sons in the Civil War. Horace Greeley attended the Fox sisters' public communications with departed spirits and judged the gatherings free from deception; his hardheaded endorsement of spiritualism appeared in the *New York Tribune*. James Fenimore Cooper became a believer. So did William Lloyd Garrison. Through a medium, Mrs. Lincoln in the White House spoke with her dead son Willie. True, Henry Ward Beecher remained skeptical; for him the dead to whose words the living so raptly attended ("Don't grieve for me, Mother; I am well and happy") substituted banalities for the Bible's inspired truth. But his brother Charles was a believer. So was Catharine Beecher. So, fervently, was Isabella Beecher Hooker.

And Harriet herself, and her husband, had long been susceptible to the enticements of spiritualism. Not the juggling and rapping and squeaking, as Mrs. Stowe made clear, or the "mountebank tricks with tables and chairs; to recite over in weary sameness harmless truisms, which we were wise enough to say for ourselves; to trifle, and banter, and jest, or to lead us through endless moonshiny mazes. Sadly and soberly we say that, if this be communion with the dead, we had rather be without it. We want something a little in advance of our present life, and not below it." But after young Henry's unregenerate death in the Connecticut River, in their anguish to know whether their child had reached bliss, Harriet and Calvin strove to sense their dead son's spirit or hear his voice. During her final trip to Europe, in 1859, Mrs. Stowe learned from her husband in Andover that their Henry's spirit had been heard across the room, plucking guitar strings. In reply Harriet reminded the hopeful father that it was his first wife, Eliza, who had signaled her presence that way: the good friend of her own youth, Eliza Tyler Stowe, dead long years ago in Cincinnati, whose birthday Harriet and Calvin had continued to observe together solemnly ever since. "One thing I am convinced of," she went on to write Calvin from Italy during the months immediately ahead, "that spiritualism is a reaction from the intense materialism of the present age." In a more spiritual time, Martin Luther had seen the devil face to face. "There is a real scriptural spiritualism," wrote Harriet, "which has fallen into disuse, and must be revived, and there are, doubtless, people who, from some constitutional formation, can more readily receive the impressions of the surrounding spiritual world. Such were apostles, prophets, and workers of miracles."

And such in America might be the many mediums who pursued the calling of the Fox sisters after 1848, when those young women first interpreted to sensational effect mysterious rappings heard in their family's farmhouse in Hydesville, New York. The sisters' demonstrations went on the road and drew large crowds. In the years following the Civil War, with spiritualism continuing to attract wide notice, Harriet would read much about it and about mysticism in general, a subject that had long been of interest to Calvin, who had scrutinized his mystical, ponderous medieval tomes for decades. Now Harriet read of spirit writing and the planchette—the small wooden triangle on casters that, when touched lightly, delivers messages from supernatural realms, as on a Ouija board. In fact, she would write a section on the planchette for her brother Charles's book *Spiritual Manifestations*; and for brother Henry's *Christian Union* she had written, in the fall of 1870, a long essay that distinguished genuine from spurious spiritualism. Her essay sought to demonstrate that genuine spiritualism has a history stretching back to biblical times.

Meanwhile, female mediums, suddenly elevated to a crucial solacing role in society as conduits for the bereaved, were preparing the way for the postwar "new woman." That more independent female presence, by seizing a position of prominence for herself and engaging in the ongoing struggle for women's rights, wove one of the few bright strands—Reconstruction efforts on behalf of blacks in the South were another—through the corrupt self-gratifications that darkened so much of the fabric of this Gilded Age.

25

MY WIFE AND I

he federal Constitution, unaltered since 1804, was amended
three times in the half decade after the Civil War. The Thir-
teenth Amendment abolished slavery; it was ratified in December
1865. The Fourteenth Amendment, adopted three years later, man-
dates (among other matters) that no state "deprive any person of
life, liberty, or property, without due process of law; nor deny to
any person within its jurisdiction the equal protection of the laws."
The Fifteenth Amendment addresses the right to vote; no state shall
abridge that right "on account of race, color, or previous condition
of servitude." This last was ratified in 1870.

The middle one of those amendments introduced the term *male*
into the Constitution, by prescribing representation in the lower
house of the federal legislature on the basis of the number of "male
inhabitants" twenty-one years of age or older in the various states.
Nowhere earlier in the document does the word appear; nor does
it appear anywhere in the twelve amendments that have followed.

The intrusion of *male* into the language of the Constitution
helped concentrate the postwar efforts of women who had been
agitating for equal rights since 1848. In that year, a group of them,
along with some fifty sympathetic men, had come together in Sen-
eca Falls, a village in upstate New York not far from Hydesville,
where the Fox sisters were conducting their earliest rappings. Thus
modern spiritualism and the movement for women's rights were
born nearly simultaneously and in towns only a few miles apart.
By 1870, women seeking their rights—to divorce, to own property
apart from their husbands', to be educated with and as well as

men—were demanding ever more vociferously to know why they had been denied the vote. The Fourteenth Amendment says that "persons born or naturalized in the United States, and subject to the jurisdiction thereof, are citizens of the United States and of the State wherein they reside." So women aren't citizens? Moreover, the Constitution itself, as early as Section 2, decrees that the House of Representatives "shall be composed of Members chosen every second Year by the People of the several States." And don't people include women? Throughout that document the same terminology occurs: "the people," or "persons." So why should female persons, one half of America's people, not be heard from? Why should women be deprived of the ballot and kept politically mute even after former slaves have been granted suffrage, in 1870?

Women were destined to win their battle for the vote, but only upon the adoption of the Nineteenth Amendment to the Constitution in 1920, a full half century in the future. It took a long time and the efforts of many reformers; and for the pioneers, the most influential woman in America expressed her admiration. Writing just after the war, in December 1865, Harriet Beecher Stowe—a longtime crusader for social justice—saluted the early suffragists in the pages of the *Atlantic Monthly*. The "Woman's Rights movement," she wrote, "with its conventions, its speech-makings, its crudities and eccentricities, is nevertheless a part of a healthful and necessary movement of the human race towards progress. This question of Woman and her Sphere is now, perhaps, the greatest of the age." As for the issue of suffrage, that boiled down to simple logic. "If the principle on which we founded our government is true, that taxation must not exist without representation, and if women hold property and are taxed, it follows that women should be represented in the State by their votes, or there is an illogical working of our government." Yet, Stowe went on, however easy the point may be to grasp, it will take the agitation of many courageous, valuable women to bring about such a change. "They are the voices crying in the wilderness, preparing the way for a coming good. They go down on their knees in the mire of life to lift up and brighten and restore a neglected truth; and we that have not the energy to share their struggle should at least refrain from criticizing their soiled garments and ungraceful action. There have been excrescences, eccentricities, peculiarities about the camp of these reformers; but the body

the green banks of which Harriet had strolled as a schoolgirl with her friend Georgiana May and where she later chose to build her villa, was known alternatively as the polluted Hog River, with once bucolic sites near Oakholm overtaken—a metaphor for the period— by factories, tenements, and railroad yards. In 1870 Harriet was obliged to sell, at a sizable loss, her dream home—the only residence she ever built for herself. And all the while, in Florida, her Mandarin cottage was siphoning off additional funds. She lost $40,000 on ventures down there involving cotton and oranges for sale, even as people in growing numbers both there and elsewhere came to depend on the bounty from her pen: Calvin, in retirement; the twins, with their taste for silken luxuries; her son Charley, coming into manhood and in need of capital; and the less lucky among Harriet's numerous siblings, nephews, and nieces, as well as relatives and friends at a further remove.

So she kept writing feverishly. In addition to all the other prose—for children, for housewives newly moneyed and befuddled, for the historically and biographically minded, for the religiously inclined—Harriet was writing novels. As at the start of the 1860s, so once more she found herself, early in the 1870s, composing not one but two novel-length serials simultaneously, having accepted assignments from two different magazines, in part for the money, in part to strengthen a literary reputation badly mauled by critical buffetings during the Byron controversy.

These new novels in the making represented yet another departure for a tireless author of considerable imaginative boldness. Neither novel was about the plight of the blacks, as *Uncle Tom's Cabin* and *Dred* had been; nor was either about Calvinist forebears in the earlier New England of *The Minister's Wooing* and *Oldtown Folks*. Stowe's new fiction was on a different subject entirely: contemporary and urban, set in New York City, vivacious serials of manners that exposed an affluent society's materialistic foibles. It was satirical subject matter that a later American novelist, Edith Wharton (then a child in New York not yet out of her single digits), would bring to a level of near-perfection. In the end Harriet Beecher Stowe wrote not two but three such society novels, considerably less telling than Wharton's, to be sure: *Pink and White Tyranny*, *We and Our Neighbors*, and—by far the best of the three, the first—*My Wife and I*.

That narrative in serial form on marriage—a "subject," as its protagonist says, "in everybody's mind and mouth, discussed on every platform, ringing from everybody's tongue, and coming home to every man's business and bosom"—ran in the pages of the *Christian Union* from November 1870 through September 1871. *My Wife and I* tells the story of Harry Henderson, tenth child of a poor country parson in the mountains of New Hampshire, who moves to the city and there makes his way in life: a love story about the so-called child wife of Harry's rural youth (a sweet little playmate who dies); about the dream wife of his college years in New England (a beauty who plays him false, choosing instead to align her fate with an empty-headed son of wealth); and about his true wife, with whom in the novel's late pages he sets up an exemplary home in Manhattan. The plot follows a familiar Algeresque curve: a narrative of luck and pluck as an honest country youth in the big city meets romantic and professional adventures on his way to success. Moreover, by entering the world of magazine publishing—about which the author of *My Wife and I* was by this time thoroughly informed— Harry undertakes journalistic labors that permit him, plausibly, to become involved in issues of importance to postwar America.

Among those issues (ostentation, snobbishness, the decline of principle, the increasing power of moneyed interests), women's rights are explored through various female characters whom the narrator comes to know. Early on in this first-person account, Harry offers his opinion: "The woman question of our day, as I understand it is this.—Shall MOTHERHOOD ever be felt in the public administration of the affairs of state? The state is nothing more nor less than a collection of families, and what would be good or bad for the individual family, would be good or bad for the state." Thus through her fictional spokesman Stowe expresses her own recipe for social reform. Of course women should have the vote, in order to bring feminine virtues to bear on influencing male-driven public policy for the better.

Or that was how the author felt in the early eventful months during which her serial was appearing in the *Christian Union*. As the story unfolded, however, Stowe came to qualify her views on the woman question. Harry's true wife, Eva Van Arsdel—a name signaling her fine old Knickerbocker pedigree—has for a sister the independent-minded Ida, who exhibits no interest in getting mar-

ried, and whose worthwhile pursuits nevertheless set an example
for similarly enlightened women to follow. Another young woman—
Caroline, Harry's cousin—is equally attractive and just as committed to fulfilling her nature without a husband's help. Marriage, then,
is not for everyone: "the day is now come, thank God," as one of
the characters acknowledges, "when a woman as well as a man can
have some other career besides that of the heart. Let her study her
profession—expand her mind, broaden her powers—become all
that she can be." Accordingly, the self-reliant sister of Harry's be-
trothed, having prepared for adversity in this era of boom and bust,
is able to look with equanimity on financial troubles threatening
her wealthy father. "I have absolutely refused," the resolute Ida
announces, "to be made such a helpless doll as young girls in our
position commonly are. I have determined that I would keep my
faculties bright, and my bodily health firm and strong; and that all
these luxuries should not become a necessity to me, so but what I
could take care of myself"—through industry, energy, and self-
denial—"and take care of others, without them."

One hears Stowe's own voice in that declaration of independence: largely self-educated as she had been (and well educated,
too), now as for many years taking financial care of herself and
others. Yet the author's admirable mouthpiece, Ida, addressing the
question of votes for women late in the book—after *My Wife and I*
had run in the *Christian Union* for many months—appears of a
different mind on that subject than had Harry, another, more ap-
proving mouthpiece, earlier. Now Ida professes herself "on the
whole, very well pleased that there is no immediate prospect of the
suffrage being granted to women until a generation with superior
education and better balanced minds and better habits of consecu-
tive thought shall have grown up among us." Society, she suggests,
should change through evolution, not revolution; accordingly, she
concludes that "the gift of the ballot will come at last as the result
of a superior culture and education. And I am in no hurry for it
before."

Neither, presumably, by this time was Ida's creator. So what
had intervened between Harry Henderson's early endorsement of
the vote for women and his sister-in-law's later view that women
might well wait awhile to achieve their goal? From Stowe's perspec-
tive, no less than an alarming tremble of revolution had shaken the

interval. During the opening two years of the 1870s (time of the French Communards), the women's movement in America appeared to adopt a more revolutionary program, joined by what a character in *My Wife and I* describes as "that radical part of strange creatures who rant and rage about progress in our time." Those creatures distressed a Mrs. Stowe grown ever more traditional, even as her reputation in the wake of her revelations about Byron had turned scandalously extreme. But the excesses of the women's movement troubled many others as well: programs that advocated divorce, that agitated for women to assume all the untrammeled liberties of men, that endorsed free love. In addition, those same female reformers to excess, not feminine at all, appeared bent on abolishing the possessive pronouns *my* and *thy*. "Marriage," they were preaching communistically, "is an old effete institution, a relic of barbarous ages. There is to be no *my* of husband and wife, and no *my* of children." Such views, new to the women's movement, provided excrecences, eccentricities, and peculiarities iconoclastic enough to give Mrs. Stowe serious pause. In the later pages of her novel, accordingly, she has in mind the "very alarmingly rational women-reformers" when she takes pains to include a character's musings that "Woman was meant to be more than a worker; she was meant for the poet and artist of life." Woman's role, in short, is not fulfilled by her aspiring to be as manly as men, but rather by her remaining true to a femininity that softens the rigors of living and brings poetry into life. Precisely that, Harry's bride Eva concludes, "is what I call woman's genius. To make life beautiful, to keep down and out of sight the hard, dry, prosaic side, and keep up the poetry—that is my idea of our 'mission.'"

Critics at the time were by no means universally kind to this new novel of Mrs. Stowe's. In a brief unsigned review, the intellectually fashionable *Nation* condescended to its sequel, *We and Our Neighbors* (1875), which related further doings of Mr. and Mrs. Harry Henderson in their model residence amid Manhattan society. The reviewer, Henry James, then in his early thirties, noted flaws in the sequel that had appeared as well in its predecessor. Stowe was not at home among New York's upper crust; one need only visit the sparkling *Age of Innocence*—by an aristocratic Edith Newbold Jones, to the manner born, grown up, wife of and divorced from Teddy Wharton—to feel the contrast between an authentic representation of high society in New York in the late nineteenth century and the Yankee-inflected version that Stowe offers us, observed not from within but without, and with only partial understanding. Moreover, in James's perceptive words: if we are to believe Stowe's representation, "the language used by good society in New York is a singular amalgam of the rural Yankee dialect (so happily reproduced by Mrs. Stowe in some of her tales), the jargon of the Southern negroes," and the style of the ladies' magazines.

But even apart from its dubious upper-class dialogue, *My Wife and I*—though the best of the author's three fictional works that undertake to describe New York society—is hardly a major achievement. Its talkative characters are often undifferentiated; its ideas are conventional (divorce is strongly disapproved of: think the matter over carefully *before* marriage, not after); and its late chapters are prolonged—in the manner of many serial stories—beyond several opportune endings before limping to a feeble close. Of course there are interesting moments in the narrative; Stowe was too practiced and intelligent an author to write otherwise. And the character of Harry's colleague Bolton, hiding a secret in his work-focused asceticism, makes for a memorable portrait. Bolton turns out to be a recovering alcoholic, constantly on his guard; the case of Fred Stowe, vanished in the Far West, has furnished the author with hard-won knowledge and a remarkably modern understanding of that character's treacherous disease. It was as if a vessel no longer responded to the rudder, the shipmaster aboard unable to prevent its gradually, horrifyingly succumbing to the slow, accelerating movement of the whirlpool, while the sun overhead shone in a blue sky, and the nearby shore—"with its green trees and free birds and blooming flowers"—remained in view, the ship in its whirl sliding relentlessly "past the church with its peaceful spire, past the home cottages, past the dwelling of friends and neighbors, past parents, brothers, and sisters who stood on the shore warning and shrieking and entreating; helpless, hopeless."

Noncritical readers in Stowe's own day, unlike the captious reviewers, were more than satisfied with *My Wife and I*. They were delighted with the author's new, lively story, full of current concerns and up-to-the-minute social detail. During the months that the serial ran in its pages, the *Christian Union* doubled its subscription list; and the editors found themselves happily obliged, halfway through, to reprint a special issue of the story thus far for eager readers who had missed earlier numbers. According to her own testimony, Harriet Beecher Stowe had written no novel since *Uncle Tom's Cabin* that elicited so much mail from her readers as *My Wife and I*. And one thing those readers were wondering about was this: had the author based her characters on real people? In particular, might Audacia Dangyereyes have a real-life counterpart making news even then in New York's daily press?

26

SCANDAL

When J. B. Ford and Company issued the completed serial *My Wife and I* as a book in late 1871, Mrs. Stowe added a preface addressing the matter of whether the characters in her novel were intended as portraits of living individuals. They are not, the author pronounces categorically, and people who think they are misunderstand the principles of dramatic composition. A writer of fiction creates a character out of composites, "guided in this creation by the knowledge and experience of men and women," but making use of "individual instances and incidents only to assure himself of the possibility and probability of the character he creates." True, if the author succeeds in bringing a character to life, readers may confuse the fiction with somebody they know or have read about. "But to apply to any single living person such delineation is a mistake, and might be a great wrong both to the author and to the person designated."

Yet despite this early specimen of disclaimer ("any resemblance to persons living or dead . . . "), Audacia Dangyereyes in Stowe's new novel could hardly have existed without the existence in real life of a similarly audacious woman, of whom New Yorkers had been made abruptly aware in the early months of the preceding year, and in remarkable ways. No less a figure than Commodore Cornelius Vanderbilt, hardheaded owner of ferryboat, steamship, and railroad lines, then in his late seventies and New York's wealthiest financier, had taken under his wing two young women, sisters out of nowhere—Victoria Woodhull and Tennessee Claflin—and set them up in their own brokerage firm in the city's financial district. These were the first of the fair sex to enter that fast-paced, risky profession; and the women, with the support of their gruff tycoon—a personification of the immediate postward period—made a success of Woodhull & Claflin, Brokers, at 44 Broad Street. Mrs. Woodhull was in her early thirties; her sister Tennie was twenty-five; and on the evidence of surviving photographs, both young female stockbrokers were strikingly handsome. As for their professionalism, the *New York Herald* reported on the "extraordinary coolness and self-possession" of the two, while marveling that their "evident knowledge of the difficult role they have undertaken is far more remarkable than their personal beauty and graces of manner, and these are considerable"—so considerable that old Vanderbilt, fond of both, had grown infatuated with Miss Claflin, the younger of his protégées.

Thus, while Tennie Claflin looked after her commodore, the older sister, the clever, beautiful, magnetic Mrs. Victoria Woodhull, managed the new brokerage house. And under Vanderbilt's sponsorship, money poured in. Some of those funds the sisters devoted to starting a newspaper, *Woodhull & Claflin's Weekly,* and a very good newspaper it proved to be. The first issue appeared in May 1870, printed in a handsome font on superior stock; and through the weeks that followed—indeed, for six years—New Yorkers were treated, in each issue of sixteen cleanly printed four-column pages, to articles on (among much else) financial news, women's suffrage, the rights of labor, current divorce laws, and spiritualism, along with less weighty considerations of fashion, drama, and sports (boating, baseball), all offered under the motto, "Progress! Free Thought! Untrammeled Lives! Breaking the Way for Future Generations."

That two young women should launch a successful metropolitan weekly was as unprecedented as that they should dare to run a brokerage house. But editing their newspaper was by no means the end of Woodhull and Claflin's unprecedented public behavior. Early in 1871, while Mrs. Stowe's new serial *My Wife and I* was delighting readers of the *Christian Union,* Victoria Woodhull shattered precedent yet again, arriving in Washington to testify before a congressional committee. No female had ever done that before, and this witness made a splendid impression. Mrs. Woodhull was appearing, on January 11, 1871, before the Judiciary Committee of the United States House of Representatives in order to urge that her sex be given the vote. "The American nation, in its march on-

ward and upward, cannot publicly choke the intellectual and political activity of half its citizens by narrow statutes," the witness
admonished representatives on the committee in a clear, strong
voice. "The will of the entire people is the true basis of republican
government, and a free expression of that will by the public vote of
all citizens, without distinctions of race, color, occupation or sex,
is the only means by which that will can be ascertained."

Among the thirty-two-year-old Victoria Woodhull's sponsors was
a doting Representative Benjamin Butler of Massachusetts; and in
her audience in the Capitol that morning sat various suffragists,
adherents of their cause having convened elsewhere in Washington.
Susan B. Anthony made time to come over to the legislative chamber, as did Isabella Beecher Hooker, Harriet's half sister, now active
and well regarded in the swelling movement for women's rights. Belle,
in her late forties, was entranced by this new recruit to the banner
of reform, this star with whom she had already had a two-hour private interview. Indeed, the influential Mrs. Hooker recorded herself
as profoundly impressed by Mrs. Woodhull, later adjudging the crusader to have been "heaven sent for the rescue of woman from her
pit of subjection." Woodhull, she wrote, "has ever since appealed to
me as then"—during these early days in Washington—"as a womanly woman, yet less a woman than an embodiment of pure thought,
soul and reason—a prophetess, full of visions and messages to the
people which it would be woe unto her to refrain from proclaiming,
even though martyrdom were sure to follow."

Another person who found Victoria Woodhull impressive at about
this time was the prominent editor Theodore Tilton, to the extent of
committing himself to preparing an adulatory biography of the reformer during the summer and fall of 1871. In its pages the Byronically
handsome Tilton praised Mrs. Woodhull as one "whose position
as a representative of her sex in the greatest reform of modern times
renders her an object of peculiar interest to her fellow-citizens, and
whose character (inasmuch as I know her well) I can portray without color or tinge from any other partiality save that I hold her in
uncommon respect." Tilton, a longtime associate of Henry Ward
Beecher, concluded this appraisal of the beautiful Victoria Woodhull
by asserting that "to see her is to respect her—to know her is to
vindicate her." In short, she is "one of the sincerest, most reverent, and divinely-gifted of human souls."

Woodhull does appear to have been amazing. That fall, for the first time attending a spiritualist convention, in Troy, New York, she addressed the assembly—"I have been a spiritualist and a recipient of heavenly favors ever since I can remember"—to such effect that the group spontaneously, by acclamation, elected her president of the national organization. Nor was that all, for she had already announced, in *Woodhull & Claflin's Weekly,* her candidacy for president of the United States of America—assuredly an unprecedented aspiration—and would attempt, defiantly if futilely, to vote in November 1871. Six months later, in Apollo Hall in New York City, on May 10, 1872, the Equal Rights Party in convention assembled endorsed Victoria Woodhull as its candidate for America's chief executive in the national elections scheduled for later that year.

And why not? Why not have Victorias as rulers of the two great Anglo-Saxon nations on either side of the Atlantic? Woodhull's platform included planks favoring women's suffrage; a graduated income tax; the regulation of monopolies; laws to protect laborers; reform of the civil service; public ownership of mineral, land, and water rights; guaranteed full employment; and a fairer redistribution of wealth. Her supporters comprised suffragists, spiritualists, labor reformers, freethinkers, Greenbackers, socialists, populists, anarchists, communists, vegetarians, and free lovers—for Victoria Woodhull had already stood on the stage in Steinway Hall, the largest hall in New York City, in November 1871, to speak on behalf of what she called freedom of the affections. "And are you a Free Lover?" The charming, impassioned speaker posed "the almost incredulous query" rhetorically. Then answered it: "I am; and I can honestly, in the fullness of my soul, raise my voice to my Maker, and thank Him that *I am.*"

Her worshipful biographer Tilton (on whom his subject, with her liberal views of social freedom, appears to have bestowed comforting intimacies) would explain that to Mrs. Woodhull, free love meant something other than mere promiscuousness. Rather, she understood the term to connote that "marriage is of the heart and not of the law, that when love ends marriage should end with it, being dissolved by nature, and that no civil statute should outwardly bind two hearts which have been inwardly sundered." More bluntly, Mrs. Woodhull herself insisted on her natural, inalienable right "to love whom I may, to love as *long* or as *short* a period as I can; to *change* that love *every day* if I please, and with that right neither *you* nor any *law* you can frame have *any* right to interfere."

So is this where votes for women would lead us? Little of the reformer's program endeared so radical a theorist to Harriet Beecher Stowe, a devout believer in the sacred, eternal covenant of marriage, even as she was lamenting the law's failure to protect wives from brutal husbands and sexual slavery. Nor would her half sister Belle's obsession with the promoter of such radical views fail to grieve the author of *My Wife and I*. "No one could understand," Mrs. Stowe wrote at the end of 1872, privately, bitterly, of Woodhull, "the secret of her influence over my poor sister—an incredible infatuation continuing even now. I trust God will in some way deliver her." For Isabella "was and is a lovely woman," a perplexed Harriet insisted, and before "this witch" took possession of her, "we were all so happy."

The beautiful, bewitching candidate had spent the summer and fall of 1872 seeking to raise funds, establish so-called Victoria Leagues of support, and invigorate a quixotic presidential campaign, appearing at Cooper Institute in New York and, in September, before the National Association of Spiritualists in Boston. This matter of women speaking in public was, incidentally, a new phenomenon. Saint Paul had opposed such public exhibitions by the weaker sex: *"Let your women keep silence in the churches,"* he counseled the Corinthians, *"for it is not permitted unto them to speak; but they are commanded to be under obedience, as also saith the law."* Thus on Catharine Beecher's behalf, one or another of her brothers had read her numerous lectures aloud to audiences; and when Harriet set out on her triumphal tour of England and Scotland in 1853, Calvin came along expressly to respond to any public tributes—the author of *Uncle Tom's Cabin* merely acknowledging the applause and cheers before taking her seat in genteel silence. Now, however, with the rising prominence of female mediums and the appearance of advocates for women's rights accustoming postwar audiences to higher-voiced lecturers in skirts, Stowe was enticed at last into performing in public herself. In the manner of Dickens, the popular Hartford author would set out in the fall of 1872 on a reading tour, intent on making a tidy sum of money before fleeing the northern winter yet again in favor of her usual months-long annual retreat to warm, sunny Mandarin, Florida.

Thus she spent autumn on the road. Mrs. Stowe's first reading was in Springfield, Massachusetts, on September 13. Over the next three months she read in more than thirty other New England cities and towns and in New York City, ending her tour in mid-December. It was an impressive performance on the part of a woman past sixty, undertaking such demands for the first time and without prior training or experience. She handled it all with aplomb—simply (as she wrote to Annie Fields) speaking her piece and taking her money. According to newspaper reports, those lucky enough to hear her shared in a "mint of genuine fun." For fifty or seventy-five cents they were treated to selections in her own voice from her own writings by the "most noted woman in America," "the world-famous author of 'Uncle Tom's Cabin,'" a "distinguished lady whose works have been read wherever the English language is spoken," on occasions that were billed as the Great Event of the Season.

So there at the lectern in person, in the flesh, stood a slight lady tastefully turned out in gray or black silk or velvet; her gloves either lavender or white; wearing a brooch, corsage, or collar pin; her gray hair accentuating the brightness of her blue eyes; her manner untroubled by stage fright; her voice slightly husky, low, and musical, well suited to rendering the various Yankee dialects of her readings. Stowe's program was invariably in two parts: first, passages from *Uncle Tom's Cabin,* which she delivered with pathos, tenderness, and humor; second, selections from her New England short stories or *The Pearl of Orr's Island.* Scarcely glancing at her text, she would perform in lecture rooms, theaters, music halls, and opera houses; and if, as on November 2 in Bangor, Maine, her voice proved inadequate to the space, "the people rose from their seats and crowded round her, standing gladly, that no word might be lost." More often, however, her Yankee voice proved sufficient to gratify listeners, who might number anywhere from 150 to 1,500 in attendance. In Bangor a deaf woman, having journeyed fifty miles and well satisfied without hearing a word, had approached Mrs. Stowe afterward to tell her: "I come jist to see you. I'd rather see you than the Queen." By the time the author had reached Framingham, she was writing back to her family about her "amazing" audiences, and "how they do laugh! We get into regular gales." In fact, despite her absence from home, the loneliness and weariness of travel, and the rigors of reading aloud night after night, she was able to conclude that on the whole, "it is as easy a way of making money as I have ever tried, though no way of making money is perfectly easy."

Gamely, Mrs. Stowe repeated her ordeal the following fall, of 1873, for the same reason—to make money—and to comparable acclaim, although this time farther afield. She journeyed by ferry, steamboat, and railroad to Pittsburgh, Columbus, Chicago, Zanesville, Dayton, and Cincinnati. The audience in Cincinnati, like others before, "all seemed delighted and begged me to come again." And on that occasion the author made time to revisit Walnut Hills. She was driven to the site by George Beecher, the Georgy who as a child of eleven had been of the party on her triumphal tour in Europe after *Uncle Tom's Cabin*. Now he was in his early thirties, this son of Harriet's beloved brother dead by his own hand long years ago in Chillicothe. His aunt Harriet had George drive her among the buildings of Lane Seminary, and to the house where her twins had been born, "and the house," she reported, "in which we afterwards lived." Left unexpressed in a letter home are the emotions that must have accompanied her on this single return to the place where some eighteen struggling years of a life had passed, in faraway times out west more than two decades gone by then.

During the earlier of Stowe's lucrative reading tours, in the fall of 1872, her brother Henry Ward Beecher was himself being enveloped in yet one more public triumph. This jubilee of the Reverend Mr. Beecher's was uniquely special. In October, Plymouth Church chose to commemorate a quarter century of dazzling success; for exactly twenty-five years earlier, in 1847, a young cleric had arrived in Brooklyn from Indiana to serve as its first pastor. Now, under the banner of "One Family in Heaven and Earth," the full congregation of what had grown into the greatest house of worship in America was devoting a well-planned week to recognizing all that had been accomplished since then.

The Reverend Mr. Beecher pleaded that the week not be about him, but inevitably it tended in that direction. Monday was Children's Day. Tuesday was Teachers' Day. Wednesday was Members' Day. Thursday was Historical Day. And Friday, the last, was Communion Day. And what an extraordinary growth those congregants were able to celebrate, from twenty-one charter members to just under 3,000 among their numbers now (at a time when the average church congregation was less than 100), the vastly increased income, the huge new organ, the employment bureau established for young men of the Plymouth congregation, the ample support provided to two mission churches, the 3,000 youthful scholars gathering every Sunday in the church's three Sunday schools—graduates of which were even then extending the influence of Beecher's benign views nationwide.

On the first of the festival days, Monday, October 7, 1872—a beautiful morning, crisp and clear—current Sunday-school children filed past their famous minister's home on Columbia Heights. Beecher himself was on the doorstep to receive their salute amid the exhilaration of drum and marching band. "Handkerchiefs were waved, banners held aloft, smiles everywhere, cheers triumphant rent the air, and to complete one of the most joyous demonstrations that any one clergyman was ever made the recipient of, a perfect shower of the choicest bouquets were cast at Mr. Beecher's feet." Each child in passing would toss a flower, so that the stout beaming cleric stood at last ankle-deep in blossoms and rose petals, one of the urchins having succeeded "with admirable precision," we are improbably told, "in planting a rosebud on Mr. Beecher's eyes." Members' Day on Wednesday resembled a huge family reunion, with flowers and music everywhere. Thursday, the tenth, Historical Day, rounded out the twenty-five years precisely. With feeling and humility, the minister addressed a vast cheering throng that overflowed the spacious church and spilled far out into the street. "I bless God," he told them, "when I look back. I have lived my life, and no man can take it from me. The mistakes that I have made—and they are many—none know so well as I. My incapacity and insufficiency none can feel so profoundly as I." Now Beecher's time was coming to a close. "Let it go down," he said, "to-day, to-morrow, whenever it may please God. I will not ask for the lengthening out of one single day. I have lived a happy life. I have been a happy pastor. I have loved you and been beloved by you."

On the following day, Friday, the jubilee concluded with over two thousand people taking communion.

It would seem, amid a good man's days, to have been a culminating moment of unalloyed public recognition and esteem. Yet the preacher, for all his smiling, was troubled. He had lately been hiding a secret, which before the month ended all of Brooklyn, all of New York City, all of a gaping, titillated nation would learn about.

The issue of *Woodhull & Claflin's Weekly* dated November 2 hit the city streets on October 28. Immediately it sold out—100,000 copies gone. People were soon paying up to $10—one person $40! an incredible amount for a single copy of a newspaper—in order to own and read a column that began on page 9, by Victoria Woodhull.

"I propose," the editor Woodhull announced there, "as a commencement of a series of aggressive moral warfare on the social question, to begin in this article with ventilating one of the most stupendous scandals which has ever occurred in any community." The editor was doing so in the interest of "officering, and in some sense conducting, a social revolution on the marriage question. I have strong convictions to the effect that this institution, as a *bond* or *promise* to love one another to the end of life, and forego all other loves or passional gratifications, has outlived its day of usefulness." Even now, a number of esteemed and virtuous citizens in our midst have to all intents and purposes discarded the institution, submitting to its limitations only ostensibly, and only "from the dread of a sham public opinion."

Mrs. Woodhull persevered. Take as an example "the character and conduct of the Reverend HENRY WARD BEECHER in his relations with the family of THEODORE TILTON. I intend," she declared, "that this article shall burst like a bomb-shell into the ranks of the moralistic social camp." But in setting off her explosion, the editor insisted that she was "impelled by no hostility whatever to Mr. BEECHER, nor by any personal pique toward him or any other person." That much said, she went on to clarify that the "immense physical potency of Mr. BEECHER, and the indomitable urgency of his great nature for the intimacy and embraces of the noble and cultured women about him, instead of being a bad thing as the world thinks, or thinks that it thinks, is one of the noblest and grandest of the endowments of this truly great and representative man." In other words, it wasn't the preacher's amativeness, which she was here exposing, that offended the editor, but rather his hypocrisy. For the Reverend Mr. Beecher, like Mrs. Woodhull herself, was a free lover, and he should step forth and admit as much. "Every great man of Mr. BEECHER's type," she asserted, "has had, in the past, and will ever have, the need for, and the right to, the loving manifestations of many women."

27

INSIDE THE HOME

O ne woman in particular was alleged to have received the Reverend Mr. Beecher's adulterous caresses over recent years. That woman was Elizabeth Tilton. Like her husband, Mrs. Tilton was a parishioner at Plymouth Church, where the couple had been joined in holy matrimony in 1855 by Beecher himself—"one of the fairest pairs that I ever married." Thereafter, into the 1860s, Theodore Tilton and Henry Ward Beecher became fast friends, so that from "my boyhood up," the younger man was moved to write to his pastor at mid-decade, "you have been to me what no other man has been—what no other man can be. While I was a student, the influence of your mind on mine was greater than all books and all teachers. . . . You are my minister, teacher, father, brother, friend, companion. The debt I owe you I can never pay. My religious life; my intellectual development; my open door of opportunity for labor; my public reputation; all these, my dear friend, I owe in so great a degree to your own kindness that my gratitude cannot be written in words, but must be expressed only in love."

None of us knows for sure what goes on behind the closed doors of even our neighbors' homes, let alone the houses of people dead over a century. Beecher himself remarks that we are all "living two lives—an exterior one and an internal one. They are not always, or often, either parallel, or morally alike. And not once in a thousand times can one infer from the outward life what is in the interior." But this first honored incumbent—in early 1872, and to great acclaim—of the Lyman Beecher Lectureship at Yale Divinity School, in this very year of Plymouth Church's triumphal silver anniversary jubilee, when his congregation extolled their pastor as never before: here, at the summit of his transcendent success, is the greatest preacher since Saint Paul to be exposed to the public and the world as, in private life, an adulterer?

The decades that have passed since then have acclimated us rather better than our forebears, alas, to immorality among the clergy, both Protestant and Catholic. But although transgressions among the godly may astonish us less, Beecher's own century was hardly pure innocence in the matter. Precisely that offense informs Hawthorne's supreme fiction (1850) concerning the Reverend Arthur Dimmesdale. And in real life some few years earlier, the same offense had—as we recall—shocked Beecher's brother-in-law Calvin Stowe, on a trip east in the 1840s, when he came upon examples not only of a New Hampshire pastor's fornicating with a member of his congregation and seducing a kitchen girl, but also of a bishop in Philadelphia who, "half boozled," had pawed young women unlucky enough to be caught alone with him, attempting their violation "to the dishonor of religion, his own unspeakable shame and anguish, and the distress unutterable of his wife and children."

Calvin Stowe's own wife knew well how rarely the real world approaches the ideal, yet in the pages of *My Wife and I* Mrs. Stowe had sought to delineate an ideal home. Outside the home lies the great prosaic terrain of commerce, a masculine, materialistic field of self-interest and raw competitiveness among cutpurses and pickpockets. But within the home is to be found, ideally, among accumulated manifestations of poetical beauty, the feminine values that place family above the individual, a noncompetitive domestic refuge of selflessness and renewal, compassionate, spiritual, empathic. Harriet's own home fell short of the ideal, of course, as every home must. For one thing, sadness kept staining its comforts. Although, for example, the Stowes hired investigators to pursue their son Fred after he disappeared in San Francisco early in the 1870s, not a trace of the young man was ever found; and meanwhile, in this same decade their daughter Georgiana, mother of Harriet's first grandchild, was given easily accessible drugs to relieve melancholia and thereafter grew dependent on them. From that time forward until her death at forty-four, Georgie's life was a grievous one.

And now this horrible charge against Mrs. Stowe's favorite brother!

But consider the source of the charge. Victoria Woodhull, abruptly materializing in New York City toward the end of the 1860s, was living at the moment in a brownstone on East Thirty-eighth Street with not one but two husbands. In addition, various family members and hangers-on had gathered under the same roof. The woman, one of a large family, had been born (it turns out) at a crossroads called Homer, Ohio. Her shiftless father, when forced to leave that hamlet under suspicious circumstances, had wandered with his brood all over the Midwest, making a living of sorts by displaying various of his young daughters as clairvoyants and healers. At fifteen, the child-woman Victoria Claflin married Dr. Canning Woodhull and duly bore him a son—the severely retarded Byron, now in his teens and a part of the brownstone coterie. That first husband was a drunk and an abuser. Presumably Victoria divorced him, for she was now married to a Colonel Blood of St. Louis, a gentlemen who had abandoned a wife and child to comply with his lover's matrimonial wishes. Of late the sodden Dr. Woodhull had reappeared and moved back into his former wife's irregular household.

Also living in this less than ideal home at 15 East Thirty-eighth Street was a man named Andrews, something of a polymath who, along with Colonel Blood and Blood's brother George, was assumed to be furnishing the intellectual content and even the wording of the scarcely schooled Victoria Woodhull's pronouncements in editorials, speeches, and congressional testimony. Besides her sister Tennie, there lived at the same address one or more additional Claflin sisters and their children, along with Victoria's charlatan father—still profiting from his two daughters' success, now as stockbrokers and editors under Commodore Vanderbilt's blessing. Recently removed to a nearby boardinghouse (her daughters paying the rent) was the Claflin mother, who in the spring of 1871 favored the public with a glimpse inside one Victorian household by means of embittered testimony in open court:

"Judge," Annie Claflin buttressed a complaint that she brought unexpectedly to the Essex Market Police Court on May 15, "my daughters were good daughters and affectionate children until they got in with this man Blood. He has threatened my life several times, and one night last November he came into the house on 38th Street and said he would not go to bed until he had washed his hands in my blood." Among other outrages, Annie Claflin went on to specify that the colonel had given offense by taking away "Vickey's affection and Tennie's affection from poor old mother." Nor was that all. "S'help me God, Judge," she cried out—and a reporter for the *Herald* was on hand to set it down and share it with the world—"I say here and I call Heaven to witness that there was the worst gang of free lovers in that house in 38th Street that ever lived—Stephen Pearl Andrews and Dr. Woodhull and lots more of such trash."

A year and a half later, in December 1872, Harriet Beecher Stowe, near the end of her first reading tour, would write in confidence to her friend Annie Fields: "Did I tell you that here in Framingham," in Massachusetts, "lives one wife of that Colonel Blood whom this wretched woman has seduced and infatuated to be her tool and slave"? The first Mrs. Blood appeared to be a lovely and, according to this witness, "accomplished woman with a daughter twelve years of age." Mrs. Blood had explained that her husband came from a fine St. Louis family, had served with honor during the war, and was a devoted father with excellent prospects until the "Woodhull woman set up in St. Louis as a clairvoyant physician and Blood consulted her as to his wife's health. Immediately this witch set her eye on him and never left practicing every diabolical art til she finally got him to give up his family, his position, his prospect in life, his wife and his child, to follow her in a life of infamy as he has been doing ever since."

And this woman had put herself forward as a candidate for the presidency of the United States? "Well," asks Harry Henderson in *My Wife and I*, "why not a woman president, as well as a woman Queen of England?" The sensible, more mature Mr. Van Arsdel, Harry's future father-in-law, provides one answer: "'Because,' said he, 'look at the difference. The woman Queen in England comes to it quietly; she is born to it, and there is no fuss about it. But whoever is set up to be President of the United States is just set up to have his character torn off his back in shreds, and to be mauled, pummeled, and covered with dirt by every filthy paper all over the country. And no woman that was not willing to be draggled through every kennel, and slopped into every dirty pail of water, like an old mop, would ever consent to run as a candidate.'"

In short, such a candidacy lacked decorum. It wasn't feminine. The character of Audacia in *My Wife and I* reveals herself to be just such an unfeminine woman, buttonholing Harry Henderson in his office downtown after reading one of his columns, barging in uninvited "to make your acquaintance." Even worse: "'My dear fellow, I have come to enlighten you,'—and as she said this she drew somewhat near to me, and laid her arm confidingly on my shoulder, and looked coaxingly in my face. The look of amazement which I gave, under these circumstances, seemed to cause her great amusement. 'Ha! ha!' she said, 'didn't I tell em' so? You ain't half out of the shell yet. You ain't really hatched.'"

This was Stowe's brazen Audacia Dangyereyes—"call me Dacia"—jaunty and dashing, "with bold blue eyes, and curling brown hair" and "a little wicked looking cap with nodding cock's feather set askew on her head," just as the real-life Victoria Woodhull was reported to favor a feathered, stylish Alpine cap over eyes that were blue and hair that was curly and brown.

But that real-life American woman *had* entered New York City's masculine world, after which she wrote defiantly to the *Herald* in 1870: "while others argued the equality of woman with man, I proved it by successfully engaging in business; while others sought to show that there was no valid reason why women should be treated, socially and politically, as being inferior to man, I boldly entered the arena of politics and business and exercised the rights I already possessed." As one consequence Victoria Woodhull was certain that prejudice against women must soon disappear, and meanwhile their vote should be understood not as a privilege to be petitioned for but rather as a constitutional right to be exercised.

The reformer also defended her private life, vigorously. "Colonel Blood never treated my mother otherwise than kind," this wife and daughter testified in court. "Sometimes when she would become violent he would utterly ignore her presence. I thought at times that she was insane and not responsible for what she said." It ended with the daughter's pitying her mother. On occasion the older woman "would come down to the table and sit on Mr. Blood's lap and say he was the best son-in-law she had. Then again she would abuse him like a thief, calling him all the names she could lay her tongue to, and otherwise venting her spleen—all without any cause whatsoever." As for a first husband living there, in the same house with the second, "Dr. Woodhull, being sick, ailing, and incapable of self-support, I felt it my duty," Mrs. Woodhull explained, "to myself and to human nature that he should be cared for, although his incapacity was in no wise attributable to me. My present husband, Colonel Blood, not only approves of this charity, but co-operates in it. I esteem it one of the most virtuous acts of my life."

Be that as may, others whom society regarded as moral exemplars found little virtue of any sort attached to Mrs. Woodhull; and notable among those others were members of the Beecher family. One of them, Catharine Beecher, had opposed votes for women on the ground (yet again) that participating in political life would rob the gentler sex of its femininity, vital in ameliorating the influence of ruthless, amoral male behavior. As time passed, Catharine spoke out directly against Woodhull's various radical views, even seeking to deny her access to lecture halls, while Catharine's sister Harriet Beecher Stowe was disseminating through her popular novel *My Wife and I* the crude caricature of the reformer as a comical absurdity, pushy and unconscionably vulgar.

A moment came when Victoria Woodhull, under attack, wrote to the eminent brother of those two ladies, Henry Ward Beecher himself. "Dear Sir: For reasons in which *you* are deeply interested as well as myself, and the cause of truth, I desire to have an interview with you, without fail at some hour to-morrow." This was in the late fall of 1871, a full year before the exposure of the Beecher-Tilton scandal in *Woodhull & Claflin's Weekly*. Mrs. Woodhull was then about to give her lecture on "The Principles of Social Freedom"—that is, on free love—at Steinway Hall, and she approached the famous minister to introduce her. "Two of your sisters have gone out of their way to assail my character and purposes," she reminded her correspondent, before adding ominously: "You doubtless know that it is in my power to strike back." Mrs. Woodhull insisted that she had no wish to do so and wanted nothing but justice. "I speak guardedly, but I think you will understand me. I repeat that I must have an interview to-morrow."

The interview took place, and—predictably—reports about it later differed over what was said. In the event, Mr. Tilton made the introduction of Mrs. Woodhull at Steinway Hall. She proceeded that evening to give her flaming speech on free love—thanking God that she *was* a free lover—with the consequence that during the following months, into and through the spring, summer, and fall of 1872, the reformer's standing with the community crumbled. She had expressed "visions and messages to the people which," as Isabella Beecher Hooker foresaw, "it would be woe unto her to refrain from proclaiming, even though martyrdom were sure to follow." And martyrdom did follow, on cue. Mrs. Woodhull's foes grew vastly in number. Her mother's unscripted, erratic behavior in court that spring furnished further means to get at her. Commodore Vanderbilt withdrew his support. Other sources of funds dried up. Respectable society washed its hands of the woman. The press turned on her. Her adherents vanished. When, in October 1872, she defied them all and published in her newspaper what she had gleaned from Tilton and others—among them Susan B. Anthony and Elizabeth Cady Stanton—about the distinctive domestic arrangements of Henry Ward Beecher, the scandal that erupted at once put an end to any further political ambitions. Anthony Comstock, a twenty-eight-year-old dry-goods salesman who was at the start of a long, self-appointed career as Suppressor of Vice, obtained a federal warrant that allowed him to have both sisters seized for using the mails to disseminate obscene literature in the form of *Woodhull & Claflin's Weekly*. Arraigned, the two were sent to the Ludlow Street jail, where they remained on election night, November 5, 1872. For a full month after General Grant's reelection to the presidency, the "Bewitching Brokers of Wall Street" were kept in cell 11, until their sympathizers posted the $16,000 bail and the young women, still defiant, went free.

What can we know for sure about private lives of people long dead? Facts made public we may learn of. Theodore Tilton, for example, was born in 1835 in New York City. In his youth he was a strict Calvinist, having been taught that all humans are miserable sinners: "I would have cut off my right hand rather than have written a letter on a Sabbath day." At Plymouth Church he had encountered, with heartfelt gratitude, the Reverend Henry Ward Beecher's gentler gospel of love. Tilton and Elizabeth Richards had been drawn to each other when he was sixteen and she seventeen. After their minister had married them, Tilton and Beecher became close friends. "Then, what hours we had together!" the younger man reminisced in 1865, writing to his reverend mentor. "What mutual revelations and communings! What interchanges of mirth, of tears, of prayers! The more I think back upon this friendship, the more am I convinced that, not your public position, not your fame, not your genius, but just your affection has been the secret of the bond between us; for whether you had been high or low, great or common, I believe that my heart, knowing its mate, would have loved you exactly the same."

Letters survive to convey to us words—the very words—of people long and forever silenced. If not what they thought exactly, at least the phrasings in which they shaped what they intended others to read. Letters, journals, court testimony, hearsay—about Beecher's own marriage: Oliver Johnson, a lifelong loyal friend of the minister's, spoke of Eunice Beecher as "one of the most jealous women that ever lived," and her husband's life with her a "hell upon earth." Henry's oldest brother, William, charged that Eunice "separated Henry Ward from his kindred, from his brothers and sisters, who were prevented from coming to the house on her account." Within that house at breakfast—a specimen of hearsay that Henry Ward is reported to have told his friend Theodore—Mr. and Mrs. Beecher's conversation together was "the vainest, the most vapid, the most juiceless, the most unsaccharine of all things."

On firmer, factual grounds, we know that Theodore Tilton proved successful in a publishing career, in part thanks to his minister's sponsorship. In 1861, when he was twenty-six, Tilton was awarded the position of assistant editor at the *Independent,* a periodical then on the point of bankruptcy. In his hands, circulation more than tripled. The young man's skills and good judgment saved the magazine and led it to prosper. Later assignments he discharged with like effectiveness. The attractive, articulate editor, imposing at six feet four inches, began taking to the road annually on profitable lecture tours; he would be gone for months at a time. Tilton's public life, as an advocate in politics, literary taste, and social reform, was busy and influential.

His private life sounds different. "I am a weak man, supposed to be strong," he writes to his wife Elizabeth in 1866, in the course of lecturing out west, "a selfish man, supposed to be the world's lover and helper; an earthly minded man, supposed to be more Christian than my fellows. I cannot endure the mockery—it breeds agony in me." She has charged him to write her his "secretest thoughts, and not to chronicle external events." He writes to his "Delicious Darling," to his "Dear Pet," and signs himself "Thine immortally," "with love inseparable and everlasting." Elizabeth responds in kind, to "My Own True Mate," for instance, on Friday night, December 28, 1866. "My beloved," she writes, "I have been thinking of my love for Mr. B considerably of late, and those thoughts you shall have." Mr. B was her pastor, Henry Ward Beecher, her husband's friend, welcomed in the restful seclusion of the Tiltons' home. "Now," writes Elizabeth to her absent Theodore, "I think I have lived a richer, happier life since I have known him. And have you not loved me more ardently once you saw another high nature appreciated me? Certain it is that I never in all my life had such rapture of enthusiasm in my love for you" as now, she suggests, in her husband's arms in recent passionate nighttimes.

It took eight years from that date, but after all the emotion through a long interval, all the avowals and suspicions, the secrets and mistrust, the tears, protestations, kisses, and outrage within and between two Victorian homes—and as introduction to the protracted anguish that followed—Theodore Tilton swore out a complaint in Brooklyn City Court against Plymouth Church's world-renowned minister, the Reverend Henry Ward Beecher, on August 24, 1874. The complaint charged defendant with having willfully alienated a wife's affections from her husband, plaintiff, and demanded $100,000 as recompense for Tilton's having wholly lost "the comfort, society, aid and assistance" of said wife.

28

TRIAL

*M*ore fully: "That the defendant, contriving and wilfully intending to injure the plaintiff and deprive him of the comfort, society, aid and assistance of the said Elizabeth, the wife of the plaintiff, and to alienate and destroy her affection for him, heretofore on or about the tenth day of October, 1868, and on divers other days and times after that day and before the commencement of this action, at the house of the defendant, No. 124 Columbia street, City of Brooklyn, and at the house of the plaintiff, No. 174 Livingston street, City of Brooklyn, wrongfully and wickedly and without the privity or connivance of the plaintiff, debauched and carnally knew the said Elizabeth, then and ever since the wife of the plaintiff, by means whereof the affection of the said Elizabeth for the said plaintiff was wholly alienated and destroyed . . ."

The trial commenced in City Court, Brooklyn, on Monday morning, January 11, 1875, Chief Justice Joseph Neilson presiding. It proved to be the sensational occurrence of the year, of the decade—indeed, except for the trial of John Wilkes Booth's accomplices, it was the most widely reported legal event in America during the later nineteenth century. At the time these struggles at law of Tilton and Beecher appeared even more momentous: "Nothing since the outbreak of the Civil War has excited such intense interest all over the United States as this case," the *New York Sun* told its readers. "All the papers, from Brooklyn to the smallest hamlet in Oregon, are talking about it, and the whole American people are anxious to know the truth." During the long duration of the trial, as many as 3,000 hopeful spectators were turned away daily, the courtroom filled with prominent public figures among a sizable crop of the less well known. The audience proved lively. Some few were arrested for disorderly conduct; Judge Neilson had to reprimand others for hissing, or applauding, or chattering among themselves when the testimony grew tedious. Those seated skipped lunch rather than risk losing their places, or they brought food from home or purchased snacks from vendors nearby. Opera glasses went on sale as well, the better to keep an eye on the principals up front.

Nearly every day Mrs. Henry Ward Beecher—the faithful, severe Eunice—appeared in her seat. Her husband attended less often. To conduct his defense, Plymouth Church's renowned minister had assembled a formidable legal team headed by William Maxwell Evarts, recently United States attorney general, future secretary of state, future senator from Massachusetts. Tilton's legal advisers were scarcely less imposing. As the trial proceeded, hundreds of pamphlets reproducing witnesses' testimony and evidential documents (among many others the "Letter of Contrition," the "Ragged Edge Letter," the "Day of Judgment Letter") were printed for sale at newsstands all over the country. Cartoons and caricatures of the courtroom adversaries decorated storefronts, saloons, and barbershops. Newspapers reported the proceedings in copious detail, with columns and columns devoted to opening statements, to the examination of witnesses, to cross-examinations, and in time to summations from both sides that took more than two weeks to deliver. As far away as Marseille, French readers followed the latest installment of *"L'afaire Beecher-Stilton, et Victoria Vodull."*

Ever since his days in Indianapolis, the great preacher under scrutiny had been known for slighting his pastoral duties, leaving to others the task of visiting the sick, the wayward, and the grieving. But in the case of his parishioners at 174 Livingston Street, the Reverend Mr. Beecher made an exception. During the winter of 1868–1869, for instance, he called on the Tilton family as many as a dozen times, and the man of the house was away lecturing during most of those visits. Earlier, Robert Bonner of the *New York Ledger* having advanced the astonishing sum of $24,000 for Beecher to write a novel, the minister had done so (not a very good novel, as it turned out) and in the process he had brought his manuscript to Mrs. Tilton to read to her. In part his *Norwood* was a love story. Hours spent thus at the Livingston Street home provided this untried fiction writer with inspiriting interludes. At the trial he described his special friendship in general terms: "During these years of intimacy in Mr. Tilton's family, I was treated as a father or elder brother . . . Children were born; children died. They learned to love me, and to frolic with me as if I was one of themselves. I loved them, and I had for Mrs. Tilton a true and honest regard. She seemed to me an affectionate mother, a devoted wife"—and also a parishioner who could turn to her pastor "with artless familiarity and with entire confidence. Childish in appearance, she was childlike in nature, and I would as soon," he said, "have misconceived the confidence of her little girls as the unstudied affection she showed me."

In August 1868, Elizabeth's infant son Paul died. The bereft mother was thirty-four; the Reverend Mr. Beecher, from whom she sought comfort in her grief, was fifty-five. From his summer home in Peekskill he came down to Brooklyn expressly to officiate at Paul's funeral. That autumn, the great preacher delivered a political speech at the Brooklyn Academy of Music in support of General Grant, the Republican candidate for president. An admiring Elizabeth Tilton sat in the front row, sad that her dead son would never hear Mr. Beecher's golden voice. The following afternoon she went to her minister's home on Columbia Heights. He was alone, preparing a sermon. Only one entry in a diary Mrs. Tilton kept then was later made public, a single entry on that Saturday, October 10, 1868: "A Day Memorable."

Nearly twenty-one months later, in the course of the summer evening of July 3, 1870, upstairs in her bedroom at their home on Livingston Street, in the very room where Paul had died, the wife confessed her infidelity to her husband. She told Theodore Tilton that Mr. Beecher had persuaded her their love was not wrong, and "therefore it followed that any expression of that love, whether by the shake of the hand or the kiss of the lips, or even bodily intercourse, since it was all an expression of that which by itself was not wrong, therefore that bodily intercourse was not wrong; that Mr. Beecher had professed to her a greater love than he had ever shown to any woman in his life; that she and I," so Tilton reprised his wife's confession at the trial, "both knew that for years his home had not been a happy one; that his wife had not been a satisfactory wife to him." In making her confession, Elizabeth revealed no sense of wrong on her part for submitting to Beecher's sexual importunities;

her wrong lay in deceiving her husband and hiding the deceit through these many months. And Tilton forgave her, explaining to a friend: "I don't think she was a free agent. I think she would have done his bidding if, like the heathen-priest in the Hindoo-land, he had bade her fling her child into the Ganges or cast herself under the Juggernaut."

Thus, despite everything, the aggrieved husband continued to regard his wife as chaste in spirit. Yet had Elizabeth Tilton really confessed in her bedroom on Livingston Street that summer evening? Beecher to the last denied debauching and carnally knowing Mrs. Tilton; and Elizabeth herself—although not called to testify during the trial—had earlier flatly repudiated the idea of ever committing adultery. She told an investigating committee convened at Plymouth Church that her husband had grown insanely jealous and lived only to destroy Henry Ward Beecher. And about the state of her own home the agitated Mrs. Tilton protested to the *Brooklyn Eagle* that any suggestion "that the harmony of the house was unbroken 'til Mr. Beecher entered it as a frequent guest and friend is a lamentable satire upon the household where he himself"—her erring Theodore—"years before, laid the cornerstone of free love and desecrated its altars up to the time of my departure, so that the atmosphere was not only godless but impure for my children. And in this effort and throe of agony, I would fain lift my daughters, and all womanhood, from the insidious and diabolical teachings of these latter days."

In consequence, shortly before bearing witness at the Plymouth Church investigation, she had fled her free-loving husband turned religious skeptic, sent their children to her mother's home in New Jersey, and come to rest with friends nearby. An interrogator at the Plymouth Church inquiry questioned Mrs. Tilton about her pastor: was she suggesting that the Reverend Mr. Beecher gave her self-respect?

"Yes," she answered, "I never felt a bit of embarrassment with Mr. Beecher, but to this day I never could sit down with Theodore without being self-conscious and feeling his sense of my inequality with him."

Indeed, as the later, civil trial in Brooklyn City Court proceeded, Theodore Tilton, despite his good looks, his accomplishments, and his forgiveness of Elizabeth, was transformed into an unattractive figure. The story becomes immensely complicated, this of the Beecher-Tilton imbroglio, taking more than a million words of court testimony and six protracted months to unfold. And as it unfolds, the cast of characters grows bulky. Major ones include the mother to whose house Mrs. Tilton sent her children after her marriage soured. Mrs. Morse, Tilton's redoubtable mother-in-law, once wrote to him, "Your slimy, polluted, brawny hand curses everything you touch," and on another occasion she lunged at her son-in-law with a carving knife: a woman both malicious and hysterical, though (on Tilton's own testimony) capable of great kindness.

The colorful cast includes Bessie Turner from Ohio, an adolescent servant who lived for eight years with the Tiltons as all but a member of the family. On the stand, Bessie provided intimate glimpses into the Livingston Street household. One night in 1867, for example, "I had not been in bed very long before Mr. Tilton came in and said he had come to kiss me good-night. I was lying on the side of the bed next the door; he went round on the other side and leaned over the bed and kissed me good-night." But having done so, the intruder lingered to stroke Bessie's forehead, then her hair, "and said what nice soft hair I had, and how nice and soft my flesh was—my forehead, and then he put his hand—was putting his hand in my neck, and I took his hand out; and he says, 'Why, Bessie, my dear, you are painfully modest'; he says, 'Why, those caresses, those are all right. People in the best society do all those things, and it is perfectly proper. Nobody but people that had impure minds think of such things as that as not being right.' And I said," Miss Turner reported stoutly to the court, "I could not help what they did in the best class of society; that I had my own ideas of what was proper and what was modest."

So who was the worse cad: Beecher or Tilton? Mr. Tilton was not on trial, yet spectators and readers judged him perforce, for that nighttime escapade as for his behavior on a different occasion with Bessie, when (the servant swore) he struck her—"gave me a terrible blow that hurled me the opposite side of the room"—coolly remarking afterward, "why, Bessie, my dear, you tripped and fell, didn't you?" The master of the house was apparently hot-tempered and abusive, and scenes emerged of bedroom doors at 174 Livingston Street locked to keep Tilton out in the hallway, fuming. Assuredly he belittled his wife's intelligence; and about Victoria Woodhull, as well, the suave editor—late her glowing biographer—testified ungallantly on the stand: "I wish to say distinctly to the jury that my relationship to Mrs. Woodhull was a foolish one and a wrong one . . . and I do not ask any man to defend me for it, but to blame me for it."

That repudiation provoked a counterblast from a celebrated feminist leader. "Victoria Woodhull's acquaintance would be refining to any man," Elizabeth Cady Stanton wrote publicly, indignantly. "In her character and person there is never anything but refinement in word and movement. She has a beautiful face—the ideal of spirituality." And, gathering steam, Mrs. Stanton charged on to challenge Tilton's disparagement at length: "Victoria Woodhull has done a work for Women that none of us could have done. She has faced and dared men to call her names that make women shudder. She has risked and realized the sort of ignominy that would have paralyzed any of us who have longer been called strong-minded. Leaping into the brambles that were too high for us to see over them, she broke a path into their close and thorny interstices, with a stedfast faith that glorious principle would triumph at last over conspicuous ignominy, although her life might be sacrificed; and when"—alluding to the reformer's recent public downfall—"with a meteor's dash, she sank into a dismal swamp, we could not lift her out of the mire nor buoy her through the deadly waters."

Victoria Woodhull herself appeared at Beecher's trial only once, briefly, to surrender certain letters deemed relevant, although on perusal the letters proved inconsequential. Mr. Beecher had earlier asserted that the world was welcome to pore over any letters of his that Mrs. Woodhull or anybody else might have in hand. In fact, that had constituted his sole response to the accusation of adultery in the pages of *Woodhull & Claflin's Weekly* in November. But not until the following summer, returning to Brooklyn from a restorative visit in the White Mountains, did the reverend minister thus finally deign to break his silence. On June 30, 1873, Beecher had written to the *Brooklyn Eagle*: "I have returned to the city to learn that application has been made to Mrs. Victoria Woodhull for letters of mine, supposed to contain information respecting certain infamous stories against me." This was his initial public acknowledgment of the scandal, his first word on it, eight months after the charge of adultery had appeared in Woodhull's newspaper. "I have no objection," Beecher now wrote, "to have the *Eagle* state, in any way it deems fit, that Mrs. Woodhull, or any person or persons, who may have letters of mine in their possession, have my cordial consent to publish them. In this connection, and at this time, I will only add that the stories and rumors which have, for some time past, been circulated about me are untrue, and I stamp them in general and in every particular as utterly untrue."

But why had the accused waited so long to speak up? Why had Mr. Beecher not come forth at once and vehemently denounced Woodhull's charges as flagrant lies? The court wondered about that. (Elizabeth Tilton had denied the adultery, true, but she might have done so in order to protect her own name, or to shield her children, or to spare the Plymouth Church congregation and preserve a world-renowned preacher's moral influence.) And why had Beecher earlier written an incriminating apology to Mr. Tilton and given it for delivery to Frank Moulton—one more colorful character whom the trial let the nation come to know. Moulton, with his Kitchener mustache, would spend eleven days on the witness stand. "My Dear Friend Moulton," Beecher had written: "I ask through you Theodore Tilton's forgiveness and I humble myself before him as I do before my God. He would have been a better man in my circumstances than I have been. I can ask nothing except that he will remember all the other hearts that would ache. I will not plead for myself. I even wish that I were dead; but others must live to suffer." The note, *"In trust with F. D. Moulton,"* dated from Brooklyn, January 1, 1871, went on to regret the pain inflicted upon "the poor child lying there and praying with her folded hands. She is guiltless —sinned against; bearing the transgression of another. Her forgiveness I have. I humbly pray to God that he may put it into the heart of her husband to forgive me."

When so private a letter became public, Beecher's half sister Isabella, Mrs. Woodhull's ardent partisan, wrote to her brother Tom in Elmira: "Now, Tom, so far as I can see it is he"—Henry—"who has dragged the dear child into the slough and left her there." The dear child was Elizabeth Tilton; and the Reverend Thomas Beecher felt inclined to agree: Mrs. Woodhull as a free lover, he responded, "only carries out Henry's philosophy, against which I recorded my philosophy twenty years ago." For in *Norwood* Henry had written what he had frequently preached: that love evolves upward, that true love "requires a greatness of nature that does not come often," and that "two natures, both large and various, yet unlike, though not discordant, are still rarer." Such large natures do sometimes meet to fulfill a high destiny—even if all the help Tom Beecher could offer his own large-natured brother in the present instance was to pray for him. "In my judgment, Henry is following the slippery doctrines of expediency," and between the two—Henry Ward Beecher and Victoria Woodhull—"Woodhull is my hero," wrote Tom, "and Henry my coward, *as at present advised*. But I protest against the whole batch and all its belongings."

In contrast, the other Beechers—Catharine, Edward, Charles, and the rest—stood solidly behind their beleaguered brother through his ordeal, and this despite the disappointing impression he made when called to the witness stand. Tilton, for all his faults, had testified with forthrightness and candor; but once Beecher's turn came, he sounded evasive, resorting some 900 times to phrases of uncertainty and forgetfulness: *I do not recollect; I will not be sure; I do not now remember distinctly.* As for his apology sent via Moulton, that had been offered, Beecher explained, only because he had disrupted Mr. Tilton's life and failed to recognize the warmth of Mrs. Tilton's feelings for her pastor. Nothing more than that— certainly not for having committed adultery!—despite the apology's tone of anguish. The minister did concede his imprudence, but never immorality; and his siblings—except for Isabella and Tom, privately—believed him.

His sister Harriet believed unshakably in Henry Ward Beecher's innocence. After the trial was over, she set down her feelings at length. "It seems now but a little time since my brother Henry and I were two young people together," she wrote. "He was my two years junior, and nearest companion out of seven brothers and three sisters. I taught him drawing and heard his Latin lessons, for you know a girl becomes mature and womanly long before a boy. I saw him through college, and helped him through the difficult love affair that gave him his wife; and then he and my husband had a real German, enthusiastic love for each other, which ended in making me a wife." Harriet was in Mandarin as she recapitulated all this, in March 1876, at "Orange-blossom time," responding to a note of sympathy from England two years old by then. Earlier she had felt unable to answer Mrs. Lewes—George Eliot. Now Mrs. Stowe exclaimed to her epistolary friend, that other, greater, but no more celebrated author: "Ah! in those days we never dreamed that he, or I, or any of us, were to be known to the world." Sister and brother *had* become famous, and controversial, with both Beechers making enemies aplenty in the process. The Civil War, which each of them played a part in bringing about, had reduced a proud planter aristocracy to resentful beggary; and Henry's reform impulses in other fields—his progressive theology, his advocacy of universal suffrage—had turned many more against him: social traditionalists, religious conservatives. "Lastly, he has had," Harriet went on with her explanation, "the misfortune of a popularity which is perfectly phenomenal. I cannot give you any idea of the love, worship, idolatry, with which he has been overwhelmed."

All that, and something else besides. "Never," she assured Mrs. Lewes, "have I known a nature of such strength and such almost childlike innocence." But innocence, credulous and trustful, had made vulnerable "a man who continuously, in every little act of life, is thinking of others, a man that all the children on the street run after, and that every sorrowful, weak, or distressed person looks to as a natural helper." She who knew her brother through and through would insist on one further point: "In all this long history there has been no circumstance of his relation to any woman," Harriet affirmed in her private missive to George Eliot, "that has not been worthy of himself,—pure, delicate, and proper; and I know all sides of it, and certainly should not say this if there were even a misgiving."

Personal testimony, heartfelt, from an astute observer of a favorite brother to an intimate friend. Yet there had been rumors, which Stowe either had never heard or had dismissed out of hand. Henry Bowen, a founder of Plymouth Church, had fallen into the arms of another founder in joyful relief upon being assured that young Henry Ward Beecher would come to them from Indianapolis—the same Reverend Mr. Beecher with whom Bowen's own wife later, even on her deathbed, was alleged to have confessed having had improper relations. And young Julia Merrill and Betty Bates in Indiana had penned letters rather more passionate than spiritual to Mr. Beecher at his setting forth for the East, and had written to him, still passionately, many years later. Despite all that—and similar whispers about Edna Dean Proctor and Chloe Beach—a doting, aching sister kept firm her faith in one whom she adored, telling George Eliot in 1876, "you see why I have not written" until after the trial was long over. "This has drawn on my life—my heart's blood. He is myself."

Was Henry Ward Beecher guilty? He stands before us in a guise different from how he appeared to his contemporaries. We who have met the Elmer Gantrys of fiction and the Jimmy Swaggarts and Jim Bakkers of fact—not to mention a succession of pedophile priests—will be likely to find Beecher's public style suspect: by turns sanctimonious, oleaginous, and veering into the hypocritical. Even among his contemporaries, one observer compared the man to a dunghill covered with flowers; others wrote of him as an overpaid, overfed perfumer of souls, dropping unctuous syllables like "soft spiritual rain from his flowery platform" onto the creamy overcoats of a shallow congregation alternately guffawing and teary. Yet for the majority back then, the trial of Henry Ward Beecher pitted Christians on one side against scoffers and infidels on the other. That was how Beecher's attorneys summed up the case, stressing the utter impossibility of their client's guilt, "the incredibility of so flagrant and heinous an imputation."

The summations ended. Judge Neilson gave the jury its charge. It was to disregard all testimony about Mr. Tilton's oddities of behavior and to pay no attention to Plymouth Church's earlier exculpation of its pastor. "In any view of the case," the judge went on, "you may be disposed to ask why Mr. Beecher, if innocent, should have garnered up in his heart all that pain and fear so long, when he might have made proclamation to the world and trampled out the scandal as with iron boots."

The jury withdrew. It comprised twelve merchants of modest means; the foreman was a dealer in flour. The twelve deliberated without leaving the building. While their deliberations dragged on, food and changes of clothing were sent in to them. At night, they took turns sleeping a few hours on a couple of mattresses in the jury room. A few came down sick, the flour dealer suffering from colic. They were out eight days.

Finally, after fifty-two ballots, the group reported back to the court on July 2, 1875. From the start, eight of the twelve had found against Tilton, and by the end one more had joined those eight, leaving three on the plaintiff's side. In his study on Columbia Heights, the Reverend Mr. Beecher was told of the deadlock: effectively he had been exonerated, with nine votes in his favor. At that, partisans from

Plymouth Church had set about ushering Mrs. Beecher home in triumph, as others of their number—normally staid gentlemen all— lingered in the courtroom "frisking from table to table" as they shared their joy at the outcome.

For his part, Theodore Tilton had left the building earlier and, "calm and placid as a lake on a summer morning," strolled into the streets of Brooklyn alone.

29

LATE YEARS

*T*hereafter, the Tiltons went their separate ways. Theodore, his path to further progress in journalism obstructed, resumed lecturing for a livelihood, on such topics as "The Human Mind" and "The Problem of Life." At first he enjoyed some success. In the fall of 1875, an overflow crowd at the Brooklyn Academy of Music gave him an enthusiastic welcome and interrupted his talk again and again with applause. But elsewhere in the country Tilton's efforts met with less warmth. Audiences grew sparse. The forsaken husband returned discouraged from a tour out west, obliged to eke out a living freelancing in the years immediately ahead. Finally he left America in 1883 for permanent exile in France. For the rest of his life Theodore Tilton lived in Paris, much of the time on Île Saint-Louis in sight of Notre Dame, a regular habitué of the Café de la Régence on the Right Bank. There, as the century wound down, the expatriate spent his days playing chess with Judah Benjamin and other exiles and telling acquaintances anecdotes of celebrities he had known in America. In addition he wrote industriously, both fiction and poetry, all forgotten now. His *Complete Poetical Works*, published by Oxford University Press and dedicated to his estranged wife, appeared in 1897, the year of Elizabeth's death back home. Theodore Tilton died a decade later, at age seventy-one, and was buried at Fontainebleau, in the Cemetière de Chailly-en-Bière. He left an estate valued at $3,000.

Elizabeth Tilton had lived out her days in quiet as well, except for a single brief moment. After the civil trial, she became a near-recluse, a zealously devout woman growing ever more pious, residing with a widowed daughter there in Brooklyn. No newspapers were allowed in their home, which a group called the Christian Friends used as a house of worship. Only on the one occasion did Mrs. Tilton emerge from her self-imposed obscurity, in 1878, three years after the end of the courtroom spectacle that her husband's complaint had initiated. On April 16 of that year, she wrote a letter to her lawyer, who turned it over to the press with her permission. The letter was published in newspapers across the country. In it the writer spoke of recent "long months of mental anguish" that had led her at last to tell friends, "whom I had bitterly deceived, that the charge brought by my husband, of adultery between myself and the Reverend Henry Ward Beecher, was true, and that the lie I had lived so well the last four years had become intolerable to me. That statement I now solemnly reaffirm, and leave the truth with God, to whom also I commit myself, my children, and all who must suffer." She concluded this final, tardy confession of guilt by acknowledging the misreadings of her motives that were bound to arise from it: that Mrs. Tilton was filled with malice, or was insane, or wanted to return to her husband. All kinds of reasons would be conjectured, she supposed, "save the true and only one—my quickened conscience, and the sense of what is due to the cause of truth and justice."

Rather surprisingly, this last public word, so definitive in its phrasing, was widely discounted. People measured what the woman was saying now alongside three earlier statements of hers: the one that her husband, at the trial, reported Elizabeth's sharing with him in private, in which on a July night in 1870 she had confessed her unfaithfulness; a second in 1874 to the Plymouth Church investigating committee, before whose members she had unequivocally denied ever committing adultery; and a third statement, after the trial, in 1875, when she again asserted her innocence of the accusation. "This weak and erring woman has so forsworn herself," the *Times* concluded in response to her final statement, in 1878, "as to forfeit all claim to attention or credence."

What really went on between Elizabeth Tilton and her pastor will never be known. We later Americans, instructed in such matters on the highest federal authority—about unrighteous lustings of the heart, about not having sex with that woman—know the slipperiness of definitions in cases of intimacy. A fanatically pious partner may come to judge as adultery behavior that the other, more liberal participant in what occurred regards as little more than impassioned gropings of affection: admittedly imprudent, but not penetrant and thus in effect hardly actionable. But whatever her sins, and despite her different accounts of them, the public at large felt mostly sympathy for Elizabeth Tilton, both during the trial and afterward. Her husband always spoke well of her in public; her pastor, though denying adultery, took the accrued blame on himself; and in court at recess that pastor's wife, the formidable Eunice Beecher, made a point of greeting Mrs. Tilton cordially. Moreover, throughout her ordeal, lank Theodore's petite, youthful-looking, onetime "Delicious Darling" had sat quietly in the legal limelight, and afterward she withdrew with her four children into the shadows of a decorous, inconspicuously pious life. Thus her ways seemed to pose no threat to the social order, which would hear little more of her until the spring of 1897. "Mrs. Theodore Tilton Dead," read the headline—in her early sixties, after a stroke, at the home of her daughter on Pacific Street in Brooklyn. "Her children," we learn, "were at her bedside when she died."

Even Harriet Beecher Stowe spoke gently of Mrs. Tilton, whose fate was far different from the one that awaited the more threatening Victoria Woodhull. In the mid-1870s, the social order had moved to crush Mrs. Woodhull and had appeared successful in doing so. A "jailbird," as Mrs. Stowe in private labeled that "witch," a living example of the deplorable consequences that result when women aspire to equality with men, the beleaguered reformer suffered in health from the campaign launched against her. These later years had left Mrs. Woodhull without funds and, apparently, without respectable friends. Her brokerage firm had closed; her newspaper had shut down. A sister she cared for, Utica, died at this time from drugs and alcohol, at thirty-one. Victoria divorced Colonel Blood in 1876. To make ends meet, she was driven, like others, onto the grueling lecture circuit.

Yet from those emotional ashes the phoenix would rise, gathering up what remained of her singular household and transporting the lot of them to England in August 1877. Once arrived overseas, the indomitable Victoria and her sister Tennie took care to provide well for themselves. The one met and married, against his family's wishes, a younger, very respectable, very wealthy bachelor banker.

The other, Tennie, married a gentleman, also solidly solvent, who in the following year was made a baronet. Victoria meanwhile had turned away from her past in America, changed the spelling of her name to Woodhall (with an *a*), renounced the doctrine of free love, and set about becoming conventionally proper in her London mansion in fashionable Hyde Park Gate and at her country seat, Norton Park, in Worcestershire. All that newly acquired square footage provided ample room to accommodate for the rest of their lives the eccentric parents of a loyal daughter, along with any siblings in need. (Woodhull's son Byron, brain-damaged at birth, lived on there until his death far in the future, at age seventy-seven, in 1932, cared for after his mother's demise by Victoria's only other child, who herself died at eighty, in 1940.)

The stylish and still handsome Mrs. Woodhall-Martin, meanwhile, had lived out her own days promoting Anglo-American understanding, serving the Red Cross in the Great War, and in war and peace riding around the countryside in her motorcar. As his letters away from her confirm, her husband had adored her to the last. John Biddolph Martin died in 1897, leaving a widow very well off. Tennie, now Lady Cook, retained Sir Francis's devotion as well, outliving that satisfied nobleman into an opulent widowhood of her own. Tennie was in her mid-seventies when she passed on, in 1923; but it was not until 1927 that Victoria Woodhall, Mrs. John Biddolph Martin, attended by her grown maiden daughter, closed her eyes a final time, in her chair, quietly, in her ninetieth year, at Norton Park one summer morning at the height of the Jazz Age. By that time sophisticated American women overseas were successfully laying claim to many of the rights for which Victoria Woodhull had once so shockingly agitated.

Woodhull's enemy, Henry Ward Beecher, had been dead forty years by then. After his long-ago court trial that ended in a divided finding, the Reverend Mr. Beecher, effectively exonerated, had emerged from his study to attend the regular Friday prayer meeting at Plymouth Church that same evening of July 2, 1875. At his appearance, waiting crowds of supporters had cheered the minister roundly, and once inside the church, when he sang with his congregation the hymn "Christ Leads Me Through No Darker Rooms Than He Went Through Before," all were moved as one to shed grateful tears. Moreover, his flock stood solidly behind their pastor through days ahead, and the church trustees voted the amazing sum of $100,000 to help pay his abundant legal bills. Of course—as Elizabeth Cady Stanton pointed out—Plymouth Church had a financial interest in insisting on Beecher's innocence; he had brought the church both wealth and international fame. Not just Lincoln, but Whitman, Thoreau, Emerson, Greeley, and many many others, resident in New York or merely visiting, were as likely to attend a Sunday service in Brooklyn to hear the great preacher as they were to call, at least once in their lives, at that other national landmark, Niagara Falls.

But after the civil trial, to make doubly sure of the innocence of the accused, Beecher's church had convened yet another investigating committee: "a council of ministers and laymen," as his sister Harriet would describe it in her later letter to George Eliot, "in number representing thirty-seven thousand Congregational Christians, to whom Plymouth Church surrendered her records,—her conduct,—all the facts of the case, and this great council unanimously supported the church and ratified her decision; recognizing the fact that, in all the investigations hitherto, nothing had been proved against my brother. They at his request, and that of Plymouth Church, appointed a committee of five to whom within sixty days any one should bring any facts that they could prove, or else forever after hold their peace." No such facts emerged. "It is thought now by my brother's friends," as of the spring of 1876, "that this thing must finally reach a close."

Beecher himself set out in 1877 on a lecture tour, for which he was promised up to $600 a lecture, an amount that no other speaker in America could command. He traveled all over the country that year and the next, and the crowds that gathered to hear him were enormous. At first many came out of curiosity, even no doubt to scoff and jeer, but so gifted a practitioner as this had long since learned how to win over hostile listeners. Soon Beecher was enjoying resounding success in Boston, Louisville, Memphis, St. Louis, San Francisco, and elsewhere across the land. He recovered his self-esteem; and by the end of the tours not only was his confidence restored, but an indebtedness that had piled up through recent difficult years was in the way of being paid off entirely. At last he seemed able to lay his burdens aside.

Henry Ward Beecher would live nearly a decade longer, still vastly popular up to the end, still the adored minister of the largest, wealthiest congregation in America. He went on writing, publishing, and being read; went on lecturing to attentive crowds on current affairs; went on drawing huge congregations to Plymouth Church on Sundays. His parishioners never lost faith in him. No doubt the scandal had tarnished his luster as a spokesman for America; so that the earlier progenitor of "Beecher's Bibles," the admired auctioneer raising money to liberate slaves before the war, the chosen speaker at Fort Sumter to celebrate the war's end, the religious guide for millions, who had helped young men of his times mediate between the amoral demands of their workplace and moral claims of their homes: the Beecher of all that influence was doubtless diminished in spiritual size toward the last. "Henry Ward Beecher is an adulterer, a perjurer, and a fraud," wrote Charles A. Dana of the *New York Sun* in 1878, "and his great genius and his Christian pretenses only make his sins the more horrible and revolting." And another well-known editor, Samuel Bowles of the *Springfield Republican* (good, rare friend of Emily Dickinson), adjudged that Beecher "has no reverence, and he inspires none, only wonder and admiration for his mental gymnastics and his physical freshness and vigor." But those were minority views, except to the extent that they registered a decline in the seriousness with which the famous preacher was regarded nationwide after the mid-1870s, even as his equally famous sister, following her Byron debacle at the start of that decade, was taken less seriously as a major figure in nineteenth-century American culture.

Despite all this, when the great man died, on March 8, 1887, the entire nation took notice. Newspapers all over the country recorded the solemn event on their front pages, where readers were gratified to learn that Eunice Beecher (who would die precisely a decade later, to the day) had been at her husband's deathbed holding his hand. President Cleveland telegraphed condolences. Tributes were recorded from a wide variety of admirers: the actor Edwin Booth, the Irish leader Charles Parnell, Andrew Carnegie, the free-thinker Robert Ingersoll, Louis Pasteur, William Ewart Gladstone, Alexander Graham Bell, the reformer Henry George, various Union and Confederate generals of the Civil War, and even busy Anthony Comstock of the New York Society for the Suppression of Vice. Overseas, Londoners were told of the demise of "one of the comparatively few Americans who enjoyed a world-wide reputation."

And six years later, long after the mammoth funeral services in a flower-bedecked Plymouth Church had ended, after the obsequies had been observed and the procession and the salutes and the burial in Greenwood Cemetery all were over and done, the *National Cyclopedia of American Biography* would opine—astonishing! how fleeting is fame, how changed the tastes of now from then!—that "it is safe to say that no man, unless it be George Washington, has ever died in America more widely honored, more deeply loved, or more universally regretted."

30

ENDINGS

*T*hree years after the Beecher-Tilton trial in Brooklyn City Court, nine years before the death of Henry Ward Beecher, that celebrity's famous sister published her last work of consequence, in 1878. Harriet Beecher Stowe could not have ended her writing career on a happier note, for *Poganuc People* may be her most serene and coherent novel. Its manageable length is appropriate to the charming story it tells; its tone, laced with abundant humor, is uniformly mellow and wise; and its characters come to full life in their vividly rendered settings. The principal of those settings is Litchfield, Connecticut—here Poganuc—in 1818. Once more Mrs. Stowe, now in her late sixties, chooses to look far back, this time to her own childhood sixty years earlier, in a New England mountain village that retains into our present day much of the beauty that her pages lovingly describe.

The author's sharp memory permits us to live through a winter of that earlier time. Seven-year-old Dolly, Hatty's surrogate, lies in bed in her cold, fireless bedchamber on "a still, clear, freezing night," listening in the deep silence as the slightest sound clinks metallically, runners of sleighs beyond the window "squeaking and crunching over the frozen road, and the lively jingle of bells. They would come nearer, nearer, pass by the house, and go off in the distance." In the morning downstairs, "frost sparkled white on the back of the big fire-place, where the last night's coals lay raked up under banks of ashes." The business of half the year is to chop fuel to keep that fire burning for the other half, where indoors through a long cold season endless chores await the inhabitants: stockings for a little girl to darn, wristbands to stitch, salt to pound, spices to grind, coffee to roast, eggs for her to beat. Outside, their world on a hilltop lovely in summer is "a howling desolation for about six months of the year, sealed down under snow and drifted over by winds that pierced like knives and seemed to search every fiber of one's garments, so that the thickest clothing was no protection." In the meetinghouse ("wide, roomy, and of a desolate plainness"), over the objections of traditionalists a stove has lately been installed to ease winter Sundays, "whereby the air was so moderated that the minister's breath did not freeze into visible clouds of vapor while speaking, and the beards and whiskers of the brethren were no longer coated with frost during service time."

The village minister is Dolly's father, Dr. Cushing, "the first gentleman of the parish" in those more hierarchical days. We learn that "the life of childhood was much more in the imagination than now. Children were let alone, to think their own thoughts." Dolly Cushing, the central figure of *Poganuc People,* youngest of the doctor's ten children, finds time through these winters to explore the three attics over the parsonage, among the catnip, boneset, tansy, and other such healing herbs hung to dry up there, among the barrels of old sermons and family papers, the discarded bonnets and spinning wheels, the broken clock, the battered copy of *The Arabian Nights* for a girl to read, reread, and treasure. And in the attics are rats, indulged at their ease as they feed on the storage bins, "with their tails hanging gracefully down, engaged in making meals on the corn or oats." Under the parsonage, in the murky cellar, apples from the family orchard are stored: Pearmains, Greenings, Golden Sweets, Seek-no-furthers. But Dolly will venture into those cavernous depths only with Nabby, the maid, or with an older brother. And sometimes, expressing "the perverse spirit which moves the male nature to tyrannize over the weaker members," her brothers "agonize her by running beyond her into the darker chambers of the old cellar, and sending thence Indian warwhoops and yells which struck terror to her soul, and even mingled their horrors with her dreams."

We hear Dolly's boisterous older brothers in the background of the story, their boots thumping on the floor overhead in preparation for another passing day as spring approaches, their minister father poring over his box of garden seeds downstairs, rereading the labels longingly: Early Lettuce, Early Cucumbers, Summer Squashes. Finally spring does arrive, if to remain only briefly. "The forest hills around Poganuc first grew misty with a gentle haze of pink and lilac, which in time changed to green and then to greener shades, till at last the full-clothed hills stood forth in the joy of re-creation, and, as of old, 'all the trees of the field clapped their hands.'" With that, children imprisoned through the winter are set free to play alongside the stream outside and to gather flowers in meadows newly abloom.

Summer brings with it the great secular holiday of July 4. "Fed-eralists and Democrats, Town Hill folk and outside folk"—that is, the wealthy in their village mansions under the elms and the farm-ers beyond the edge of town—"were all of one mind and spirit to make this a celebration worthy of Poganuc Center and the great cause of American Independence." Neighboring villagers up since midnight have journeyed through darkness over rural roads to this their county seat to take part in the festivities. Those begin in early morning with the ringing of the meetinghouse bell and the setting off of fireworks. Locals have laid aside their work clothes to don the cocked hats and gold-laced uniforms of the militia, grand in their posturing before admiring women and girls. To the sound of fife and drum the parade marches proudly past, and there are stir-ring speeches, after which Dr. Cushing offers a long evangelical prayer that these United States "might be chosen vessels, commis-sioned to bear the light of liberty and religion through all the earth and to bring in the great millennial day, when wars should cease and the whole world, released from the thraldom of evil, should rejoice in the light of the Lord."

In Stowe's pages we come to know and to care for these ear-nest yet fun-loving people, as we share their transient hopes and troubles. The rickety schoolhouse must be moved to more salubri-ous ground, but how is that to be managed? A newly established Episcopal church in the village enchants the children by prepar-ing for Christmas—fragrant spruce garlands, candles at the win-dows, and a gilt-paper star—even as puritanical Congregationalists frown in disapproval. ("No, child; nobody knows when Christ was born, and there is nothing in the Bible to tell us *when* to keep Christmas.") Tension persists between the old aristocracy—Judge Belcher, Colonel Davenport, Judge Gridley—and a new nation's humbler farmer democrats, who will not be condescended to. We watch young love develop; attend at a good woman's sickbed; go to her funeral; hear her cranky old husband, "grim and stony" in his grief, abase himself in public confession and become a God-fearing human being at last. We hear of trips to Boston taking three days over a distance now covered in a couple of hours. And when autumn comes, with the forest aflame in color, we go nutting with the Cushings up winding mountain paths, Mrs. Cushing and Nabby bringing the picnic hamper—"unlimited ginger-bread, and dough-nuts crisp and brown, and savory ham, and a bottle of cream, and coffee all ready for boiling"—as the doctor scales high trees and shakes down chestnuts, walnuts, and butternuts for the children to gather.

Winter returns, another Christmas, and so the years pass. So much life and vigor, so much simple truth; and all of it has disappeared: "all whom we knew there have passed away; all the Town-Hill aristocracy and the laboring farmers of the outskirts have gone"—the author gently concludes—"one by one, to the peaceful sleep of the Poganuc graveyard. There was laid the powdered head, stately form, and keen blue eye of Colonel Davenport; there came in time the once active brain and ready tongue of Judge Belcher; there, the bright eyes and genial smile of Judge Gridley; there, the stalwart form of Tim Hawkins, the gray, worn frame of Zeph Higgins." These are people we've come to know. "Even Hiel's cheery face and vigorous arm had its time of waxing old and passing away, and was borne in to lie quiet under the daisies. The pastor and his wife sleep there peacefully with their folded flock around them"— as Litchfield's own pastor of old, Lyman Beecher, lies elsewhere asleep in another grave. A time so filled with vitality, where now a "village of white stones stands the only witness of the persons of our story. Even the old meeting-house is dissolved and gone," with a single graceful, enchanted tale to hold in awareness a people and their way of life otherwise vanished beyond recovery.

By the time she wrote *Poganuc People,* Mrs. Stowe had taken up residence in the home where she would live out the remainder of her days. At a sizable loss she had sold her fabulous Oakholm in Hartford, her bucolic dream house that the disfigurements of post-war industry had overwhelmed. Later, in 1873, the Stowes had moved into a recently built home for sale on Forest Street, in an area known as Nook Farm, on the city's western edge. Her sister Mary Beecher Perkins had long lived there, as had their half sister Isabella, with whom Harriet and the other close-knit denizens of Nook Farm would make their peace in the years ahead. It was an altogether agreeable setting for the unfolding of a late life, with the family and younger literary friends round about: not far off the amiable Susan and Charles Dudley Warner—he was the popular travel writer and editor of the *Hartford Courant*; and right next door the Clemenses, Livy and her husband Sam, who wrote under the pen name Mark Twain. None of those friends or family members was truly rich as the Gilded Age measured wealth, but all were well off, so as to make of their comfortable joint lives something approaching an idyll: side doors were left unlocked and each neighbor welcomed in everybody else's home, amid much laughter as they took tea or dined together, played their parlor games, and watched one another's children grow and prosper.

Meanwhile, in winters for as long as she could, Mrs. Stowe, her husband, and her twin girls packed their belongings—plants from the conservatory, household rugs, furniture, linen, dishes—and with the servants made their way ritualistically south to Mandarin, to live oaks, oleanders, and the mild Florida climate. There for five months, on the bluff over the broad Saint Johns, they would live "an easy, undress, picnic kind of life, far from the world and its cares," as cardinals and mockingbirds sang in the orange trees fronting their windows.

A year arrived when, having started to pack as usual, the family was obliged to change plans and remain through the winter up north in Hartford. Professor Stowe had become too ill to travel. It was 1884; and thereafter, through his long decline, the professor's wife looked after her Old Rabbi anxiously, helping to keep him comfortable until his death of Bright's disease a half century into their married life, in August 1886.

Harriet would live on for another decade. She never returned to Florida. As far back as 1880 she had begun sorting through her papers, sifting out what seemed not worth keeping, "and so filing and arranging those that are to be kept, that my heirs and assigns may with the less trouble know where and what they are." Strange, this rereading of old letters, other people's as well as her own: "I cannot describe the peculiar feelings which this review occasions." Here was

what she had set down in Cincinnati "in the first two years of marriage, when Mr. Stowe was in Europe and I was looking forward to
motherhood and preparing for it—my letters when my whole life was
within the four walls of my nursery, my thoughts absorbed by the
developing character of children who have now lived their earthly
life and gone to the eternal one." It gave her "a sort of dizzy feeling
of the shortness of life and nearness of eternity when I see how many
that I have traveled with are gone within the veil."

She wrote thus to her son Charles, born in the tumultuous July
of 1850 in Brunswick, Maine, and destined to bring much comfort
into his mother's life, as husband of a daughter-in-law for whom
she felt affection, as father of beloved grandchildren, and as minister of the nearby Windsor Avenue Congregational Church in
Hartford. Later, starting in 1887, Charles would help Mrs. Stowe
shape her letters into a kind of autobiography, his own spare commentary welding the various pieces together to furnish a basic
source of information about one remarkable woman's days on earth.
The work was published in 1889: *Life of Harriet Beecher Stowe
Compiled from Her Letters and Journals, by Her Son Charles Edward Stowe*. A handwritten, two-page note in facsimile opens the
volume, wherein Mrs. Stowe herself—her penmanship firm and
legible—contributes a brief preface. In it she alludes to the "great
difficulty" that has attended the reaching of this advanced stage in
life, "yet now, I do not repent me of the troubles I have been at, to
arrive where I am. My sword," she ends spiritedly, "I give to him
that shall succeed me in my pilgrimage & my courage & skill to
him that can get it. Hartford, Sept 30, 1889. Harriet Beecher Stowe."

By then the author's mind, like her father's in his old age, had
grown hazy. In the following year, with a new decade opening, a
physician nephew, Isabella's son, issued a startling report for Mrs.
Stowe's inquiring public: "She is neither insane nor an imbecile,
but has reached the stage which we familiarly term 'second childhood.' She is pleased with trifles, with innocent amusements, just
as a child would be. She will meet you and chat and laugh, or even
call you by name if some one mentions it to her. Otherwise she
recognizes by name her more intimate friends alone." That same
year, 1890, Hattie, one of the unmarried twins who faithfully attended their mother to the end, responded to a correspondent seeking an interview. Anything of the sort would be impossible, because

Mrs. Stowe was "not now above a child of two or three years." On one patriotic occasion, encountering on the street a Nook Farm neighbor in his Civil War uniform, the elderly lady embraced him as her lost son Fred, troubled veteran who had disappeared in San Francisco two decades earlier.

Even so, the diminished woman enjoyed moments of clarity. During one such, as late as 1893, when she was past eighty, Harriet, writing to Oliver Wendell Holmes (three years her senior), described her brain as "tired out"; she told her old friend that she no longer used it at all. At last, "from sheer fatigue and exhaustion in the march and strife of life," she wrote, "it gave out before the end was reached. And now I rest me, like a moored boat, rising and falling on the water, with loosened cordage and flapping sail." Her ways had become what she called nomadic; "I have no fixed thoughts or objects. I wander at will from one subject to another. In pleasant summer weather I am out of doors most of my time, rambling about the neighborhood and calling upon my friends. I do not read much. Now and then I dip into a book much as a humming-bird, poised in air on whirring wing, darts into the heart of a flower, now here, now there, and away. Pictures delight me and afford me infinite diversion and interest. I pass many pleasant hours looking over books of pictures." A caregiver kept an eye on the famous author transformed into a chirpy old woman wandering innocently around the neighborhood.

Grace King, then in her late thirties, came calling on Nook Farm neighbors, the genial Charles Dudley Warners, with whom the Louisiana writer had been invited to spend several days. One morning, dressing, their guest happened to glance out her bedroom window down to the pond and garden below. Amid the flowers, she made out "a slight figure gliding rather than walking, so fast and light fell the footsteps—a woman in a light dress, whose folds vibrated in the morning breeze." Though indistinct, the woman's face appeared animated as she chattered with herself down there. "Soon she was in the house, and I could hear a pleasant voice greeting Mr. and Mrs. Warner, and they answering her." But when Miss King arrived downstairs, she was surprised to find no sign of the stranger, who she assumed had been invited for breakfast. She asked about her.

"Oh, that was Mrs. Harriet Beecher Stowe," Susan Warner explained. "She is always running around the neighborhood of a morning. You will see her often. No one pays any attention to her!"

The southerner gasped. To her dying day, forty years in the future, she would remember her astonishment at so unexpected an identification. "A cannon ball could not have astounded me more," King wrote in reminiscences near her life's end, in 1932. "Harriet Beecher Stowe! She who had brought the war upon us, as I had been taught, and all our misfortunes! *That* was Harriet Beecher Stowe! The full realization of where I was came upon me!"

"You have read her book?" Mrs. Warner asked.

"No, indeed!" replied their guest. "It was not allowed to be even spoken of in our house!"

Before the war the Kings had prospered as a successful lawyer's family, but the war had cost them everything. The family had fled New Orleans in 1862; had lived in poverty after the war; and had only gradually, through a father's relentless labors at his profession, recovered their economic standing. For through those years—from the war's end in 1865 to the end of the century and beyond—America struggled with the problems involved in putting the country back together; and the South was struggling hardest of all.

"The history of the world is made up of the individuality of a few men." As an example: "A little Yankee woman wrote a crude book. The single act of that woman's will caused the war, killed a million men, desolated and ruined the South, and changed the history of the world." The speaker, a character in a later novel, of 1902, is giving voice to what became dogma in the new South after the war was over, in a conquered land as it grappled with an issue not unfamiliar to our own times: how to integrate a large ill-educated minority into the mainstream of American life. Mrs. Durham, the character who singles out a "little Yankee woman" for blame, is but one of the "good" southern people confronting the problem up close, in a work of fiction by Thomas Dixon that would earn in its time a popularity comparable to the earlier *Uncle Tom's Cabin*.

Born toward the end of the Civil War, the son of a Baptist minister and prosperous farmer in North Carolinia—who like the Kings of New Orleans had lost everything in the war—Dixon grew up immersed in the turmoils of Reconstruction. Like other once affluent, now destitute southern whites, his preacher father joined the Ku Klux Klan in the late 1860s, bent on restoring an antebellum way of life. "We stand for one thing at least, the supremacy of Anglo-Saxon civilization." This is Charles Gaston speaking, the hero of the novel that the younger Dixon, that Klan member's son, would come to write. Thomas Dixon's novel was called *The Leopard's Spots*, published in 1902 as the first volume in a trilogy that culminated in *The Clansman*. It was *The Clansman* on which D. W. Griffith based his technically astounding film *The Birth of a Nation* (1915). But for us, Griffith's movie, despite its revolutionary cinematographic innovations, has been permanently begrimed by its virulent racism, just as has Thomas Dixon's novel from which the film derives.

Indeed, in their relentless bigotry, Dixon's three novels are hardly readable now. *Can the Ethiopian change his skin or the leopard his spots?* asks the epigraph of the first of the three on its title page. In part, the story told in *The Leopard's Spots* follows characters out of *Uncle Tom's Cabin* into the postwar era. Young Halliday, the Quaker son of Ohio parents who figure in Stowe's novel, here has his role to play, as does a former slave off the Shelby plantation in Kentucky, where Tom and his wife Chloe were working at the start of *Uncle Tom's Cabin*. In Dixon's later novel, Tim Shelby in his new freedom is revealed to have turned into an insolent buffoon, so insufferably arrogant that there is nothing for right-minded white people to do but finally lynch him from a balcony in a North Carolina town square. The son of George and Eliza Harris, whom an antebellum mother clutched as a child in her arms while she fled to freedom across the thawing Ohio River, now has moved to Boston, where he has graduated from Harvard and appears handsome, intelligent, industrious—exemplary, in fact, except for his intolerable aspiration to be loved by a certain white woman. Most prominently, the despicable Simon Legree, now somehow the opportunistic, unprincipled Yankee leader of Reconstruction efforts in North Carolina, meets well-deserved defeat in his grab for power there before returning to the North, where he mercilessly exploits poor whites in his textile mills in New Jersey, to make himself fabulously wealthy.

Dixon's novel begins at the war's end. It explores life in the South through the confusions and desolations that follow immediately after the war, with the Freedmen's Bureau and federal troops enforcing the new political and economic rights of African-Americans. And it moves on to 1900, after the troops have been withdrawn, Reconstruction having failed and prewar white supremacy having been finally, effectively, triumphantly reestablished. In telling that melodramatic tale, the novel conveys a myth by which the nation bound up its wounds and lived far into the twentieth century.

This was the myth: that the martyr Lincoln would have saved the South if a madman had not killed him; that "the Lion was dead, and the Wolf, who had snarled and snapped at him in life, put on his skin and claimed the heritage of his power"; that that Wolf, in the form of such evil politicians as Charles Sumner and Thaddeus Stevens, whispered its "message of hate, and in the hour of partisan passion became the master of the nation"; that from then until 1877, with the contested presidential election that led to a national compromise withdrawing federal troops from the South, the horror of Reconstruction raged on: black men—ignorantly, vilely corrupt—lounging barefoot and drunk in southern legislatures, beastially lusting after Dixie's fair daughters while their scalawag and carpetbagger white mentors led them to pass laws trampling on southern values and transferring power into the hands of radical Republicans. There were good blacks—like Old Nelse in the novel—who remained loyal to white masters and mistresses, longing with them for a return of the old days "befo' de wah." Under those circumstances, lamenting the Lost Cause, white worthies in a world of uppity niggers bided their time as the noble Klan gathered to redeem southern honor. In the North, meanwhile, men of feeling and sound judgment, coming at last to see the injustice of it all, extended their white hands across the Mason-Dixon Line in an act of reconciliation with their southern brothers in order to preserve forever the priceless 1,500-year-old heritage that is Anglo-Saxon civilization.

In perpetuating this myth, *The Leopard's Spots* sold over a million copies, was translated into a dozen languages, bestowed on its author international renown, and made of Doubleday Page—which brought out Dixon's novel—a major publishing firm, as its namesake remains. Dixon himself regarded the writing of *The Leopard's Spots* as "the most important moral deed of my life. It may shock the prejudice of those who have idealized or worshipped the negro as canonized in 'Uncle Tom.'" But isn't it time, the author asked, that "they heard the whole truth? They have heard only one side for forty years."

That "whole truth," as the novel tells it, rests on misrepresentations that modern historical research has thoroughly discredited.

For two examples: black legislators in the brief period of Reconstruction, from 1865 to 1877, are now understood to have conducted themselves by and large responsibly—remarkably so—passing creditable laws for the general welfare; and the Ku Klux Klan, with its terrorist means and Aryan purposes, has long been recognized as the contemptible emblem of hate-filled decades during which white supremacy was brutally enforced through an interval that ranks among the most distasteful and disgraceful in our history.

One little Yankee woman, all that while, had stood for a different, more loving truth. Although by the 1890s hardly cognizant of raging national hatreds—between northern capitalists and laborers, between the races black and white—Harriet Beecher Stowe in her prime had known well enough what hate was, this old woman wandering obliviously about the green lawns of Nook Farm. Earlier she had felt deep hatred for the foul stain of slavery, and hatred for the radical threats to family of the Woodhull witch, and hatred toward that courtesan Guiccioli, mistress to Lord Byron—as toward Byron, even the great Byron himself in the role of husband, abusing a woman whom Mrs. Stowe deeply loved.

For it was love, far more than hatred, that had been Stowe's lifelong theme: love of her Savior, of her father, of her husband, of her children, of her sisters and brothers—of Charles, poor George, Henry—of the exalted Lady Byron as of humble black people alongside whom she had worked through a lifetime. "I love everybody," she once told the temperance leader Frances Willard—rather too simply perhaps, given the complexity of her emotional makeup. But her biographer son would assert at the last that love was the key to his mother's whole life. "She was impelled by love," he wrote, "and did what she did, and wrote what she did, under the impulse of love."

Now she had grown old even beyond her age. By October 1894 the twins were noting of their mother that "in the last year her handwriting has changed very much, so as to look hardly like her own, and she herself is changed very very much. Should you meet her without knowing who she was, I don't think you would recognize her at all. Her hair is now snowywhite, her face very thin and brown and has the vague wondering expression of infancy."

So this is where it must end, a story that began in 1832 with a family's voices rising in song out of a great coach lumbering westward over country roads in Pennsylvania. It ends here, in Connecticut, in Hartford, at Nook Farm, on Forest Street, with Harriet Beecher Stowe's brilliant mind long dimmed and death coming to her at last. She has been confined to her bed with brain congestion and paralysis since Monday, sinks into a stupor on Tuesday night, and dies on Wednesday, in her eighty-sixth year. The twins are at her bedside, and the hour is just after noon on July 1, 1896.

Notes

The narrative derives details of Stowe's life from three sources principally: Charles Edward Stowe's *Life of Harriet Beecher Stowe*, prepared by the novelist's son late in her lifetime and published in 1889; Forrest Wilson's *Crusader in Crinoline* (1941); and Joan D. Hedrick's exemplary *Harriet Beecher Stowe: A Life* (1994). Below I cite all three volumes frequently and gratefully, by short title. Those and other abbreviated citations are expanded in Works Cited, pages 315–320.

1 Epigraph: C. E. Stowe, *Life*, 106.

1 WESTWARD BOUND

3 "singing hymns and songs." Hooker, "Last of the Beechers," 286.

3 *"peppering the land." Autobiography of Lyman Beecher*, 2:208–209.

4 "has her little record" too. C. E. Stowe, *Life*, 58.

4 "no place in the world." *Autobiography of Lyman Beecher*, 2:201.

4 "such a field of usefulness." Ibid.

4 "If we gain the West, all is safe." Ibid., 2:224 (7/8/30).

5 "most prominent . . . preacher in the nation." Ibid., 2:181 (10/14/30).

5 "greatest thought that ever entered my soul." Ibid., 2:184.

5 "motive in going to Cincinnati." Rugoff, *Beechers*, 78.

6 "people have to leave there to be sick." C. E. Stowe, *Life*, 54.

6 "in case we decide to come." *Autobiography of Lyman Beecher*, 2:200 (5/2/32).

6 "the letter is begun." C. E. Stowe, *Life*, 56.

7 "begging, borrowing, and spoiling." *Autobiography of Lyman Beecher*, 2:208.

7 "enemy was coming in like a flood." Ibid., 2:180–181.

7 "not a clean cap to put on." C. E. Stowe, *Life*, 57.

9 "forty-five cases of conversion." *Autobiography of Lyman Beecher*, 2:209.

9 "young empire of mind and power." L. Beecher, *Plea*, 40, 12.
9 "replete with moral oxygen." *Autobiography of Lyman Beecher*, 2:231. The recollection, in an unattributed chapter, was probably penned by Harriet's brother Charles.
9 "holding out my hand." C. E. Stowe, *Life*, 50.
10 "sport of morbid feeling." Ibid., 66.
10 "those that I love differently." Ibid., 51–52.

2 CINCINNATI

11 "cheerfulness and hilarity." Fields, *Life*, 42; *Autobiography of Lyman Beecher*, 1:396.
11 "proved lifelong in its constancy." C. E. Stowe, *Life*, 32.
12 "I do nothing right." Ibid., 36–37.
12 "live in the external one." Hedrick, *Stowe*, 73.
12 "intelligent, New England sort of folks." *Autobiography of Lyman Beecher*, 2:200.
13 "wonderful and inexhaustible beauty." Martineau, *Retrospect*, 2:56.
13 "fresh dripping from the kennel." Trollope, *Manners*, 68.
14 "actually got upon the back of one." C. E. Stowe, *Life*, 63.
14 "literally speaking, a *city of pigs*." From Mrs. Houstoun's *Hesperos: or Travels in the West* (London, 1850), quoted in Harlow, *Cincinnatians*, 79.
15 "green calash and long plaid cloak." Description in *Philadelphia Sun*, quoted Ibid., 123.
15 "pigs'-tails and jawbones." Trollope, *Manners*, 69.
16 "the jog of common English." C. E. Stowe, *Life*, 69–70.
17 "the labor of our new school." Ibid., 66.
18 "in bad taste and indiscreet." L. Beecher, *Plea*, 66.
19 Lane Debates. Thomas, *Weld*, 70–87; Rugoff, *Beechers*, 146–151; *Autobiography of Lyman Beecher*, 2:240–249.
20 "could have *gone over* with the waters." C. E. Stowe, *Life*, 75.
20 "sins of uncleanliness and intemperance." New York State, *Messages from the Governors, Comprising Executive Communications to the Legislature* . . . (Albany, 1909), 3:395, quoted in Rosenberg, *Cholera Years*, 41.
21 "can we go through with this!" Hedrick, *Stowe*, 95 (8/12/34); *Autobiography of Lyman Beecher*, 2:275.
21 "within reach of woman's love." Hedrick, *Stowe*, 96.
21 "I should *bleed to death*." Ibid., 97 (5/24/35).
22 "I feel *nothing at all*." Fields, *Life*, 91; C. E. Stowe, *Life*, 76.

3 PROFESSOR STOWE

23 "Your own, H. E. B." C. E. Stowe, *Life*, 76.
23 "certainly fall in love with you." Ibid., 106.
23 "There is no woman like you." Ibid., 102.

24 "immoderately attached to books." Ibid., 436–437.

24 "account of a most singular delusion." Ibid., 422ff.

28 "thought it was one of my visions!" Fields, *Life*, 307.

28 "the sight of innumerable aerial beings." C. E. Stowe, *Life*, 435–436.

29 "I got hold of 'Faust.'" To George Eliot, 3/26/82, ibid., 420–421.

29 "kept myself in tolerable health." Ibid., 422.

30 "as domestic as any pair of tame fowl." Ibid., 78.

4 EARLY MARRIED LIFE

32 "never was happier on the whole." Hedrick, *Stowe*, 112.

32 "walk in a beaten track." Katherine (Mrs. William) Beecher to Beecher family, 4/3/37, ibid., 111.

32 "a genius & a blue stocking." Ibid., 112–113 (c. 4/16/37).

32 "so superior to most." Ibid., 141 (7/4/52).

32 "Bravo, you noble creature." Ibid., 112 (1/23/37).

33 "tired & sleepy at both periods." Ibid., 113 (c. 4/16/37).

33 "real good talks together." Ibid., 122 (4/30/42).

34 "1) I am naturally anxious." Ibid., 124–125 (9/29/44).

35 "the best English and French goods." Quoted in Harlow, *Cincinnatians*, 109.

35 "then he had but two children." Esther Beecher to Harriet Beecher Stowe, 7/7/37, Hedrich, *Stowe*, 113–114.

35 "our *last* Semi-colon." Harriet Foote to Roxana Foote and family, ibid., 114. Roxana Foote was Harriet Beecher Stowe's grandmother.

36 "throw Lane Seminary to the dogs." Calvin to Harriet, 7/22/37, ibid., 113.

37 "We are in debt—& embarrassed." To Mary Dutton, 12/38, ibid., 136.

37 "the mother of three children!" C. E. Stowe, *Life*, 90–92 (6/21/38).

40 "I *do* it for *the pay*." Hedrick, *Stowe*, 136 (12/38).

40 "need a mother's whole attention." C. E. Stowe, *Life*, 104 (from Hartford, 1842).

40 "making money very fast." Calvin Stowe to his mother, 10/27/47, Hedrick, *Stowe*, 136.

40 "You must be a *literary woman*." C. E. Stowe, *Life*, 102 (spring 1842).

40 "I must have a room to myself." Ibid., 104 (from Hartford, 1842).

40 "fresh, youthful female beauty." Quoted in E. Wilson, *Patriotic Gore*, 19.

41 "No man can love and respect his wife more." Ibid., 20.

41 "no offences of this kind." Quoted in Rugoff, *Beechers*, 243 (6/44).

41 "with an almost *insane* love." E. Wilson, *Patriotic Gore*, 22.

42 "write an occasional business letter." C. E. Stowe, *Life*, 101 (12/40).

5 AGONIES

43 "seemed in very cheerful spirits." From Harriet's account in the form of a circular letter to "Dear Brothers and Sisters all," 7/4/43, Schreiner, *Beechers*, 123.

44 "lifeless bleeding form on the sofa." Ibid., 124.

44 "not the tears of the father." *Autobiography of Lyman Beecher*, 2:345.

44 "entire emptiness of this world." Schreiner, *Beechers*, 125.

44 "heart secrets before undreamed of." To Thomas Beecher, 6/2/45, *Autobiography of Lyman Beecher*, 2:371.

44 "garrulous & filled with laughter." Hedrick, *Stowe*, 160 (6/13/44).

44 "Will no experience . . . teach you"? Ibid., 160 (7/19/44).

45 "exceedingly sensitive and rebellious." Ibid., 163 (7/17/44).

45 "the ability to nourish her myself." To Sarah Buckingham Beecher, 9/23/[43], ibid., 155.

45 "sew every day for a month." C. E. Stowe, *Life*, 110.

45 "dark, sloppy, rainy, muddy." Ibid., 111–112; Hedrick, *Stowe*, 169.

47 "You would laugh to see him." To Georgiana May, F. Wilson, *Crusader*, 221.

47 "richness of God's mercy." C. E. Stowe, *Life*, 113.

47 Watercures. For studies of this nineteenth-century enthusiasm, see Cayleff, *Wash and Be Healed*; and Weiss and Kemble, *Great American Water-Cure Craze*.

49 John Knight's diet. Weiss and Kemble, "Forgotten Water-Cures," 173.

50 "everything agrees with me." Quoted in Wagenknecht, *Stowe*, 96.

50 "we will come together again." Hedrick, *Stowe*, 180 (12/46).

50 "It is enough to kill any man." Ibid., 180 (n.d. [1847]).

50 "a baby that I can *nurse myself.*" Schreiner, *Beechers*, 144.

51 "You are so proud of your baby." Hedrick, *Stowe*, 188 (7/14/48).

51 "kisses upon my rough old face." Ibid., 180–181 (7/31/49).

51 Cholera. See Rosenberg, *Cholera Years*: symptoms, 1–3; causes, 121–122, 170–171; treatment, 151; end of cholera in America, 226.

52 "sensitive and rebellious" stomach. Hedrick, *Stowe*, 163.

52 "little Charley was taken ill." C. E. Stowe, *Life*, 122 (7/10/49).

53 "yours is a heart that never fails." Hedrick, *Stowe*, 190 (7/9/49).

53 "watching all day by the dying bed." C. E. Stowe, *Life*, 123 (7/23/49).

53 "soothe nor do one thing, not one." Ibid., 124 (7/26/49); F. Wilson, *Crusader*, 230.

6 CALL TO BOWDOIN

54 "I get out of patience." To Henry Ward Beecher, 2/1/[72?], Hedrick, *Stowe*, 424, n. 36.

55 "My health has not been good." C. E. Stowe, *Life*, 128 (2/6/50).

57 "a quiet and agreeable passage." From Brooklyn, 4/29/50, ibid., 130.

58 "have raised his salary to $3,300." Ibid.

58 "no doubt that they will do it." Ibid., 129 (2/6/50).

59 "My health is already improved." Ibid., 130.

59 "to push my way through hurrying crowds." From Boston, 5/18/50, ibid., 131.

59 "seeing to bedsteads, tables, chairs." Ibid., 132.

60 "I never doubt or despair." Ibid.

60 "Not a harsh word or hasty expression." Ibid., 133 (5/29/50).

60 "poke it into the stove, & proceed." To Sarah Buckingham Beecher, 12/17/50, Hedrick, *Reader*, 484.

61 "he was my *'summer child.'*" To Sarah Allen, 12/2/[50]; Hedrick, *Stowe*, 199.

61 "called off at least a dozen times." To Sarah Buckingham Beecher, 12/17/50; ibid., 195.

62 "more than anybody . . . would have thought." Ibid., 197.

62 "I dont do anything." To Sarah Buckingham Beecher, 12/17/50, quoted ibid.

62 "if I could use a pen as you can." C. E. Stowe, *Life*, 145.

7 POLITICS

63 "the baby sleeps with me nights." C. E. Stowe, *Life*, 146; Hedrick, *Stowe*, 207 (n.d. [12/50]).

63 Healthiest years of her life. As testified to her daughter-in-law, Susie Munroe Stowe, 1/5/79, Hedrick, *Stowe*, 193.

64 Successful vegetable garden. F. Wilson, *Crusader*, 253.

64 "write a piece for some paper." C. E. Stowe, *Life*, 147–148.

64 "dry as a pinch of snuff." To Eliza Cabot Follen, 2/16/53, ibid., 197–198; Fields, *Life*, 172; Hedrick, *Stowe*, 239–240.

64 Harriet's good health from Brunswick on. Gossett, *Culture*, 90.

65 Admitting children to public schools. Litwack, "Dilemma," 68ff.

65 Condition of free people of color. Ibid., 50.

67 "Those terrible things which were going on." Isabella Jones (Mrs. Edward) Beecher to Charles Edward Stowe, C. E. Stowe, *Life*, 145.

68 Slavery with us forever. Gossett, *Culture*, 122–123.

69 "persons owing service or labor." The text of the Fugitive Slave Act is available online: for example, at the Avalon Project of the Yale Law School, www.yale.edu/lawweb/avalon/fugitive.htm.

69 "hold their patients out of a window." Diary of William Hoyt, quoted in Collison, *Minkins*, 112.

70 "with his clothes half torn off." Dana, *Journals*, 2:412.

70 "if I could use a pen as you can." C. E. Stowe, *Life*, 145.

70 "'I will if I live.' Ibid.

71 "material for that portion of the story." Ibid., 71; F. Wilson, *Crusader*, 119–120.

71 A fugitive slave in the Stowe household. C. E. Stowe, *Life*, 44.

71 "the mob tore down his press." Ibid., 85.

72 "hit 'em in the legs!" Henry Howe, *Historical Collections*, 1:825, quoted in Henry, *Puritan*, 237.

72 Enslaved to menial drudgeries. The point is made in Rourke, *Trumpets*, 79.

73 Daguerreotype of Charley. A reproduction appears in Hedrick, *Stowe*, among illustrations that follow 236.

73 "is this a thing to be defended"? "Concluding Remarks," Stowe, *Uncle Tom's Cabin*, 514–515.

8 UNCLE TOM'S CABIN

74 "he sends me one hundred dollars." C. E. Stowe, *Life*, 148 (1/12/51).

75 "utterly beyond human hope or help." Ammons, *Critical Essays*, 62 (quoted in Charles Dudley Warner, "The Story of *Uncle Tom's Cabin*," reprinted from *Atlantic Monthly* 78 [7/96]).

75 "Would to God I could do something." To Henry Ward Beecher, 2/1/51, quoted in Kirkham, *Building*, 66.

75 "the rushing of a mighty wind." C. E. Stowe, *Life*, 148.

75 "at present occupied upon a story." Kirkham, *Building*, 66–67; F. Wilson, *Crusader*, 259–260.

76 "up from table . . . to warm feet and fingers." To Calvin Stowe, 12/29/50. C. E. Stowe, *Life*, 147.

76 "I am projecting a sketch for the 'Era.'" Ibid.; Hedrick, *Stowe*, 206 (1/27/[51]).

77 "sure to be rattling the latch." C. E. Stowe, *Life*, 147.

77 "the character of a negro catcher." To Richard Henry Dana, 11/9/52, quoted in Collison, *Minkins*, 112.

77 "A New Story by Mrs. Stowe." Kirkham, *Building*, 69–70.

78 "we send off Mr. Stowe and Harriet." To Mary Beecher Perkins, 9/51, ibid., 118–119.

79 "the sensibilities of the slave states." Stowe's introduction to an edition of *Uncle Tom's Cabin* of 1878, reprinted in Riverside edition (Boston, 1896), xxxii.

80 "she and her husband would be in Boston." Kirkham, *Building*, 143. See also Geary, "Stowe, Jewett," 349–351.

81 "almost with my hearts blood." Kirkham, *Building*, 172 (3/20/52).

81 "nobody would hear, nobody would read." Stowe's 1878 introduction for *Uncle Tom's Cabin*, reprinted in Riverside edition, (Boston, 1896), xxxvii.

82 "I was not altogether such a fool." F. Wilson, *Crusader*, 622.

9 RECEPTION

83 *Scarlet Letter* sales: Crowley, *Critical Heritage*, 11. Sales of *Moby-Dick*: Delbanco, *Melville*, 178.

83 Publishing success of *Uncle Tom's Cabin*. F. Wilson, *Crusader*, 622; Ammons, *Critical Essays*, 35–42 ([Charles Briggs], "Uncle Tomitudes," reprinted from *Putnam's Monthly*, 1 [1/53]).

83 Specific responses to *Uncle Tom's Cabin*. Dickens in Ashton, *Reference*, 7 (*Household Words*, 9/18/52); George Sand in Ammons, *Critical Essays*,

3; Tolstoy in Ashton, 66 ("What Is Art?" *Works* [1913], 20:145); Choate in Gossett, *Culture* 184 (quoting from *Independent*, 4 [8/26/52]); Longfellow and Emerson in Gossett, 166–167 (quoting from "Success," Emerson, *Works* [1904], 7:286; S. Longfellow, *Life of HWL*, 2:222–223, 233); Whittier in Gossett, 166 (to W. L. Garrison, 5/52, in *Letters of JGW* [1975], 2:191); James in Ammons, 286 (*A Small Boy and Others* [1913], 158–160).

85 De Forest's and *Nation's* responses. Gossett, *Culture*, 340.

85 "the ethical sense, not the aesthetical sense." Howells, *Literary Friends*, 102.

85 Southern response to *Uncle Tom's Cabin*. George F. Holmes in Ammons, *Critical Essays*, 7–24. See also Gossett, *Culture*, 190ff; Weinstein, "South," 40; Roppolo, "New Orleans," 347.

87 Baldwin on *Uncle Tom's Cabin*. Ammons, *Critical Essays*, 92–97 (James Baldwin, "Everybody's Protest Novel," reprinted from *Partisan Review*, 16 [June, 1949]). The citations are at 92, 94–95.

87 Wilson and Lynn on *Uncle Tom's Cabin*. E. Wilson, *Patriotic Gore*, 5 and passim; Lynn, *Visions*, 32, 31.

88 Jane Smiley on *Uncle Tom's Cabin*. Her article, "Say It Ain't So, Huck: Second Thoughts on Mark Twain's 'Masterpiece,'" appeared in *Harper's Magazine*, January 1996, 61–67. Citations in the text are at 64–65, 67.

88 Anthony Burgess. Ammons, *Critical Essays*, 124, 127 (Anthony Burgess, "Making de White Boss Frown," reprinted from *Encounter*, 27 [July 1966]).

89 *Uncle Tom's Cabin* as a play. See Gossett, *Culture*, 283, 367–373; Birdoff, *Hit*, passim.

89 "Take the children." From the show bill for a production of the play in Longbottom, Ohio, in 1866; quoted in Gossett, *Culture*, 368.

90 The novel as movie and ballet. Birdoff, *Hit*, 395, 404, 406, and passim. Prominent in the stage version, Phineas Fletcher appears in Stowe's novel of forty-five chapters all but exclusively in ch. 17. Shirley Temple played Little Eva in *Dimples* (1936); Judy Garland played Topsy in *Everybody Sing* (1938).

10 DARK PLACES

93 "babes were torn from them." C. E. Stowe, *Life*, 149.

94 "as fast as they got big enough." Stowe, *Uncle Tom*, 255.

95 Stowe as a racist. Ammons, *Critical Essays*, 128–134 (Thomas Graham, "Harriet Beecher Stowe and the Question of Race"); Otter, "Stowe and Race"; Sundquist, introduction to *New Essays*, 3–7, 23–35, and passim.

95 "affectionate, easily touched." Channing, "The African Character," in *The Anti-Slavery Picknick . . .*, John A. Collins, ed. (Boston, 1842), 56–58, quoted in Litwack, "Dilemma," 60.

95 "splendid, rich, and fanciful," Stowe, *Uncle Tom*, 195.

96 "rest on a higher power." Ibid., 213.

96 "yearning toward the simple and childlike." Ibid., 176.

96 "my brother Quashy is ignorant and weak." Ibid., 261.

96 "can't buy every poor wretch I see." Ibid., 259.

97 "a perfect behemoth." Ibid., 198, 34.

97 "I never will do a cruel thing." Ibid., 442.

97 "What! ye blasted black beast!" Ibid., 414.

97 "crowned with thorns, buffeted and bleeding." Ibid., 435–436.

98 "little, feeble, timid-looking woman." To Mary Longfellow Greenleaf, 4/53, Wagenknecht, *Mrs. Longfellow,* 193.

98 twenty-six languages of *Uncle Tom's Cabin.* By the 1930s the novel had been translated into thirty-seven (L. B. Stowe, *Saints Sinners,* 190); and by the end of the century, according to information from the Stowe Center in Hartford, it had been translated into around sixty languages in all.

99 Epigraph: Schreiner, *Beechers,* 125.

11 TO ENGLAND

101 "his grace the duke of Buckingham." C. Beecher, *Journal,* 3. Citations describing the voyage to Liverpool are taken from this source. The sketch of Charles Beecher derives from Joseph S. Van Why's introductory remarks in the *Journal* (xxv–xxxii) and from Rugoff, *Beechers,* 204–213, 407–415, 519–524, and passim.

102 "blue-black, foamy sparkling sea." C. Beecher, *Journal,* 7.

104 "a voyage . . . free of expense." C. E. Stowe, *Life,* 197.

104 "We humbly confess it before Almighty God." Text of the "Address" is in Stowe's "Reply," and the vellum page itself, with its elaborate illumination, is reproduced in color as the frontispiece to C. Beecher, *Journal.*

105 "oath to disclose the sins of those dearest." C. E. Stowe, *Life,* 188.

106 *New York Courier and Enquirer.* The article, which appeared in the issue of 11/5/52, is reprinted in Stowe, *A Key,* 67–68. For sales of *A Key,* see Geary, "Stowe, Jewett," 345.

106 "THE POWER OF THE MASTER." Judge Thomas Ruffin of North Carolina, quoted in Stowe, *A Key,* 71. "We cannot allow the *right* of the matter to be brought into discussion in the courts of justice. The slave, to remain a slave, must be made sensible that there is NO APPEAL FROM HIS MASTER," ibid.

107 "NO INFLUENCES OUT OF THE CHURCH." Stowe, *A Key,* 219.

107 "stir the dead in their graves." Ibid., 128.

107 "the most marvelous literary phenomenon." Quoted in Fisch, "Uncle Tom," 78.

108 "much to my astonishment." Stowe, *Sunny Memories,* 1:18.

108 "People came and stood in their doors." C. E. Stowe, *Life,* 214–215.

108 "all smiling and bowing." Ibid., 215; Stowe, *Sunny Memories,* 1:76.

109 "steaming in the rain and cold." C. Beecher, *Journal*, 59.

109 "A great and glorious cause." Ibid., 53

109 "funny way of taking things." Ibid., 56.

109 "never was so tired in my life." Ibid., 70.

110 "I never saw the like." Ibid., 105 (5/16/53).

110 a "very pleasant, friendly conversation." C. Stowe, *Life*, 226; Stowe, *Sunny Memories*, 1:266. At the gathering in Exeter Hall, 4,000 people were in attendance, some having lined up for twenty-four hours to get in. E. Wilson, *Patriotic Gore*, 61.

110 "a deep impression on his mind." C. Stowe, *Life*, 226.

111 "such quality as one seldom hears." Stowe, *Sunny Memories*, 2:106.

12 CULTURE

112 "how strange . . . that I should *know* you." C. E. Stowe, *Life*, 314 (6/5/57).

112 *"make a child say, 'I believe.'"* Stowe, *Lady Byron Vindicated*, 210–211.

113 "really the only topic." Duchess of Devonshire to her son, undated, but probably late March or April, 1812, Marchand, *Byron*, 334.

113 "Whilome in Albion's isle." *Childe Harold's Pilgrimage*, 1:2, in Byron, *Poetical Works*, 2:9.

114 "the deep war-drum's sound." Ibid., 2:513, Byron, *Poetical Works*, 2:62.

114 "secret woe." Ibid., "To Inez," line 841, following 1:84, in Byron, *Poetical Works*, 2:39.

114 "this poetry . . . filled my heart." Stowe, *Lady Byron Vindicated*, 44.

114 *The Corsair*'s success. Marchand, *Byron*, 433.

114 "astonished and electrified." *Autobiography of Lyman Beecher*, 1:393.

115 "hanging over the back of her chair." Reverend A. G. L'Estrange, *The Literary Life of the Rev. William Harness* (1871), quoted in MacCarthy, *Byron*, 250.

115 "The separation of Lord and Lady Byron." Lady Anne Barnard's account, quoted in Lord Lindsay's letter published in *London Times*, 9/7/69. The letter is reprinted among Miscellaneous Documents in the appendix of Stowe, *Lady Byron Vindicated*, 451–458. See also Fox, *Mystery*, 72 and passim; *Stowe-Byron Controversy*, 5ff.

116 "Fare thee well!" Byron, *Poetical Works*, 3:380.

116 "destined to set people by the ears." Byron, *Letters and Journals*, 5:92.

117 European reactions to Byron's death. In her admirable biography of Byron, MacCarthy discusses these and the cult that developed around the poet in two fascinating chapters: 29 ("The European Byronists") and 30 ("The Byronic Englishman"), 544–574—Hugo is at 546, Heine at 547, Carlyle at 555, Bulwer-Lytton at 560.

117 "how it might be with his soul." Fields, *Life*, 38–39.

117 "misanthropy and irreligious gloom." *North American Review*, 34 (1/32):76, quoted in Kleinfield, "Infidel," 183.

118 "enjoyed a thick, foggy night." C. E. Stowe, *Life*, 435–436.

119 "the *flies had got to her.*" Stowe, *Uncle Tom,* 257.

119 Lady Byron's appearance. Stowe, *Lady Byron Vindicated,* 206.

120 "vast, wild, and sublime." Gilbertson, *Stowe,* 204.

120 "melting away like snow." Hedrick, *Stowe,* 246 (7/31/53).

120 "statuettes, bonbons, playthings." Stowe, *Sunny Memories,* 2:423.

13 LOOKING BACK

122 "rapidly be fitted for the press." L. Beecher, *Works,* Preface, 1:ix.

122 "wander off into a reverie." *Autobiography of Lyman Beecher,* 1:50.

122 "they could not come up to us." Ibid., 1:156–157.

123 "light, and joy, and praise." Ibid., 1:202.

123 "this characteristic more prominent." Ibid., 1:282.

124 "earthly father to a Heavenly One?" Catharine Beecher, *Religious Training of Children in the School, the Family, and the Church,* 242, quoted in Caskey, *Chariot of Fire,* 381.

124 Legends of Dr. Beecher. *Autobiography of Lyman Beecher,* 2:88.

124 "no such seminary as Andover then." Ibid., 1:44.

124 "the least degree of selfishness." Ibid., 1:59.

125 "Shall I hide the truth?" Ibid., 1:71; L. B. Stowe, *Saints Sinners,* 33.

125 In a "heavenly" state of mind. *Autobiography of Lyman Beecher,* 1:216.

125 "a most moving scene." Ibid., 1:217–218.

126 "messenger from the court of Heaven.'" Ibid., 1:266.

126 "so fair, so delicate, so elegant." Ibid., 1:267.

126 "except Boston Mall." Ibid., 1:271.

126 "of great cheerfulness and comfort." Ibid., 1:270–271.

126 " loves to be laughed at." Ibid., 1:301.

126 "Harriet reads every thing." Ibid., 1:344.

126 "a spirit of cheerfulness and hilarity." Ibid., 1:396.

127 "seventy-two villainous sects." To Francis Hodgson, 9/3/11, Byron, *Letters and Journals,* 2:89.

127 "What a harp he might have swept!" *Autobiography of Lyman Beecher,* 1:393.

128 "my consolations are neither few nor small." To Catharine Beecher, 9/26, quoted in Schreiner, *Beechers,* 69.

128 "all the six years he labored in Boston." C. Stowe, "Sketches and Recollections," 229.

128 "I have responded to the call of Providence." L. Beecher's address at his inauguration as president of Lane Seminary, in *Cincinnati Journal,* 1/4/33, quoted in Henry, *Puritan,* 162.

129 "as if he could not die in peace." To Henry Ward Beecher, 5/21/56, quoted ibid., 260.

129 "How did they live in those days?" *Autobiography of Lyman Beecher,* 1:13–14.

130 The "infamous Nebraska bill." Stowe, *Sunny Memories,* xxxi, n.

14 RETURN TO EUROPE

132 "not a woman in the United States." Originally published in *Independent*, 2/23/54, Hedrick, *Reader*, 453. C. E. Stowe prints with minor variants in *Life*, 256.

133 "twilight of the feudal ages." Stowe, *Dred*, 3.

134 "drunken, swearing, ferocious set." Ibid., 512.

134 "the great wail of human sorrow." Ibid., 512–513.

134 "hebraistic phrases, names, and allusions." Ibid., 509.

134 "a desperate sort of sad look." Ibid., 9.

135 "help us in our struggle for Kansas." C. E. Stowe, *Life*, 268.

135 "I mean . . . the harlot Slavery." "The Crime against Kansas." Sumner, *Works*, 4:144, 239–240 (5/19–20/56).

136 "fashion of the chivalry of South Carolina." Stowe, *Dred*, 493.

137 "our tribute to it as a great novel." Ammons, *Critical Essays*, 43–44 (George Eliot in *Westminster Review* 10 [10/56]).

137 "who cares what critics say?" C. E. Stowe, *Life*, 279.

137 "an accidental, done-on-purpose meeting." Ibid., 271.

138 "I rather dreaded reading your book!" Ibid., 308–309 (6/1/57).

138 "how to value communion with you." Ibid., 274–275 (9/10/56); Stowe, *Lady Byron Vindicated*, 216–217.

139 "we shall love each other *forever*." C. E. Stowe, *Life*, 314.

15 HEARTBREAK

140 "cautious how they meddle with her." Hedrick, *Stowe*, 263.

140 "all end . . . in abortions." Ibid., 273.

140 "I give you warning." Ibid., 246.

141 "all manner of fun & mischief." To Mrs. D. H. Allen, 10/22/54, quoted in Wagenknecht, *Stowe*, 68.

141 Fred and "tobacco." Hedrick, *Stowe*, 254–255.

141 "indolent and self indulgent." Ibid., 254.

141 Calvin "gave out." Ibid., 265.

141 "disparages the minister, quizzes the deacon." Gilbertson, *Stowe*, 217.

141 "as every true man ought to live." Hedrick, *Stowe*, 276; C. E. Stowe, *Life*, 317.

142 "I write one word." Hedrick, *Stowe*, 274–275.

143 "he would have been a sinner." Ibid., 275–276.

143 "burst out into an amazing cry." Sewall, *Diary*, 1:345–346.

144 "a powerful and delightful day." Gilbertson, *Stowe*, 36 (11/1/25).

144 "theological wrestlings and surgings . . ." Stowe, "New England Ministers," 487.

145 "I shall never forget it." C. Beecher, *Journal*, 18.

145 "the strivings of the Spirit." *Autobiography of Lyman Beecher*, 1:355.

146 "how different her lot might have been." C. Beecher, *Journal*, 18–19.

146 "in a week or two." C. E. Stowe, *Life*, 316.
146 "There he lay so calm, so placid." To Duchess of Sutherland, 8/3/57, ibid., 316.
146 "it was my mother's gift to me." Ibid., 317.
146 "He died with that dear thought." Ibid., 319.
147 "I never knew how much I loved him." To her children, 8/24/57, ibid., 323.
147 "I am so miserable." To "My Darling Children," 9/1/57, ibid., 324.
148 "So do not mistake me." Ibid., 340–341 (2/12/59).

16 THE MINISTER'S WOOING

149 Faults "in the artistic department." C. E. Stowe, *Life*, 308–309 (6/1/57).
150 "How did they live in those days?" *Autobiography of Lyman Beecher*, 1:14.
150 "sanded with whitest sand." Stowe, *Minister's Wooing*, 536.
151 "magnet drives off sticks and straws." Ibid., 576.
151 "a new flower blossomed in the kingdom." C. E. Stowe, *Life*, 33–34.
152 "trace almost all my sins back to it." Ibid., 36–37.
152 "the entire emptiness of this world." Schreiner, *Beechers*, 125.
152 "what a father!" Ibid. (7/4/43).
152 "long-expected and wished help." To Thomas Beecher, 3/16/44, Hedrick, *Stowe*, 155.
153 "You trusted in God, did you?" C. E. Stowe, *Life*, 321–322.
153 "Well, it's just like that with me." Stowe, *Minister's Wooing*, 569.
154 "unconditional submission to Infinite Wisdom." Ibid., 726.
155 "the bells should toll for every wedding." Ibid., 733–734.
156 "to enjoy the light of the gospel." Ibid., 510.
156 "selfishness is the root of all moral evil." Ibid., 562.
156 "as many trials in life as her neighbors." Ibid., 560.
156 "providential witness of its justice." Ibid., 615.

17 CIVIL WAR

157 Reading with "intense interest." C. E. Stowe, *Life*, 344; Stowe, *Lady Byron Vindicated*, 226–227.
157 "Take mine if they will serve you." Stowe, *Lady Byron Vindicated*, 229–231.
158 "a worse clog than before." Wagenknecht, *Stowe*, 69.
158 "smart bright lively boy." To Mrs. D. H. Allen, 10/22/54, Wagenknecht, *Stowe*, 68. A sense of Mrs. Stowe's time in Italy on this occasion, as recalled by a friend who shared it with her, is conveyed in Howard, *Remembrance*, 96–110.
158 "carry my love to those that wait." C. E. Stowe, *Life*, 314.
159 "together on deck in pleasant weather." Ammons, *Critical Essays*, 290 (Annie Fields, "Days with Mrs. Stowe," reprinted from *Atlantic Monthly* 78 [8/96]).

159 "tired far into the future." Gilbertson, *Stowe*, 46.

159 "far-away dreaming eyes." Ammons, *Critical Essays*, 288.

160 "my dissatisfied fellow countrymen." Lincoln, *Works*, 4:262–271.

160 "a general jollification." C. E. Stowe, *Life*, 364–365.

161 "The hour has come, and the man!" F. Wilson, *Crusader*, 474.

161 "Very truly and sadly yours." Ibid., 475.

161 "freeing some and leaving others alone." Lincoln, *Works*, 5:388 (8/22/62).

162 "it helps to free the oppressed." Hedrick, *Reader*, 472. The parody appeared originally in *Independent*, 9/11/62, under the title "Will You Take a Pilot?"

162 "the chief corner-stone of its edifice." Stowe, "Reply," 130.

163 "And what do you mean to do?" Ibid., 133.

163 "at the little end of the horn." To James T. Fields, 11/13/62, Hedrick, *Stowe*, 304.

163 "So this is the little woman." L. B. Stowe, *Saints Sinners*, 205; Fields, *Life*, 269.

164 "Mrs. Stowe! Mrs. Stowe." F. Wilson, *Crusader*, 486–487.

164 "Sincerely Yours, Nath'l Hawthorne." Hawthorne, *Letters*, 515 (1/4/63).

165 "on whom I could lean all my cares." Quoted in Wagenknecht, *Stowe*, 32.

165 "among scenes of terrible suffering." F. Wilson, *Crusader*, 493.

166 "greatest sign and marvel of our day." Stowe, *Men of Our Times*, 59.

18 POSTBELLUM

167 "all sorts of roses & posies." Hedrick, *Stowe*, 311–312 (11/3/63).

168 "driving at every body's heels." To Hattie Stowe, 4/9/64, ibid., 316.

168 "lying boxed and promiscuous." F. Wilson, *Crusader*, 500.

170 Mandarin. See Graff, *Mandarin*, 44 and passim.

172 "Nobody thought of staying away." Stowe, *Oldtown Folks*, 926.

173 "a severe and unsympathetic being." Ibid., 1249.

173 "chronicle of a race." Parrington, *Main Currents*, 2:372.

173 "understanding American culture." Miller, quoted in Foster, *Rungless Ladder*, Preface, ix.

173 "indeed of American, literature." Ibid., 224.

173 "never put so much work." F. Wilson, *Crusader*, 528 (12/24/68).

173 "triumph of insight and true tolerance." C. E. Stowe, *Life*, 443 (7/11/69).

174 "fresh fields and new men and times." "Mrs. Stowe's 'Oldtown Folks,'" *Nation* 8 (1869):437–438.

175 "She is pretty—a great Coquette." Byron, *Letters and Journals*, 6:185 (7/26/19).

175 "his heart would have endured everything." [Guiccioli], *Recollections*, 2:230.

176 "It cannot be justified." Ibid., 2:240.

19 A VINDICATION

177 Prying open the poet's desk. Medwin's *Conversations of Lord Byron*, derided for its inaccuracies, appeared in 1824, the year of the poet's death. Medwin's charge is on p. 42 of the reprint edition in Works Cited; Lady Byron's denial ("The whole of this page is false") is in a note on p. 44. *Don Juan* does contain the lines, "She [Donna Inez, a much fictionalized Lady Byron] kept a journal, where his faults were noted, / And open'd certain trunks of books and letters." (*Don Juan*, 1:28, in Byron, *Poetical Works*, 5:17. See facsimile of page proof opposite p. 17 and note to line 218 on p. 675 of this source. [The poet's friend Hobhouse has underlined "And open'd certain trunks," noting in the margin, "There is some doubt about this." To which Byron responds, "It is at least poetically true—why apply everything to that absurd woman. I have no reference to living characters"—in a poem that is filled with such references]). For Stowe's rejection of the charge, see *Lady Byron Vindicated*, 312–313.

178 "The world needed to know." Howells, *Life*, 1:150.

178 "slight or even imaginary ones." [Guiccioli], *Recollections*, 240.

178 "benumbs the public to everything else." Howells, *Life*, 1:147.

179 "every natural charm, gift, and grace." Stowe, "True Story," 295. Citations from Stowe's summary of the countess's argument are from this page.

179 "It is within the writer's recollection." Ibid., 296.

180 "All the actors in the scene." Ibid., 300.

180 "adulterous intrigue with a blood relation." Ibid., 302.

180 " moral Clytemnestra." "Lines on Hearing that Lady Byron Was Ill," in Byron, *Poetical Works*, 4:44 (line 37).

181 "summer hours in her stormy life." Stowe, "True Story," 304.

181 "I am too truly your friend." Ibid., 306.

181 "an hour of revelation." Ibid., 304.

181 "would not longer have her about him." Ibid., 306–307.

182 "howls of rejection." Howells, *Life*, 1:147.

182 Fifteen thousand readers. In 1870 the *Atlantic*'s subscription list dropped from 50,000 to 35,000. "The decrease . . . may have been in part owing to new competition." Mott, *Magazines*, 2:505. See also Austin, *Fields*, 290–295, for a succinct account of Stowe, Byron, and the *Atlantic*.

182 "far exceeded anything I had anticipated." To John Lothrop Motley, 9/26/69, Morse, *Holmes*, 2:183–184.

183 "of stormy discussion and of much invective." Stowe, *Lady Byron Vindicated*, 1.

183 "to be judged as literary efforts?" Ibid., 4.

183 "to utter anything but the truth." Ibid., 5.

184 "I *certainly* knew her innocent." Ibid., 2. "Years ago, it was said far and wide, that Lady Byron was doing more good than anybody else in England; and it was difficult to imagine how anybody could do more." Stowe

(quoting from article by Harriet Martineau in *Atlantic Monthly,* 7 [2/61]:193), ibid., 147. See also ibid., 450, for "most remarkable woman."

184 "she told me *how* it was done." Ibid., 241.

184 "a few lines in the usual form." MacCarthy, *Byron,* 263. The text of the "Dearest Duck" letter is on this page. The several excellent biographies of Byron all re-create his tumultuous marriage, but a particularly vivid, brief, and appalling evocation of the wedding night and the groom's subsequent misbehavior is in Praz, *Romantic Agony,* 72–73.

185 Donna Inez as Lady Byron. The stanzas quoted are in *Don Juan,* 1:22, 23, in Byron, *Poetical Works,* 5:15–16. The phrases cited are at 1:16, 17, in ibid., 13–14.

185 "Mrs. Leigh never lost position." Stowe, *Lady Byron Vindicated,* 74.

186 "carefully-prepared proofs and documents." Ibid., 190–191.

186 "the story is not true." Ibid., 350–351.

186 "guilty of incest with his sister!" Ibid., 235.

186 "silence a confirmation of a lie"? Ibid., 359.

20 AFTERMATH

187 "Wish Mrs. Stowe was in the pillory." Dickens, *Letters,* 12:418.

188 "making the dead revile the dead." "The Byron Revelations," *Independent* (8/26/69), 8–9. Clipping in "Scrap Book" of the Byron Controversy at Stowe Center, Hartford.

188 "worse than Byzantine abomination." Ammons, *Critical Essays,* 171 (Justin McCarthy, "Mrs. Stowe's Last Romance," reprinted from *Independent,* 8/26/69).

188 "when I think of going where he is." Stowe, *Lady Byron Vindicated,* 251.

188 "the sanctimonious imbecility." Ammons, *Critical Essays,* 171.

188 "odious charge against a dead man." Ibid., 172.

189 "most infamous and malignant libels." *New York Herald,* 9/4/69, quoted in Ashton, "Filthy Story," 377.

189 a "deluge of nastiness." *New York World,* 10/6/69, 4, col. 2.

189 "sanctimonious, but viperous, Yankee self." Ibid., 12/27/69, 11, col. 3.

189 "every lying scandal." Emerson Bennett, "Stowe-Byron Scandal," eight-column article beginning on p. 12, from a contemporary newspaper source not identified, in "Scrap-Book" of the Byron Controversy, Stowe Center, Hartford.

189 "as heinous a piece of bawdy." Quoted in Lentricchia, "Whirlwind," 224 (9/3/69).

189 "Lady Byron's assertion is not answered." Ammons, *Critical Essays,* 189,188 (George [William] Curtis, "From the Editor's Easy Chair at *Harper's:* In Defense of *Lady Byron Vindicated,*" reprinted from *Harper's New Monthly Magazine,* 39 [1869]).

190 Mark Twain and the *Buffalo Express.* Baender, "Mark Twain," 469 and passim.

190 "how base, filthy and mean Byron was." Howells, *Life,* 150.
190 "it is the most moral of poems." To John Murray, 2/1/19, Byron, *Letters and Journals,* 6:99.
192 "confess—you dog—and be candid." To Douglas Kinnaird, 10/26/19, ibid., 6:232.
192 Current scholarship on Byron. On Byron's heterodox sexual tastes, see, for example, MacCarthy, *Byron,* 73–76, 90, 146–147, and passim; Eisler, *Byron,* 39–41, 144–146, 486–502, 599, 729, and passim; Grosskurth, *Byron,* 96, 103.
193 Teresa Guiccioli's later life. See Anne Barton's informative review of *Lord Byron's Life in Italy* in *New York Review of Books,* 12/15/2005, 22–26.
194 "I seem to be powerless." Wagenknecht, *Stowe,* 70.
194 "no bliss . . . to compare with a baby." Ammons, *Critical Essays,* 296 (Annie Fields, "Days with Mrs. Stowe," reprinted from *Atlantic Monthly,* 78 [8/96]).
194 Fred Stowe's final days. F. Wilson, *Crusader*; L. B. Stowe, *Saints Sinners,* 223.

195 Epigraph: To Calvin Stowe, 9/3/44, Elsmere, *Indiana,* 228.

21 THE BEECHERS

197 Beecher family. The most substantial, reliable account of the family as a whole is Milton Rugoff, *The Beechers: An American Family of the Nineteenth Century.* See also Schreiner, *Beechers*; and White, *Beecher Sisters,* passim.
198 "that viscus, the supposed organ of emotion." Roppolo, "New Orleans," 355–356 (3/10/72).
198 "children might be trained up for God." *Autobiography of Lyman Beecher,* 1:217 (9/27/16). Roxana's daughter Harriet lived only briefly, three years before her namesake, from February to March 1808. Harriet Porter's son Frederick, the first of her children, lived from 1818 to 1820; her next child, Isabella, was born in 1822.
202 "most perfect old gentleman." Wagenknecht, *Stowe,* 34.
202 "singing songs in the night." Schreiner, *Beechers,* 237.
203 "hardly came under the parental hand." *Tilton vs. Beecher,* 2:729, quoted in Waller, *Beecher and Tilton,* 20.
203 "a single child's toy as a gift." Stowe, "Henry Ward Beecher," in *Men of Our Times,* 508. Description of Roxana's funeral, ibid. and *Autobiography of Lyman Beecher,* 1:224.
204 "this bashful, dazed-looking boy." Stowe, "Henry Ward Beecher," in *Men of Our Times,* 510.
205 "gloomy and moody, restless and irritable." Ibid., 517.
205 "My heart sinks within me." *Autobiography of Lyman Beecher,* 1:288 (2/6/19).

22 RELIGION

206 *Except a man be born again.* John 3:15, 17.

207 "hell hounds fly upon their prey." Edwards, *Works,* 14:209–210. The sermon was delivered late in 1727. Quoted in Marsden, *Edwards,* 121.

208 *"by the washing of regeneration."* Ephesians 2:8–9; Titus 3:5.

208 "a multitude of blossoms." Marsden, *Edwards,* 136.

209 "if absolute truth could be got at." Stowe, *Oldtown Folks,* 1238.

209 *"the world through him might be saved."* John 3:17.

210 "this fountain of love." Marsden, *Edwards,* 191.

210 "he loved me as a son." *Autobiography of Lyman Beecher,* 1:27.

211 "whatever God requires." L. Beecher, *Works,* 2:243 (Sermon 7: "The Faith Once Delivered to the Saints," *Sermons Delivered on Various Occasions*).

211 "I was reared in the household of faith." Abbott, *Beecher,* 1.

212 "make interest to get you an appointment." Rugoff, *Beechers,* 120.

213 "THE WEST is my 'hearts desire.'" Hedrick, *Stowe,* 68.

214 "brightest thing I shall look back upon." Abbott, *Beecher,* 1–2.

214 "shouting like a good Methodist." Truman J. Ellinwood, ed., *Autobiographical Reminiscences of Henry Ward Beecher* (1898), 45–46, quoted in Elsmere, *Indiana,* 42. See also Applegate, *Famous Man,* 133–134.

23 BROOKLYN

215 "But Christ stands my *manifest* God." Abbott, *Beecher,* 14–15.

216 "I did not ring the bell." Ibid., 47.

216 Henry's activities in Indianapolis. Elsmere, *Indiana,* 238ff.

217 "going somewhat in father's track." Quoted in Schreiner, *Beechers,* 119.

217 "shocks of heat & prickly sensation." To Calvin, 7/16/44, Elsmere, *Indiana,* 224ff.

217 "I have had such a delightful visit." To Calvin, 9/3/44, ibid., 228.

218 *"publish* much to benefit the world." Ibid., 279.

218 "grey headed—toothless old woman." To Harriet Beecher Stowe, 12/27/46; Applegate, *Famous Man,* 192; Elsmere, *Indiana,* 271.

218 "come! you must come!" Elsmere, *Indiana,* 291.

219 "like a couple of school-boys." Ibid., 293.

219 "horse and carriage worth $600." C. E. Stowe, *Life,* 130.

219 Henry Ward Beecher's appearance. Applegate, *Famous Man,* 173–176 and passim; Shaplen, *Free Love,* 20, 22–23; Marshall, *True History,* 81–83.

220 "his exuberant and rollicking humor." Quoted in Clark, *Spokesman,* 109 (7/17/58).

220 "By God, he's got him." Shaplen, *Free Love,* 20.

220 Harriet on her brother's preaching. Wagenknecht, *Stowe,* 37, 39.

223 "LET US HAVE FAITH." Lincoln, *Works,* 3:550.

224 "You sockdologizing old mantrap." Kunhardt, *Twenty Days*, 29. The opening chapter, 1–17, of Applegate, *Famous Man*, vividly re-creates Beecher's exuberant Fort Sumter triumph of April 1865.

24 CHANGING AMERICA

225 "the whole guilt of this war." W. C. Beecher and Scoville, *Beecher*, 454.

226 "The freedmen must take their march." To Charles G. Halpine et al., 8/30/66, ibid., 468.

227 "their willing hand drops the musket." Ibid., 454.

227 "the question becomes only this." H. W. Beecher, *Star Papers*, 299 ("Christian Liberty in the Use of the Beautiful").

228 Elm tree analogy. H. W. Beecher, *Norwood*, 213–214.

228 "cholera did not depend on natural agencies." H. W. Beecher, *New Star Papers*, 219 ("Natural Laws and Special Providences").

229 "this makes it impossible to doubt." To Duchess of Argyll, 2/10/66, C. E. Stowe, *Life*, 395–396.

230 "the most unfortunate and misleading terms." H. W. Beecher, *New Star Papers*, 183, quoted in McLoughlin, *Meaning*, 39.

231 "Any map of the world will show you." From Andover, to Martha (Wetherill) Young, 12/15/60, Van Why, ["Letters . . . Wetherill"], 10–12.

232 "some peculiarity in the nervous system." Quoted in Wagenknecht, *Stowe*, 47.

233 *"in my flesh shall I see God."* Job 19:26.

233 Henry Ward Beecher on spiritualism. W. C. Beecher and Scoville, *Beecher*, 363.

233 "tricks with tables and chairs." C. E. Stowe, *Life*, 485–486.

234 "the intense materialism of the present age." Ibid., 351 (1/16/60).

234 Stowe on the planchette. C. Beecher, *Spiritual Manifestations*, 25–36.

25 MY WIFE AND I

236 "This question of Woman and her Sphere." Stowe, "The Chimney-Corner," *Atlantic Monthly*, 16 (12/65):673.

236 "excrescences, eccentricities, peculiarities." Stowe, "The Chimney-Corner," *Atlantic Monthly*, 16 (11/65):573–574, quoted in Wyman, "Topical Novel," 385.

237 "if he proves disagreeable to her." Stowe, "The Woman Question," *Hearth and Home*, 8/7/69, 520, quoted in Hedrick, *Stowe*, 360.

237 "things that make me dizzy & blind." Quoted in C. Beecher and Stowe, *Home*, introduction, xvii. The title *Little Foxes* alludes to the Song of Solomon, 2:15.

238 "movement of the human race towards progress." "The Chimney-Corner," *Atlantic Monthly*, 16 (12/65):673

240 "in everybody's mind and mouth." Stowe, *My Wife and I,* 3.

240 "The woman question of our day." Ibid., 37–38.

241 "career besides that of the heart." Ibid., 418.

241 "I would keep my faculties bright." Ibid., 375.

241 "no immediate prospect of the suffrage." Ibid., 261.

242 "strange creatures who rant and rage." Ibid., 302.

242 "effete institution, a relic of barbarous ages." Ibid., 436.

242 "alarmingly rational women-reformers." Ibid., 431.

242 "what I call woman's genius." Ibid., 428.

243 "entreating; helpless, hopeless." Ibid., 315. James's *Nation* review (7/22/75) of Stowe's *We and Our Neighbors* is reprinted in *Literary Criticism,* 618–620.

26 SCANDAL

245 Mrs. Stowe's disclaimer. Stowe, *My Wife and I,* Preface, iii–iv.

246 "personal beauty and graces of manner." Johnston, *Mrs. Satan,* 57.

246 "Free Thought! Untrammeled Lives!" Mott, *Magazines,* 3:445.

247 "the true basis of republican government." Woodhull, *Reader,* "Congressional Reports on Woman Suffrage . . . the Woodhull Memorial," 40D.

247 "an embodiment of pure thought." Quoted in Underhill, *President,* 101.

247 "to see her is to respect her." Tilton, *Woodhull,* 3, 35.

248 "a recipient of heavenly favors." Underhill, *President,* 174.

248 "And are you a Free Lover?" Woodhull, *Reader,* "A Speech on The Principles of Social Freedom . . . November 20, 1871," 23.

248 "marriage should end with it." Tilton, *Woodhull,* 32.

249 "*change* that love *every day* if I please!" Woodhull, *Reader,* "A Speech on The Principles of Social Freedom . . . November 20, 1871," 23.

249 "we were all so happy." Quoted in Caskey, *Chariot of Fire,* 117.

249 "*Let your women . . . keep silence.*" 1 Corinthians 14:34.

249 speaking her piece and taking her money. Ammons, *Critical Essays,* 299 (Annie Fields, "Days with Mrs. Stowe," reprinted from *Atlantic Monthly,* 78 [8/96]).

250 a "mint of genuine fun." Trautmann, "Readings," 281.

250 "that no word might be lost." Ibid., 286.

250 "rather see you than the Queen.'" Ibid., 283; C. E. Stowe, *Life,* 493.

250 "We get into regular gales." C. E. Stowe, *Life,* 495.

251 "begged me to come again." Ibid., 498.

251 Revisiting Walnut Hills. Ibid., 499.

251 Changes at Plymouth Church. Clark, *Spokesman,* 193.

252 "a rosebud on Mr. Beecher's eyes." Waller, *Beecher and Tilton,* 29–30.

253 "burst like a bomb-shell." Woodhull, *Reader,* "Complete and Detailed Version of the Beecher-Tilton Affair," 3.

253 "Every great man of Mr. BEECHER's type." Ibid., 9, 20.

27 INSIDE THE HOME

254 "one of the fairest pairs that I ever married." Shaplen, *Free Love*, 27.

254 "my gratitude cannot be written in words." *Tilton vs. Beecher*, 2:11 (11/30/65).

254 each of us "is living two lives." *Independent*, 12/8/59, quoted in *Hibben Beecher*, 173.

255 Greatest preacher since Saint Paul. Wagenknecht, *Stowe*, 14; Joseph Bucklin Bishop, quoting John Hay, in *Notes and Anecdotes of Many Years* (New York 1895), 43, cited in Hibben, *Beecher*, 311.

257 "unspeakable shame and anguish." Quoted in Rugoff, *Beechers*, 243 (6/44).

257 "S'help me God, Judge." Underhill, *President*, 134.

257 "this witch set her eye on him." Quoted in ibid., 140–141.

257 "why not a woman president"? Stowe, *My Wife and I*, 262–263.

258 "You ain't half out of the shell yet." Ibid., 240.

258 "I boldly entered the arena of politics." Underhill, *President*, 77–78.

258 "I thought . . . she was insane." Ibid., 137–138.

259 "most virtuous acts of my life." Ibid., 143.

259 "I must have an interview." *Beecher and Tilton War*, 83–84.

260 "martyrdom were sure to follow." Underhill, *President*, 101. Events surrounding Mrs. Woodhull's career as a broker, journalist, and politician from Anthony Comstock's rather different, vice-obsessed point of view are recounted in Broun and Leech, *Comstock*, 93–127.

260 "I would have cut off my right hand." Quoted in Shaplen, *Free Love*, 39.

260 "what hours we had together!" *Tilton vs. Beecher*, 2:11 (11/30/65).

261 "prevented from coming to the house." Hibben, *Beecher*, 207, quoting from *Chicago Post and Mail*, 7/24/74.

261 "the most unsaccharine of all things." Shaplen, *Free Love*, 37.

261 "it breeds agony in me." Waller, *Beecher and Tilton*, 52.

261 tell her his "secretest thoughts." R. Fox, *Intimacy*, 259.

262 "thinking of my love for Mr. B." *Tilton vs. Beecher*, 1:493 (12/7/66).

262 "lost the comfort, society and assistance." Ibid., 1:3.

28 TRIAL

263 "wholly alienated and destroyed." *Tilton vs. Beecher*, 1:3.

263 "anxious to know the truth." Charles A. Dana's judgment, quoted in Hibben, *Beecher*, 312.

264 "*L'afaire Beecher-Stilton.*" Shaplen, *Free Love*, 207.

265 "she was child-like in nature." Marshall, *True History*, 257.

265 "bodily intercourse was not wrong." Shaplen, *Free Love*, 61–62.

266 "heathen-priest in the Hindoo-land." *Tilton vs. Beecher*, 1:619.

266 "his sense of my inequality with him." Marshall, *True History*, 197.

267 "Your slimy, polluted, brawny hand." Ibid., 532.

267 "I had not been in bed very long." *Tilton vs. Beecher,* 2:474.

267 "gave me a terrible blow." Ibid., 2:477.

268 "but to blame me for it." Ibid., 1:415.

268 "buoy her through the deadly waters." Johnston, *Mrs. Satan,* 238–239.

269 "in every particular as utterly untrue." Marshall, *True History,* 30.

269 "He would have been a better man." *Beecher and Tilton War,* 75; Marshall, *True History,* 119.

270 "two natures, both large and various." H. W. Beecher, *Norwood,* 171, quoted in McLoughlin, *Meaning,* 94.

270 "I protest against the whole batch." From Elmira, 11/5/72, Marshall, *True History,* 335. Isabella's letter, from Hartford on 11/3/72, is at 333.

271 Harriet's letter to George Eliot. C. E. Stowe, *Life,* 473–482.

272 syllables like "a soft spiritual rain." Shaplen, *Free Love,* 178.

272 "so flagrant and heinous an imputation." Ibid., 249.

272 "trampled out the scandal as with iron boots." Ibid., 251.

273 "calm and placid as a lake." Ibid., 235. Tilton was not in the courtroom when the actual finding came down, Applegate, *Famous Man,* 451.

29 LATE YEARS

274 Tilton's last years. R. Fox, *Intimacy,* 11–15; Hibben, *Beecher,* 329–331; *American National Biography,* "Tilton, Theodore."

275 "the charge brought . . . was true." R. Fox, *Intimacy,* 39.

275 "erring woman has so forsworn herself." *New York Times,* 4/16/78, quoted in ibid., 40.

276 "MRS. THEODORE TILTON DEAD." See ibid., 10, a fascsimile of the newspaper clipping.

277 Victoria Woodhull's death. Johnston, *Mrs. Satan,* 301.

277 "No Darker Rooms Than He Went Through." Ibid., 234.

278 "thirty-seven thousand Congregational Christians." C. E. Stowe, *Life,* 479.

279 Charles A. Dana on Beecher. *New York Sun,* 4/16/78, quoted in Hibben, *Beecher,* 250.

279 Samuel Bowles. George Spring Merriam, *Life and Times of Samuel Bowles* (New York, 1885) 2:49, quoted in ibid., 101.

279 "Americans who enjoyed a world-wide reputation." Carter, *Crisis,* 111.

280 "no man, unless it be George Washington." Quoted ibid., 113.

30 ENDINGS

281 Sleighs passing beyond the window. Stowe, *Poganuc People,* 42.

281 "frost sparkled white." Ibid., 91

282 Wintertime chores. Ibid., 207.

282 "thickest clothing was no protection." Ibid., 72.

282 "roomy, and of a desolate plainness." Ibid., 70.

282 "first gentleman of the parish." Ibid., 121.

282 "Children were let alone." Ibid., 48.

282 "making meals on the corn or oats." Ibid., 177.

282 "mingled their horrors with her dreams." Ibid., 176.

283 trees "clapped their hands." Ibid., 183.

283 July 4 festivities. Ibid., 185ff.

283 Dr. Cushing's prayer. Ibid., 197.

283 "nothing in the Bible to tell us." Ibid., 55.

284 husband "grim and stony." Ibid., 306.

284 Chestnutting. Ibid., 220ff.

284 "white stones . . . the only witness." Ibid., 374.

285 Nook Farm. Andrews's classic account, *Nook Farm*, re-creates this singular and in many ways enviable world both vividly and comprehensively.

285 "easy, undress, picnic kind of life." To George Eliot, 3/18/76, C. E. Stowe, *Life*, 474.

286 "how many that I have traveled with." Ibid., 507–508 (9/30/80).

286 "neither insane nor an imbecile." Quoted in Wagenknecht, *Stowe*, 19.

287 Writing to Oliver Wendell Holmes. Ibid., 20 (2/5/93).

287 Grace King sees Harriet Beecher Stowe. King, *Memories*, 76–77.

288 "A little Yankee woman." Dixon, *Leopard's Spots*, 262.

288 "We stand for one thing at least." Ibid., 309.

290 "The Lion was dead." Ibid., 83.

290 "Is it not time they heard the whole truth?" Ammons, *Critical Essays*, 143 (quoted in Thomas P. Riggio, "*Uncle Tom* Reconstructed: A Neglected Chapter in the History of a Book," reprinted from *American Quarterly* 28 [spring, 1976]).

291 "She was impelled by love." C. E. Stowe, *Life*, 52.

291 "I don't think you would recognize her." Van Why, "[Letters . . . Wetherill]," 13.

Works Cited

THE LIST CONTAINS ONLY WORKS REFERRED TO IN THE NOTES.

Abbott, Lyman. *Henry Ward Beecher.* Boston, 1903.

Ammons, Elizabeth. *Critical Essays on Harriet Beecher Stowe.* Boston, 1980.

Andrews, Kenneth R. *Nook Farm: Mark Twain's Hartford Circle.* Cambridge, Mass., 1950.

Applegate, Debby. *The Most Famous Man in America: The Biography of Henry Ward Beecher.* New York, 2006.

Ashton, Jean Willoughby. *Harriet Beecher Stowe: A Reference Guide.* Boston, 1977.

———. "Harriet Stowe's Filthy Story: Lord Byron Set Afloat." *Prospects: An Annual of American Cultural Studies* 2 (1976):373–384.

Austin, James C. *Fields of* The Atlantic Monthly: *Letters to an Editor, 1861–1870.* San Marino, Calif., 1953.

Autobiography of Lyman Beecher, ed. Barbara M. Cross, 2 vols. Cambridge, Mass., 1961.

Baender, Paul. "Mark Twain and the Byron Scandal." *American Literature* 30 (1959):467–485.

The Beecher and Tilton War . . . A Book of Reference. New York, 1874.

Beecher, Catharine, and Harriet Beecher Stowe. *The American Woman's Home,* intro. Nicole Tonkovich. New Brunswick, N.J., and Hartford, 2002. Originally published 1869.

Beecher, Charles. *Harriet Beecher Stowe in Europe: The Journal of Charles Beecher,* ed. Joseph S. Van Why and Earl French. Hartford, 1986.

———. *Spiritual Manifestations.* Boston, 1879.

Beecher, Henry Ward. *New Star Papers; or, Views and Experiences of Religious Subjects.* New York, 1859.

———. *Norwood; or, Village Life in New England.* New York, 1868.

———. *Star Papers; or Experiences of Art and Nature.* New York, 1855.

Beecher, Lyman. *Plea for the West.* Cincinnati, 1835.

———. *Works,* 3 vols. Boston, 1852–1853.

Beecher, William C., and Samuel Scoville, assisted by Mrs. Henry Ward Beecher. *A Biography of Henry Ward Beecher.* New York, 1888.

Birdoff, Harry. *The World's Greatest Hit: Uncle Tom's Cabin.* New York, 1947.

Broun, Heywood, and Margaret Leech. *Anthony Comstock: Roundsman of the Lord.* New York, 1927.

Byron, George Gordon (Lord Byron). *Byron's Letters and Journals,* ed. Leslie A. Marchand, 12 vols. Cambridge, Mass., 1973–1982.

———. *The Complete Poetical Works,* ed. Jerome J. McGann, 6 vols. Oxford, 1980–1991.

Carter, Paul A. *The Spiritual Crisis of the Gilded Age.* DeKalb, Ill., 1971.

Caskey, Marie. *Chariot of Fire: Religion and the Beecher Family.* New Haven, Conn., 1978.

Cayleff, Susan E. *Wash and Be Healed: The Water-Cure Movement and Women's Health.* Philadelphia, 1987.

Clark, Clifford E., Jr. *Henry Ward Beecher: Spokesman for a Middle-Class America.* Urbana, Ill., 1978.

Collison, Gary. *Shadrach Minkins: From Fugitive to Citizen.* Cambridge, Mass., 1997.

Crowley, J. Donald, ed. *Hawthorne: The Critical Heritage.* New York, 1970.

Dana, Richard Henry, Jr. *Journals of Richard Henry Dana, Jr.,* ed. Robert F. Lucid, 3 vols. Cambridge, Mass., 1968.

Delbanco, Andrew. *Melville: His World and Work.* New York, 2005.

Dickens, Charles. *The Letters of Charles Dickens,* ed. Madeline House et al., 12 vols. Oxford, 1965–2002.

Dixon, Thomas. *The Leopard's Spots: A Romance of the White Man's Burden—1865–1900.* New York, 1902.

Edwards, Jonathan. *Works,* ed. Perry Miller et al., 23 vols. Vol. 14, ed. Kenneth P. Minkema. New Haven, Conn., 1957–2004.

Eisler, Benita. *Byron: Child of Passion, Fool of Fame.* New York, 1999.

Elsmere, Jane Shaffer. *Henry Ward Beecher: The Indiana Years, 1837–1847.* Indianapolis, Ind., 1973.

Fields, Annie. *Life and Letters of Harriet Beecher Stowe.* Boston, 1897.

Fisch, Audrey. "Uncle Tom and Harriet Beecher Stowe in England," in *The Cambridge Companion to Harriet Beecher Stowe,* ed. Cindy Weinstein. Cambridge, 2004, 96–112.

Foster, Charles H. *The Rungless Ladder: Harriet Beecher Stowe and New England Puritanism.* Durham, N.C., 1954.

Fox, Sir John C. *The Byron Mystery.* London, 1924.

Fox, Richard Wightman. *Trials of Intimacy: Love and Loss in the Beecher-Tilton Scandal.* Chicago, 1999.

Geary, Susan. "Harriet Beecher Stowe, John P. Jewett, and Author-Publisher

Relations in 1853," in *Studies in the American Renaissance,* ed. Joel Myerson. Charlottesville, Va.,1977, 345–367.

Gilbertson, Catherine. *Harriet Beecher Stowe.* New York, 1937.

Gossett, Thomas F. *"Uncle Tom's Cabin" and American Culture.* Dallas, Tex., 1985.

Graff, Mary B. *Mandarin on the St. Johns.* Gainesville, Fla., 1953.

Graham, Thomas. "Harriet Beecher Stowe and Race." *New England Quarterly* 46 (December 1973):614–622.

Grosskurth, Phyllis. *Byron: The Flawed Angel.* Boston, 1997.

[Guiccioli, Countess Teresa]. *My Recollections of Lord Byron; and Those of Eye-Witnesses of His Life,* 2 vols. London, 1869.

Harlow, Alvin F. *The Serene Cincinnatians.* New York, 1950.

Hawthorne, Nathaniel. *The Letters, 1857–1864.* Vol. 18 of *The Centenary Edition of the Works of Nathaniel Hawthorne,* ed. Thomas Woodson et al., Columbus, Ohio, 1987.

Hedrick, Joan D. *Harriet Beecher Stowe: A Life.* New York, 1994.

———, ed. *The Oxford Harriet Beecher Stowe Reader.* New York, 1999.

Henry, Stuart. *Unvanquished Puritan: A Portrait of Lyman Beecher.* Grand Rapids, Mich., 1973.

Hibben, Paxton. *Henry Ward Beecher: An American Portrait.* New York, 1927.

Hooker, Isabella Beecher. "The Last of the Beechers: Memories of My Eighty-Third Birthday." *Connecticut Magazine* 9 (1905):286–298.

Howard, John Raymond. *Remembrance of Things Past . . .* New York, 1925.

Howells, Mildred. *Life in Letters of William Dean Howells,* 2 vols. Garden City, N.Y., 1928.

Howells, William Dean. *Literary Friends and Acquaintance,* ed. David Hiatt and Edwin Cady. Vol. 32 of *The Howells Edition: The Approved Text of the Modern Language Association of America.* Bloomington, Ind., 1968.

James, Henry. *Literary Criticism: Essays on Literature, American Writers, English Writers.* New York: Library of America, 1984.

Johnston, Johanna. *Mrs. Satan: The Incredible Saga of Victoria C. Woodhull.* New York, 1967.

King, Grace. *Memories of a Southern Woman of Letters.* New York, 1932.

Kirkham, E. Bruce. *The Building of Uncle Tom's Cabin.* Knoxville, Tenn., 1977.

Kleinfield, H. L. "Infidel on Parnassus: Lord Byron and the *North American Review." New England Quarterly* 33 (1960):164–185.

Kunhardt, Dorothy Meserve, and Philip B. Kunhardt Jr. *Twenty Days: A Narrative in Text and Pictures of the Assassination of Abraham Lincoln.* New York, 1965.

Lentricchia, Frank, Jr. "Harriet Beecher Stowe and the Byron Whirlwind." *Bulletin of the New York Public Library* 70 (1966):218–228.

Lincoln, Abraham. *The Collected Works of Abraham Lincoln,* ed. Roy P. Basler, 9 vols. New Brunswick, N.J., 1953–1955.

Litwack, Leon F. "The Abolitionist Dilemma: The Antislavery Movement and the Northern Negro." *New England Quarterly* 34 (1961):50–73.

Lynn, Kenneth. *Visions of America: Eleven Literary Historical Essays.* Westport, Conn., 1973.

MacCarthy, Fiona. *Byron: Life and Legend.* New York, 2002.

Marchand, Leslie A. *Byron: A Biography,* 3 vols. New York, 1957.

Marsden, George M. *Jonathan Edwards: A Life.* New Haven, Conn., 2003.

Marshall, Charles F. *The True History of the Brooklyn Scandal: Being a Complete Account of the Trial of the Rev. Henry Ward Beecher.* Philadelphia, 1874.

Martineau, Harriet. *Retrospect of Western Travel,* 2 vols. London, 1838.

McLoughlin, William G. *The Meaning of Henry Ward Beecher: An Essay on the Shifting Values of Mid-Victorian America, 1840–1870.* New York, 1970.

Medwin, Thomas. *Conversations of Lord Byron,* ed. Ernest J. Lovell Jr. Princeton, N.J., 1966.

Morse, John T., Jr. *Life and Letters of Oliver Wendell Holmes,* 2 vols. Boston, 1896.

Mott, Frank Luther. *A History of American Magazines 1741–1930,* 5 vols. Cambridge, Mass., 1930–1968.

Otter, Samuel. "Stowe and Race," in *The Cambridge Companion to Harriet Beecher Stowe,* ed. Cindy Weinstein. Cambridge, 2004, 15–38.

Parrington, Vernon Louis. *Main Currents in American Thought: An Interpretation of American Literature from the Beginnings to 1920,* 3 vols. New York, 1930.

Praz, Mario. *The Romantic Agony,* trans. Angus Davidson. London, 1933.

Roppolo, Joseph P. "Harriet Beecher Stowe and New Orleans: A Study in Hate." *New England Quarterly* 30 (1957):346–362.

Rosenberg, Charles E. *The Cholera Years: The United States in 1832, 1849, and 1866.* Chicago, 1962.

Rourke, Constance. *Trumpets of Jubilee: Henry Ward Beecher, Harriet Beecher Stowe, Lyman Beecher, Horace Greeley, P. T. Barnum.* New York, 1927.

Rugoff, Milton. *The Beechers: An American Family in the Nineteenth Century.* New York, 1981.

Schreiner, Samuel A. *The Passionate Beechers.* Hoboken, N.J., 2003.

Sewall, Samuel. *The Diary of Samuel Sewall,* ed. M. Halsey Thomas, 2 vols. New York, 1973.

Shaplen, Robert. *Free Love and Heavenly Sinners.* New York, 1954.

The Stowe-Byron Controversy: A Complete Résumé of Public Opinion; with an Impartial Review of the Merits of the Case. Compiled by the editor of "Once a Week." London, 1869.

Stowe, Calvin. "Sketches and Recollections of Dr. Lyman Beecher." *Congregational Quarterly* 6 (1864):221–235.

Stowe, Charles Edward. *Life of Harriet Beecher Stowe Compiled from Her Letters and Journals.* Boston, 1889.

Stowe, Harriet Beecher. *Dred: A Tale of the Great Dismal Swamp*. New York; Penguin Classics, 2000.

——. *A Key to Uncle Tom's Cabin: Presenting the Original Facts and Documents upon Which the Story Is Founded*. Boston, 1853.

——. *Lady Byron Vindicated: A History of the Byron Controversy, from Its Beginning in 1816 to the Present Time*. Boston, 1870.

——. *Men of Our Times; or Leading Patriots of the Day*. Hartford, Conn., 1868.

——. *The Minister's Wooing*, in *Three Novels (Uncle Tom's Cabin, The Minister's Wooing, Oldtown Folks)*. New York: Library of America, 1982.

——. *My Wife and I: or, Harry Henderson's History*. Chicago, 2004. (Reprinted from the 1872 edition.)

——. "New England Ministers," review of W. B. Sprague's *Annals of the American Pulpit*, in *Atlantic Monthly* 1(2/58):485–492.

——. *Oldtown Folks*, in *Three Novels (Uncle Tom's Cabin, The Minister's Wooing, Oldtown Folks)*. New York: Library of America, 1982.

——. *Poganuc People*. Hartford, Conn., 1987. (Reprinted from the 1878 edition.)

——. "A Reply to 'The Affectionate and Christian Address of Many Thousands of Women of Great Britain and Ireland to Their Sisters the Women of the United States of America.'" *Atlantic Monthly* 11 (January 1863): 120–133.

——. *Sunny Memories of Foreign Lands*, 2 vols. New York, 1854.

——. "The True Story of Lady Byron's Life." *Atlantic Monthly* 24 (September 1869):295–313.

——. *Uncle Tom's Cabin*, in *Three Novels (Uncle Tom's Cabin, The Minister's Wooing, Oldtown Folks)*. New York: Library of America, 1982.

Stowe, Lyman Beecher. *Saints Sinners and Beechers*. Indianapolis, Ind., 1934.

Sumner, Charles. *The Works of Charles Sumner*, 15 vols. Boston, 1870–1883.

Sundquist, Eric J., ed. *New Essays on Uncle Tom's Cabin*. Cambridge, Mass., 1986.

Theodore Tilton vs. Henry Ward Beecher. Action for Crim. Con. Tried in the City Court of Brooklyn, Chief Justice Joseph Neilson, Presiding. Verbatim Report of the Official Stenographer, 3 vols. New York, 1875.

Thomas, Benjamin. *Theodore Weld, Crusader for Freedom*. New Brunswick, N. J., 1950.

Tilton, Theodore. *Victoria C. Woodhull: A Biographical Sketch. The Golden Age*, Tract No. 3. New York, 1871.

Trautmann, Frederick. "Harriet Beecher Stowe's Public Readings in New England." *New England Quarterly* 47 (1974):279–289.

Trollope, Mrs. [Frances]. *Domestic Manners of the Americans*, intro. James E. Mooney. Barre, Mass., 1969.

Underhill, Lois Beachy. *The Woman Who Ran for President: The Many Lives of Victoria Woodhull*. Bridgehampton, N.Y., 1995.

Van Why, Joseph S. ["Letters of Harriet Beecher Stowe to Martha and Rebecca Wetherill"]. *The Stowe, Beecher, Hooker, Seymour, Day Foundation Bulletin* 1, no. 3 (1961):2–14.

Wagenknecht, Edward. *Harriet Beecher Stowe: The Known and the Unknown.* New York, 1965.

——, comp. *Mrs. Longfellow: Selected Letters and Journals of Fanny Appleton Longfellow (1817–1861).* New York, 1956.

Waller, Altina L. *Reverend Beecher and Mrs. Tilton: Sex and Class in Victorian America.* Amherst, Mass., 1982.

Weinstein, Cindy. "Uncle Tom's Cabin and the South," in *The Cambridge Companion to Harriet Beecher Stowe.* Cambridge, 2004.

Weiss, Harry B., and Howard R. Kemble. "The Forgotten Water-Cures of Brattleboro, Vermont." *Vermont History: Proceedings of the Vermont Historical Society* 37 (1969):165–176.

——. *The Great American Water-Cure Craze: A History of Hydropathy in the United States.* Trenton, N.J., 1967.

White, Barbara A. *The Beecher Sisters.* New Haven, Conn., 2003.

Wilson, Edmund. *Patriotic Gore: Studies in the Literature of the American Civil War.* New York, 1962.

Wilson, Forrest. *Crusader in Crinoline: The Life of Harriet Beecher Stowe.* Philadelphia, 1941.

Woodhull, Victoria. *The Victoria Woodhull Reader,* ed. Madeleine B. Stern. Weston, Mass., 1974. (The facsimiles that this collection comprises are not sequentially paged. Citations in my notes are identified by a relevant title and the appropriate page number; the selection must then be located in the table of contents at the beginning of the *Reader.*)

Wyman, Margaret. "Harriet Beecher Stowe's Topical Novel on Woman Suffrage." *New England Quarterly* 25 (1952):383–391.

Acknowledgments

Joan Bingham, executive editor, and Luba Ostashevsky, assistant editor, have indulged me in my authorial idiosyncrasies, for which I'm grateful. I'm grateful as well to John Reazer, librarian and archivist of the Stowe Center in Hartford, for kindnesses during my several visits there. On each of those visits, Don and Patti Cantor opened their West Hartford home to me, adding to accumulated generosities that have assumed by now a value beyond what I could ever repay. As with my book on Hawthorne, so with this present one: I've gained from the help of Leslie Perrin Wilson and her assistant, Conni Manoli-Skocay, of Special Collections in the Concord (Massachusetts) Free Public Library. Sandy and Lucille Stott made Brunswick, Maine, a happy destination for me and my wife—the same dear Patricia who has been as unfailingly and enlighteningly supportive in the writing of this as of my other books. Herman Gollob, friend of a lifetime, has once again kept my course steady. And again, as for the last thirty years, the Boston Athenaeum has provided the resources, the genial staff, and the quiet environment that have made writing possible and pleasurable. The literature on Stowe and her times is voluminous, hardly less so than that on Hawthorne, and is only very partially indicated in Works Cited. I'm grateful to all the scholars and critics who have dealt with the subject to my profit, in particular to Joan Hedrick for her marvelous life of Harriet Beecher Stowe. Mrs. Stowe is blessed to have earned the interest of a biographer so sensitive, so formidably knowledgeable, and so eloquent.

Index